THE
GENERATIVE
SOCIETY

THE GENERATIVE SOCIETY

CARING FOR FUTURE GENERATIONS

EDITED BY

Ed de St. Aubin

Dan P. McAdams

Tae-Chang Kim

AMERICAN PSYCHOLOGICAL ASSOCIATION

WASHINGTON, DC

Published by
American Psychological Association
750 First Street, NE
Washington, DC 20002
www.apa.org

To order
APA Order Department
P.O. Box 92984
Washington, DC 20090-2984
Tel: (800) 374-2721; Direct: (202) 336-5510
Fax: (202) 336-5502; TDD/TTY: (202) 336-6123
Online: www.apa.org/books/
Email: order@apa.org

In the U.K., Europe, Africa, and the Middle East, copies may be ordered from
American Psychological Association
3 Henrietta Street
Covent Garden, London
WC2E 8LU England

Typeset in Goudy by Stephen McDougal, Mechanicsville, MD

Printer: Data Reproductions, Auburn Hills, MI
Cover Designer: Berg Design, Albany, NY
Technical/Production Editors: Jennifer L. Zale and Dan Brachtesende

The opinions and statements published are the responsibility of the authors, and such opinions and statements do not necessarily represent the policies of the American Psychological Association.

Library of Congress Cataloging-in-Publication Data

The generative society : caring for future generations / edited by Ed de St. Aubin,
Dan P. McAdams, and Tae-Chang Kim.— 1st ed.
        p. cm.
Includes bibliographical references and indexes.
    ISBN 1-59147-034-X (alk. paper)
    1. Adulthood—Psychological aspects. 2. Children and adults. 3. Social psychology.
I. De St. Aubin, Ed. II. McAdams, Dan P. III. Kim, Tae-Chang.

    BF724.5.G45 2003
    155.6—dc21   2003011064

British Library Cataloguing-in-Publication Data
A CIP record is available from the British Library.

Printed in the United States of America
First Edition

To Talbot Rae, and her generation.

CONTENTS

CONTRIBUTORS

Don Browning, PhD, Divinity School, University of Chicago, Chicago

E. Gil Clary, PhD, Department of Psychology, College of St. Catherine, St. Paul, MN

Ed de St. Aubin, PhD, Department of Psychology, Marquette University, Milwaukee, WI

Michele Dillon, PhD, Department of Sociology, University of New Hampshire, Durham

Kai Erikson, PhD, Department of Sociology, Yale University, New Haven, CT

Lawrence J. Friedman, PhD, Department of History, Indiana University, Bloomington

Takatoshi Imada, PhD, Graduate School of Decision Science and Technology, Department of Value and Decision Science, Tokyo Institute of Technology, Tokyo, Japan

Tae-Chang Kim, PhD, Institute for Integrated Study of Future Generations, Muromachi-Higashi-Iru, Shimogyo-Ku, Kyoto, Japan

John Kotre, PhD, Department of Psychology, University of Michigan, Dearborn

Charles S. Lanier, PhD candidate, School of Criminal Justice, State University of New York at Albany

Thomas P. LeBel, PhD candidate, School of Criminal Justice, State University of New York at Albany

Regina L. Logan, PhD, Foley Center for the Study of Lives, Northwestern University, Evanston, IL

Ronald J. Manheimer, PhD, North Carolina Center for Creative Retirement, University of North Carolina at Asheville

Shadd Maruna, PhD, Institute of Criminology, University of Cambridge, Cambridge, England

Dan P. McAdams, PhD, School of Education and Social Policy and Foley Center for the Study of Lives, Northwestern University, Evanston, IL

Bonnie J. Miller-McLemore, PhD, Divinity School, Vanderbilt University, Nashville, TN

Bill E. Peterson, PhD, Department of Psychology, Smith College, Northampton, MA

Takeshi Sasaki, PhD, President, University of Tokyo, Tokyo, Japan

Mark Snyder, PhD, Department of Psychology, University of Minnesota, Minneapolis

Paul Wink, PhD, Department of Psychology, Wellesley College, Wellesley, MA

Yoko Yamada, PhD, Department of Developmental Psychology, Graduate School of Education, Kyoto University, Kyoto, Japan

ACKNOWLEDGMENTS

The editors thank the Foley Family Foundation of Milwaukee, Wisconsin; the Future Generations Alliance Foundation of Kyoto, Japan; and the Kyoto Forum for their support of the work collected in this volume. The Foley Family Foundation has provided funding to Dan P. McAdams and Northwestern University to establish the Foley Center for the Study of Lives, a research center whose main mission is to examine social and personality development in adulthood. The Foley Family Foundation has supported a number of research projects on generativity, and it provided funding for the 1999 Northwestern conference, "Who Cares? Moral Commitment and Creative Lives in Contemporary America." The Future Generations Alliance Foundation and the Kyoto Forum sponsored the 1999 Kyoto conference, "Generativity Crisis and Our Responsibilities to Future Generations." Under the leadership of Tae-Chang Kim and Katsuhiko Yazaki, the Future Generations Alliance Foundation and the Kyoto Forum have organized symposia and conferences all over world, with the aim of promoting international cooperation and raising consciousness regarding the responsibilities we have today for the generations of human beings who may inhabit the earth in the future.

I

INTRODUCTION

1

THE GENERATIVE SOCIETY: AN INTRODUCTION

ED dE ST. AUBIN, DAN P. McADAMS, AND TAE-CHANG KIM

At the mid-point of the 20th century, Erik Erikson burst onto the scene with a new way of thinking and talking about human development. In *Childhood and Society*, Erikson (1950) set forth a theory of the human life course that profoundly influenced the social sciences and inspired a generation of young people to examine their souls and their societies in the search for *identity*. The concept of identity made Erikson famous and made *Childhood and Society* one of the most widely read and widely discussed books on college campuses in the 1950s, 1960s, and early 1970s (Friedman, 1999). American college students in their late teens and early 20s wrapped their doubts about conventional authority, their growing distrust of government and church, their explorations of alternative lifestyles and ideologies, and their aspirations for love, for work, and for personal meaning around Erikson's concept of the identity crisis. In late adolescence and young adulthood, Erikson taught, we must break from the stale conventions of childhood to find new and more coherent ways of understanding who we are and where we will ultimately fit within the adult world. The search for identity can be both exhilarating and disorienting, deeply satisfying and painfully disturbing. For many, identity marks a *crisis* in psychosocial development—a crisis that ushers in the daunting challenges of living meaningfully as an adult in the modern world (Giddens, 1991).

In the modern story of adult development, identity is the opening act. But what happens later? The American baby-boomers who so assiduously absorbed Erikson's ideas about the identity crisis are now well into middle age, and many have teenage children of their own. In the aging societies that characterize contemporary Western Europe, Japan, and the United States, Erikson's ideas about the postidentity years, about midlife and beyond, now take on a special salience. After the identity stage, Erikson argued, is the psychosocial challenge of *intimacy*—of finding a life partner with whom to share the joys, responsibilities, and challenges of adult life. And then? The bulk of adult life—the long, main, middle act of the modern adult story—is, for Erikson, the stage of *generativity*. In and through generativity, adults aim to create, build, and care for a new generation and assure a positive world for those people and institutions that they will leave behind. In the long middle of the human life course, adults make their most important contributions to their families, communities, society, and culture.

GENERATIVITY AND SOCIETY

Generativity is the adult's concern for and commitment to the next generation, as expressed through parenting, teaching, mentoring, leadership, and a host of other activities that aim to leave a positive legacy of the self for the future (McAdams & de St. Aubin, 1992). In adolescence and young adulthood, we discover who we are; in our middle adult years, we extend that discovery into a legacy. Through generativity, we seek to care for and contribute in positive ways to the world we live in and the people we will leave behind. In *Gandhi's Truth*, Erikson (1969) explored the vicissitudes of generativity in the life of the great religious leader of India—a man whose generativity script expanded to take on the care of an entire nation. And Erikson wrote eloquently about the challenges, struggles, and ambiguities of generativity in most of his later works (e.g., Erikson, 1978, 1982). But it was not until the last decade of the 20th century that the concept of generativity began to enjoy both public attention and empirical scrutiny. In the 1990s, generativity finally emerged as a topic for empirical research among life span developmental psychologists, personality psychologists, and sociologists (Kotre, 1999; McAdams & de St. Aubin, 1998; Rossi, 2001; Snarey, 1993). Researchers have studied the developmental course of generativity, its implications for mental health and well-being, and its relationships to a wide range of psychologically and socially consequential outcomes (McAdams, 2001). Generativity is now a central idea in some forms of psychotherapy, as well, especially in family counseling (Dollahite, Slife, & Hawkins, 1998). The year 1999 also saw the first international conference devoted solely to the exploration of generativity. Titled "Generativity Crisis and Our Responsibilities to Future Generations," the 3-day gathering brought social scientists and public intellectuals of many different stripes to Kyoto, Japan, to consider the meaning and relevance of generativity for life in contemporary modern societies.

A half century after Erikson introduced the world to the concept of identity, therefore, we are now turning our attention to a second Eriksonian idea whose importance for psychology and for society may be even more significant today. Generativity is a central concern for many midlife adults living at the dawn of the 21st century. It is clear that as the large post-World War II cohorts in Europe, Japan, and the United States move through the middle and later periods of the adult life course, the psychology of generativity will continue to attract more and more scientific and lay attention (Lachman, 2001).

What is perhaps less clear, however, is the extent to which generativity becomes an even more timely and urgent issue when we move from the psychology of the individual to generativity *in society*. Adults express generativity in social contexts and through social institutions. Generativity is shaped by political, economic, religious, and cultural forces. Furthermore, it makes good sense to consider how social institutions themselves, and even societies writ large, may or may not function in generative ways (Moran, 1998). In the realms of family, religion, politics, education, and social and economic policy, we need to consider carefully and critically the ways in which societies do, and do not, promote the well-being of future generations.

Can there be any more significant issue today than the well-being, and for that matter the very survival, of future generations of human beings? Adults in most all societies have surely faced problems in generativity since the dawn of civilization. How can I be the best possible parent for my children? How can I assure their survival, their happiness, their progeny? But on a societal and a global level, the threats to generativity that we face in the first years of the third millennium would appear to be as formidable as any we have ever known. Since the advent of nuclear weapons, people have realized that there may indeed be no future generations to inhabit the earth. Even setting aside the possibility of nuclear cataclysm, the world today faces stupendous challenges and constraints—from global warming to finite energy sources—that raise the strong possibility that there soon may be no viable world to leave to future generations.

One impetus behind the Kyoto Conference was the belief that Japanese society in particular is experiencing a generativity crisis. Some feared that Japan was becoming a *shoshika shakai* (childless society) as increasing numbers of women were opting not to have children. Many who are mothers are also part of the increasing numbers of Japanese women joining the labor force. This has dramatically transformed patterns of child care. Furthermore, the Japanese generativity crisis is seen in the extinguishing of traditional art forms and the decay of cultural traditions. The generative forces that have maintained these practices in the past as each was passed on to successive generations are no longer as vital as they once were. Finally, generative leaders—those with a vision for the future and a concern for the citizenship of tomorrow—are increasingly rare in Japan. The sectors of society that have provided such leaders in the past—political, social, and economic—seem to have lost the ability to generate such leaders.

It may be that certain societies in our world, such as Japan, are experiencing a more profound generativity crisis, but the problem does indeed appear to be a global one. In a 1993 statement, the Union of Concerned Scientists asserted, "A great change in our stewardship of the earth and the life on it is required, if vast human misery is to be avoided and our global home on this planet is not to be irretrievably mutilated" (p. 1). In a special issue of the journal *American Psychologist*, Oskamp (2000) and Howard (2000) considered how psychologists and social scientists may address the urgent problem of "a sustainable future for humanity" (Oskamp, 2000, p. 496). A "sustainable society" is "one that satisfies its current needs without jeopardizing the prospects of future generations," wrote Howard (2000, p. 509). At a minimum, it would seem, a generative society should seek to be sustainable.

But for generativity's sake, we typically imagine ends that greatly exceed the mere survival of future generations. We hope the lives of our children and their children will be *good*, will have meaning and value. Erikson taught that generativity involves much more than procreation and providing for the physical needs of our progeny. Generative adults are teachers, leaders, mentors, and what George Vaillant has called the "keepers of the meaning" (Vaillant & Milofsky, 1980). They seek to pass on the most valued traditions of a culture, to teach the most valued skills and outlooks, to impart wisdom, to foster the realization of human potential in future generations. As adults move into and through their midlife years, they may become increasingly concerned with giving something back to the world, perhaps as gratitude for the care and good fortune they have received. The generative gifts that adults have to offer are shaped and mediated by the cultures within which they live and their lives have meaning. A generative society provides institutional support and reinforcement for the generative efforts of adults. In their influential book, *The Good Society*, sociologist Robert Bellah and his colleagues (Bellah, Madsen, Sullivan, Swidler, & Tipton, 1991) proposed that American society needs to develop a "politics of generativity." According to Bellah et al., the most pressing problems facing large-scale American institutions—schools, churches, and governing bodies—center on

> what the psychologist Erik Erikson called "generativity," the care that one generation gives the next. Generativity is a virtue that Erikson ideally situates in the concern of parents for children, but he extends it far beyond the family so that it becomes the virtue by means of which we

care for all persons and things we have been entrusted with. What kind of society will we endow our children and our children's children, what kind of world, what kind of natural environment? By focusing on our immediate well-being (are you better off than you were four years ago?), and by being obsessively concerned with improving our relative income and consumption, we have forgotten that the meaning of life derives not so much from what we have as from what kind of person we are and how we have shaped our lives toward future ends that are good in themselves. (Bellah et al., 1991, p. 274).

In *The Good Society*, Bellah and his colleagues (1991) were not the first to pit generativity against self-centered and obsessive consumption. Erikson wrote that many adults are too self-preoccupied to be generative. So concerned are they with caring for their own well-being that they are unable or unwilling to extend that care to others. At the levels both of the individual and society, the self-centered pursuit of material wealth and personal aggrandizement is a great enemy of generativity. Ever since the 19th-century robber barons made their fortunes in industry, critics of American society have taken the United States to task for its grasping materialism and its celebration of the advancement of self. We live in a "culture of narcissism," wrote Christopher Lasch back in 1979—an indictment that would seem to be even more fitting for the 1990s. And yet even the most craven apologists for the hegemony of American capitalism express ambivalence about gaping inequalities in material well-being and the inability of wealth to buy happiness and meaning. In *The Good Society*, Bellah et al. (1991) wrote that Americans have a difficult time expressing their inchoate longings for community and for nobler ends that transcend the advancement of self (see also Bellah, Madsen, Sullivan, Swidler, & Tipton, 1985; Wuthnow, 1991). We have little by way of language, little by way of a comfortable discourse for expressing generative inclinations. Even when we talk about making a good life for *our* children, the words sound selfish.

At its emotional core, generativity may indeed draw on selfish (as well as selfless) motives (Kotre, 1984; McAdams, 1985). But culture has the power to transmute even the most self-centered propensities into nobler and higher ends. The most powerful discourses for generativity may come from the great religious traditions, from the noblest civic engagements and commitments, from the grand and encompassing, as well as the local and particular, meaning systems rooted in culture. In the aftermath of the September 11, 2001, terrorist attacks on the United States, many journalists and cultural observers have noted an upsurge of patriotism and religious conviction in American society. Time will eventually tell us whether or not the September 11 events will mark a watershed in American cultural history. But one cannot help but be struck by how public discourse in the United States has become rather more hospitable to a language of generativity. How do we assure a world that is safe for our children? How do we safeguard the most cherished institutions of American society? How do we protect democratic ideals and individual rights for future generations? How do we commit ourselves to the higher pursuits of a modern and tolerant democratic society? Of course, there is always a dark side to these kinds of questions, for they can readily be answered in ways that promote a society's hegemony and the conviction that *my* society, *my* religious tradition, *my* lifestyle is the only true and good alternative, and all others are evil. As Erikson pointed out, generativity can devolve into *pseudospeciation*—the conviction that one's own people are God's (or evolution's) chosen and that all rivals are akin to other (inferior) species. Still, a generative society must link its people to the great cultural questions and traditions. It must empower them to participate in the generation and regeneration of cultural forms that aim to promote the advancement and well-being of future generations.

The central aim of this book is to explore the complex relationships between generativity and society. We have brought together scholars and scientists from a wide range of disciplines to discuss the role of generativity in contemporary society. We have asked the authors to consider the political, economic, religious, educational, and cultural dimensions of generativity. We have asked them to integrate empirical research, scientific and cultural theory, and their own informed observations and speculations regarding generativity in society. A number of the chapters evolved from presentations first made at the 1999 Kyoto Conference, "Generativity Crisis and Our Responsibilities to Future Generations." One other chapter was modeled on a presentation given at a 1999 conference at Northwestern University, "Who Cares? Moral Commitment and Creative Lives in Contemporary America." Still other chapters were commissioned specifically for this volume. Although most of the chapters reflect the perspectives of American writers, three chapters are written by Japanese scholars. The overall result is, we believe, a rich and stimulating exchange about the multifaceted role of generativity in human life and in society.

ORGANIZATION OF THE BOOK

Following this introductory chapter, in chapter 2, Dan McAdams and Regina Logan organize recent research and theory on the psychology of generativity under 10 basic propositions. McAdams and Logan present a summary of the scholarship that has addressed the concept of generativity, the majority of which has examined generativity at the level of the individual. Taken together, these first two chapters set the stage for what is to come in the remainder of the book.

The next five chapters are clustered together in Part II: Generativity in Society and Culture. In chapter 3, John Kotre asks what makes any culture— a school culture, church culture, sports culture—generative? Among the key components of a thriving generative culture, he argues, is a rich and inspiring store of *narratives* that people can draw on to provide their lives with meaning and purpose. Among other things, a generative society passes on and transforms narratives that affirm some aspect of the shared past while inviting people to move confidently into a welcoming future, even if they do not know what exactly the future will bring.

The one author in this volume who knew Erik Erikson the best—his son Kai Erikson—adopts a sociological perspective in chapter 4 to reflect on the complexities and the ambiguities of generativity in society. In this provocative chapter, Erikson provides several examples from history to demonstrate the manner in which social forces (such as immigration, technological changes, and ethnic conflicts) contour the specific form that generativity may take in a given society and at a given historical moment. Among other effects, Erikson's chapter casts a sobering perspective on the discussion of generativity and society, suggesting that generativity can sometimes have a dark side and that one group's or society's generative projects can work against the well-being, and even threaten the survival, of rival groups and societies. Of special note here is the threat of pseudospeciation—a danger that can stem even from well-intentioned generative efforts.

The manner in which generative efforts are contoured by cultural context is the focus of Ed de St. Aubin's chapter 5. In this chapter, de St. Aubin compares generative expressions in two different societies, Japan and the United States. He focuses on two delimited realms of generativity: caring for young children and the mentoring of artistic talent. The intriguing differences that de St. Aubin reveals serve as a testament to the overarching power of culture to shape the means and even the ends of generativity. Chapter 6 is authored by Takatoshi Imada, one of several Japanese scholars represented in this book. Imada suggests that the concept of generativity helps to elucidate the dynamics inherent in intergenerational transmission that lead to societal continuity and change.

Part II concludes with Yoko Yamada's chapter 7, wherein she contrasts linear Western and more contextualist Eastern perspectives on both generativity and the human life course. Psychological theorizing in America has recently focused attention on the distinction between independent (think: Western, individualistic) and interdependent (think: Eastern, collectivist) construals of self and society (e.g., Markus & Kitayama, 1991; Triandis, 1997). Yamada offers interesting new twists to this discussion through her research and observations regarding traditional Japanese folktales.

Part III focuses on Generativity and Social Institutions. In chapter 8, Ronald Manheimer examines one aspect of the educational institution as he considers the role of generativity in emerging institutes for lifelong learning in aging societies. In the United States and Canada, close to 300 Institutes for Learning in Retirement encourage older participants to plan curricula, teach courses, and help govern these increasingly popular organizations. Similar programs are flourishing in Europe and parts of Asia. While these programs aim to enhance the learning and development of retired men and women, they serve the equally important and generative function of bringing different generations together.

In chapter 9, Shadd Maruna, Thomas LeBel, and Charles Lanier focus on the criminal justice institution and reforms aimed at *strengths-based corrections*. Desistance from crime in the United States and Great Britain often involves the construction of society-affirming personal narratives that contain generative desires and "redemptive truths." Not only do reformed ex-convicts find sustenance and strength in generativity, but strengths-based correctional reforms place the encouragement and development of generativity at the heart of the correctional enterprise.

In chapter 10, Michele Dillon and Paul Wink examine the ways in which participation in religious institutions enhances and reinforces generativity in American society. Their longitudinal data, furthermore, show that even nontraditional forms of religious activity, such as the spiritual-seeking characteristic of many young and middle-age Americans today, provide links to the awakening and realization of generativity. In chapter 11, Bonnie Miller-McLemore, a professor of pastoral theology, considers the institution of the family and the ways in which generativity in the family is contoured by gender. Her critical appraisal draws on psychology, ethics, and religion to reveal how the hidden gender politics of generativity work to distort care giving in the family.

In chapter 12, Bill Peterson examines the political institution as he takes up Bellah's concept of a "politics of generativity." In such a politics, the children of a society emerge as the prime constituencies. Peterson considers how generative political institutions might generate public policy dealing with issues of child care, intergenerational relations, and immigration. And he asks what kind of personal features might indeed characterize a *generative politician*. From his standpoint as a social scientist and now as the president of Tokyo University, Takeshi Sasaki in chapter 13 reinforces Peterson's desire to place children at the center of generative politics. But Sasaki goes further in contending that even those not-yet-born generations—the people of the distant future—deserve some kind of political representation in a generative society. In arguing for a radical transformation of political institutions to assure that the well-being of future generations moves to the center of political discourse and deliberation, Sasaki underscores the extent to which generative individuals and a generative society must eschew the seductions of "now-ism" and adopt instead a perspective on life that considers the *very* long term.

In chapter 14, Mark Snyder and E. Gil Clary return the focus to American society and to a social form that has been described as characteristically American ever since the time of de Tocqueville. Volunteerism is a quintessentially American pathway for the expression of generative impulses.

Snyder and Clary examine the psychosocial dynamics of volunteerism as an expression of adult generativity in society.

Generativity connects past, present, and future as traditions and rituals are maintained and recreated in attempts to benefit future generations. In this spirit, the final section of the book (Part IV) is Looking Forward, Looking Backward. In chapter 15, theologian Don Browning contends that generativity may serve as the guiding ethic for the 21st century. Building on ideas he first introduced almost 30 years ago in a groundbreaking book titled *Generative Man* (Browning, 1973), Browning argues that implicit in virtually any discussion of a generative society is the idea that generativity itself is more than a psychological or social concept. It is also a concept laden with ethical meaning, both when it is applied to individual lives and when it is applied to the workings of society and societal institutions. Browning deconstructs Erikson's concept of generativity to show that it mixes elements from diverse and competing philosophical traditions. The result is a concept with strong *moral validity*, well designed to provide adults with the ethical resources they need to adapt to the challenges and strains of life in modern societies.

In chapter 16, Lawrence Friedman looks back to the life lived by Erik Erikson. Friedman draws on his full-length biography of Erik Erikson (Friedman, 1999) to situate the concept of generativity within Erikson's own life and in the context of the social and political forces that shaped his life and his theory in the years immediately following World War II. *The Generative Society* ends with chapter 17, wherein we provide brief reflections on recurrent themes, implications that emerged in our readings of the chapters, and our thoughts about where social-scientific inquiries into generativity and society might move in the future.

REFERENCES

Bellah, R. N., Madsen, R., Sullivan, W. M., Swidler, A., & Tipton, S. M. (1985). *Habits of the heart*. Berkeley: University of California Press.

Bellah, R. N., Madsen, R., Sullivan, W. M., Swidler, A., & Tipton, S. M. (1991). *The good society*. New York: Knopf.

Browning, D. (1973). *Generative man*. New York: Dell.

Dollahite, D. C., Slife, B. D., & Hawkins, A. J. (1998). Family generativity and generative counseling: Helping families keep faith with the next generation. In D. P. McAdams & E. de St. Aubin (Eds.), *Generativity and adult development: How and why we care for the next generation* (pp. 449–481). Washington, DC: American Psychological Association.

Erikson, E. H. (1950). *Childhood and society*. New York: Norton.

Erikson, E. H. (1969). *Gandhi's truth: On the origins of militant nonviolence*. New York: Norton.

Erikson, E. H. (1978). Reflections on Dr. Borg's life cycle. In E. H. Erikson (Ed.), *Adulthood* (pp. 1–31). New York: Norton.

Erikson, E. H. (1982). *The life cycle completed*. New York: Norton.

Friedman, L. (1999). *Identity's architect: A biography of Erik H. Erikson*. New York: Pantheon Books.

Giddens, A. (1991). *Modernity and self-identity: Self and society in the late modern age*. Stanford, CA: Stanford University Press.

Howard, G. S. (2000). Adapting human lifestyles for the 21st century. *American Psychologist, 55*, 509–515.

Kotre, J. (1984). *Outliving the self: Generativity and the interpretation of lives*. Baltimore: Johns Hopkins University Press.

Kotre, J. (1999). *Make it count: How to generate a legacy that gives meaning to your life*. New York: Free Press.

Lachman, M. (2001). (Ed.). *Handbook of midlife development*. New York: Wiley.

Lasch, C. (1979). *The culture of narcissism: American life in an age of diminishing expectations*. New York: Norton.

Markus, H., & Kitayama, S. (1991). Culture and the self: Implications for cognition, emotion, and motivation. *Psychological Review, 98*, 224–253.

McAdams, D. P. (1985). *Power, intimacy, and the life story*. New York: Guilford Press.

McAdams, D. P. (2001). Generativity in midlife. In M. Lachman (Ed.), *Handbook of midlife development* (pp. 395–443). New York: Wiley.

McAdams, D. P., & de St. Aubin, E. (1992). A theory of generativity and its assessment through self-report, behavioral acts, and narrative themes in autobiography. *Journal of Personality and Social Psychology, 62*, 1003–1015.

McAdams, D. P., & de St. Aubin, E. (1998). (Eds.). *Generativity and adult development: How and why we care for the next generation*. Washington, DC: American Psychological Association.

Moran, G. (1998). Cares for the rising generation: Generativity in American history, 1607–1900. In D. P. McAdams & E. de St. Aubin (Eds.), *Generativity and adult development: How and why we care for the next generation* (pp. 311–334). Washington, DC: American Psychological Association.

Oskamp, S. (2000). A sustainable future for humanity? How can psychology help? *American Psychologist, 55*, 496–508.

Rossi, A. (2001). (Ed.). *Caring and doing for others: Social responsibility in the domains of family, work, and community*. Chicago: University of Chicago Press.

Snarey, J. (1993). *How fathers care for the next generation: A four-decade study*. Cambridge, MA: Harvard University Press.

Triandis, H. C. (1997). Cross-cultural perspectives on personality. In R. Hogan, J. Johnson, & S. Briggs (Eds.), *Handbook of personality psychology* (pp. 439–464). San Diego, CA: Academic Press.

Union of Concerned Scientists. (1993, April). *World scientists' warning to humanity* [Statement]. Cambridge, MA: Author.

Vaillant, G. E., & Milofsky, E. (1980). The natural history of male psychological health: IX. Empirical evidence for Erikson's model of the life cycle. *American Journal of Psychiatry, 137,* 1348–1359.

Wuthnow, R. (1991). *Acts of compassion: Caring for others and helping ourselves.* Princeton, NJ: Princeton University Press.

2

WHAT IS GENERATIVITY?

DAN P. McADAMS AND REGINA L. LOGAN

The psychoanalytic theorist Erik Erikson introduced the concept of *generativity* over 50 years ago (Erikson, 1950). But it was not until the 1980s that the idea of generativity caught the imagination of psychological theorists, researchers, and clinicians (e.g., Kotre, 1984; McAdams, 1985; Stewart, Franz, & Layton, 1988; Vaillant & Milofsky, 1980). Since then, the concept of generativity has evolved in a number of different directions, and we have learned a great deal about the meanings and the manifestations of generativity in human lives. The purpose of this chapter is to lay out what we have learned about generativity as a *psychological* construct—a construct that is situated in the psychology of individual lives. We present what we know in terms of 10 propositions about the psychology of generativity. This chapter, then, sketches a broad-brush portrait of our current understanding of generativity, drawing from a wide range of theoretical offerings and research programs. With the psychology of generativity as our background, we can then proceed to consider, as do many of the chapters that follow, the idea of generativity *in society*.

The work described in this chapter has been supported by grants to Dan P. McAdams from the Spencer Foundation and from the Foley Family Foundation.

GENERATIVITY IS THE CONCERN FOR AND COMMITMENT TO THE WELL-BEING OF FUTURE GENERATIONS

Erikson (1950, 1969) viewed generativity as an especially important psychological quality in the lives of adults. In the adult years, he argued, mature men and women work to assure the well-being of their own children in particular and the next generation more generally. Generativity, therefore, is expressed in parenting and family life. But the generative adult may also operate on a larger scale and outside the realm of his or her own family by working for the well-being of future generations through various kinds of activities and enterprises in churches, schools, neighborhoods, communities, organizations, and society writ large. Generativity may be expressed in teaching, mentoring, volunteer work, charitable activities, religious involvements, and political activities. Promoting society's traditions, taking on the responsibilities of good citizenship, even paying taxes—these may be seen as expressions of generativity. At the same time, generativity can be expressed in efforts for social change and even in behaviors that defy the status quo, as in the efforts of some individuals to change conventions or transform societal institutions toward the end of making society or indeed the world a better place for future generations. Therefore, generativity may be expressed both in the conservation and nurturance of that which people deem to be good in life and in the transformation of that which people believe to be in need of improvement, with the common aim of fostering the development and well-being of future generations (McAdams & de St. Aubin, 1992).

Kotre (1984) distinguished among biological (reproduction), parental (caring for children), technical (teaching skills), and cultural (passing on meaning systems) forms of generativity. The various forms of generativity are often expressed within particular social roles and domains—in family or work roles, for example, in political and civic domains, or even in leisure-time pursuits (MacDermid, Franz, & De Reus, 1998). Within and across these different role domains, furthermore, generativity can manifest itself in activities aimed at generating or producing new things and people, in caring for people and maintaining those most valued aspects of society, and in eventually offering up or letting go of those people and things that have been generated and cared for (McAdams & de St. Aubin, 1992). The task of letting go, of granting autonomy to one's biological, parental, technical, and societal progeny, is one of the great challenges of generativity, as many parents know.

GENERATIVITY IS A DEVELOPMENTAL CHALLENGE FOR THE MIDDLE-ADULT YEARS

Erikson considered generativity to be the psychological centerpiece of the seventh stage in his eight-stage model of human development. According to this developmental view, the stage of generativity versus stagnation is preceded by the late-adolescent (fifth) stage of identity versus role confusion (wherein the person ideally achieves a workable adult identity) and the young-adult (sixth) stage of intimacy versus isolation (wherein the person ideally commits him- or herself to another in a long-term bond of love). Erikson believed that once a person has a clear sense of who he or she is (identity) and has established a relationship of intimacy, then he or she is psychologically ready to focus energies on promoting the well-being of the next generation. Although a person, therefore, can have generative feelings and inclinations at virtually any point in the life span, it is in the middle-adult years, Erikson believed, that generativity is likely to rise to the fore as a central issue in living. Furthermore, it would be expected that generative inclinations would decrease in later adulthood (never clearly demarcated by Erikson), as the person moves into the last (eighth) stage, ego integrity versus despair.

In middle adulthood, Erikson argued, the person may confront significant opportunities, challenges, and frustrations in the realm of generativity. In terms of frustrations, midlife adults may experience a sense of *stagnation*—a sense that they cannot produce or generate and that their lives are not having the positive impact on others that they wish they might. Another failing in generativity is what Erikson called *self-preoccupation*. For many different reasons, both psychological and social, some adults may be unable or unwilling to direct their generative and caring impulses in the direction of others. Instead, they may become their own generative objects. The self-preoccupied person focuses his or her caring on the self, investing a tremendous amount of time and psychic energy on maintaining and promoting his or her own well-being rather than the well-being of those who are younger, weaker, or more in need of care. Economic and cultural issues play a large role in this matter. For example, wrenching poverty can undermine generativity. The individual who does not know when he will next eat a good meal may not have the psychosocial luxury to worry about the next generation. In some cases, self-preoccupation may be less a matter of narcissism and more a matter of survival.

A considerable amount of research has examined Erikson's contention that generativity marks a discrete midlife *stage* of development. Predictably, these studies have examined the relation between age and various measures of generativity, including measures of generative behaviors, attitudes, and self-attributions. The results of these studies vary, from a few showing no relation between generativity and age (e.g., Whitbourne, Zuschlag, Elliot, & Waterman, 1992) to others that have documented a smooth stage sequence (e.g., Snarey, 1993; Vaillant & Milofsky, 1980). The best estimate, however, probably lies somewhere between these two extremes. A number of studies, including a recent nationwide survey of over 3,000 U.S. citizens, suggest that generativity concerns and behaviors may peak in the midlife years (e.g., Keyes & Ryff, 1998; McAdams, de St. Aubin, & Logan, 1993; Peterson & Stewart,

1990
still s
(Coh
gest t
there
is not
more,
over t
that t
but th
desire:
that g
but ge
adult l

vity is
forces
ɔ sug-
idlife,
ment
ther-
times
nown
nood,
ative
ere is
llife,
the

[handwritten annotation: "Important proposition for Creation of a/b text." "Agency and Communion" 18]

GENERATIVITY MAY SPRING FROM DESIRES THAT ARE BOTH SELFLESS AND SELFISH

One of the most interesting paradoxes about generativity is how it blends narcissism and altruism. A number of scholars have linked generativity to a desire for symbolic immortality (Becker, 1973; Kotre, 1984; McAdams, 1985). Even after death, an individual can "live on," in a sense, through his or her generative products—for example, through children, through the family business, through one's books or paintings, one's reputation, one's family name, and so on. A deep and strong impetus for some forms of generative action may be a desire to extend the self beyond its mortal life. Indeed, Kotre (1984) suggested that such a desire is at the heart of generativity when he defined generativity as "the desire to invest one's substance in forms of life and work that will outlive the self" (p. 10). At the same time, generativity involves the relatively selfless nurturance of and caring for the next generation, even to the point of giving one's self up for one's children, one's community, or one's people.

The fullest expressions of generativity involve the manifestation of what Bakan (1966) called the contrasting tendencies of *agency* and *communion*. Agency is the organismic tendency toward self-expression, self-expansion, self-protection, self-development, and all other goals promoting the individual self. Communion is the organismic tendency toward sharing the self with others, merging the self in community, giving up the self for the good of something beyond the self. Generativity calls on adults to generate products and offspring in a powerful and agentic fashion and to care for that which has been generated in a loving and communal fashion. Generativity challenges adults to be highly agentic and communal at the same time. Research has shown that highly generative adults tend to express especially strong needs for both agency and communion in their narrative accounts of their own lives (de St. Aubin & McAdams, 1995; Mansfield & McAdams, 1996; McAdams, Ruetzel, & Foley, 1986; Peterson & Stewart, 1993). Some evidence also suggests that these two kinds of motives—self-oriented agentic motives and other-oriented communal motives—can sometimes conflict with each other, and that highly generative adults sometimes find it especially difficult to satisfactorily fulfill these strong and discordant needs (McAdams, 1993).

GENERATIVITY IS SHAPED BY CULTURE

The ultimate sources of generativity are doubtlessly biological and cultural. The agentic and communal desires that people feel and express through generative activity may be the outgrowth of evolutionarily grounded and biologically mediated urges, ultimately working to promote survival and reproduction (Tooby & Cosmides, 1992). But generativity is also expressed in a cultural context, and cultural forces decisively shape how people orient themselves to the next generation. The generative adult must work within the economic and ideological frameworks made available by society if he or she is to assume such generative roles as parent, teacher, mentor, healer, arbiter, advocate, leader, activist, organizer, and citizen.

Different societies set up different expectations regarding generativity. In any given society or cultural group, generativity may be strongly contoured along the lines of class (Keyes & Ryff, 1998), race/ethnicity (Cole & Stewart, 1996), or gender (Logan, 1993). With regard to gender, many traditional societies mandate that women's generative expressions focus mainly on the family, whereas men are expected to direct their generative inclinations outward, toward society as a whole. In some more modern societies, sex roles are becoming more fluid and flexible, and gender may be rather less significant as a determinant of generativity. All societies hold expectations regarding the *timing* of generativity. As people move through young adulthood and toward midlife, their peers and their community typically hold greater and greater expectations regarding generative action and commitment. By contrast, most societies do not typically set forth high expectations for generativity in the very young and the very old. Still, societies differ dramatically with respect to what potentially generative actions they deem appropriate at given times in the life course. In the middle-class and professional strata of the United States, for example, young women today are typically expected to put off childbearing until well into their 20s and beyond. Yet in many cultural contexts, beginning one's biological and parental projects in the teenage years may be viewed very favorably, and even encouraged (Belsky, Steinberg, & Draper, 1991).

The forces of culture shape the meanings of generativity in many interesting ways. In traditional societies, generativity may take the form of passing on the eternal truths and wisdom of the ages that are embedded in religious and civic traditions. The well-being of future generations is tied explicitly to expectations about continuity of the past. By contrast, modern societies tend to emphasize scientific progress, the questioning of convention, and an optimistic belief that the future can be better than the past (Giddens, 1991; McAdams, 1997). Under conditions of swift cultural change, as we witness today in many modern and developing societies across the globe, generativity becomes a balancing act between tradition and innovation. Amidst the dizzying cultural change experienced in many societies today, youths may no longer value the wisdom of their elders, for that wisdom may be seen as specific to a bygone world. An older generation may seek to be generative through passing on traditional values of life, but the targets of their efforts—the younger generation—may want and need guidance and resources that better address new challenges in the future. Parents are not always able to give children what they need, and children do not always value what parents have to offer. Although generativity mismatches are surely as old as civilization itself, they appear to take on added salience under conditions of rapid social and cultural change (McAdams, Hart, & Maruna, 1998).

THE STRENGTH OF GENERATIVITY DIFFERS ACROSS INDIVIDUALS

While Erikson underscored the idea that generativity is a universal stage in the human life cycle, he also contended that in any group of same-age adults there are likely to be significant individual differences in the strength of generative inclinations. Put simply, some adults are more generative than others.

Over the past 15 years, researchers have developed a number of different measures of individual differences in various aspects of generativity. Some researchers have used clinical ratings (Bradley, 1997; Snarey, 1993; Vaillant & Milofsky, 1980) to assess the extent to which different adults have achieved developmental tasks associated with generativity. Others have used the Q-sort ranking procedure to evaluate the extent to which an individual's overall profile of personality traits exhibits features indicative of generativity (Himsel, Hart, Diamond, & McAdams, 1997; Peterson & Klohnen, 1995). Still others have used content analysis procedures designed to detect generativity themes in imaginative and autobiographical narratives (Peterson, 1998; Peterson & Stewart, 1990).

Our own research program has focused on three interrelated aspects of generativity: generative concern, generative goals, and generative actions (McAdams & de St. Aubin, 1992; McAdams et al., 1993, 1998). On the Loyola Generativity Scale (LGS), adults rate the extent to which they agree or disagree with 20 statements designed to assess the strength of a person's overall concern for the next generation. To measure generative goals, we have used a procedure developed by Emmons (1986) for identifying the person's most important daily strivings—the things that a person is typically trying to accomplish in daily life. To measure acts, we present people with a checklist of behaviors indicative of generativity (e.g., "read a story to a child," "performed a community service") and ask them to determine how many times they have indeed performed each act in the past 2 months. Measures of generative concern, generative goals, and generative acts tend to be positively correlated with each other. However, the correlations are not so strong as to suggest that these three measures are assessing exactly the same thing. Rather, different measures of generativity appear to tap into different features of the construct.

INDIVIDUAL DIFFERENCES IN GENERATIVITY ARE RELATED TO QUALITY OF PARENTING

The prototype of generativity is the bearing and nurturing of offspring. But are adults who score high on generativity more effective as parents than those who score low? Recent empirical evidence suggests that they may be.

In a large-scale study of parents whose children were enrolled in a major metropolitan school system in the United States, Nakagawa (1991) found that mothers and fathers with high scores on a short version of the LGS tended to be more involved in their children's schooling than parents scoring lower. Parents scoring high on generativity tended to help their children with their homework more, showed higher levels of attendance at school functions, and evidenced greater knowledge about what their children were learning and doing in school, compared with parents scoring lower in generativity. In another study of parents, researchers found that high levels of generativity were associated with valuing trust and communication with one's children and viewing parenting as an opportunity to pass on values and wisdom to the next generation (Hart, McAdams, Hirsch, & Bauer, 2001). In a study asking adults to tell socialization stories for adolescent children, those adults scoring high on the LGS constructed narratives that manifested a stronger investment in personal values and that emphasized learning important lessons from the past (Pratt, Norris, Arnold, & Filyer, 1999). These studies all suggest that highly generative parents prioritize education and values in their approach to socialization and that they take advantage of opportunities in parenting to impart lessons and pass on wisdom to the next generation.

Two recent studies suggest that generativity is associated with an *authoritative* parenting style. Peterson, Smirles, and Wentworth (1997) found that middle-aged parents of college students expressed more authoritative attitudes about parenting if they were high in generativity. Pratt, Danso, Arnold, Norris, and Filyer (2001) found that generativity among mothers of teenage children predicted authoritative styles, but generativity among fathers was unrelated to parenting style. Authoritative parenting combines an emphasis on high standards and discipline with a warm, child-centered, and caring approach to raising children. Authoritative parents provide their children with a good deal of structure and guidance, but they also give their children a strong voice in making family decisions. In studies done primarily in the United States, authoritative patterns of parenting have been consistently associated with a number of positive outcomes in children, including higher levels of moral development and greater levels of self-esteem (Maccoby & Martin, 1983). In Peterson et al. (1997), authoritative parenting predicted attitudinal similarity between parents and college-age children, and it was negatively associated with parent–child conflict.

INDIVIDUAL DIFFERENCES IN GENERATIVITY PREDICT A RANGE OF SOCIAL INVOLVEMENTS

Because parenting is closely associated with generativity, it is intriguing to note that Erikson chose as his exemplary personification of generativity a man whose generative accomplishments were played out in the bright light of public action rather than in the private realm of the family. Although Mahatma Gandhi generated biological children of his own, Erikson viewed him as a paragon of generativity because of his mission to deliver and care for an entire nation. Indeed, Gandhi knew many failings as a father of his own children. But his commitment to the well-being of his people, the nation of India, defined a life whose generativity was as impressive and exemplary as any witnessed in the 20th century. In *Gandhi's Truth*, Erikson (1969) showed how generativity may be expressed in public political actions as well as in the crucible of the family.

If parenting within the family is seen as the most private and local realm of generative expression, social involvements among one's peers, in churches and synagogues, and in the community offer opportunities for a more public expression of generativity. In a study of over 270 American adults between the ages of 35 and 65 years, Hart et al. (2001) found that high levels of generativity were associated with more extensive networks of friends and social support in the community and greater levels of satisfaction with social relationships. In addition, generativity was positively associated with church attendance and with involvement in church activities. Adults scoring high in generativity, furthermore, were more likely than those scoring lower to have voted in the last U.S. Presidential election, to have worked for a political party or campaigned for a candidate, and to have called or written to a public official about a social concern or problem. Cole and Stewart (1996) found that generative concern among both African American and Euro American women in midlife correlated highly with measures of sense of community and political efficacy, suggesting that adults with strong generative concerns also tend to express strong feelings of attachment and belongingness in their communities and tend to view themselves as effective agents in the political process. Peterson et al. (1997) found that generativity is positively associated with interest in political issues. And Peterson and Klohnen (1995) found that highly generative women showed more prosocial personality characteristics.

The most impressive documentation of generativity's role in both family and public life comes from a recently completed nationwide study of over 3,000 American adults, ranging in age from 25 to 74 years (Rossi, 2001). One of the primary goals of the National Survey of Midlife Development in the United States (MIDUS) was to determine what demographic, social, and psychological factors are predictive of "caring and doing for others," that is, "social responsibility in the domains of family, work, and community" (Rossi, 2001, title page). Using items from the LGS, the researchers found that, even controlling for age and other demographic factors, generativity was the single strongest and most consistent predictor of many dimensions of socially responsible behavior, including volunteerism and contributing one's time and one's money to family members and to community concerns.

GENERATIVITY PROMOTES PSYCHOLOGICAL WELL-BEING

Erikson believed that generativity was good for society and for the individual, too. The benefits of generativity should be seen in the strengthening of social institutions and the linking of individuals to both benevolent cultural traditions and progressive social change. At the same time, generativity should benefit the generative individual him- or herself. Erikson viewed generativity to be a sign of both psychological maturity and psychological health in the adult years. But what do the data show?

The data show that Erikson was probably right. Longitudinal studies conducted by Vaillant (1977) and Snarey (1993) have shown that ratings of generativity are positively associated with such things as the use of mature coping strategies during times of stress and measures of psychosocial adaptation in adulthood. In a number of studies, we have found that measures of generativity are positively, though modestly, associated with self-reports of life satisfaction, happiness, self-esteem, and sense of coherence in life and negatively associated with depression among midlife men and women, both Euro American and African American (de St. Aubin & McAdams, 1995; McAdams et al., 1998). Similarly, Ackerman, Zuroff, and Moscowitz (2000) showed that generativity was positively associated with positive affectivity, satisfaction with life, and work satisfaction among midlife adults. Among young adults, generativity predicted positive affect at home. Among midlife adults, self-report generative concern is negatively correlated with trait measures of neuroticism (de St. Aubin & McAdams, 1995; Peterson et al., 1997). In longitudinal studies done at the University of Michigan and Radcliffe College, Stewart and Ostrove (1998) reported that, among a host of variables, quality of midlife roles and generativity were the only significant direct predictors of later midlife well-being.

Finally, Keyes and Ryff (1998) reported that measures of generativity were positively associated with a number of measures of psychological and social well-being in the MIDUS nationwide sample. The authors wrote that "generative behavior, generative social obligations, and generative self-definitions are key ingredients in the recipe for psychological wellness" (Keyes & Ryff, 1998, p. 249). The authors also examined interactions with education, arguing that higher education may "motivate generativity by instilling social concern and engendering the desire for reciprocity" (p. 237). In other words, more educated and (assumedly) successful people may be more motivated to "give something back" to society. Higher levels of education, therefore, should predict higher levels of generativity, which in turn should predict well-being. Keyes and Ryff provided strong empirical support for these linkages, and their statistical analyses, furthermore, showed that a significant portion of the variation in well-being associated with education can be accounted for by generativity. Generativity components explained between 30% and 40% of the relationship between education and well-being in the nationwide data analyzed by Keyes and Ryff.

GENERATIVITY IS EXPRESSED IN THE STORIES PEOPLE CONSTRUCT TO MAKE SENSE OF THEIR LIVES

A growing number of philosophers, psychologists, social scientists, and social critics have argued in recent years that adults living in modern societies strive to provide their lives with some sense of unity and purpose by constructing self-defining *life stories* (Bruner, 1990; Giddens, 1991; MacIntyre, 1981; McAdams, 1985; Polkinghorne, 1988; Taylor, 1989). Indeed, Erikson's conception of identity can be reconceived from a narrative point of view (McAdams, 1985). Erikson conceived of identity as, among other things, a personalized and self-defining configuration of drives, talents, values, and expectations that positions the young adult in historical time and within society. Beginning in late adolescence, the person constructs and internalizes this configuration to provide his or her life with some sense of unity, purpose, and meaning. From the standpoint of narrative theory, the identity configuration is itself a personal narrative—an internalized and evolving self-story that imaginatively reconstructs the past and anticipates the future. McAdams (1985, 1993) has identified a number of distinctive features of identity narratives, including characteristic thematic lines of agency and communion, ideological settings or backdrops of belief and value, nuclear episodes or key scenes that stand out as high points or turning points in the plot, and self-ascribed protagonists or "imagoes" that function as idealized main characters in the story. He has also shown that generativity functions as a main idea in many life narratives, especially as individuals move into middle age.

Generativity is an important theme in the life stories of midlife adults. A common version of the theme in American society is expressed as a realization that because others have provided me with care in the past it is now my turn "to give something back" to my family, my people, or my society (Kotre, 1999; McAdams, 1985). The idea of generativity, furthermore, can be appropriated into life stories to provide people with a meaningful understanding of their narrative's "ending." Virtually all stories move toward a more-or-less satisfying ending that resolves plot tensions and brings a sense of closure (Kermode, 1967). As adults move into and through midlife, they may become especially cognizant of their own mortality, and they may come to ponder how their lives may eventually end and what legacies they will leave behind. In that generativity is aimed toward future generations, it is natural that people's anticipations of their own life endings should be informed by their sense of generativity. The prospect of imagining how one's life will end is not a welcome one for most individuals. The narrative beauty of generativity, however, is that it provides a way of thinking about the end of one's own life that suggests that the end is not *really* the end. I may die, but my children will live on. My own story may end, but other stories will follow mine, due in part to my own generative efforts. Generativity helps to script how people see the end of their own lives, helping them to construct identities in which endings give birth to new beginnings.

THE LIFE STORIES OF HIGHLY GENERATIVE ADULTS AFFIRM THE POWER OF HUMAN REDEMPTION AND RENEWAL

A common theme in the life stories of highly generative adults is the transformation of bad life scenes into good outcomes (McAdams & Bowman, 2001; McAdams, Diamond, de St. Aubin, & Mansfield, 1997; McAdams, Reynolds, Lewis, Patten, & Bowman, 2001; for a related finding in the area of social responsibility, see Colby & Damon, 1992). In describing how they reconstruct their own past and anticipate their own future, highly generative adults (e.g., those scoring high on self-report measures of generativity, such as the LGS) are much more likely than their less generative counterparts to highlight scenes in their life stories in which extremely bad events (e.g., death, loss, failure, frustration) are followed by good outcomes (e.g., revitalization, improvement, growth, enlightenment). This way of telling a story about one's life is what we call a *redemption sequence*. A bad scene is redeemed, salvaged, made better by that which follows. The opposite sort of sequence in narrative is what we call a *contamination sequence*, whereby an extremely good scene is ruined, spoiled, or sullied by a bad scene that follows it. Highly generative adults rarely construct contamination sequences in accounting for their own lives, whereas less generative adults are more likely to speak of good scenes turning bad.

What is the connection between redemption and generativity? First, some adults see their own generative efforts as explicit attempts to redeem their own lives. A striking example of this phenomenon is documented in Maruna's (1997) study of published autobiographies of ex-convicts. Maruna found that men and women who eventually desist from crime after spending many years in criminal activity tend to create life narratives that document how they achieved redemption through generativity. They then seek to tell their stories to young people who may be headed toward antisocial behavior. In Maruna's research, the life story of the ex-convict often becomes dominated by a generativity script that affirms the author's redemption and provides a cautionary tale aimed to protect the next generation.

Second, generativity itself entails an implicit understanding of human redemption. The hard work that the highly generative adult displays in his or her efforts to promote the well-being of future generations may entail a good deal of pain, suffering, and sacrifice. But the hardships of today may pay off in good dividends in the future. Scenes of sacrifice and hard work, therefore, may lead to scenes of blessing and reward—a redemption sequence of sorts. Generativity is often about progress, improvement, transforming the bad into good. At the same time, however, generativity challenges people and societies to preserve that which is good from the past in order to benefit the future. In this case, the effort to preserve the good is often viewed to be difficult or onerous. It is not easy to pass on the good from one generation to the next. There is always a battle to be fought with the forces that oppose such a transmission. The discourse of generativity, therefore, is full of stories about people suffering and making sacrifices in order that the future will be good (McAdams, 1993). These stories are variations on a more general theme of transforming bad into good—the essence of redemption.

A universal theme in the world's religions (James, 1902/1957), redemption underscores what Erikson believed to be a key ingredient in generativity, what he called a "belief in the species" (Erikson, 1963, p. 267). The life stories of highly generative adults suggest a deep and abiding faith in the fundamental worthwhileness of the human enterprise. Despite human depravity and a precarious world, humans can redeem themselves, or be redeemed. Adults who shape their life narratives in terms of generativity build identities on the foundation of their faith in humankind, affirming their hope for the future and supporting their convictions that their own lives have ultimate meaning and significance by virtue of their connection to the generations that will follow.

CONCLUSION

The 10 propositions we have discussed in this chapter address the manifestations and meanings of generativity in individual adult lives. We have attempted to highlight the most well-established theoretical offerings and empirical findings on the psychology of generativity. The psychology of generativity begins with individual lives. But part of the beauty and the power of the generativity concept is its wide-ranging applicability, how it speaks to issues that are much larger than individual lives—issues pertaining to education, politics, society, culture, and history. Generativity is shaped by and expressed through cultural norms, social movements, societal institutions, and public policy (Bellah, Madsen, Sullivan, Swidler, & Tipton, 1991). As do individuals, societies themselves may differ dramatically with respect to the content and the form of generative expression (Moran, 1998). Generativity happens in society. Yet until very recently, psychologists and other social scientists have not thought systematically about the societal dimensions of generativity. This chapter has provided a sketch of the best theoretical offerings and empirical findings concerning the psychology of generativity in individual lives. With this background in mind, we are now well prepared to consider generativity in a broader context and to examine the complex relationships between generativity and society.

REFERENCES

Ackerman, S., Zuroff, D., & Moscowitz, D. S. (2000). Generativity in midlife and young adults: Links to agency, communion, and well-being. *International Journal of Aging and Human Development, 50,* 17–41.

Bakan, D. (1966). *The duality of human existence: Isolation and communion in Western man.* Boston: Beacon Press.

Becker, E. (1973). *The denial of death.* New York: Free Press.

Bellah, R. N., Madsen, R., Sullivan, W. M., Swidler, A., & Tipton, S. M. (1991). *The good society.* New York: Knopf.

Belsky, J., Steinberg, L., & Draper, P. (1991). Childhood experience, interpersonal development, and reproductive strategy: An evolutionary theory of socialization. *Child Development, 62,* 647–670.

Bradley, C. (1997). Generativity–stagnation: Development of a status model. *Developmental Review, 17,* 262–290.

Bruner, J. (1990). *Acts of meaning.* Cambridge, MA: Harvard University Press.

Cohler, B. J., Hostetler, A. J., & Boxer, A. M. (1998). Generativity, social context, and lived experience: Narratives of gay men in middle adulthood. In D. P. McAdams & E. de St. Aubin (Eds.), *Generativity and adult development: How and why we care for the next generation* (pp. 265–309). Washington, DC: American Psychological Association.

Colby, A., & Damon, W. (1992). *Some do care: Contemporary lives of moral commitment.* New York: Free Press.

Cole, E. R., & Stewart, A. J. (1996). Meanings of political participation among Black and White women: Political identity and social responsibility. *Journal of Personality and Social Psychology, 71,* 130–140.

Dannefer, D. (1984). Adult development and social theory: A paradigmatic reappraisal. *American Sociological Review, 49,* 100–116.

de St. Aubin, E., & McAdams, D. P. (1995). The relations of generative concern and generative action to personality traits, satisfaction/happiness with life, and ego development. *Journal of Adult Development, 2,* 99–112.

Elder, G. H., Jr. (1995). The life course paradigm: Social change and individual development. In P. Moen, G. H. Elder, Jr., & K. Luscher (Eds.), *Examining lives in context: Perspectives on the ecology of human development* (pp. 101–139). Washington, DC: American Psychological Association.

Emmons, R. A. (1986). Personal strivings: An approach to personality and subjective well-being. *Journal of Personality and Social Psychology, 51,* 1058–1068.

Erikson, E. H. (1950). *Childhood and society.* New York: Norton.

Erikson, E. H. (1963). *Childhood and society* (2nd ed.). New York: Norton.

Erikson, E. H. (1969). *Gandhi's truth: On the origins of militant nonviolence.* New York: Norton.

Giddens, A. (1991). *Modernity and self-identity: Self and society in the late modern age.* Stanford, CA: Stanford University Press.

Hart, H. M., McAdams, D. P., Hirsch, B. J., & Bauer, J. (2001). Generativity and social involvements among African Americans and White adults. *Journal of Research in Personality, 35,* 208–230.

Himsel, A. J., Hart, H. M., Diamond, A., & McAdams, D. P. (1997). Personality characteristics of highly generative adults as assessed in Q-sort ratings of life stories. *Journal of Adult Development, 4,* 149–161.

James, W. (1957). *The varieties of religious experience.* New York: New American Library. (Original work published 1902)

Kermode, F. (1967). *The sense of an ending.* New York: Oxford University Press.

Keyes, C. L. M., & Ryff, C. D. (1998). Generativity and adult lives: Social structural contours and quality of life consequences. In D. P. McAdams & E. de St. Aubin (Eds.), *Generativity and adult development: How and why we care for the next generation* (pp. 227–263). Washington, DC: American Psychological Association.

Kotre, J. (1984). *Outliving the self: Generativity and the interpretation of lives.* Baltimore: Johns Hopkins University Press.

Kotre, J. (1999). *Make it count: How to generate a legacy that gives meaning to your life.* New York: Free Press.

Logan, R. L. (1993). *Gender differences in the expression of generativity.* Unpublished doctoral dissertation, Human Development and Social Policy, Northwestern University.

Maccoby, E., & Martin, J. (1983). Socialization in the context of the family: Parent–child interaction. In P. Mussen (Ed.), *Handbook of child psychology* (4th ed., Vol. 4, pp. 1–102). New York: Wiley.

MacDermid, S. M., Franz, C. E., & De Reus, L. A. (1998). Generativity: At the crossroads of social roles and personality. In D. P. McAdams & E. de St. Aubin (Eds.), *Generativity and adult development: How and why we care for the next generation* (pp. 181–226). Washington, DC: American Psychological Association.

MacIntyre, A. (1981). *After virtue.* Notre Dame, IN: University of Notre Dame Press.

Mansfield, E. D., & McAdams, D. P. (1996). Generativity and themes of agency and communion in adult autobiography. *Personality and Social Psychology Bulletin, 22,* 721–731.

Maruna, S. (1997). Going straight: Desistance from crime and life narratives of reform. In R. Josselson & A. Lieblich (Eds.), *The narrative study of lives* (Vol. 5, pp. 59–93). Newbury Park, CA: Sage.

McAdams, D. P. (1985). *Power, intimacy, and the life story: Personological inquiries into identity.* New York: Guilford Press.

McAdams, D. P. (1993). *The stories we live by: Personal myths and the making of the self.* New York: William Morrow.

McAdams, D. P. (1997). The case for unity in the (post)modern self: A modest proposal. In R. Ashmore & L. Jussim (Eds.), *Self and identity: Fundamental issues* (pp. 46–78). New York: Oxford University Press.

McAdams, D. P. (2001). Generativity in midlife. In M. Lachman (Ed.), *Handbook of midlife development* (pp. 395–443). New York: Wiley.

McAdams, D. P., & Bowman, P. J. (2001). Narrating life's turning points: Redemption and contamination. In D. P. McAdams, R. Josselson, & A. Lieblich (Eds.), *Turns in the road: Narrative studies of lives in transition* (pp. 3–34). Washington, DC: American Psychological Association.

McAdams, D. P., & de St. Aubin, E. (1992). A theory of generativity and its assessment through self-report, behavioral acts, and narrative themes in autobiography. *Journal of Personality and Social Psychology, 62,* 1003–1015.

McAdams, D. P., de St. Aubin, E., & Logan, R. L. (1993). Generativity among young, midlife, and older adults. *Psychology and Aging, 8,* 221–230.

McAdams, D. P., Diamond, A., de St. Aubin, E., & Mansfield, E. D. (1997). Stories of commitment: The psychosocial construction of generative lives. *Journal of Personality and Social Psychology, 72,* 678–694.

McAdams, D. P., Hart, H. M., & Maruna, S. (1998). The anatomy of generativity. In D. P. McAdams & E. de St. Aubin (Eds.), *Generativity and adult development: How and why we care for the next generation* (pp. 7–43). Washington, DC: American Psychological Association.

McAdams, D. P., Reynolds, J., Lewis, M., Patten, A., & Bowman, P. J. (2001). When bad things turn good and good things turn bad: Sequences of redemption and contamination in life narrative, and their relation to psychosocial adaptation in midlife adults and in students. *Personality and Social Psychology Bulletin, 27,* 472–483.

McAdams, D. P., Ruetzel, K., & Foley, J. M. (1986). Complexity and generativity at midlife: Relations among social motives, ego development, and adults' plans for the future. *Journal of Personality and Social Psychology, 50,* 800–807.

Moran, G. (1998). Cares for the rising generation: Generativity in American history, 1607–1900. In D. P. McAdams & E. de St. Aubin (Eds.), *Generativity and adult development: How and why we care for the next generation* (pp. 311–334). Washington, DC: American Psychological Association.

Nakagawa, K. (1991). *Explorations into the correlates of public school reform and parental involvement.* Unpublished doctoral dissertation, Human Development and Social Policy, Northwestern University.

Peterson, B. E. (1998). Case studies in midlife generativity: Analyzing motivation and realization. In D. P. McAdams & E. de St. Aubin (Eds.), *Generativity and adult development: How and why we care for the next generation* (pp. 101–131). Washington, DC: American Psychological Association.

Peterson, B. E., & Klohnen, E. C. (1995). Realization of generativity in two samples of women at midlife. *Psychology and Aging, 10,* 20–29.

Peterson, B. E., Smirles, K. A., & Wentworth, P. A. (1997). Generativity and authoritarianism: Implications for personality, political involvement, and parenting. *Journal of Personality and Social Psychology, 72,* 1202–1216.

Peterson, B. E., & Stewart, A. J. (1990). Using personal and fictional documents to assess psychosocial development: A case study of Vera Brittain's generativity. *Psychology and Aging, 5,* 400–411.

Peterson, B. E., & Stewart, A. J. (1993). Generativity and social motives in young adults. *Journal of Personality and Social Psychology, 65,* 186–198.

Polkinghorne, D. (1988). *Narrative knowing and the human sciences.* Albany, NY: SUNY Press.

Pratt, M. W., Danso, H. A., Arnold, M. L., Norris, J. E., & Filyer, R. (2001). Adult generativity and the socialization of adolescents: Relations to mothers' and fathers' parenting beliefs, styles, and practices. *Journal of Personality, 69,* 89–120.

Pratt, M. W., Norris, J. E., Arnold, M. L., & Filyer, R. (1999). Generativity and moral development as predictors of value-socialization narratives for young persons across the adult life span: From lessons learned to stories shared. *Psychology and Aging, 14,* 414–426.

Rossi, A. S. (2001). (Ed.). *Caring and doing for others: Social responsibility in the domains of family, work, and community.* Chicago: University of Chicago Press.

Snarey, J. (1993). *How fathers care for the next generation: A four-decade study.* Cambridge, MA: Harvard University Press.

Stewart, A. J., Franz, E., & Layton, L. (1988). The changing self: Using personal documents to study lives. In D. P. McAdams & R. L. Ochberg (Eds.), *Psychobiography and life narratives* (pp. 41–74). Durham, NC: Duke University Press.

Stewart, A. J., & Ostrove, J. M. (1998). Women's personality at middle age: Gender, history, and midcourse corrections. *American Psychologist, 53,* 1185–1194.

Stewart, A. J., & Vandewater, E. (1998). The course of generativity. In D. P. McAdams & E. de St. Aubin (Eds.), *Generativity and adult development: How and why we care for the next generation* (pp. 75–100). Washington, DC: American Psychological Association.

Taylor, C. (1989). *Sources of the self.* Cambridge, MA: Harvard University Press.

Tooby, J., & Cosmides, L. (1992). The psychological foundations of culture. In J. H. Barkow, L. Cosmides, & J. Tooby (Eds.), *The adapted mind: Evolutionary psychology and the generation of culture* (pp. 19–136). New York: Oxford University Press.

Vaillant, G. E. (1977). *Adaptation to life.* Boston: Little, Brown.

Vaillant, G. E., & Milofsky, E. (1980). The natural history of male psychological health: IX. Empirical evidence for Erikson's model of the life cycle. *American Journal of Psychiatry, 137,* 1348–1359.

Whitbourne, S. K., Zuschlag, M. K., Elliot, L. B., & Waterman, A. S. (1992). Psychosocial development in adulthood: A 22-year sequential study. *Journal of Personality and Social Psychology, 63,* 260–271.

II

GENERATIVITY IN SOCIETY
AND CULTURE

3

GENERATIVITY AND CULTURE: WHAT MEANING CAN DO

JOHN KOTRE

In the memorable metaphor of Geertz (1973, p. 5), culture is a symbolic "web of significance" that humans spin and on which they live their lives. There are many kinds of cultures—Geertz lists art, religion, ideology, science, law, morality, and common sense—but all have in common the element of shared meaning. Those of us who study lives are quick to ask how such meaning affects the young. It is a short step from there to asking whether cultures themselves are, or can be, "generative."

In the reflections that follow I take up this question, working with a metaphor of culture as an "atmosphere," rather than a web, of meaning. The choice of metaphor matters, for an atmosphere is shared, whereas a web is not (except, perhaps, by the victims of its solitary predator). An atmosphere has greater extension than a web: Changes on one side of the globe inevitably affect the other. It has greater duration: Its air is breathed by a succession of generations, each of which can affect it profoundly. Such is the present circumstance, one could argue, of the shared systems of meaning we call culture.

The reflections unfold as follows. First, I contrast two isolated cultures to illustrate what meaning can do: the difference, that is, that meaning can make in the lives of future generations. Then I suggest, at greater length, how meaning can do it: how certain kinds of stories can inspire generative desire and how certain kinds of people can embody cultural values. Finally, because this is a time when cultures are "moving and mixing" (Hermans & Kempen, 1998), I ask what kind of stance a generative culture might take toward cultures that are different from it, and toward the global culture that is now taking shape. The assumption throughout is that the earth's atmosphere of meaning is as vital to the well-being of future generations as its atmosphere of nitrogen and oxygen—and as much in need of care.

CONTRASTING CULTURES

What does it mean to say that a culture is generative? This is a complex question because cultures are so diverse and because each of us participates in so many of them. When I was growing up in Chicago in the 1940s and 1950s, I participated in a school culture, a church culture, a sports culture, a neighborhood culture, an urban culture, and a national culture. I was exposed to a number of ethnic cultures. Later, when I attended graduate school in that same city, I encountered an intellectual culture unlike any I had known before; it was often at odds with the cultures of my childhood and adolescence. Because all of these cultures overlapped in my mind, it would have been difficult indeed to identify which were generative and which were not—and why.

So let me approach this question of a culture's generativity a little differently—in layers, if you will. And let me begin by turning to history and contrasting a culture that was clearly generative, at least for a time, with one that was not—again, for a time. In the early 17th century, two groups of English settlers came to America and established colonies on its East Coast. One of the colonies came to be known as Virginia and the other, about 500 miles to the north, as New England. The Virginians and the New Englanders crossed the same ocean at the same time, but the meaning of their migrations could not have been more different. And that meaning, according to Moran (1998), mattered greatly to the young in their midst.

The Virginians represented "the very antithesis of a generative culture," wrote Moran (1998, p. 315). They were adventurers, traders, and mercenaries seeking to bring wealth back to England. After establishing their colony in 1607, they discovered how much money could be made by growing tobacco. So they began importing young men from England to work the land, taking them on as indentured servants for contracted periods of 7 years. The young men involved lost all connections with their past. In particular, they lost an important element of culture: the protection of labor laws regulating the treatment of servants like themselves. In England they were afforded such protection, but in Virginia they were at the mercy of their masters.

The results were deadly. Well over 50% of the youths who came to Virginia died before their 7 years of servitude were up. Few of the remainder married or had children, mainly because women in Virginia were so scarce. Those who did marry were unlikely to live long enough to see their children reach adulthood.

In stark contrast to the Virginians stood the New Englanders, who came to America in the 1630s not to make money for investors but to preserve a culture and to find a safe haven for their children. The culture in question was Puritanism, a religious reform movement that had developed in the mid-16th century to "purify" the English church. Unlike the Virginians before them, the Puritans came in family groups, not as isolated individuals, and they brought their culture with them.

That culture is known today for its harshness, and for its self-righteous treatment of those who were deviant. But, as Kai Erikson (1966, p. 188) reminded us, Puritan punishment "was in many ways less severe than in other parts of the contemporary world." The success of their settlement was unquestionable. In New England, the Puritans found abundant land and stayed relatively free of disease. They produced completed families averaging over seven children. As Moran (1998) observed:

> Nowhere else in England, Europe, or in the West for that matter did completed families approach the size of those in Puritan America. . . . In some communities, the under age ten population was as high as 35 percent of the total, and the under age twenty population was as high as 60 percent of the total. (p. 318)

What makes a culture generative? The first and most obvious answer to that question is this: The culture creates an atmosphere in which children survive—survive in the most basic physical sense. Perhaps no elements of culture were more decisive in this regard than legal ones: In contrast to Virginian youths, who lost the protection of the law, Puritan children gained it. In 1641 the New Englanders enacted a document on the "Liberties of Children" that prohibited parents from exercising "any unnatural severity" toward their offspring and that gave children "free liberty" to seek redress. The act was the first of its kind in the Western world, and it came at a time when children were routinely maltreated.

Puritan culture, of course, addressed far more than the physical survival of children. Indeed, the Puritans had come to America to rescue their children from what they saw as the moral corruption of England. Above all, they wished to preserve a way of life, and they wished to do so through the mechanism of the family. "As a Biblical people," wrote Moran (1998), "they viewed the family as God's vehicle for perpetuating faith and religious obligations" (p. 316). Puritanism gave fathers absolute authority, and it placed severe generative demands on them. Not only were fathers to feed, clothe, and shelter their children, but they were to teach them how to read and write, and they were to see to their religious and moral education. As New England grew in size, schools were created to assist in this education. In 1647 a law was passed requiring a form of public schooling for every town over 50 families in size. A decade before, while immigrants were still arriving by shiploads, Harvard College had been created—an astonishing achievement in the history of colonization. From their very beginnings in America, the New Englanders created an atmosphere of meaning that pervaded every aspect of a child's life and every stage of the child's development.

In his theory of the life cycle, Erik Erikson (1963, pp. 249–260) concentrated not on the physical survival of children but on their psychosocial development, and he emphasized how important culture was at every step of the way. Parents, he said, had to "represent to the child a deep, almost somatic conviction that there is a meaning to what they are doing"; to do so they needed the "trusted framework" of a culture. Parents needed religion, or at least some "institutionalized form of reverence," to support their child's ability to *trust* in life (the first stage in psychosocial development). They needed "the principle of law and order" to affirm and delineate their child's growing *autonomy* (the second stage). They needed the assistance of what we today call role models, "ideal adults recognizable by their uniforms and functions" to channel a child's *initiative* (the third stage). And they needed the right kind of "technological ethos" to underwrite the development of personal *industry* in their child (the fourth stage). Frustrations at any of these stages could be endured, Erikson wrote, if a culture provided an interpretation for them—if the frustrations, that is, led "toward a final integration of the individual life cycle with some meaningful wider belongingness." At the time they settled in America, the Puritans seem to have been generative in all these respects.

Not so the Virginians, who had no interest in maintaining a culture that would support the development of their young. Continuing to import indentured youths throughout the 17th century, they cut off all connections with the past. "Each generation of Virginians seems to have started anew, paying little attention to what had preceded it," observed Breen (1980, p. 165). "[They] focused their attention on what they called the colony's 'present state.'" Even when Virginia became more stable in the 18th century, it showed little concern for educating its young. Although the system of indentured servitude was eventually abolished in Virginia, it was soon replaced with something far worse—African slavery.

As we can see from the example of the American New Englanders, generative cultures are concerned not only with the physical survival of their children but with their psychological and moral development as well. But the story of the New Englanders comes with a caveat, a reminder that no culture is *permanently* generative. As time wore on, there was a cooling of the generative intensity that originally brought the Puritans to America. The early school laws they enacted were gradually ignored. Harvard College declined both quantitatively and qualitatively. Puritan fathers proved to be excessively authoritarian (Peterson, this volume, chap. 12), disinheriting the child who chose the wrong occupation, married the wrong spouse, or in other ways displeased them. As the second generation became adults, many chose not to follow the religious path of their parents. As Murrin (1972, p. 239) stated, "Only unusual Puritans seem to have been capable of raising children who knew how to love their fathers." In the absence of this love, it was difficult for Puritan children to embrace the beliefs of their forebears.

As it began to experience a steady sequence of generations, Virginian culture moved in the opposite direction. It began "to raise prospects of generativity," noted Moran (1998, p. 315). The fate of both cultures should make us aware that cultures, like individuals, have their moments—moments to which they rise, moments from which they fall. It's not just a matter of whether cultures are generative, but when.

STORY TYPES

The failure of Puritan culture with adults of the second generation takes us to a second level of inquiry. Here we ask: What does a culture need to keep the young connected to its traditions, even as it welcomes youthful reform? What will lead the young to create a generative *identity* (the fifth stage in Erikson's scheme) and arouse in them what is now called generative *desire*?

What is generative desire? Listen to this 23-year-old woman:

> I don't think one day goes by that I don't worry about what my path is going to be. I keep coming back to the idea that I want to somehow make my mark. I want to help a person who is struggling. If I can't do that as a therapist, I would like to reach people with my writing.
>
> I'm not sure if I will have children, but I want to make a difference in a child's life even if he or she is not my own. Maybe, if I'm lucky, I can say that I changed someone's life for the better. Maybe there's a term for being my age and being concerned with the legacy that I hope to leave. (Kotre, 1999, p. 158)

Generative desire is evident in the phrases "to make my mark . . . to help . . . to reach people . . . to make a difference." It is evident in this young woman's hope to change someone's life for the better and her concern with legacy-making. Other young people will use expressions such as "making my life matter" or "making it count" or "giving something back to my community." As a teacher, I am amazed—and reassured—when I see such desire arising faithfully with each new generation, especially when it does so in someone whose early years have been troubled.

Stewart and Vandewater (1998) have begun to investigate generative desire. They found high levels of it in two samples of college-educated women in their mid-20s and early 30s. They also found that as time went on, these women experienced increases in the capacity for generativity and in actual generative accomplishment. They found outlets for their desire, in other words, and as they did, the desire became less urgent. The women, it would appear, had established a generative identity.

Both Erikson and McAdams have made it clear that identity needs culture—needs what Erikson (1963, p. 263) called an "ideological outlook" and McAdams (1985, p. 247) an "ideological setting." In a parallel fashion, I would suggest that generative desire needs something particular *in* culture, something like the oxygen in air. Oxygen is the element responsible for combustion; it is what makes a match burn when you strike it. What is the corresponding element in culture? What will set imaginations ablaze, creating generative desire?

As a way of opening up this question, I would suggest that if a culture is to spark desire, it must shape its meaning in certain ways—not only in the form of prescriptions but also in the form of stories, and stories of at least five types.

The first type is the *epic*. When the Puritans made their migration from England, they brought with them Biblical accounts like the Exodus, the story of the Jews migrating from Egypt. The Puritans were able to interpret their hardships in light of these Biblical narratives, to attach their experiences to them, and so to feel Erikson's "wider meaningful belongingness." The Exodus is a kind of epic, a story of great deeds done by great people in the past. Epics come in many forms, and the kind of deed they celebrate will of course depend on the nature of the culture involved. The deed could well be the crossing of an ocean, but it could just as well be a breakthrough in science, a spiritual revelation, a courageous act in wartime, an artistic innovation, a political revolution. As adolescents develop their first life stories—their "Personal Fables" (Elkind, 1981) or their "Dreams" (Levinson, Darrow, Klein, Levinson, & McKee, 1978)—they need to come into contact with greatness. They need to feel that they can touch it and be a part of it. They need the blend of history and myth that epics have to offer.

Related to the epic is a second narrative form, the *origin myth*. Origin myths are accounts of how the world came to be, of how "our" people did, of why we embrace each newcomer as our own. Families have such stories; communities do; nations do. As Long (1963, p. 18) has pointed out, origin myths express what a collectivity believes to be important *now*, in the present rather than in the past; they express "what is most essential to human life and society by relating it to a primordial act of foundation." Through its origin myths a culture says, "This is the way things are because this is the way they began. This is what we must do now."

It has been suggested by writers such as Lyotard (1979) that "grand narratives" like epics and origin myths are losing their credibility in the postmodern world; people no longer trust them. And yet the popularity of a movie series like *Star Wars* suggests to me that people long for such narratives. Indeed, I believe that any time a culture approaches a generative moment, it comes into possession of one, whether through rediscovery or reinvention.

A third type of narrative that can foster generative desire is the *story of real life*, the account of ordinary people struggling to live the great virtues, sometimes succeeding, sometimes failing, but always doing so in a way that pays homage to the virtue. The protagonist in this kind of narrative is not a distant predecessor but a fellow traveler, someone who is very human and therefore very reachable as an exemplar, someone "just like you." In contrast to the powerful figure who is the subject of the epic, the leading character of the real-life story is a figure with whom one can be close. Both types of figures are needed if a culture is to inspire generativity. Together, they offer greatness *and* ordinariness, power *and* intimacy—precisely those elements that research has found to coexist in the personalities of generative adults (Mansfield & McAdams, 1996; McAdams, Ruetzel, & Foley, 1986; Peterson & Stewart, 1996).

Growing up in Chicago, I often heard stories from my parents about the economic depression of the 1930s. These were stories about people working for nothing more than the *hope* of being paid, or stories about children working for pennies and then giving what they earned to their parents. On one occasion my father told me about finding a $20 bill (a fortune at the time) and having no choice but to hand the money over to his mother. My mother would tell me about her cleaning duties in a boarding house that her mother tried to run after her father was killed in an accident; she and her three sisters ended up moving from apartment to apartment, sometimes on welfare, sometimes not. These stories of real life were about honesty and hard work, about personal sacrifice and family loyalty. Now, some 70 years later, stories like them are taking on the proportions of an epic, as evidenced by the recent publication of books such as Brokaw's *The Greatest Generation* (1998).

A fourth type of story with generative potential is the *parable*, the teaching tale that is found in so many of the world's cultures. The characters in a parable may be great or ordinary, but their actions will be clear and direct, though often paradoxical in intent. In the simplest of ways and in the briefest of plots, parables depict what happens over the long run. They encapsulate a knowledge of all the mysterious forces that shape human destiny, and they suggest ways of moving on when life is paralyzed. Because parables are open to interpretation, they invite the projections of those who hear them. Making the projections, in fact, is how listeners "get" the message. It is how parables bring wisdom and guidance to generative desire.

The parables I grew up on were the ones I heard in church, and today I see in them a great deal of wisdom about generativity. There is a story about a woman who finds a treasure in a field and sells all that she has to purchase the field; she illustrates a phase of the generative process that I call *selecting*

(Kotre, 1999). There is another story about planting a seed but allowing it to grow on its own; it illustrates a phase called *letting go* (Kotre, 1999). There are stories about evil growing up in the midst of good, like weeds in the midst of wheat, and stories that reconcile one to the fact that much of what is sown fails to bear fruit. And there are ones with the message: Eventually you will die, but something will spring up from you.

A fifth vehicle of wisdom and guidance is the *cautionary tale*, the account of one who goes astray and abandons cultural ideals, or the account of a culture itself that goes astray. The story of the colonial Virginians may be regarded as an example. Another, which I have recently written about (Kotre, 1999), is that of an American minister named Jim Jones who in the 1960s and 1970s became a surrogate father to thousands of abandoned people, only to lead many of them—and their children—to their deaths.

Cautionary tales keep us alert to what I call the "dark side" of generativity (Kotre, 1984). They warn us not to ignore the destructive tendencies that are present in our cultures. By providing examples of how things go wrong, they show how evil can be resisted in its earliest stages, before it gains momentum.

I suspect that the five kinds of stories I have been describing can be found in cultures of all types, even those in which narrative has no formal role. I once wrote a brief piece arguing that some of the classic experiments in social psychology, a discipline that prides itself on being scientific, were actually parables in modern guise, and that this was the reason for their influence (Kotre, 1992). And I recently heard an astronomer speak movingly of the fact that she herself was made up of the very elements created in the universe's original Big Bang. Something from that founding event had flowed outward to produce her, and now she was privileged to study it. She was connecting her life's work to an origin myth that had no place in formal scientific method. But there it was in science's mythic substrate.

Given my own love of narrative, and given the rise in America of narrative psychology, it is not surprising that stories should head my list of cultural forms that can inspire and guide generative desire. As the extensive work of McAdams (1985, 1993) demonstrates, it makes a good deal of sense these days to think of personal identity as a life story, one that depends on an ideological setting. I believe that a culture's stories can provide such a setting. I believe they have the power to ignite generative desire and steer it in the direction of a generative identity.

LIVING FORMS

In the 20th century we have seen the development of new media—radio, television, movies, and now the Internet—that offer unprecedented means of disseminating a culture's stories. Media are "machineries of meaning," in the words of Hannerz (1992), and the new ones are having an impact on the world's thinking as great as that of the printing press. Those of us who work with these machines have a responsibility to uncover the stories in our cultures that have generative power and bring them to the world.

Ironically, it is the advent of the new information technologies that leads us to a third level of reflection on generativity and culture. For while these technologies offer unprecedented opportunities for the dissemination of culture, they also offer an unprecedented threat: that culture will become nothing but "virtual" reality. As Imada (1999, p. 245) wrote of the situation, "Distinctions between original and copy and between reality and unreality become vague. The essentially fictitious is taken as reality. In extreme cases, reality is recognized only in fiction." Often enough in today's world, the media image that seems to be authentic turns out to be anything but. Cyberspace becomes phony space.

Even as cultures make use of the new technologies, then, they will have to protect a very ancient form of expression. That "form" is the human person—the individual who is a living embodiment of a culture's stories, and so of its values. By "living" I mean "not deceased," but I also mean "not imaged."

The living forms that culture needs are of many types; research is only beginning to identify them. One is the *keeper of meaning*. As described by Vaillant and Milofsky (1980), this is a person located between the seventh and eighth of Erikson's stages (between *generativity* and *ego integrity*, that is) who is concerned with preserving a culture's traditions. I once interviewed a woman who felt a need to preserve such traditions in her very person. At certain times in her life, she said, she had tried to "present" a paradox, "exemplify" a virtue, or "stand" for something. Indeed, she saw her whole life as a "statement of" or a "testimony to" certain beliefs. She was a keeper of meaning.

I also include in this category people who become "living legends" or "legends in their own time." Even before their death, anecdotes build up around them and begin to create a myth. Icons such as Albert Einstein and Mother Theresa are clear examples, but there are others closer to home. A young woman once told me about a great-grandmother who had developed a reputation for "knowing things" (Kotre, 1995, p. 231). She had intuitions about family members that always seemed to come true; her premonitions were becoming legendary. Well known or not, living legends like her command our respect, not only because of the gifts they possess but also because their lives ring true to cultural values.

If the keeper of meaning is a cultural beacon, a second figure, the *mentor*, is a practical guide. The mentor is a host who welcomes an initiate into a new world; an exemplar who provides a model for emulation; a teacher who passes on skills; a counselor who provides guidance and moral support; a sponsor who facilitates a protege's advancement; and, above all, someone who believes in a young person's Dream (Levinson et al., 1978). To this description we must add what is in the interest of culture: that in their role as teachers, the very best mentors see that crafts are passed on with integrity, that the art in question is not compromised. They also seek out students in whom special talent, special virtue, or special ideas are struggling to emerge, for cultures need the fresh eyes and the fresh blood that these students possess.

To be generative, cultures also need a third figure, one that Kathy Kotre and I (1998) have called an intergenerational *buffer*, but one who in a larger context might simply be called a reformer. This is a person who has firsthand knowledge of a culture's destructive tendencies and stands in the way of them, absorbing the damage and protecting future generations from their impact. The role of buffer may be clearest in families, in which many parents who suffered at the hands of their own parents vow that their children will not suffer as they did. These mothers and fathers stop the intergenerational transmission of damage. They break the cycle of abuse.

Similar stands are taken outside the family in a variety of cultural contexts. A gynecologist who worked to stop the practice of automatic and unnecessary hysterectomies served as a vicarious buffer, as did a woman who worked to change the prohibition against birth control in her church when she saw the damage it was creating in the lives of married couples. In our study of these buffers, Kathy Kotre and I learned that, as important as the role is, it is fraught with difficulty, for a culture's adherents rarely agree on what is damaging and what is not, and therefore what is or is not in need of reform.

Research in a number of areas has also underscored the importance to culture of *fellow travelers*, even though it has not called them such, preferring instead the terms *peer group* or *support group*. Groups of this kind (the fourth kind of cultural mediators) have been found to be beneficial in coping with loss, illness, and a host of other significant life changes. More to the point, they appear to help gifted individuals achieve their creative breakthroughs. Studying shapers of the 20th century such as Einstein and Freud, Gardner (1993) was surprised by the intense social and affective forces that surrounded his subjects at critical moments. Confidants, collaborators, lovers, and other kinds of fellow travelers provided emotional support and intellectual understanding during the time of the creator's breakthrough.

In this brief and admittedly incomplete list of figures that mediate culture, there is the same blend of power and intimacy that appeared in the preceding list of story types. The intimacy is especially important if we recall the failure of Puritan fathers to evoke love from their children. Intimacy gives the young—it gives us all—someone to touch, and not just through technology. It gives the abstract values of culture a human face. These days we need more than electronic belonging. We need it in the flesh.

CULTURES LOOKING OUTWARD

Up to this point I have probed inward and described characteristics of a generative culture in relation to "its" young. Such a culture, I have said, creates a milieu in which children not only survive but develop the Eriksonian virtues of trust, autonomy, initiative, and industry; in which adolescents develop generative desire; and in which young adults develop a generative identity. It is a milieu full of stories and living embodiments of those stories.

In the 21st century, however, it will become more and more difficult for any culture to speak of the young who belong to "it" and to no one else. The reason is that, because of travel, commerce, and the new media, the earth's cultures are losing their connections to particular places. They are becoming "deterritorialized," in the words of one observer (Appadurai, 1990). They are "moving and mixing," forming "hybrids," in those of others (Hermans & Kempen, 1998; Pieterse, 1995). A complex global culture is emerging and beginning to penetrate local ones, a phenomenon for which one scholar created the composite term "glocalization" (Robertson, 1995). We live increasingly in one world, and that world is coming to our doorsteps.

Hermans and Kempen (1998, p. 1113) have seen the signs of cultures connecting:

> Mexican schoolgirls dressed in Greek togas dancing in the style of Isadora Duncan, a London boy of Asian origin playing for a local Bengali cricket team and at the same time supporting the Arsenal football club, Thai boxing by Moroccan girls in Amsterdam, and Native Americans celebrating Mardi Gras in the United States.

In view of this extraordinary development, let us ask a concluding question. How can a culture look *outward* and be generative? How can it take care of the meaning that envelops not just "its" young, but the world's?

Such care, I believe, would have to begin with the conviction that we need to protect the earth's idea pool as much as we do its gene pool, and that such protection begins at home. A generative culture, then, would store its own ideas the way a botanist stores seeds. It would conserve its stories, venerate the living persons who embody them, and keep fresh the many aspects of culture I have failed to touch on here. It would do so not because of the historical interest of these cultural elements, though that is reason enough to preserve them, but because a time may come when the earth has need of them.

Take the word *generativity*, which was coined in 1950 by Erikson. Generativity was a new word, but the idea behind it was very old, perhaps one of the oldest in existence. Seeds of Erikson's concept are now being found in many cultures—ways of thinking about the self, for example. From Korea comes the idea of a nuclear self (*na*) that maintains a spiritual relationship with others (*nam*), with one's nation (*nara*), and with the world (*nuri*). As Chung (1999) pointed out, the linguistic embeddedness of the root *n* reminds us of the actual embeddedness of the self in these larger collectivities. From Japan, and specifically from the Kyoto School, comes the idea of the self as betweenness (*ba* or *ma*; Kim, 1999). This is a self keenly aware of contextual or atmospheric influences—keenly aware, it seems to me, of the meaning that surrounds it.

Ways of thinking about time have also been unearthed. From the Huayan School of Buddhism comes the idea that the future is able to affect the past as well as the past the future. The point is that generations to come are not simply downstream from us; they are upstream, "ancestors of the future" (Leighton, 1994, p. 197). An African proverb captures the same idea: "The world was not left to us by our parents. It was lent to us by our children" (Villacorta, 1994, p. 75). So does a statement from the Great Law of the Native American Iroquois: "In our every deliberation, we must consider the impact of our decisions on the next seven generations" (Jones, 1994, p. 47). Had these ancient proverbs and policies not been preserved, they would not have been open to discovery at a time when the world needed to hear them. Not only will a generative culture in the 21st century preserve its ideas, it will encourage cross-fertilization with those from other parts of the world—this, in the hope of bringing new ideas into being.

To find an example of what can happen when different cultures meet, one need go no further than the life of Erik Erikson (Coles, 1970). A child psychoanalyst trained under Sigmund Freud's daughter Anna, Erikson left Europe for the United States in 1933. A few years later, he was in some of the remotest regions of the American wilderness asking the grandmothers of Sioux and Yurok Indians how they raised their children. In these conversations, psychoanalysis interacted with the cultures of buffalo-hunting and salmon-fishing Native Americans. In them, the wisdom of Anna Freud interacted with that of old shaman women who were just as keen in their observations of children. Cultures and ideas mixed in Erikson's mind, and from the mix came a new vision of the life cycle, one containing the very idea that is the subject of this book.

Scholars have pointed out that such cross-fertilization is already taking place in contact zones at cultural boundaries. As Kim (1994, p. 322) wrote, this is not a new phenomenon:

> The creation of new value systems throughout history has always taken place at the peripheries, and not in the "world centers" of the time. The founders of all new value systems (e.g., Jesus Christ, Buddha, Confucius) did not appear, serve, or teach in the political, economic, cultural or religious centers of their times. . . . We should recognize and utilize the potential and energy which peripheries possess in value creation.

I would add, however, that those working at the peripheries need themselves to be deeply centered—committed, that is, to a value system—while recognizing that there are indeed other centers. Otherwise, a contact zone becomes a place in which everything is fluid and nothing foundational, a place where it is difficult to generate much of anything.

This view of individual cultures standing in a generative relationship to a global culture takes us beyond *cultural absolutism*, which has led to terrible assaults on many of the world's indigenous cultures. But it also takes us beyond *cultural relativity*, which, in its embrace of diversity, has ignored the hybridization of cultures and overlooked their dark side. It is a view of *cultures contributing* their ideas, their stories, and even their living representatives to something larger.

When we ask whether a culture is generative, we must be aware that few cultures today exist in the kind of isolation experienced by America's early Puritans and Virginians. Culture, in contemporary life, is like the earth's atmosphere: Meanings originate locally, then spread rapidly, as if they were carried on currents of air. A generative society will therefore take care of its culture—its cultures, I should say—as well as it does the air above it. It will be concerned not only with the meaning that "its" young breathe but also with the meaning that the world's young do.

REFERENCES

Appadurai, A. (1990). Disjuncture and difference in the global cultural economy. In M. Featherstone (Ed.), *Global culture: Nationalism, globalization, and modernity* (pp. 295–310). London: Sage.

Breen, T. H. (1980). *Puritans and adventurers: Change and persistence in early America.* New York: Oxford University Press.

Brokaw, T. (1998). *The greatest generation.* New York: Random House.

Chung, Y.-J. (1999). "Transindividuality" in modern Korean philosophies, and some implications for future generations. In T.-C. Kim & R. Harrison (Eds.), *Self and future generations: An intercultural conversation* (pp. 260–284). Cambridge, England: White Horse Press.

Coles, R. (1970). *Erik H. Erikson: The growth of his work.* Boston: Little, Brown.

Elkind, D. (1981). *Children and adolescents.* New York: Oxford University Press.

Erikson, E. H. (1963). *Childhood and society.* New York: Norton. (Original work published 1950)

Erikson, K. T. (1966). *Wayward Puritans: A study in the sociology of deviance.* New York: Wiley.

Gardner, H. (1993). *Creating minds: An anatomy of creativity seen through the lives of Freud, Einstein, Picasso, Stravinsky, Eliot, Graham, and Gandhi.* New York: Basic Books.

Geertz, C. (1973). *The interpretation of cultures: Selected essays.* New York: Basic Books.

Hannerz, U. (1992). *Cultural complexity: Studies in the social organization of meaning.* New York: Columbia University Press.

Hermans, H., & Kempen, H. (1998). Moving cultures: The perilous problems of cultural dichotomies in a globalizing society. *American Psychologist, 53*, 1111–1120.

Imada, T. (1999). Self-identity in a postmodern age. In T.-C. Kim & R. Harrison (Eds.), *Self and future generations: An intercultural conversation* (pp. 235–259). Cambridge, England: White Horse Press.

Jones, C. (1994). Cosmic Gaia and future generations. In T.-C. Kim & J. Dator (Eds.), *Creating a new history for future generations* (pp. 43–59). Kyoto, Japan: Institute for the Integrated Study of Future Generations.

Kim, T.-C. (1994). Toward a new theory of value for the global age. In T.-C. Kim & J. Dator (Eds.), *Creating a new history for future generations* (pp. 319–342). Kyoto, Japan: Institute for the Integrated Study of Future Generations.

Kim, T.-C. (1999). Cambridge, future generations and self. In T.-C. Kim & R. Harrison (Eds.), *Self and future generations: An intercultural conversation* (pp. 285–313). Cambridge: White Horse Press.

Kotre, J. (1984). *Outliving the self: Generativity and the interpretation of lives.* Baltimore: Johns Hopkins University Press.

Kotre, J. (1992). Experiments as parables. *American Psychologist, 47*, 672–673.

Kotre, J. (1995). *White gloves: How we create ourselves through memory.* New York: Free Press.

Kotre, J. (1999). *Make it count: How to generate a legacy that gives meaning to your life.* New York: Free Press.

Kotre, J., & Kotre, K. (1998). Intergenerational buffers: "The damage stops here." In D. McAdams & E. de St. Aubin (Eds.), *Generativity and adult development: How and why we care for the next generation* (pp. 367–389). Washington, DC: American Psychological Association.

Leighton, T. (1994). Meeting our ancestors of the future. In S. Shimizu & K. Yazaki (Eds.), *Thinking about future generations* (pp. 197–213). Kyoto, Japan: Institute for the Integrated Study of Future Generations.

Levinson, D., Darrow, C., Klein, E., Levinson, M., & McKee, B. (1978). *The seasons of a man's life.* New York: Knopf.

Long, C. (1963). *Alpha: The myths of creation.* New York: Braziller.

Lyotard, J.-F. (1979). *La condition postmoderne* [The postmodern condition]. Paris: Minuit.

Mansfield, E., & McAdams, D. (1996). Generativity and themes of agency and communion in adult autobiography. *Personality and Social Psychology Bulletin, 22*, 721–731.

McAdams, D. (1985). *Power, intimacy, and the life story: Personological inquiries into identity.* Homewood, IL: Dorsey.

McAdams, D. (1993). *The stories we live by: Personal myths and the making of the self.* New York: Morrow.

McAdams, D., Ruetzel, K., & Foley, J. (1986). Complexity and generativity at midlife: Relations among social motives, ego development, and adults' plans for the future. *Journal of Personality and Social Psychology, 50*, 800–807.

Moran, G. (1998). Cares for the rising generation: Generativity in American history 1607–1900. In D. McAdams & E. de St. Aubin (Eds.), *Generativity and adult development: How and why we care for the next generation* (pp. 311–333). Washington, DC: American Psychological Association.

Murrin, J. M. (1972). Review essay. *History and theory, 21*, 226–272.

Peterson, B., & Stewart, A. (1996). Antecedents and contexts of generativity motivation at midlife. *Psychology and Aging, 11*, 21–33.

Pieterse, J. N. (1995). Globalization as hybridization. In M. Featherstone, S. Lash, & R. Robertson (Eds.), *Global modernities* (pp. 45–68). London: Sage.

Robertson, R. (1995). *Globalization: Social theory and global culture.* London: Sage.

Stewart, A., & Vandewater, E. (1998). The course of generativity. In D. McAdams & E. de St. Aubin (Eds.), *Generativity and adult development: How and why we care for the next generation* (pp. 75–100). Washington, DC: American Psychological Association.

Vaillant, G., & Milofsky, E. (1980). Natural history of male psychological health: IX. Empirical evidence for Erikson's model of the life cycle. *American Journal of Psychiatry, 137*, 1348–1359.

Villacorta, W. (1994). Creative vision for future generations: Accepting the invitation to dream. In T. -C. Kim & J. Dator (Eds.), *Creating a new history for future generations* (pp. 73–86). Kyoto, Japan: Institute for the Integrated Study of Future Generations.

4

REFLECTIONS ON GENERATIVITY AND SOCIETY: A SOCIOLOGIST'S PERSPECTIVE

KAI ERIKSON

Generativity encompasses a profound concern on the part of human adults not only for their own children but also for the next generation of which those children are a part (McAdams & Logan, this volume, chap. 2). Its reach extends well beyond the family to include society and its institutions. In this chapter I consider the concept from a sociologist's viewpoint and suggest that a true generativity is more complex than is often supposed.

Among living creatures everywhere, the first generative task of parents is to assure that their offspring—the inheritors of their genes—survive in sufficient number to enter the vast elimination tournament of life known as natural selection. Biologically speaking, that is their fundamental reason for existence. They are the trustees of certain genetic material, and their responsibility is to see that it is passed on to the next generation. Observations of animal ethologists suggest that adults in most species are on the whole extremely solicitous of their own offspring but that they can be relatively indifferent (and sometimes even a real danger) to the offspring of other parents. Indeed, they tend to be relatively indifferent even to their own offspring once those offspring leave the nest, literally or figuratively, and approach adult life. Their generative careers are for the most part simple ones.

For the human species, however, the generative task is far more complex. Human parents, like all parents, normally accept responsibility for nourishing and cherishing their own children and for equipping them as best they can for adult life. Our reasons for doing so may have deep instinctual roots, but they involve a complex package of motives, varying somewhat from place to place and from time to time, that can include a deep sense of love for the children we produce, a sense of obligation to the family or lineage to which we belong, and so on. Unlike other animals, however, human beings are also expected to accept responsibility for the welfare of ever wider circles of people—the young of their own communities, of larger national and religious groupings, and, most abstractly, of the species as a whole. And, unlike other creatures, human beings have been either blessed (or is it cursed) by an ability to sense the passing of time, and thus know that what we do in the present can reverberate down the years and affect the lives of persons born in a distant future. This poses a number of dilemmas for humankind. I discuss three of them below.

WHAT IS PASSED ON?

The first dilemma is that the lessons one generation is prepared to pass on to the next are, by definition, attuned to realities that are very likely to change at least a little by the time the new generation has replaced the old. It makes a very great difference, then, whether the lessons parents try to convey to their children reflect a wisdom derived from a wide range of human experiences or are simply the reactions of a given generation of people to the particularities of their own time and place. This has always been true up to a point, but it is a more critical matter now than it has been at other times in human history because the pace of technological change and the growth of human information systems have accelerated so dramatically in recent times.

The concept *generativity* is often traced to the work of Erik H. Erikson, and since that name has a way of coming up in discussions of this topic, as it has in this volume, it might make sense for me to refer to his life span in making a point that was implicit in much of what he wrote. Erik Erikson was born in 1902 and entered adulthood in the years immediately following World War I, a period that large numbers of people in Europe and in the West generally came to see as the beginning of a new era. He did not die until 1994, so he can be said to have been an observer of and a participant in that era for most of the century. I think that he would have agreed with the following.

At the time of his birth, the generative task of most human parents throughout the world was to introduce their children to those patterns of tradition and belief, those ways of perceiving reality, that the parents had learned in their turn. Human infants, of course, do not enter life with instinctual blueprints laying out for them how to behave or how to raise offspring when they become adults in their own turn. The social and cultural settings in which they are born, rather, substitute for those blueprints by offering guides to social life, kept alive in the memories of elders and reflected in the lores and legends and ceremonies that a people share. So the generative task for most adults who lived in the time of my father's parents, and for uncounted millennia before that, was to ensure that their children became participating members of the communities into which they had been born.

That circumstance had changed decisively by the time of Erik Erikson's death in those parts of the world he lived in and studied. Please note that I am trying to be very careful how I phrase that thought here because I am acutely aware that I can only speak of the West. I must leave it to others to consider whether the point I am making has application elsewhere. In those portions of the world I am speaking of now—the United States being very much a case in point—the chances are increasing with bewildering speed that children will need to become attuned to a very different set of realities than was the case for their parents.

For one thing, as I noted a moment ago, the pace of technological change and the growth of human knowledge are now climbing so sharp an incline almost everywhere in the world that the skills and outlooks of the present generation may be of limited value for the worlds their children will soon occupy. Erik Erikson was an immigrant, and as so often happens in such circumstances, his children learned some of the ways of his new land more rapidly than he did. So I was often his teacher in matters having to do with the complexities of American life, just as my children are often my teachers in matters having to do with the complexities of modern life. Moreover, people move with such fluid ease now through social space—migrating laterally across the surfaces of the earth, moving vertically up and down social class hierarchies—that today's children are far more likely than their counterparts at any time in the past to follow different callings, observe different cultural values, and aspire to different social standings than did their parents, and even to adhere to different norms, marry people of different faiths, live in different lands, and speak different languages. To the extent that those conditions obtain, of course, one must ask how well equipped most of the world's parents really are intellectually or even psychologically to serve as mentors of their own young.

In some ways, at least, my country received an advance look at what is now becoming a more universal phenomenon. Erik Erikson came to the United States on the crest of one of the last waves of migration from Europe to America. Between 1830 and 1930, some 35 million persons left Europe for the United States. They came from many parts of what Americans came to call the Old World—Ireland, Germany, Norway, Poland, Italy—but they shared much in common. Although the majority of them came from rural backgrounds, they found themselves being drawn by a force almost like gravity into urban centers of their new country. Many of them found life bewildering in those unfamiliar surroundings, and quite a number suffered from illness and alcoholism and other pathologies as a result. But the deepest of their sorrows, often, was the realization that they had so little to pass on to their children. The skills they had learned in the rural countryside and the moralities that had been a part of their cultural background offered little guidance to their children as they tried to adjust to a new set of realities. In a traditional village, children are expected to inherit their parents' customs, their parents' holdings, their parents' standing in the community, and their parents' outlook on life. Who knows more than parents about the land the children will one day work? Who knows more than parents about the patterns of life the children will one day follow? So young people become apprentices to their elders. The lessons learned by the parents over a lifetime become their curricula. That, clearly, was not to be the case among many immigrant families in America, because the children were moving into worlds their parents could neither fully understand nor fully enter. No one knew less about the intricacies of this new land than parents, and no one was a less adept role model for children seeking new opportunities, moving into new occupations, and learning new ways of behaving.

The most poorly adjusted of those immigrants, in their confusion, came to rely ever more sullenly on familiar old ways of doing things, which only proved to their children that they were relics of a time past. And so the gulf between them sometimes widened, to the sorrow of both. The wisest of them, however, knew something that is well worth remembering: The best way for parents to help children adjust to the realities of a world about which they know very little is to teach them not *what* to think but *how*, not what particular moral values they should observe but what a sense of values *really is*, not what words they should say or what acts to perform in the presence of others but what respect and compassion and caring consist of, not what articles of faith should be defended but what it means to stand for something.

Any examples I offer, of course, come from Western experience, but the general point I am making—applicable, I would hope, to cultures other than my own—is that the most useful traditions in today's times are those that promote *general attitudes* and *mind-sets*, rather than those that promote fixed rules of behavior and thought. The first form of instruction readies the mind for sorting through new experiences; the second only equips it with automatic reflexes that are often obsolete as soon as they are learned.

WHO PROFITS?

Generativity speaks of a concern for and a commitment to future generations at several levels of abstraction: (a) one's own offspring; (b) younger members of the community, or nationality, or any other social grouping to which one sees oneself as belonging; and (c) the species itself. These are not the only levels of abstraction that might be identified, of course, but I make the distinction because it helps introduce another level of dilemma—the fact that these generative tasks are not only *different* in kind but potentially *contrary*.

In the first place, to provide one's children with whatever leverage in life one can afford to bestow on them is a different kind of activity—and may be drawn from a different chamber of the human mind, so to speak—than looking out for the welfare of a whole generation. These are not always opposing pursuits, to be sure, but they often are. If you or I were given the choice of either providing our own offspring with special advantages in life or assuring an equitable distribution of opportunities and resources throughout the younger generation more generally, we would be facing a very difficult choice. Would I relinquish an extra measure of medicine for my ailing child, for example, if I was told that a fairer apportioning of that precious stuff would serve the species better? I doubt it. Nor, for that matter, would I expect it of anyone else. Most of us, caught in such a dilemma, would adopt a form of moral reasoning that denied the very premise of the question (a strategy for which the human mind has proved to be very well adapted). This is one reason why the promptings of even the most generous of hearts have to be supplemented by the workings of social institutions. Parents who cherish their own offspring deeply enough cannot always be counted on to have the best interests of the larger generation utmost in mind.

And the reverse can be true as well. People who devote a good deal of love and energy to the care of whole communities or societies or nations often do so at the cost of neglecting their own children. As McAdams and Logan note in chapter 2, Mohandas Gandhi was as benevolent a parent to his people as it is possible to imagine, but he seems to have had few reserves left over for the care of his own offspring. The Catholic Church has long required that parish priests have no families of their own so that nothing can divert them from the care of the community as a whole. I do not know how true this is in other religious traditions. But the issue is clear: Trying to care for a whole generation while at the same time trying to care for one's own children can pose conflicts of several kinds.

The second point I want to raise in this connection moves closer to the heart of the matter. In English, when one speaks about "the next generation," one is usually referring to the young of a particular community or nation or people. It is important to keep in mind, then, that looking out for the welfare of a specified class of young people—Muslims, Jews, Japanese, Americans—is different from, and can be contrary to, looking out for the interests of the species in general. In this regard, Erik Erikson (1966, 1984) spoke of a process he called *pseudospeciation*, which was meant to refer to the fact that mankind, while one species, has divided itself throughout its history—territorially, culturally, politically—into various groupings that permit their members, at decisive times, to consider themselves, more or less consciously or explicitly, the only truly human species, and *all* others (and especially *some* others) as less than human. (Erikson, 1984, pp. 481–482)

He then went on to say that:

[M]ankind from the very beginning has appeared on the world scene split into tribes and nations, castes and classes, religions and ideologies, each of which acts as if it were a separate species created or planned at the beginning of time by supernatural will. Thus each claims not only a more or less firm sense of distinct identity but even a kind of historical immortality. Some of these pseudospecies, indeed, have mythologized for themselves a place and a moment in the very center of the universe, where and when an especially provident deity caused it to be created superior to, or at least unique among, all others. (Erikson, 1984, pp. 481–482)

At its best, Erikson thought, this sense of special significance can bind people together, evoke feelings of loyalty and devotion in them, and inspire the best poetry and art the human soul is capable of. At its worst, however, this sense of special significance can become a "potential malignancy of universal dimensions" because

in times of threat and upheaval the idea of being the foremost species tends to be reinforced by a fanatic fear and hate of other pseudospecies. The feeling that those others must be annihilated or kept "in their places" by warfare or conquest or the force of harsh custom can become a periodical and reciprocal obsession of humankind. (Erikson, 1984, p. 482)

Those thoughts have returned to me lately because I have been studying the breakup of Yugoslavia and the effects of that disaster on the people of the Balkan countryside. As everyone now knows, deep fissures have opened up across that land separating Serbs from Croats and both from Muslims, and it is hard to look at that troubled landscape without revisiting the idea of pseudospeciation. This is just as true, of course, if one contemplates any of the other ethnic and national conflicts that have exploded into being in recent times—Northern Ireland and Central Africa, along with Yugoslavia, serving as prominent examples. In light of these recent events, I would propose the following:

Human beings, like all social animals, have an innate tendency to gather into collectivities containing individuals who regard themselves as being of *like kind*. That is, it is in our nature to seek communion with other human beings. But the ways in which we do so, the people to whom we find ourselves drawn, and the groupings that emerge from all this must be understood as products of social life. The members of a collectivity may see themselves as joined together by traceries of kinship, and so assume that their fellowship is somehow created by nature. But even those social groups that make the strongest claims about common ancestry or speak the most passionately about bonds of blood are rarely consanguineous in any meaningful sense of the term. The ties are an invention of the social world.

Most people belong to a number of such domains. These different aspects of our layered selves are like concentric circles, radiating out from their center like ripples in a pond—each of those widening circles enclosing a "we" to which one feels a sense of relation and in which one feels a sense of membership. For most people, one's immediate family or household occupies the innermost ring, and as the circles radiate outward, they enclose ever larger domains such as village, parish, neighborhood, place of work, community, city, region, or country, as well as a number of other rings representing ethnicity, faith, and so on. We cannot afford to be too exact here, because the domains that appear on any particular set of maps, and the way they are nested within each other, will vary by time, place, and culture.

This way of looking at matters makes it easier for me to make two points. First, human beings tend to invest a good deal more in some of those domains than they do in others. And, second, those investments are subject to change from one domain to another, especially during unsettling times.

The most important question one can ask of these nested identities is: which of them are crucial enough at any given time to provide a sense of communion, a sense of security, a sense of being at home among one's own kind? Or, to put it more dramatically, which are so central to one's feelings of selfhood that one would kill for them, die for them, or—this is the acid test—willingly risk the lives of one's own children for them? These can be called *master identities* for our purposes here. The family, presumably, offers that kind of shelter everywhere on earth, and most adults are prepared to defend it at any cost. That is a reflex so deep in the human grain—so deep, really, in animal nature—that nothing more needs to be said about it.

The only other domains in modern times that draw on that kind of emotional investment—that touch people, literally, to the quick—are those denoting one's *country* or one's *nationality*. In many parts of the world (Japan is often cited as an example), state and nation are for the most part the same. In other parts of the world, however, that is not necessarily the case, and when the state can no longer provide a sufficient measure of emotional protection—when it weakens as a source of master identity—people are likely to withdraw into defensive enclosures that *they* think of as defined by an even closer form of national or ethnic kinship. This, obviously, is what happened in the former Yugoslavia. Most of the people who now call themselves "Serbs" or "Croats" do not really suppose that they belong to a distinct genetic strain, but they have been invited to assume that they share a common ancestry, belong to much the same world of experience, and in that sense have a place in a kind of family genealogy.

Why people in places like the Balkans have more confidence in those attachments than they do in ties of place, class, guild, ideology, and sometimes even in religious faith, is not immediately obvious. That is among the wonders of human life that we social scientists ought to ponder more often than we do. But the evidence that this tendency is not only strong but growing in appeal is hard to escape in this age of growing national fervor.

It has been frequently noticed by social scientists that whatever the centers of gravity that act to draw people together into ethnic clusters, the groupings that result derive their shape and definition less from the positive qualities of the "we's" who occupy the center of group space than from the negative qualities of the "they's" who press in on that domain from the outside and thus mark its edges. In a very real sense, then, "they," the outsiders, identify and give substance to "we," the insiders. Indeed, there probably cannot *be* any "we" in the absence of a "they."

To the extent that this can be said to be true, feelings of difference and otherness—even of outright contempt and enmity—are the very soul of nationalism. The drawing of an ethnic boundary generally involves a process in which people on one side of the dividing line come to see people on the other side as so unlike them morally and sometimes even physically that it seems reasonable to treat them as a different order of being, maybe even a species apart. And that, of course, brings us back to pseudospeciation.

This has been a relatively long detour, but the point I want to make is that the expression "next generation" in most of what was once Yugoslavia—and this is true for many other parts of the world as well—has come to mean the young of a particular ethnic community. When a community of adults speak of "their" young, that is almost always what they have in mind, and it is increasingly the case that the moral education they are ready to provide for that incoming generation involves an almost murderous level of contempt for those ethnic others who were so recently (and could so easily have been again) their neighbors. The result of this in Croatia and Bosnia and Kosovo has been that many of the most promising members of the incoming generation have been killed or wounded or maimed so severely psychologically that they are consumed by hatred and a deep conviction that it is their obligation to exact revenge on other young people who are exactly like them in every important respect.

People move into these defensive encirclements in the first place to protect themselves and their children's future. It is important to note for our purposes here, then, that the impulses that brought them there can be called "generative" on at least one level. But it is hard to think of an activity, at least on the surface of things, that is more destructive to the long-range prospects of humankind in general. It is not just that the most promising of the young kill each other in frightening numbers, but that those who survive lose their sense of security and their confidence in the workings of both the natural and the social world. That is what trauma does to people. And it has the further consequence that people who grow into adulthood and become parents in such times as these find it ever harder to summon a nourishing sense of generativity themselves.

No matter how one understands the process of natural selection, then, it seems impossible to make a case that this bitterness, even under the most benign of circumstances, can contribute to the welfare of the species as a whole. But when one adds that these "pseudo-species" may one day be armed with weapons that have the capacity to kill vast numbers of those despised others—and, of course, the rest of us in the bargain—the situation appears more critical yet.

Erik Erikson was deeply concerned by this potentiality, of course, and spoke hopefully of a time when a "species-wide identity," based on a "truly universal ethos," might replace the all-too-human tendency for people to splinter into ethnic enclaves of one kind or another. "Only thus," he wrote, "can humankind truly become in spirit what it already is in fact: one species" (Erikson, 1984, p. 486). He left the matter there, alas, and turned his attention to other matters, leaving us the problem of imagining how such a revolution in human sensibility might take place.

WHEN ARE THE BENEFITS REALIZED?

I would like to now turn to a third dilemma. The ability of human beings to maintain a concern for younger generations well into the future varies considerably from one cultural setting to another, but it is limited. In the United States, it is fair to say, the vast majority of people feel a deep sense of commitment to their own children, whom they know and love as persons, and to their children's children, whom they know or expect to know or at least can imagine as living creatures with names and personalities and needs. When they are asked to contemplate generations more distant than those, however, they often find themselves thinking in dry abstractions. People who feel a strong sense of concern about the continuation of a particular family line, say, or a particular religious tradition, may be able to think further into the human future. But even then the distance they can project themselves over time is relatively short.

I have served for many years as a consultant in matters having to do with the disposal of high-level nuclear waste. The disposal strategy favored by the government of the United States is to place those wastes at the bottom of a deep hole in the living body of the earth in the hope that they will remain untouched and secure for the tens of thousands of years it will take them to lose their radioactive potency. Most of the worrying about this matter has been done by scientists and engineers and other technical persons who are expert in calculating how long particular rock formations or particular man-made barriers can be expected to remain intact. But virtually no attention has been given to what seems to me the most essential of questions: What impact is this solution likely to have on future generations of people? We have been treated to the remarkable spectacle of scientists and engineers trying to imagine how safe those wastes will be from human intrusion many millennia from now when they haven't the slightest idea what technologies will be available to the generations then inhabiting the earth or what they are likely to be thinking.

The absurdity of these discussions, however, helps emphasize a crucial issue. What shall we say is the generative task of those of us entrusted with trying to look out for our progeny of ten, twenty, fifty thousand years hence? Is there anything we can do given our limited resources and limited understanding to help them protect themselves from the most concentrated package of destructive energy our age knew how to assemble? My own solution to that problem would be to leave those wastes on the surface as long as humanly possible in the hopes that future generations will develop a better strategy than we have thus far devised for dealing with the dreadful legacy we have left to them. But the main point I want to raise is something else. I think it very likely that future generations will look with disdain upon the wastes we bequeathed them and conclude that our brief adventure with nuclear energy in the second half of the 20th century was not worth the costs it imposed on the future. And if they look into the matter closely, they will learn that virtually no one in our time was given the task of even *thinking* about the nature of those costs. The nuclear age had been under way for more than two decades before responsible authorities gave any thought to the wastes being generated, and they did not undertake a serious discussion about the human dimensions of the disposal problem for another two decades. There was scarcely a trace of what we call generativity in that process, at least as seen in the long term. But the people who lurched into the nuclear age with so little thought to the future had their children and their children's children in mind as they did so, and we need to ask how often in human affairs this happens—that short-term generosities blind people to long-term generosities.

In recent years, it is true, many thousands of hours have been devoted in those councils to calculating the chances that some natural event will disturb the wastes and endanger the people then occupying the world. Those impulses, too, can be understood as generative, at least in the sense that their object is to protect the people who follow them, as the old Iroquois saying goes, even unto the 7th, or in this case the 70th generation. But decades passed before the issue was even broached, partly because no one in modern governments is assigned the task of thinking about, or speaking for, the needs of future generations. Joanna Macy (1991) once suggested that the Congress of the United States reserve two seats for delegates whose responsibility it would be to represent the needs of people yet unborn. This suggestion is not a very practical one, as Macy knows perfectly well, but it does underscore an important point: When official discussions take place in the capitals of the world about how scarce resources should be apportioned or how the environment should be preserved, the voices of those who will be affected the most by what we do are not represented in any formal way.

In this chapter, I have asked questions rather than offered answers. I think it is critical to note that while generativity itself can be seen as an essential quality for addressing problems of the human future, it must also be seen as one of those problems.

REFERENCES

Erikson, E. H. (1966). Ontogeny of ritualization in man. *Philosophical transactions of the Royal Society of London, 251*, 337–349.

Erikson, E. H. (1984). Reflections on ethos and war. *The Yale Review, 73*, 481–486.

Macy, J. (1991). *World as lover, world as self*. Berkeley, CA: Parallax Press.

5

THE PROPAGATION OF GENES AND MEMES: GENERATIVITY THROUGH CULTURE IN JAPAN AND THE UNITED STATES

ED dE ST. AUBIN

The drive to create offspring and to care for the young of one's species certainly has bioevolutionary roots. Whether it is the male emperor penguin that forgoes weeks of nourishment as he protects an egg balanced on the top of his feet or the conger eel that lays a brood of millions but then departs (Allport, 1997), adult members of all species are compelled to reproduce so that one's inherited genetic code may survive in successive generations. The assurance of a genetic legacy is accomplished through reproduction and by maintaining the health of one's offspring such that these may in turn mature to reproductive capabilities that result in the downstream flow of one's genes within the endless river of generations. Less evolutionarily fit adults do not make for good replicators of genes in that they are less able to produce offspring or to assure the survival of those they do create (Pinker, 1997). These well-known dynamics of natural selection and parenting within the evolutionary process are the biological bases of generativity, which is a psychological concept capturing a human adult's desire to invest in the well-being of younger and future members of one's species (McAdams & de St. Aubin, 1998).

With humans, of course, the generativity process becomes more interesting for at least two basic reasons: higher levels of consciousness and the existence of cultures. First, we are aware of so much more than our nonhuman neighbors. We know, for instance, that regardless of our species' incredible achievements in medicine and technology, each of us will one day die (Becker, 1973). This fact does not please us (Goldenberg, Pyszczynski, Greenberg, & Solomon, 2000). And we find little comfort in the knowledge that our genes will indeed survive through future generations. Along with a genetic legacy, humans seek to achieve a symbolic immortality by creating a legacy of a different kind and through means other than the purely biological. For our species, generativity operates both within and beyond the biological level.

Although we propagate genes like other species, our generativity also entails the creation and nurturance of memes. A *meme* is an idea, behavior, style, or usage that spreads from person to person within a culture (Merriam-Webster, 2002). Just as one's genetic code is transmitted through genes, we pass our values and ideas to others through memes (Blackmore, 1999; Dawkins, 1976). This is why Erikson was careful to point out that generativity entails so much more than parenting and why he suggested that creativity was closely related. The childless adult may not be procreative in the strictly biological sense, but such an adult can surely be considered generative if he or she has participated in any one of a number of meme-propagating endeavors such as maintaining traditions, creating new products, or mentoring the young. As humans, our intellectual abilities compel us to propagate memes as well as genes. We wish to be remembered for our unique contributions to the worlds of ideas and values and products more so than for the genetic endowment we bequeath to our progeny. Given the choice between a daughter who embodies one's cherished values (meme propagation) or a daughter who possesses a nose crook similar to one's own (gene propagation), most of us would choose the former. This is one reason generativity is so fascinating to study. Each adult offers a unique portrait of generativity. No two meme legacies are the same. And even within any one adult, generativity often changes over time (Stewart & Vandewater, 1998). Most of the scholarship regarding generativity to date has focused on these individual differences and intraindividual developmental patterns (McAdams, 2001a).

Human generativity is further compounded by the existence of cultures. Both the meaning we assign to specific memes (*cow* as sacred, lazy, smart, food, beautiful; *child* as possession, labor, evil, innocent) and the processes by which generativity is enacted (effective pedagogy, proper parenting, creativity, mentoring) are determined to a great extent by cultural dynamics. The ancient Spartan tradition of beating male children with switches (deMause, 1974) is a form of generativity as is the contemporary parent playing Mozart to a fetus to improve the spatial-temporal abilities of the forth-coming child. The former generative practice results from the Spartan image (meme) of the adult male as soldier and a belief in authoritarian and harsh training tactics. It has to do with Spartan culture. Likewise, the misguided parent with the Mozarted fetus exists in a culture that prizes proactive parenting aimed at advancing a child's intellectual abilities but also one that fails to value the results of empirical science (which has repeatedly demonstrated the futility of this practice; Chabris, 1999). It is difficult to imagine a U.S. school in the 21st century regularly beating its male students or a Spartan mother playing certain music to her embryo so as to facilitate the intellectual growth of her coming child. Generative practices and products vary by culture.

Simply noting the cross-cultural differences in generative practices (beat-ing male children considered abusive in one culture and effective in another) is an important first step, but a more meaningful enterprise would seek to discern the manner in which culture influences these differences in generativity. Psychologists have been implored to move beyond simple cross-cultural comparisons of content or magnitude and to begin unlocking the meaning and psychological processes inherent in cultural dynamics (Markus, 2001). Simply stating that culture A exhibits a different form of generativity than culture B is no longer satisfying. It would be like reporting that males tend to be more aggressive than females and not discussing *why* this is so (antecedents, biological factors, contextual demands) or *how* this occurs (forms of aggression, dynamics). To understand the manner in which culture con-tours the expression of human generativity, we must examine specific cul-tures at a deep level.

In sum, the biological base of generativity is the drive to pass on genes. Given their advanced cognitive sophistication, human adults are generative in the realm of memes as well. This leads to individual differences and to temporal shifts in one's own generativity. Finally, variation in human generativity is due, in part, to cultural differences. Although each adult ex-presses generativity in a unique manner, culture imposes parameters within which one operates as memes and genes are propagated through generativity. In this chapter, I address a rather straightforward question and use two cul-tures (Japan and the United States) as comparison cases: How does culture influence the manifestation of generativity? Japan and the United States are chosen as comparison cases because of their similarities (technology, eco-nomic), their very real differences (histories, politics, demographics, values), and the increasing availability of research addressing Japanese culture.

INVESTIGATIVE STRATEGY

A cross-cultural investigation of generativity might take any one of several approaches. One could administer well-established measures of generativity such as the Loyola Generativity Scale (LGS) or the Generativity Behavioral Checklist (GBC) to groups of U.S. and Japanese adults. Although the findings might be interesting at some level (Are U.S. adults as a group higher in generative *concern* [LGS]? Do Japanese adults *act* [GBC] in a more generative manner?), this type of investigation would ultimately reveal very little about the cultural influences on generativity. Such cross-cultural studies of quantitative differences in aggregated individual data are common in psychology (Matsumoto, 2000), but our discipline must move beyond this methods paradigm if we are to offer a vital voice in discussions of culture.

A second approach would be to compare generativity in Japan and the United States with the use of one of the various models of generativity that have been produced. One could rely on Erikson's (1969, 1982) writings here or turn to the seven-faceted model developed by McAdams and de St. Aubin (1992) or to Kotre's (1984, 1999) four-type scheme. Regarding the last, for instance, one might discuss the differences between Japan and the United States in *technical* generativity, the third of Kotre's four types. As useful as these models have been in scholarly investigations of generativity, such a top-down approach to cross-cultural work would ultimately fail to capture the specific generativity dynamics unique to a particular culture. Starting with an established model a priori and trying to fit it to different cultures limits our ability to advance generativity theory.

The wisest approach, it seems to me, would be to start with the culture itself, not with predesigned measures or models. Much like the grounded theory approach (Glaser & Strauss, 1967; Strauss & Corbin, 1998), the starting point of this investigation is an immersion in actual cultural practices. This is necessary if one is to truly respect the meaning and processes within a culture. Further, looking "from within a culture" (Ogbu, 1994) in this way allows for the "emergence of new understandings" (Geertz, 1979) of generativity.

Although the method followed here is unique, it was inspired by Shweder and colleagues' (Shweder et al., 1998) use of a *custom complex* (initially conceived by Whiting & Child, 1953) as the unit of analysis in cultural psychology. Shweder begins with a customary practice that all cultures must address, such as sleeping arrangements within a dwelling. He describes this "practice" in as much detail as possible, outlining the typical relevant behaviors for a given culture. I would add that one should note important variations and nuances within the culture. From this thick description of a customary practice, Shweder builds a custom complex that specifies the beliefs, values, sanctions, rules, and motives associated with it. By building from bottom (actual behavior in a specific culture) to top (cultural values, modes) in this way, Shweder's approach is an *inductive process* (the context of scientific discovery) rather than a *deductive technique* (context of justification; McAdams, 2001b).

66   *ED dE ST. AUBIN*

I have chosen two custom practices that are central to the generativity process: caring for one's young children and the mentoring of artistic talent. As Erikson (1950) and others (Snarey, 1993) have declared, parenting is the quintessential act of generativity. It concerns the propagation of both genes and memes. Parents pass on genes to offspring but also seek to instill values and create memories for their children. Human newborns are completely dependent on caregivers for survival (unlike the conger eel mentioned earlier), and so parents are required to invest considerable resources toward the survival and well-being of their offspring. Noting the different parenting "practices" in Japan and the United States will allow for the construction of a generativity "complex" that articulates the cultural dynamics (beliefs, sanctions, motives, etc.) either shared or unique to each culture that shape the generativity process. This review focuses primarily on maternal caregiving because mothers in both cultures, but particularly in Japan, provide a disproportionate amount of care to children.

But the investigation would be incomplete if it did not attempt to also address the nonprocreative aspect of generativity as it exists in Japan and the United States. The mentoring of artistic talent is typically not enacted between biological relatives. Yet it is a generative endeavor in that it both concerns creativity and involves the teaching of artistic skills to younger individuals. It is all about the propagation of memes and not at all about genes. By comparing the practices involved with the passing on of creative skills in these two cultures, we should be able to add to the generativity complex that had begun to take shape in the investigation of parenting.

The coverage of both these custom practices begins with discussions of how each is manifested in Japanese culture. Further, more space is allocated to the generativity practices and generativity complexes as these exist in Japan as I assume that the reader is likely less familiar with the Japanese cultural context.

CARING FOR ONE'S YOUNG CHILDREN

Japanese mothers maintain prolonged physical contact with their infants (Rothbaum, Weisz, Pott, Miyake, & Morelli, 2000) and are likely to make great use of proximity-promoting equipment such as snugglies or slings that hold the child against one's chest (Bornstein, Tal, & Tamis-LeMonda, 1991). This extensive body contact (skinship) between mother and infant characterizes the sleeping patterns, lengthy bathing episodes, and breast-feeding encounters (beyond the intake of nourishment) and is most likely to occur during times of infant distress (Rothbaum, Pott, Azuma, Miyake, & Weisz, 2000). Newborns in Japan spend approximately 2 hours per week in nonmaternal care, whereas U.S. babies typically experience 23 hours (Barratt, Negayama, & Minami, 1993).

Research portrays Japanese mother–infant interactions as focusing the infant on social stimulation (particularly the mother) as opposed to material objects (e.g., toys; Rothbaum, Pott, et al., 2000) and maternal speech as more emotion-laden than informational (Rose, 1999). Japanese mothering has been described as indulgent (Power, Kobayashi-Winata, & Kelley, 1992), protective (Rose, 1999), and symbiotic (Rothbaum, Pott, et al., 2000). The relationship between mother and infant is best captured by the term *amae*, described over 40 years ago to Western audiences by Doi (1962) as a loving dependence that a Japanese child feels toward his or her parent (particularly the mother). *Amae* refers to the indulged child's presumption and dependence on mother's benevolence.

To achieve *amae*, or the child's "basking in another's indulgence" (Doi, 1962, p. 8), Japanese mothers cater to each need of their child (Rothbaum, Pott, et al., 2000), anticipating necessary changes to the environment before circumstances should cause any distress to the infant. Children are protected and sheltered. A mother rarely allows direct conflict or negative feelings to occur between herself and her child as this would weaken the emotional connection she hopes to engender.

The resulting *amae* encourages in the child a sense of dependence on others (Power et al., 1992) and motivates attempts to please his or her mother. What is seen as normal and healthy *amae* in Japan would likely be classified as insecure ambivalent attachment by U.S. psychologists (Rothbaum, Pott, et al., 2000) in that it involves helpless dependency, blurring of boundaries between self and others, nonexploration, excessive babyish behaviors, passivity, and extensive clinging. Japanese mothers impose few demands on their young children (Rose, 1999) and are more tolerant of misbehaviors, unless these relate to breaking the *amae* bond by turning against the mother in any way. In these instances, the typically permissive Japanese mother is most likely to resort to physical punishment (Power et al., 1992).

The behaviors associated with Japanese parenting captured by the term *amae* are highly aligned with the values of cultural collectivism that exists in Japan. As described by Triandis (1997, 2001) and others (Uleman, Rhee, Bardoliwalla, Semin, & Toyama, 2000), collectivist cultures emphasize interdependency between group members and place importance on the group over the individual. Cultures with a predominance of individualism such as the United States, in contrast, value individual autonomy and the pursuit of individual goals and achievements.

Mothers' care for infants in the United States is significantly different on every one of the behaviors discussed so far in this section. Rather than changing environmental factors in anticipation of the child's possible distress, U.S. mothers are more likely to wait until an infant communicates a need and then to react to it (Rothbaum, Pott, et al., 2000). Mother–child interactions in the United States are characterized by information-based speech regarding the world of objects (Bornstein et al., 1991) and the early encouragement of independent exploration of the environment (Rose, 1999). Such independence training results in the child's having much input into the socialization process (Power et al., 1992), such as discussions regarding appropriate discipline for misbehaviors. U.S. mothers are more prone to maintain a distal eye contact (as opposed to a "skinship") and to make use of distance-promoting equipment such as walkers and swings (Rothbaum, Pott, et al., 2000).

Outside of the specific mother–child interactions, Japanese mothers are distinct in their high levels of anxiety (Kazui, 1997), particularly as it relates to their parenting role (Kameguchi & Murphy-Shigematsu, 2001). Further, Japanese mothers conduct approximately 80% of the parenting and 90% of all household chores (Strom, Strom, Strom, Makino, & Morishima, 2000). Finally, Japanese mothers tend to seek advice from other mothers, whereas U.S. mothers are more likely to consult expert guidance from sources such as pediatricians or parenting books (Kakinuma, 1993).

Although empirical research has demonstrated all of these differences between U.S. and Japanese mothering, it is important to keep in mind that these two groups of mothers are more alike than different (as would be true if mothers of any other culture were compared). Around the world, mothers feed, soothe, encourage, and discipline their young children more similarly than differently. Cross-cultural psychology has failed to appreciate the significance of such intercultural similarity (Stevenson-Hinde, 1998) just as it has not adequately addressed intracultural differences (Power et al., 1992). We know, for instance, that not all Japanese mothers behave identically, and that some of these intracultural differences are systematic, such as comparisons of Japanese mothers from different age cohorts (Rothbaum, Pott, et al., 2000).

Nonetheless, there is indeed cultural variation in the *custom practice* of caring for one's infant. By moving up from this behavioral level to the custom complex that specifies the beliefs, values, sanctions, and motives associated with it, we will begin to discover the cultural forces that shape generativity in these two countries. The cultural dynamics that result in parenting practices also contour the manifestation of generativity.

Many of the cultural influences that shape parenting (and generativity) have clear and deep historical roots (Shwalb & Nakazawa, 1997). The Tokugawa Shogunate that had closed Japan to foreigners for nearly 300 years was replaced by the Meiji government, which opened Japan to foreign contact in 1868 and drafted the Meiji Civil Law in 1873. Activated in 1890, this set of domestic laws codified and enforced patriarchy. Primogeniture was strictly imposed. Women were to stay at home (and men, by law, were not allowed in the kitchen), and their main function was to raise a son so as to extend the family lineage. Kazui (1997) has referred to women's position during this time as provisional in that a man could easily divorce an infertile wife without contention and women held the lowest position in the family structure—expected to endure whatever hardships were needed to ensure the well-being of her children. Meiji Civil Law was abolished at the end of World War II but many of the cultural dynamics it instituted remain strong forces today.

Responsibility for parenting and household labor still falls almost exclusively to women in Japan. Further, basic beliefs have been influenced by these past laws, with 77.9% of contemporary Japanese parents opining that parenting is naturally woman's work (compared with 42.6% for U.S. parents; reported in Kazui, 1997). Note that this section on caring for one's young child has not included much on fathering. This is because so few men in Japan take part in parenting activities. The Japanese Ministry of Health initiated a National Fatherhood Campaign in 1999 with the slogan "if you are not involved in childrearing, you cannot be called a father" (Strom et al., 2000), but the impact of this has yet to be seen.

With the end of Meiji Law after World War II, women were no longer legally forced to center their lives on their children, but the incredibly strong work ethic imposed on men in the rapidly growing Japanese industries was filtered toward women and their roles in the home. Just as men were increasingly expected to dedicate much of their time and energy to being a productive worker, women were to find their *ikigai*, or "purpose in life," as devoted mothers. Thus the legacy of legally imposed patriarchy and the dominant gender-specific virtue of a strong work ethic since World War II has influenced the current gendered division of household labor and the pressures Japanese women experience in their mothering roles.

The gender specificity and high anxiety in mothering that is part of the custom practice of parenting in Japan is aligned with the cultural values of patriarchy and the expectations regarding women. This pressure to be a good mother begins during pregnancy, when Japanese women are issued a *Boshitecho* ("Mother–Child Handbook") (Kazui, 1997) and expected to adhere to the regulations outlined. As the child develops, a mother's anxiety is increasingly based on her child's academic success (Kameguchi & Murphy-Shigematsu, 2001) in which she is seen as the motivator and monitor. Having one's worth yoked so closely to the achievements of one's child has resulted in very serious stress in the mothering role. Yamada (1998) found Japanese women scored lower than any others from several countries on satisfaction with mothering. This is not to say that patriarchal modes are nonexistent in U.S. culture, for they surely are. But U.S. patriarchy is not nearly as predominant as in Japan, nor as deeply rooted in history, nor as codified in law. The democratic political system that prevails in the United States (imperfect and noninclusive as it is—for example, with regard to slavery and women's fight for suffrage) is remarkably different from the imperial authority (1868–1941) and constitutional monarchy (1941–present) of Japan—both of which explicitly support patriarchy.

Japan's history is that of a dense and stable population, with more than 130 million people living in a country slightly smaller than California (and with much of the land being uninhabitable mountains and volcanoes; Shelley, 1993). This has led to a communal form of raising children (Kakinuma, 1993) wherein girls are socialized in close proximity to several mothers, and mothers are closely supervised both by other mothers and by older women. The United States, in contrast, presents a history of migration (e.g., the East to West frontier settlement; the rural South to urban North movement of many African Americans in the early 20th century) and several waves of immigration. A woman in the United States was much less likely to be raising children in a context that included her own mother or several other women with identical backgrounds but was more probably (compared with Japan) in an isolated area (the frontier) or one populated by people quite different from herself. And the United States continues to be much more pluralistic than the predominantly homogeneous Japan (Shigaki, 1983). This is one reason middle-class U.S. women rely more on expert advice and Japanese women find guidance from other mothers (Kakinuma, 1993). The *well-side conference* is still a term used in Japan to describe the gathering of young mothers, even though few wells exist in modern Japan (Kakinuma, 1993). Mothers in the U.S. were less likely to turn to neighbors for mothering advice (and more likely to consult distant experts or books), as these neighbors often held quite different values and came from separate backgrounds.

Though modernization has shaped both cultures, these historical forces maintain an influence on differences in parenting. Both countries, for instance, have available today any number of parenting magazines but those in Japan tend to contain articles based on other mothers' input (60% compared with 10% of American magazines; Kakinuma, 1993). Whereas the U.S. publications are filled with child-rearing information and professional advice, the Japanese magazines prominently feature letters from other mothers telling funny stories or exchanging ideas informally—similar in content to discussions taking place at a well-side conference.

These historical (political, geographic, population) dynamics are part of the custom complex that exists in each culture as each speaks to the parenting practices in the United States and Japan. These custom complexes that are being constructed here relate to possible cultural differences in generativity. We begin to see, for instance, that the manifestation of generativity in Japan is highly gendered and communal. We also begin to understand that generativity in Japan likely occurs through an adherence to traditional ways and through a conforming to the modes in one's environment. Generativity in the United States, in contrast, may be both more individual-centered in that one is less likely to be guided by the behaviors of those in close physical proximity and more paradigmatic in that one follows the guidance of a distant authority. Generativity in Japan focuses more on meme maintenance (the continuance of traditional values and manners or the revitalization of these), whereas meme modification and creation (based on an individual's needs and circumstances) are more common forms of generativity in the United States.

One set of memes that have been sustained in Japan relates to the image of the ideal person. When asked what aspirations one has for one's students, Japanese teachers usually respond with hopes that each will be *ningen-rashii kodomo*, or a "humanlike child" (Shigaki, 1983). Such a person is one who promotes harmonious human relationships. This is well aligned with the dominating cultural values in Japan that emphasize interdependency and social harmony. Cultural norms stress responsiveness to social signals; acceptance of group goals, social etiquette, and respect for authority; compliance with others' wishes; dependence on others, self-effacement; and emotional restraint (one is to stifle hostile feelings so as to preserve social harmony; Power et al., 1992; Rothbaum, Pott, et al., 2000). In Japan, competency is defined in terms of one's ability to perceive social cues and then to direct one's resources to accommodating these.

These cultural values and modes are part of the custom complex that we see clearly manifested in the Japanese practice of caring for one's young child, which includes directing the child's attention to social stimuli, the establishment of close interpersonal bonds, and the encouragement of a dependency on others. The contrasting parenting practices in the United States speak to differences in cultural values and beliefs. Whereas the Japanese believe that the assertive and autonomous person is immature (Rothbaum, Pott, et al., 2000), such a person is viewed as the epitome of psychosocial health in U.S. culture. Further, relying on others is seen as weak in the United States but as the ideal path in Japanese culture. Parenting in the U.S. promotes independent and assertive modes with its early encouragement of environment exploration, the use of distance-promoting equipment, the maintenance of distal eye contact, the expectation that a child must somehow (vocalization, crying) ask for what is desired, and speech centered on information about the world of objects.

The historical dynamics and contemporary values outlined here are the cultural forces that shape the manifestation of generativity. Generativity in Japan is enacted through behaviors that are much more prescribed and monitored by one's community. The generative adult in Japan is ever mindful of social cues and ready for opportunities to facilitate social harmony by accommodating the desires of others. Although the range of possible generative behaviors may be limited (e.g., more gender-specific parenting; nothing so unusual as to shame one's family) in that the Japanese adult is to conform to social expectations, the depth of generativity that exists is great, as one's generative actions are so deeply rooted in history and so closely tied to one's core self (which is founded on interdependency and group membership). The essence of generativity occurs in the psychosocial space between people (McAdams & de St. Aubin, 1992) and so the embeddedness of the individual within the community in Japanese culture results in a deeply ingrained generativity. Whereas U.S. psychologists sometimes speak of certain adults as being nongenerative (de St. Aubin, 1998), Japanese scholars find this concept untenable (Y. Yamada, personal communication, November 5, 1999), for their cultural experiences make it impossible for them to consider that an adult would be unconcerned with the well-being of others and with the maintenance of traditions passed on from previous generations.

The incredible diversity of the U.S. population combined with the strong guiding values of individualism and assertiveness results in a different manifestation of generativity. The generative adult in the United States has both the liberty and the burden of being less intimately tied to a unifying set of community standards. With a core self based on individual strivings and unique accomplishments, U.S. adults manifest generativity in less rooted ways. Generative projects are more likely to entail the blending of traditions (e.g., Kwanzaa and Christmas), the modification of what has been passed on (e.g., different child-rearing styles than one's parents), or attempts at creating new generative products and processes.

THE MENTORING OF ARTISTIC TALENT

Much of the intergenerational transmission of artistic creativity in Japan today occurs in the lineage schools that are based, as are so many institutions in Japan, on the family structure. The Japanese *ie* translates as "household," and *iemoto* refers to one of the lineage schools in the arts or to the head of such a school (Smith, 1998). Whereas the sanctity of the U.S. family is based on the sacred bond between man and woman, for the Japanese it is the connection between the current head of household and his ancestors (thus "lineage" schools). The family is never to expire, nor is the *iemoto* skill (painting, poetry, dance, acting, pottery, etc.) and its particular form (separate *iemotos* teach different styles of painting, poetry, etc.) that is being passed from master to student. As Smith (1998) noted, each *iemoto* is "conceived to have originated far in the past and destined to persist into the future as its members die and are replaced by their successors in each generation. In theory, no household should ever die out" (p. 24). Many *iemotos* claim lineages dating back hundreds of years and actually keep track of the number of generations that have participated in the training methods. Master Tamehito Reizei of the Reizei *iemoto* for Tanka poetry traces his lineage back 800 years and through 50 separate generations (Reizei, 1999).

The traditional *iemoto* system is structured through a strict authoritarian hierarchy with student ranks, titles, rites of passage, and always the unquestioned authority of the master *iemoto* whose power rests on his authentic place in the lineage (DeCoker, 1998). But he need not be connected to his *iemoto* ancestry through biology. In a form of symbolic primogeniture, the *iemoto* master chooses which student is most likely to have the character to maintain the lineage and the exclusive form of art it represents (Smith, 1998). The master poet mentioned above, Tamehito Reizei, is one such example: He married into the Reizei family and then was chosen as the successor to the *iemoto*. Once a master is chosen, all are expected to accept the fiction that he is the genealogical rightful leader (a form of fictive kin; Smith, 1998). This assures the continuance of the *iemoto*. Though the lineage schools present the image of a family history with successive heirs to the master position, it is in fact only a simulation. It is not biology (gene propagation) but the continuation of a certain art form (meme propagation) that is paramount.

At the core of the *iemoto* system of training in the arts is the master–student relationship, which secures the continuity of both the *iemoto* and the particular skill it teaches. Whereas an art teacher in the United States spends considerable time with students providing explanation about the particular craft (color theory, technique, etc.), most of the discussion between master and student in a Japanese *iemoto* has very little to do with the particular skill that is being learned (Rimer, 1998). One reason for this is that the master assumes partial paternalistic and spiritual responsibilities and so conversation includes a much wider range of topics. This is also true because skills are passed on through disciplined observation and copying, not through verbal instruction. *Funponshugi*, or the doctrine of the copybook method, has been used to pass Kano painting from master to student since the 15th century (Jordan, 1998). Students watch closely as the master paints and attempt to steal his "secrets," which can only be done by paying very close attention to every gesture. Training in "*no*" theatre (which combines singing, dancing, mime, acting, chanting, mask, and costume design) follows a similar teaching process (Rimer, 1998). In a curriculum defined as "training by doing," *no* apprentices learn by copying the movements and sounds of the master.

By repeated observation and copying (a life-long practice for a Japanese artist), an ability becomes internalized. This principle of internalization remains central to all training. A great artist no longer needs to think about what he is doing. His craft has become a ritualized practice (Rimer, 1998). This training method has kept these traditions alive as a specific skill or performance is reborn in each generation. The emphasis is not on the individual talent or the uniqueness of one's product (a painting, a poem, a performance) but on the tradition itself. This stands in stark contrast to the United States where art is ultimately about an artist's individual personality and how this is uniquely expressed (Rimer, 1998). Most U.S. opera divas refuse to listen to recordings of others as this may influence their own performance of the same lyrics. As Rimer (1998) put it, "In the Japanese case, on the other hand, it is precisely this self-conscious personality that is to be set aside, or, to put it in a more appropriate perspective, to be harnessed and shaped for service toward a larger goal" (p. 36).

It is not that individual variance within an art form is not allowed in the Japanese mentoring of creative expressions, for it certainly is. Such "happy accidents" (Jordan, 1998) are noted and celebrated to some extent, but these are less valued as it is not possible to pass these on to successive generations of artists. The rapid modernization that Japan has experienced since World War II has led to somewhat of a "Westernization" of the culture and with this has indeed come evidence of more individualistic leanings (Rosenberg, 1992). Although there is more of a tension between individual achievements and the submission of self into a tradition (Kelly, 1998), most arts training still favors a balance of honed skills (planned production) over more individual creativity (happy accidents; Jordan, 1998).

Recent critics of the *iemoto* system charge that its feudal structure stifles the country from moving ahead toward a democracy (Smith, 1998). Others contend that the dogmatic orthodoxy of the *iemoto* system fails to allow for spontaneity and creativity, modes that are vital to the progress of any culture's arts (Jordan, 1998). And there is much contention over the commoditization and commercialism of the system (Singleton, 1998). The laws and business practices surrounding *iemoto* rights and the requirement for family approval in the issuance of certificates and titles have led to an absurd situation wherein some *iemoto* families no longer practice or teach the art attached to their name but simply sell others the rights to do so (Smith, 1998).

Despite the criticisms and the changes, traditional art and training still retain their power and importance in Japan today. There is still plenty of haiku and waka poetry written; *no* is still watched and performed; wood cutting is still a respected craft. Further, the *iemoto* system of mentoring artistic talent still dominates in modern Japan, if not through actual authentic *iemotos* dating back hundreds of years, then through the basic dynamics established in these and still maintained today. Several recently opened schools claim an "*iemoto*-like" system of pedagogy (Smith, 1998). Even though some of the arts traditions (pottery is a good example here; Singleton, 1998) have been infused with entrepreneurial values and have developed commercial components (such as tourism), the basic methods of transmitting artistic abilities from master to student (observation → copying → internalization) still dominates. The structure and dynamics inherent to the *iemoto* system continue to pervade arts and crafts training in Japan. In fact, these procedures are evident in the instruction that occurs outside of the arts as well. In her field work at a neighborhood garage in Japan, Madono (1998) found clear evidence of *iemoto* processes such as hierarchical structure, paternalism, and learning through observation between master and apprentice. Further, Kelly (1998) discovered *iemoto*-like master–student relationships existing in Japan between baseball coach and player.

The practices surrounding the mentoring of artistic talent in Japan are marked by the sanctity of the particular tradition, a reverence for the *iemoto* master connected to that lineage, the spiritual and paternalistic responsibilities of the master toward the student, the copying method of internalizing a talent, and the relinquishing of self-strivings for the promotion of the art.

These modes define the generative practice of mentoring artistic talent in Japanese culture. They also speak to the custom complex that stipulates the relevant cultural forces that shape the expression of generativity.

The generativity process in Japanese arts begins not with the talent of the individual but with the larger form of art he or she performs. The energy behind Japanese generativity is much greater than the individual or even than the current generation. Much as individuals are viewed as mere vessels to the selfish gene that will live on through reproduction and recombination (Pinker, 1997), the tradition (be it *no* acting, Tanka poetry, or mingei pottery) lives on as it is replicated in each student who has internalized the skill through copying the master. Just as genes might be viewed as the central characters in the evolutionary narrative, the memes surrounding a particular skill take center stage in Japanese generativity.

Scholars in the U.S. have often used the metaphor of the gift in trying to capture the two-phase process of generativity (McAdams, 2001a). The first phase consists of an adult fashioning a unique gift through an *agentic* mode. Here, the midlife man or woman creates a gift based on one's talents and proclivities. The gift is seen as an extension of self, a generative product with the unique mark of the individual. Then, the second phase of generativity entails the *communal* mode wherein the adult offers this gift up to others, typically to younger and future generations. Based in part on one's belief in the worthiness of the gift's recipients, the adult lets it go in a selfless move and allows the generative product to become what it may (a young adult child leaving home; a book published and open now to critique and interpretation).

As helpful as this metaphor has been to advancing our understanding of generativity, the investigation of generativity within the Japanese *iemoto* system clearly suggests that this model is rife with Western assumptions of individualism and assertiveness. The gift metaphor proposes that generativity begins with individual volition, that some generative product must first be created and then passed on. If there is any history to the generative process, most U.S. psychologists would likely search for it in the previous psychosocial stages of the individual: Had this adult successfully resolved earlier psychosocial stages (e.g., initiative vs. guilt, industry vs. inferiority) such that virtues were gained (purpose, competence) that would lead to one's ability to be generative (as opposed to stagnating)?

The history of a particular generative act in Japanese culture dates back not to the childhood of the individual but to the inception of an art form (or parenting technique, or teaching style, or method of food preparation) that may have occurred centuries ago. In a type of proactive passivity, the generative adult in Japan surrenders the self to the continuation of a particular tradition. The individual's contribution is secondary. He or she does not "make a generative gift" but instead attempts to tap into the generative force that currently resides within the master. Through observation and imitation the student begins to embody generativity. This parallels Kim's (1999) assertion that generativity in Japan often involves the maintenance of that which already exists and the injection of vitality into traditions. Generativity does not necessarily involve the creation of something completely new. The subordinate relation existing in the creation process (the object of creation is subordinate to the creator) does not exist within the generativity that Kim observed in Japan. According to Kim's understanding of generativity, it is the individual who is subordinate to the lineage.

There is not unconditional subordination between student and master. As deferential as a student is to the master in an *iemoto*, it is well understood that the authority of the master is completely contingent on his connection to the past. His value comes from the fact that the generative tradition currently resides within him. For the developing student to embody this generativity, he or she must observe the ways of the master. Generativity within the Japanese culture is "stored" within individuals and passed on through observation and social modeling.

The "renovating shrine" in Japan was first built over 1,200 years ago but it has been completely rebuilt, stone by stone, every 20 years since that time. Master builders work alongside novice apprentices who observe closely the particular skills needed to carry out the task. Each novice knows that he will be passing these skills on to younger generations in another 20 years. In this way, the craftsmanship lives on indefinitely as generations of men observe it, practice it, and model it for others. The particular men will surely die, but the memes (knowledge, skills) surrounding the building of the shrine continue. Japanese culture results in a generativity wherein the particular tradition supersedes the individual adult.

CONCLUSION

There is no doubt that the manifestation of generativity varies by culture. The two generative practices examined here attest to the culture-specific expressions of generativity. Child-rearing practices differ in these two cultures as does the mentoring of artistic talent. By examining these custom practices closely, we begin to understand the manner in which cultural forces influence the generativity processes. Cultural differences in generativity are the result of separate value systems; discrepant meanings of the self; and distinct historical, political, and geographical realities that define Japan and the United States.

These cultural forces in Japan have led to a generativity that is highly gendered, communally based, rooted in history, modeled on those in close physical proximity, more narrow in range of possibilities, closely connected to one's interdependent and group-oriented self, a surrendering of self to a larger tradition, and likely to entail the maintenance of traditional methods and rituals or the infusion of vitality into these. Generativity in the United States is less tied to unified community standards and more centered on individual volition and achievements. It is enacted on the basis of given circumstances and more distal models of conduct. Further, it is more likely to entail the integration or modification of what has been passed on or the attempt to create new generative processes or products.

Imagine that the intergenerational flow of genes and memes that we call generativity is a large river with a steady current. The Japanese might be said to navigate this river of generativity with a kayak whereas those in the United States traverse it with a gondola boat, using a pole against the river's bottom. A kayaker is propelled forward by the river's natural currents. For the Japanese, all energy in the generativity enterprise is derived from the larger traditions that define the intergenerational stream of memes. The individual enters into the process through disciplined actions modeled on others. She submits to the power of the river that carries her forward, and as her skills improve, others begin to imitate her actions as they tap into the endless stream of generativity. Rather than move with the natural flow of the river in this way, the gondola moves according to the efforts of the handler. A gondola driver is able to cut against the river's currents or to make dramatic turns as required by the given terrain at any one time and place. The path of generativity in the United States is relatively less directly tied to larger intergenerational flow of traditions and more contingent on individual decisions and proclivities. To fully understand generativity, we must examine both the individual (the boat pilot) as U.S. scholars have and the larger traditions and skills (the river) being passed from generation to generation (see Imada, chap. 6, this volume).

This river of generativity in Japan has been altered by the rapid modernization that has occurred since World War II. As if historical processes were accelerated, Japan has quickly moved toward a technology-based economy and has experienced an infusion of "Western" values such as materialism, consumerism, me-ism, now-ism, and efficiency (Okonogi, 1999). Although this has certainly complicated the manner in which generativity is performed, the inclusion of these values in some segments of society in no way marks a clear shift in the dominant cultural beliefs and modes. Most middle-age Japanese adults today were raised by parents whose childhood was spent under the authoritarian Meiji regime. Further, the strong emphasis on conformity and group-based identification make for cultural shifts in values a very slow process. The allegro pace by which technology and commercialism have advanced has not been matched by a complete revamping of cultural beliefs and modes, despite some highly publicized incidents of the Americanization of Japan. All of the cultural differences highlighted in this chapter regarding the generativity practices of caring for one's young child and the mentoring of artistic talent were found in empirical studies conducted within the past 5 years. Despite economic and technical similarities, the two cultures maintain profoundly different histories, demographics, philosophies, politics, and ideals.

These contrasting cultural contexts influence the manifestation of generativity. Unlike other species that simply propagate genes through biologically based reproductive and parental instincts, ours is both entitled and condemned to seek a symbolic immortality through the propagation of memes. Cultural modes and values set parameters that contour individual adults' generative efforts to propagate genes and memes.

REFERENCES

Allport, S. (1997). *A natural history of parenting.* New York: Harmony Books.

Barratt, M., Negayama, K., & Minami, T. (1993). The social environments of early infancy in Japan and the United States. *Early Development and Parenting, 2,* 51–64.

Becker, E. (1973). *The denial of death.* New York: Free Press.

Blackmore, S. (1999). *The meme machine.* Oxford, England: Oxford University Press.

Bornstein, M. H., Tal, J., & Tamis-LeMonda, C. (1991). Parenting in cross-cultural perspective: The United States, France, and Japan. In M. Bornstein (Ed.), *Cultural approaches to parenting* (pp. 69–81). Hillsdale, NJ: Erlbaum.

Chabris, C. F. (1999). Prelude or requiem for the "Mozart effect"? *Nature, 400,* 826–827.

Dawkins, R. (1976). *The selfish gene.* Oxford, England: Oxford University Press.

DeCoker, G. (1998). Seven characteristics of a traditional Japanese approach to learning. In J. Singleton (Ed.), *Learning in likely places: Varieties of apprenticeship in Japan* (pp. 68–84). Cambridge, England: Cambridge University Press.

deMause, L. (1974). *The history of childhood.* New York: Harper & Row.

de St. Aubin, E. (1998). Truth against the world: A psychobiographic exploration of generativity in the life of Frank Lloyd Wright. In D. McAdams & E. de St. Aubin (Eds.), *Generativity and adult development: How and why we care for the next generation* (pp. 391–427). Washington, DC: American Psychological Association.

Doi, T. (1962). Amae: A key concept for understanding Japanese personality structure. In J. Smith & R. K. Beardsley (Eds.), *Publications in anthropology* (pp. 132–139). New York: Viking Fund.

Erikson, E. H. (1950). *Childhood and society.* New York: Norton.

Erikson, E. H. (1969). *Gandhi's truth: On the origins of militant nonviolence.* New York: Norton.

Erikson, E. H. (1982). *The life cycle completed: A review.* New York: Norton.

Geertz, C. (1979). From the natives' point of view: On the nature of anthropological understanding. In P. Rabinow & W. M. Sullivan (Eds.), *Interpretive social science* (pp. 225–241). Berkeley: University of California Press.

Glaser, B. G., & Strauss, A. L. (1967). *The discovery of grounded theory: Strategies for qualitative research*. Chicago: Aldine.

Goldenberg, J., Pyszczynski, T., Greenberg, J., & Solomon, S. (2000). Fleeing the body: A terror management perspective on the problem of human corporeality. *Personality and Social Psychology Review, 4*, 200–218.

Jordan, B. G. (1998). Education in the Kano school in nineteenth-century Japan: Questions about the copybook method. In J. Singleton (Ed.), *Learning in likely places: Varieties of apprenticeship in Japan* (pp. 45–67). Cambridge, England: Cambridge University Press.

Kakinuma, M. A. (1993). A comparison of the child rearing attitudes of Japanese and American mothers. *Childhood, 1*, 235–242.

Kameguchi, K., & Murphy-Shigematsu, S. (2001). Family psychology and family therapy in Japan. *American Psychologist, 56*, 65–70.

Kazui, M. (1997). The influence of cultural expectations on mother–child relationships in Japan. *Journal of Applied Developmental Psychology, 18*, 485–496.

Kelly, W. W. (1998). Learning to swing: Oh Sadaharu and the pedagogy and practice of Japanese baseball. In J. Singleton (Ed.), *Learning in likely places: Varieties of apprenticeship in Japan* (pp. 265–285). Cambridge, England: Cambridge University Press.

Kim, T. (1999, November). *Why generativity and future generations now?* Paper presented at The International Conference Commemorating the 10th Anniversary of the Kyoto Forum, Kyoto, Japan.

Kotre, J. (1984). *Outliving the self: Generativity and the interpretation of lives*. Baltimore: Johns Hopkins University Press.

Kotre, J. (1999). *Making it count: How to generate a legacy that gives meaning to your life*. New York: Free Press.

Madono, K.E. (1998). Craft and regulatory learning in a neighborhood garage. In J. Singleton (Ed.), *Learning in likely places: Varieties of apprenticeship in Japan* (pp. 134–152). Cambridge, England: Cambridge University Press.

Markus, H. (2001, August). Opening remarks. In H. Markus (Chair), *Cultural models: Implicating content in psychological process*. Symposium conducted at the 109th Annual Convention of the American Psychological Association, San Francisco.

Matsumoto, D. R. (2000). *Culture and psychology* (2nd ed.). Stamford, CT: Wadsworth.

McAdams, D. P. (2001a). Generativity in midlife. In M. Lachman (Ed.), *Handbook of midlife development* (pp. 395–443). New York: Wiley.

McAdams, D. P. (2001b). *The person: An integrated introduction to personality psychology* (3rd ed.). New York: Harcourt.

McAdams, D. P., & de St. Aubin, E. (1992). A theory of generativity and its assessment through self-report, behavioral acts, and narrative themes in autobiography. *Journal of Personality and Social Psychology, 62*, 1003–1015.

McAdams, D. P., & de St. Aubin, E. (1998). *Generativity and adult development: How and why we care for the next generation*. Washington, DC: American Psychological Association.

Merriam-Webster. (2002). *Merriam-Webster dictionary and thesaurus*. Retrieved May 1, 2001, from http://www.m-w.com/

Ogbu, J. (1994). From cultural differences to differences in cultural frames of reference. In P. M. Greenfield & R. R. Cocking (Eds.), *Cross-cultural roots of minority child development* (pp. 3–391). Hillsdale, NJ: Erlbaum.

Okonogi, K. (1999, November). *Generativity crisis and new view of self*. Paper presented at The International Conference Commemorating the 10th Anniversary of the Kyoto Forum, Kyoto, Japan.

Pinker, S. (1997). *How the mind works*. New York: Norton.

Power, T. G., Kobayashi-Winata, H., & Kelley, M. L. (1992). Childrearing patterns in Japan and the United States: A cluster analytic study. *International Journal of Behavioral Development, 15*, 185–205.

Reizei, T. (1999, November). *Preserving a culture generatively*. Paper presented at The International Conference Commemorating the 10th Anniversary of the Kyoto Forum, Kyoto, Japan.

Rimer, J. T. (1998). The search for mastery never ceases: Zeami's classic treatises on transmitting the traditions of the no theatre. In J. Singleton (Ed.), *Learning in likely places: Varieties of apprenticeship in Japan* (pp. 35–44). Cambridge, England: Cambridge University Press.

Rose, G. M. (1999). Consumer socialization, parental style, and developmental timetables in the United States and Japan. *Journal of Marketing, 63*, 105–119.

Rosenberg, N. R. (1992). Introduction. In N. R. Rosenberg (Ed.), *Japanese sense of self* (pp. 1–20). Cambridge, England: Cambridge University Press.

Rothbaum, F., Pott, M., Azuma, H., Miyake, K., & Weisz, J. (2000). The development of close relationships in Japan and the United States: Paths of symbiotic harmony and generative tension. *Child Development, 71*, 1121–1142.

Rothbaum, F., Weisz, J., Pott, M., Miyake, K., & Morelli, G. (2000). Attachment and culture: Security in the United States and Japan. *American Psychologist, 55*, 1093–1104.

Shelley, R. (1993). *Culture shock*. Portland, OR: Graphic Arts Center.

Shigaki, I. S. (1983). Child care practices in Japan and the United States: How do they reflect cultural values in young children? *Young Children, 38*, 13–24.

Shwalb, D. W., & Nakazawa, J. (1997). Guest editors' commentary: Japanese socialization research in review. *Journal of Applied Developmental Psychology, 18*, 527–530.

Shweder, R. A., Goodnow, J., Hatano, G., LeVine, R.A., Markus, H., & Miller, P. (1998). The cultural psychology of development: One mind, many mentalities. In W. Damon (Ed.), *Handbook of child psychology* (5th ed., Vol. 1, pp. 865–937). New York: Wiley.

Singleton, J. (1998). Craft and art education in Mashiko pottery workshops. In J. Singleton (Ed.), *Learning in likely places: Varieties of apprenticeship in Japan* (pp. 122–133). Cambridge, England: Cambridge University Press.

Smith, R. (1998). Transmitting tradition by the rules: An anthropological interpretation of the iemoto system. In J. Singleton (Ed.), *Learning in likely places: Varieties of apprenticeship in Japan* (pp. 23–34). Cambridge, England: Cambridge University Press.

Snarey, J. (1993). *How fathers care for the next generation: A four-decade study*. Cambridge, MA: Harvard University Press.

Stevenson-Hinde, J. (1998). Parenting in deferent cultures: Time to focus. *Developmental Psychology, 34*, 698–700.

Stewart, A. J., & Vandewater, E. A. (1998). The course of generativity. In D. P. McAdams & E. de St. Aubin (Eds.), *Generativity and adult development: How and why we care for the next generation* (pp. 75–100). Washington, DC: American Psychological Association.

Strauss, A., & Corbin, J. (1998). *Basics of qualitative research: Techniques and procedures for developing grounded theory* (2nd ed.). Thousand Oaks, CA: Sage.

Strom, R. D. Strom, S. K., Strom, P. S., Makino, K., & Morishima, Y. (2000). Perceived parenting success of mothers in Japan. *Journal of Family Studies, 6*, 25–45.

Triandis, H. C. (1997). Cross-cultural perspectives on personality. In R. Hogan, J. Johnson, & S. Briggs (Eds.), *Handbook of personality psychology* (pp. 439–464). San Diego, CA: Academic Press.

Triandis, H. C. (2001). Individualism–collectivism and personality. *Journal of Personality, 69*, 907–924.

Uleman, J. S., Rhee, E., Bardoliwalla, N., Semin, G., & Toyama, M. (2000). The relational self: Closeness to ingroups depends on who they are, culture, and the type of closeness. *Asian Journal of Social Psychology, 3*, 1–17.

Whiting, J. W. M., & Child, I. (1953). *Child training and personality*. New Haven, CT: Yale University Press.

Yamada, M. (1998). *The Japanese family in transition*. Tokyo: Foreign Press Center.

6

GENERATIVITY AS SOCIAL RESPONSIBILITY: THE ROLE OF GENERATIONS IN SOCIETAL CONTINUITY AND CHANGE

TAKATOSHI IMADA

Generativity is not only a psychological phenomenon; it is also a sociological one. That is, generativity not only gets expressed as the result of an intrapsychic press or developmental crisis but also functions as a sociological force. How the individuals within a society pass on and inherit the legacies of the past, consider the present, and anticipate the future is an expression of generativity. The role of generational interaction has traditionally been considered as either a force for change or a force for continuity. I suggest it is not an either/or but a both/and process. In this chapter, I argue that it is the psychosocial nature of generational exchange, expressed as generativity, that results in both continuity *and* change within society. That is, it is through the intersection of generativity and generation that we find the mechanism by which a society's legacy is shaped.

I first consider the nature of social responsibility and suggest its relationship to generations. Second, I address the problem and significance of generation from the standpoint of the sociology of knowledge (see Mannheim, 1952).

Next, I discuss how the significance of generational effects has been minimized through operational recasting by socialization theory. Then, I point out how the concept of generativity, first proposed by Erikson (1963), contributes to a reconceptualization of the problem of generations. Finally, I show how social responsibility as a generational response relates to generativity.

SOCIAL RESPONSIBILITY

Social responsibility, sometimes conceived of as "publicness," is defined here as the ethical and moral obligations of the citizens of a society to each other and to the society itself. Social responsibility has typically been viewed as a spatial dimension of society. In other words, social theorists have tended to emphasize the connections and duties that tie people together within a particular social ecology at a given point in time. However, social responsibility is not limited to a spatial dimension but includes a temporal dimension. Arendt (1972) and Habermas (1990), two pioneers of the theory of publicness, limited their discussions to its spatial nature, disregarding the temporal aspect of publicness. The temporal dimension of social responsibility, that is, how social responsibility exists in time (and thus, within and between generations), has continued to be overlooked in the literature.

A key to understanding the temporality of social responsibility lies in the social construction of time. Time is perceived as both physical (i.e., "real time") and social. Giddens (1987) pointed out three forms of temporality related to structuring social life: duration of day-to-day life, duration of the life span, and duration of institution. By repeating actions in their day-to-day lives, individuals experience not only reversible time as it underlies the structure of social order but also irreversible time that relates the duration of day-to-day life to the duration of the life span from birth to death. These two forms of duration interweave with the duration of institution beyond the life span of any particular individual. Unlike physical time, social time is not linear from the past to the present and the future. In fact, social time is experienced in relation to the continuity or change of social order and self-identity. This helps to explain the evolving nature of social institutions and values.

Individuals play out their responsibility to society through generational exchange. That is, the generations that constitute society pass on and inherit cultural capital through generational exchange, which exists in both physical and social time. Thus, social responsibility must have a temporal aspect. Furthermore, generation is germane to the formulation of the temporal dimension of social responsibility.

THE IMPORTANCE OF GENERATION

Generation refers generally to a set of people (collectivity) who were born and have grown up in the same period and have common values and lifestyle. According to this definition, generation has the mixed effects of age and historical time. In other words, generation means a set of people formed as a result of the interaction between the effect of age, which is a particular point in the life stage, and the effect of the times, which is a particular point in history. People of the same generation share the experiences of continuity and change under the simultaneous effects of age and historical time. The notion of generation is critical to a fundamental understanding of social structure. Both continuity and change are manifested in society through the process of new generations entering and old generations exiting. The explanatory power of the concept of generation has not been considered thoroughly within social theory. Generation plays a central role in understanding how a society inherits the legacy of the past, considers the present, and moves into the future. Thus, generation is one of a few concepts that includes social time as distinguished from physical time.

Generation is a concept that typically represents what Giddens (1987) and Mead (1932) called *social temporality*. Phenomena of generation are differentially experienced by the old and new generations and also by the next generation. Through generational change, the legacy of the old generation is inherited and recreated as it is passed on to the new generation. Thus, legacy is processed and transformed as both continuity and change within day-to-day life, the life span, and institutions.

A PERSPECTIVE FROM THE SOCIOLOGY OF KNOWLEDGE

Mannheim (1952) was the first to seriously address the concept of generation. He regarded the problem of generations as an indispensable index to understanding social change. Mannheim suggested that generation may be understood in three ways. The first is *generation location* (*Generationslagerung*) in which people belong to the same birth cohort and are constrained by similar historical and social situations. This is generation in the broadest sense. Mannheim contrasts generation location with *generation as actuality* (*Generationszusammenhang*), which he construes as people of the same birth cohort participating in a common destiny. Generation as actuality has particular features that can no longer be reduced to age group. Mannheim further defined same-age individuals as an actual generation to the extent they participate in the characteristic social and intellectual currents of their society and period. In addition, there is generation in a narrow sense, which is called the *generation unit* (*Generationseinheit*). This means a state in which uniformity of response to certain social phenomena has been established as a result of common experiences among the members. This uniformity represents a concrete solidarity such as similarity of consciousness and same orientation toward historical problems, and it forms characteristic value orientations and cultural styles specific to a certain generation. Its examples are groups that manifest innovative consciousness such as the "Youth Romanticists" of early 20th century Germany, "Political Youths" in the Meiji era Japan, or the American Peaceniks of the 1960s.

Each member of society can participate only in a temporally limited section of the historical process. Therefore, the object of generational research is to clarify the process by which accumulated cultural heritage is or is not transmitted from generation to generation. The continuous emergence of new generations results in some loss of accumulated cultural heritage. That is, some, but not all, cultural heritage is successfully transmitted from generation to generation. To explain the continuity and change between generations, Mannheim proposed *structures of memory* at the individual and social levels. Memories that restrict the individual's actions are those produced by him- or herself in the process of personal growth. Memories acquired during the initial life stages are taken as a certain attitude toward the world, the so-called *natural attitude* (*naturliches Weltbild*), whereas those obtained during later stages are understood and adopted after being checked against the initial memories. Therefore, memories are constructed of layers. Mannheim claimed that the differences in "the stratification of experiences" (*Erlebnisschichtung*) in memories produce the differences between generations. An experience makes only one of the stratified memories for the older generation, whereas the same experience makes a memory that forms the fundamental consciousness for the younger generation. According to Mannheim, there are two ways by which people incorporate a cultural experience in social memories: (a) as consciously recognized models to determine the direction of their behaviors or (b) as unconsciously condensed patterns. He added that most of social memories are formed by unconscious adaptation, thus the difference in culture between generations stems from the difference in the initial experience in the individual memory structure and sharing of culture from the unconscious adaptation in the initial experience of the new generation.

A CRITIQUE OF MANNHEIM

Mannheim's theory of generation provides a strong foundation for the study of generations. However, his theory is incomplete. There are several areas in which Mannheim's argument falls short. First, Mannheim paid little attention to the fact that the culture created by the new generation encounters control by the old generation. As socialization theory (see below) asserts, the old generation exerts control of the new generation in the crucial early stages of the life span through the internalization of existing values and culture, primarily by the family and school. Society is maintained by the internalization of the culture accumulated in the past and transmitted by the former generations to the new generation. Mannheim emphasized that the new generation created cultural and social change. However, he overlooked the power of cultural inheritance and the continuity of culture. The culture created by the new generation cannot constitute an entirely new social order, as Mannheim maintained, because the generative process partly entails the passing on of that which is valued from one generation to the next. Thus societal continuity occurs as younger generations incorporate that which is passed on.

My second critique of Mannheim is his concept of stratification of experience in the memory structure, which I find too simplistic. Although I agree that experiences and memories are accumulated in layers, Mannheim overlooks conscious adaptation. As life-cycle theory suggests, people are faced with psychological issues and the corresponding conscious responses in each stage of development (see discussion on Erikson, below). For example, most people learn language and discipline in childhood, work on a sense of identity in adolescence, commit to an intimate relationship in early adulthood, create a legacy in midlife, and try to integrate their life experiences in old age. Contrary to Mannheim, then, culture is shared not simply through the unconscious adaptation of initial experience but also through self-conscious processes. Perhaps a prime example of this is the generative midlife adult who consciously attempts to nurture and mentor members of the younger generation.

Furthermore, there are other problems in the "initial experience" that Mannheim claims provide the basis of difference and sharing of culture between generations. First, it is difficult to identify what the initial experience is. Second, there is an inherent contradiction in attributing the difference and sharing of culture solely to the initial experience. If the difference of culture between generations is attributed to the difference in the initial experience and the sharing of culture to the unconscious sharing of initial experience, all phenomena related to generations will be reduced to an ambiguous concept of initial experience. This leads to a sort of determinism in that the theory predicts that culture will be transformed with each successive generation but it fails to explain the process of continuity and change within society.

AN APPROACH FROM SOCIALIZATION THEORY

The standard definition of socialization is that it is the process, from the viewpoint of society, of fitting newly born individuals into institutionalized lifestyles and teaching them the society's cultural traditions, and at the same time, from the viewpoint of the individual, of developing a self through interaction with others. Socialization contributes to two functions: transmission of social legacy and creation of personality. According to socialization theory, individuals who are born into a society (i.e., the new generation) internalize values and norms transmitted from the preceding generations primarily through family and schooling, thus contributing to the continuity of society. Their activities are constrained by the preceding generations in this process. Thus, the conscious orientation by the preceding generations has great influence on the value formation of the next generations. Socialization theorists assume individuals' active commitment to the formation of personality and self, thus socialization infers an interaction between society and individuals. However, the key conception of socialization lies in the notion of internalization, that is, control by socializing agents. There are no conceptual problems when the objects of internalization are the basic "equipment" for social life, such as mastering a language, toilet habits, and postponement of direct satisfaction for the sake of a long-term goal. It becomes problematic, however, when socialization concerns more complex phenomena, such as one's sense of values and cultural tastes. It is at this point that socialization theory becomes controversial. As Shibano (1977) pointed out, socialization theory focuses primarily on conformity, and creative formation is ignored. After examining the concept of socialization from various aspects, Shibano concluded that socialization (a) encompasses acquiring a social membership, (b) is fundamentally a learning experience, (c) is a process to link personality to society through interactions, and (d) serves as a functional requisite of social systems. The last characteristic is specifically emphasized in the Parsonsian functionalist approach. These four common characteristics indicate how the emphasis is placed more on the social aspects than on the individual aspects. In fact, Parsons (1951) described the significance of socialization for the social system as follows:

> The socializing effect will be conceived as the integration of ego into a role complementary to that of others in such a way that the common values are internalized in ego's personality, and their respective behaviors come to constitute a complementary role-expectation-sanction system. (p. 215)

If the essential point of socialization is to perform a normative function of the social system, then socialization necessarily functions to maintain the equilibrium and order of the social system through the mechanisms of role expectations and sanctions. This assumes that common values are clear and stable. However, this is rarely the case. Thus, the functionalist perspective might be useful for describing the maintenance and reproduction of existing values in a stable society, but not so in a rapidly evolving society in which common values are in flux.

Moreover, socialization theorists consider deviant behaviors to be a result of ineffective socialization. As such, they are deemed undesirable, necessitating control in order to return to the normal equilibrium. However, even the proponents of socialization theory admit that deviant behaviors include creative ones that may lead to social innovation and reform. Nonetheless, as

Parsons (1951) claimed, a theoretical framework does not exist to explain creative deviant behaviors, which tend to receive strong negative sanctions. Parsons went on to say that social control is required as a reaction to force conformity to recover equilibrium. This is irrespective of whether the deviance has creative aspects. Thus, socialization paired with social control results in conditions that maintain the social system.

In contrast to Mannheim's view, which emphasizes differences between generations, socialization theory underscores the sharing and continuity of culture between generations. In an effort to understand the causes of difference and similarity between generations, Bengtson and Kuypers (1971) studied the socialization of values. They proposed the following hypothesis to explain the differences between generations: As people age, they are haunted by a myth that the significance of their existence will be lost; thus they want to transmit the values and institutions that have defined their lives to the next generations. By engaging in such generative behaviors, the adult generation seeks to achieve a symbolic immortality (McAdams, 2001). Therefore, the older generation wishes to keep the difference between generations to a minimum, because they are strongly vested in the inheritance of their values and institutions. In contrast, young people have a strong desire to establish their own identities. Bengtson and Kuypers argued that young people fear the inheritance desired by their elders would lead to a loss of identity. As a result, young people would tend to reject the values and institutions of the previous generation. If adults are inclined to stress the importance of passing on their values and institutions, the young eschew them so that they may form an autonomous identity. This may be one of the dynamics that leads to a "generation gap."

To examine this hypothesis, Bengtson (1975) analyzed generation (birth cohort) and family (lineage) effects on the generation gap. His overall results question whether the generation gap really exists. His findings indicate more homogeneity between generations than previously thought. However, Bengtson also cautioned that similarity between generations may be a reflection of a common social location and not the direct transmission of values. Nonetheless, Bengtson's findings may be interpreted to support the notion of social control as suggested in socialization theory and, consequently, may imply that the sociology of knowledge excessively emphasizes differences between generations. Bengtson's findings would appear to contradict Mannheim (1952), who suggested that the greater influence of the "spirit of the age," including historical events such as war, and ideological and cultural movements cannot be reduced to effects measured by calendar year or birth cohort. Even if the difference between generations is only a subtle fluctuation, it will resonate with the spirit of the age to amplify changes. When this is taken into account, socialization theory underestimates the difference between generations compared with the sociology of knowledge.

The above two opposing approaches to the problem of generations indicate a difference in social recognition, in that one focuses on change and the other on continuity. Both approaches must be appreciated in the sense that they clarify important aspects of the generation phenomenon. However, as each focuses on one of two conflicting perspectives, neither can sufficiently clarify the generational dynamics that lead to societal change and continuity. The rest of this chapter focuses on the paradox of how continuity and change coexist through generative exchange between generations.

IDENTITY AND GENERATIVITY:
A PSYCHOSOCIAL APPROACH TO GENERATION THEORY

Erik Erikson (1963, 1982) proposed a theory of eight stages of psychosocial development through the life cycle. His view of the relationship between generations is vastly different from the sociology of knowledge insistence on generational discontinuity and from socialization theory's stance on generational control. As I argue below, Erikson's concepts of adolescent identity and adult generativity interrelate in such a way as to shed new light on the problem of generations and the mechanisms of continuity and change in society.

Erikson suggests that the life cycle is comprised of the following stages: infancy, early childhood, play age, school age, adolescence, young adulthood, middle adulthood, and old age. According to his model, there are psychosocial developmental issues or conflicts that arise at each stage. How these issues are resolved contributes to a more or less ideal character formation or ego development. However, this is a secondary concern for Erikson. The important point is the dynamism of conflict and crisis encountered at each stage. His basic viewpoint is that people unconsciously encounter psychological crises at each life stage, which they must resolve to acquire certain ego strengths or "virtues" such as hope, will, purpose, competence, fidelity, love, care, and wisdom.

The Eriksonian life stages relevant to this chapter are *identity* (Stage 5) in adolescence and *generativity* (Stage 7) in middle adulthood. Understanding the relationship between these two stages is critical to an understanding of the generations, as discussed below. Adolescents face the conflict "identity versus role confusion" and acquire the virtue of fidelity by resolving the identity crisis. At the adolescence stage, youths seek to discover their own set of values and norms. Erikson (1963) observed that

> growing and developing youths . . . are now primarily concerned with what they appear to be in the eyes of others as compared with what they feel they are, and with the question of how to connect the roles and skills cultivated earlier with the occupational prototypes of the day. (p. 261)

The concept of adolescent identity crisis was exemplified in the late 1960s when student power was at a peak. Adolescent identity crisis was linked to the reform of the establishment. In this era, young people selected the ideology of antiestablishment as their object of fidelity. Erikson (1964) said, "fidelity is the ability to sustain loyalties freely pledged in spite of the inevitable contradictions of value systems" (p. 125). In other words, fidelity is the core of identity that is confirmed by peers through a commitment to a common ideology. Although it may sound paradoxical, the antiestablishment movement by students was an opportunity to inspire and develop the virtue of fidelity.

Midlife adults face the conflict "generativity versus stagnation" and acquire the ego strength (virtue) of care in its resolution. In contrast to the well-known identity crisis of adolescence, generativity in adulthood has only recently been widely discussed (see McAdams & Logan, this volume, chap. 2). Generativity not only refers to bearing and nurturing children but also includes creativity, that is, the production of new works and things, and generating new ideas. In other words, to be generative is to give birth to and bring up children, produce new things, and create ideas and culture. Generativity also pertains to the interrelationship of different generations. Erikson (1964) described the virtue of "care" obtained through the expression of generativity as "the widening concern for what has been generated by love, necessity, or accident; it covers the ambivalence adhering to irreversible obligation" (p. 131). Generativity represents help and assistance expressed in activities such as taking care of children, mentoring, and volunteer activities. The virtue of care ties together different generations, promotes exchange between generations, and passes on values from generation to generation. Thus, generativity includes both *creating* and *caring*.

The entire expression of generativity requires *letting go* in addition to creating and caring. McAdams (1998) contended that generativity involves not only creating but also releasing. Generative adults seek to create and maintain that which is potentially good, but they must be willing to offer up to the world the fruit of their generative labors. Generative adults do not hold on to what they have created. As children grow up, for example, parents have less and less control. Eventually, parents let go of their children who leave and become independent. In the same way, generative adults release what they have created and entrust it to others.

THE CYCLE OF GENERATIONS

Erikson extended discussions of virtues, or ego strengths, from the individual life cycle to the cycle of generations. Virtues develop through the interaction between successive generations to produce the driving forces that compose society. Erikson (1964) stated,

For man's psychosocial survival is safeguarded only by vital virtues which develop in the interplay of successive and overlapping generations, living together in organized settings. Here, living together means more than incidental proximity. It means that the individual's life-stages are "interliving," cogwheeling with the stages of others which move him along as he moves them. (p. 114)

Any virtue acquired in the resolution of psychosocial issues is not limited to a particular life stage but is seen at all stages. Problems of identity and generativity are in principle related to all life stages, not just adolescence or adulthood. Nonetheless, the conflicts identified in each stage are thought to be most salient at that stage. The acquisition of a virtue is not unidirectional but is evidenced through the interaction between generations. This suggests that the relation between generations should be understood as a mutually self-organizational mechanism in that one activates and changes itself by activating the other.

As discussed previously, there are two opposing theoretical perspectives on generation: one emphasizing change and the other, continuity. In the above discussion, two generations have been implicitly assumed: adulthood, when people are inclined more to continuity; and adolescence, when people tend to seek changes. Of course, these tendencies are relative in that neither continuity nor change is ascribed completely to one or the other generation. However, both the sociology of knowledge and socialization theory assume that the younger generation wants change and the older one seeks continuity.

Erikson's approach to generational exchange provides insight into the problem of generations and the growth of cultural capital. As a psychologist, his perspective differs from that of the sociology of knowledge and socialization theory. His description of identity and generativity provides an understanding of the problem of generations and thus how societies evolve. His psychosocial model can help explain both the individual, intrapsychic press and the collective, societal response. For example, when the current baby-boomer generation was at the adolescence stage, the problem of generations was refocused on adolescent identity crisis. It was conceptualized as being limited to the individual's life cycle as a conflict faced in the transition from adolescence to adulthood. Indeed, this conflict posed an enormous problem between generations in the sense that it caused alienation of youths from the adult generation and the resultant adult apprehension of youths. However, issues of identity were still considered a phenomenon within a generation. In contrast, generativity is essentially a phenomenon between generations, in that the caring generative impulse results in the creation and release to the next generation of that which is potentially good, thereby linking the generations together. Erikson's model of the cycle of generations goes beyond the individual's life cycle. The notion of the cycle of generations is extremely useful in discussing the problem of generations.

The cycle of generations starts when the generative urges of the preceding generation (adults) interact with the needs for identity formation in the next generation (youths). To reiterate, generativity is to create and release one's legacy, whether that be within the individual or within an entire generation. However, this does not mean controlling the next generation or demanding adherence to the preceding generation's values and institutions. Generativity is to support the next generation to form its identity by releasing (letting go) the already created. The new generation will adopt or reject the values of the preceding generation and in so doing will develop its own unique identity (see Kotre, 1998). It is the very expression of the older generation's generativity that calls forth the new generation's identity.

Socialization theory, which admits the linkage between different generations and addresses the inheritance of culture and formation of the self, suggests that social control is a mechanism for the learning of existing values and norms. In contrast, the Eriksonian notion of the cycle of generations assumes care for the younger generation and the releasing of values and institutions created by the older to the younger generation. Therefore, it does not imply social control. The cycle of generations is thus a framework to convert the relationship between generations from controlling to caring.

GENERATIVITY: GENERATION RESPONSIBILITY AS SOCIAL RESPONSIBILITY

Generativity based on the virtue of care leads to a new dimension of social responsibility. In his book *Gandhi's Truth*, Erikson (1969) remarked that the contribution of Gandhi to the Indian people is an unrivaled example of generativity. One expression of generativity is to bear and rear children. However, as seen in the life of Gandhi, generativity plays out beyond the private domain of family and is expressed at a societal level in the public sphere as social responsibility. Kotre (1984) clarified four domains in which generative responsibility is expressed: biological, parental, technical, and cultural. The first two domains represent the responsibility for bearing and caring for children. The third, the technical domain, concerns the responsibility of teaching others critical skills, including the use of tools, ranging from writing with pencils to performing surgery. In the fourth domain falls the responsibility for maintaining, innovating, and creating the meaning system (i.e., values, beliefs, customs, and systems of symbols). The expression of generativity as a parent or as a transmitter of technologies and culture is a commitment to social responsibility in the sense that it contributes to the sustainability of society. Even if the generative impulse originates from one's private needs, the fulfillment is public insofar as it has been implemented with the responsibility for the next generation as a result. For example, parents' efforts to educate their children and transmit cultural capital to them have been regarded as private. This way of thinking comes from the perspective that social responsibility occurs exclusively within a spatial dimension (public space). However, activities such as the education and training of children also disclose the temporal (generational) dimension of social responsibility because the expression of generativity allows for the next generation to form and reform an ongoing society. In this sense, constructing social responsibility as generational responsibility opens the way to the public expression of generativity for the family, which had previously been confined to the private domain.

CONCLUSION

Neither the sociology of knowledge nor socialization theory is sufficient to explain continuity and change within society. I have suggested that a more robust explanation may be found in the Eriksonian model of psychosocial development—more explicitly, in the notion of the exchange between generations evidenced as the response to the crises of identity in adolescence and generativity in midlife. In particular, it is in the ways that adults demonstrate social responsibility, in both private and public ways, disclosing both the temporal and spatial nature of the call to be socially responsible, that cultural capital is exchanged between the generations. It is through care, not control, that the older generation is linked to the younger one. Just as the expression of generativity as a psychological dynamic is paradoxical in that it is both creating and releasing, so does generativity as a societal mechanism permit both continuity and change between generations.

REFERENCES

Arendt, H. (1972). *Crises of the republic*. New York: Harcourt Brace Jovanovich.

Bengtson, V. L. (1975). Generation and family effects in value socialization. *American Sociological Review, 40*, 358–371.

Bengtson, V. L., & Kuypers, J. A. (1971). Generational differences and the developmental stake. *Aging and Human Development, 2*, 249–260.

Erikson, E. (1963). *Childhood and society* (2nd ed.). New York: Norton.

Erikson, E. (1964). *Insight and responsibility: Lectures on the ethical implications of psychoanalytic insight*. New York: Norton.

Erikson, E. (1969). *Gandhi's truth: On the origins of militant nonviolence*. New York: Norton

Erikson, E. (1982). *The life cycle completed*. New York: Norton.

Giddens, A. (1987). *Social theory and modern sociology*. Stanford, CA: Stanford University Press.

Habermas, J. (1990). *Moral consciousness and communicative action*. Cambridge, MA: MIT Press.

Kotre, J. (1984). *Outliving the self: Generativity and the interpretation of lives*. Baltimore: Johns Hopkins University Press.

Kotre, J. (1998, November). *The generative way of life: Practical perspective*. Paper presented at the meeting of the Study of Public Philosophy, Kyoto, Japan.

Mannheim, K. (1952). The problem of generations. In P. Kecskemeti (Ed.), *Essays on the sociology of knowledge* (pp. 276–320). London: Routledge & Kegan.

McAdams, D. P. (1998, November). *What is generativity?* Paper presented at the meeting of the Study of Public Philosophy, Kyoto, Japan.

McAdams, D. P. (2001). Generativity in midlife. In M. Lachman (Ed.), *Handbook of midlife development* (pp. 395–443). New York: Wiley.

Mead, G. H. (1932). *The philosophy of the present*. La Salle, IL: Open Court.

Parsons, T. (1951). *The social system*. New York: Free Press.

Shibano, S. (1977). Shakaika-ron no saikento: Shutaisei keisei katei no kousatsu [Reexamination of recent socialization theories: Inquiry into the formation process of subjectivity]. *Japanese Sociological Review*, *27*(3), 19–34.

7

THE GENERATIVE LIFE CYCLE MODEL: INTEGRATION OF JAPANESE FOLK IMAGES AND GENERATIVITY

YOKO YAMADA

Think not forever of yourselves
nor of your own generations,
Think of continuing generations of our families,
think of our grandchildren
and those yet unborn whose faces
are coming from beneath the ground

—*Native American Elder*

When we think of the life of a person, it may be necessary to draw a map of his or her life in such a way that it starts not from birth, but from going back to the past, and concludes not with death but extends toward the future. What a person is born into in this world does not mean only his or her birth. We should see that he or she is born under the large shadow of the cycle of people which includes everyone, and even after death, there is something in succession.

—*Kenzaburo Oe (1986)*

It is my intention to critique a set of assumptions in developmental psychology and propose a new model of the life cycle. As a researcher in life-span developmental psychology, I would like to suggest a paradigm shift in our view of human beings and their development. The model I propose grows out of the traditional Japanese worldview, but it seeks to integrate perspectives that are both Eastern and Western, and both traditional and modern. The linchpin for my integration is Erik Erikson's (1950) conception of *generativity*. In bringing together perspectives from different cultural traditions, I ultimately seek to redefine generativity and to expand and enrich its conceptualization.

I begin by critiquing the underlying assumptions of *individualism* and *linear progression* as they exist in Western developmental theories. In com-

I am very grateful to Ed de St. Aubin, Dan McAdams, and Regina Logan for kind comments and helpful advice regarding a draft of this chapter. This study was supported by Grant-in-Aid for Scientific Research from the Japanese Ministry of Education, Science, Sports, and Culture (No. 13410081) and by the 21st Century COE Program (D-2 to Kyoto University), Japan.

parison with this individual model, I describe a contextual model drawn from traditional Japanese culture, with its central notion of cyclical development. I then comment on Erikson's life cycle model, focusing on the idea of generativity, as it relates to this traditional developmental scheme. I propose a new model: the generative life cycle model (GLCM), based on a blending of Western assumptions, concepts drawn from Japanese traditional folk culture, and selected segments of my own research. I conclude with a discussion of how the GLCM can contribute generally to life-span developmental psychology and specifically to a new understanding of generativity.

INDIVIDUALISM AND LINEAR PROGRESSIVISM

One of the main constructs undergirding Western developmental theory is the primacy of the individual (Miller, 1993). Models developed by Freud and Piaget, for example, reflect the individualistic view of human beings in Western culture that originated with the ancient Greek philosophers. The word *individual* has the same etymology as the word *atom*, which means an ultimate entity that cannot be further divided. But in modern physics, an atom is no longer treated as an ultimate simple substance. Nonetheless, in the field of psychology, the emphasis on the individual persists as the basic unit of study (Sampson, 1989). It has often been assumed that each individual can be understood independent of his or her context and that a person's identity is consistent, despite changes in the natural or social environment. In this individual model for psychology, the ecological, cultural, social, and historical contexts are downplayed or ignored. The careful study of these contexts is left to sociologists, economists, and historians. In fairness, some recent Western theories of development have sought to offer more ecologically contextual viewpoints (e.g., Bronfenbrenner, 1994; Elder, 1995). And certain feminist perspectives have suggested human interdependence as a developmental goal (Gilligan, 1982). Nonetheless, the dominant thrust of developmental theorizing in the West tends to separate out the individual from social and historical contexts.

A second basic assumption that has dominated Western developmental models is linear progressivism. Development is understood to involve movement forward and upward, a progression through which earlier and simpler stages are left behind as the individual moves upward, onward, and toward greater complexity in life (Loevinger, 1976). According to such thinking, time is progressive, irreversible, and unidirectional; stagnation has a negative meaning, and regression implies failure or an abnormality. Regardless of the pace of development of individuals, it has been assumed that basically all development takes the same course in the same direction, whether development is treated as a process of continuous change (Bandura, 1977) or as one divided into many stages (Kohlberg, 1969). Developmental psychology has historically been a science closely associated with great Enlightenment values of progress, evolution, and expansion.

Rooted in conceptions of child and adolescent development, developmental progressivism considers positive change to involve the process of ascending, rising, improvement, competence, or advancement with age, at least until adulthood. Developmental psychology has historically covered the period from infancy to adolescence. This perspective places primacy on the first half of life with the implication that the second half of life, from middle age on, which may be characterized by degeneration and decline, is somehow less significant. Excessive emphasis on childhood and adolescence is a reflection of the modern, progressivism-centered attitude toward life. Beginning in the 1960s, developmental psychology began to expand into life-span developmental approaches (e.g., Jacques, 1965; Neugarten, 1968). Indeed, Baltes (1987) pointed out that social, cultural, and historical contexts were important, and that what was needed was a multidimensional model including not only acquisition and ascent but also loss and decline. Nonetheless, currently popular conceptions of "successful aging" still represent an extension of the individual and progressive view of human development (Baltes & Baltes, 1990).

As indicated by the expression *successful aging*, which is frequently used in life-span developmental psychology, there is an inherent assumption that development equates with "progress," which implies acquisition, struggle, and success. These terms are used to describe the first half of life and are thus assumed to continue into adulthood. Why should we think of life metaphorically as struggle and winning, which also connotes losing? Why do we believe that we should continue to succeed or progress? Who decides whether our lives are "successful"? We could select other words such as *meaningful* or *tasteful* to represent our lives. Kanji characters of the Japanese word *meaning* involve *Aji*, which translates as "taste, flavor, sense, impression, appreciation, enjoyment, and experience." Even if a person's life ended in what others might judge as complete failure, the "failed" person might still assess his or her life as he or she would assess the taste of food, using a variety of adjectives such as bitter, sour, salty, spicy, smoky, and so on. Though the person may not appear to have been successful, his or her life could have a great depth of meaning and been rich in human experience. Just as we cannot proclaim which is the most delicious food—fruits, vegetables, fish, or meat— we cannot presume to define success or progress for any person's life.

The individual and progressive view is apparent even in the writings of Levinson (1978), who was a strong critic of conventional developmental psychology. Levinson criticized the conventional approach of developmental psychology as characterized by the special treatment accorded to infancy and adolescence and insisted on the importance of development in the adult years. Taking the four seasons as an analogy for life, he argued that, just as it was meaningless to say that spring, for example, is better than autumn, in the same way, no stage of life should be given special priority over any other stage. However, despite his metaphorical expression of the four seasons of life, what Levinson proposed as a developmental model for the adult years ended up being a stepped progressivism, as indicated in Figure 7.1. Recent trends toward a perspective of life-span development mean that more attention is now paid to development in the latter half of life. Despite such a shift to life-span perspectives, however, models of development, like Levinson's, are still mainly based on assumptions of individualism and progressivism.

CONTEXTUALISM AND CYCLICAL IMAGERY

In contrast to the modern conception of developmental psychology based on an image of individual progression, let us consider an alternative view, drawn from traditional Japanese images and from Buddhism—a view that conceives of the person as being enveloped in his or her context. Ancient Japanese tradition holds the belief that humans are embedded in nature, as found in religious beliefs such as the Kami (Harris, 2000). The Kami are animistic gods perceived both in all aspects of nature such as trees, waterfalls, and mountains, and in human activities and practices such as cultivating, cleaning, and crafting. The Kami are gods who live together with deified ancestral and historical figures. Another source of Japanese tradition is Buddhism. A fundamental idea of Buddhism is to describe reality in terms of process and relation rather than entity or substance. The central Buddhist teaching of nonself (*anatman*) asserts that there is no independent existence and all phenomena arise in interrelation with causes and conditions.

As pointed out by Aries (1960), the way the life cycle is depicted in art and folklore may reflect a culture's collective understanding in a given time period. Accordingly, the stages of human life are depicted in a chart of Kanshin Jukkai Mandala (Daienji Temple; Amino, Onishi, & Satake, 1999). This chart was used by Buddhist missionary nuns in the 17th–19th centuries to teach those people who could not read sutras to narrate religious lessons orally. In this chart, the images of life between the personal world and the natural world are represented as parallels. In the limited space of this painting, seasonal changes are symbolically depicted as the context or background for personal development. The composition is intended to show that human beings change according to what surrounds them—a house, mountains, fields, the seasons.

Humans are not depicted as individuals isolated from nature; their clothing and personal belongings reflect the social, cultural, and historical contexts in which they live. The people in this art are not represented in an individualistic fashion; rather, they reflect the human life as being wrapped in meaningful contexts. Furthermore, identities of people are changed from one stage to another. At the beginning and end of life, gender is not exhibited, but in the middle there is a mix of both male and female. People wear

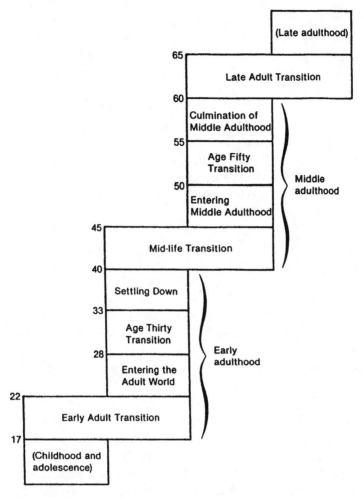

Figure 7.1. Levinson's stage model. From *The Seasons of a Man's Life* (p. 57) by D. Levinson, 1978, New York: Knopf. Copyright 1978 by Alfred A. Knopf, a division of Random House, Inc. Reprinted with permission.

different costumes, indicating the diversity of their social classes. The painting portrays a social representation of various groups of people on different time axes, rather than focusing on the consistent identity and development of any particular individual (Yamada, 2002).

This artistic chart includes not only the first half of the individual's life but also the latter half, subsuming the process of decline to death. The average life expectancy at the time this picture was originally drawn in the 17th century was only around 40, less than half the expected life in contemporary Japan. In the 17th century, very few people lived into old age. Nevertheless, it should be noted that the way in which old people have bent backs or carry their canes is carefully observed and expressed in detail in the limited space of the picture. We may presume that because there is as much detail devoted to old age as to youth, the fading process is also valued in life.

Now, I reconsider the linear progressive model of development that is related with the concept of time. Different understandings of time seem to coexist in many cultures. For example, in ancient Europe the time seemed to be linear in the Hebraic period but cyclic in the Hellenistic period. In East Asia, ancient Chinese also had two concepts of time (Loewe 1999). Time was seen as a thread or line that linked past and present. It provided a starting point toward which men and women could trace their ancestry and permanent existence of their kin, stretching from one generation to another. A separate image of time was the cyclical track: the repetitive cycle of birth, death, and rebirth charted alike in the movement of the stars, the growth and decay of vegetation, the births of sons and daughters, and the deaths of grandfathers and grandmothers.

These images have been transformed by scientific notions but still pervade fundamental thought. The Japanese concepts of time (*toki*), age (*toshi*), and generation are viewed as cyclic images. They are combined with the meanings "cyclic change of nature" and "seasonal transition." An appreciation of the natural world has always been an intrinsic part of Japanese culture. In particular, they value a sense of awareness regarding the seasonal changes, with their fleeting or fading beauty and attendant promises of renewal. New Year is a most important festival. The sense of starting afresh, returning to the origin, and regenerating life is a key concept of Japanese religious beliefs and daily life.

The cyclic time perspective seems to be combined with loss and renewal. One example of Japanese concepts of cyclic change and continuity is to be found at the highly sacred imperial shrine of Ise, a seventh-century building that is carefully rebuilt every 20 years. The regular reconstruction means both destroying the old building and preserving the original style of architecture freshly and continuously for over 1,000 years. It means both a repetition of loss and renewal of life and an eternal succession of life.

TOWARD AN INTEGRATION:
ERIKSON'S MODEL AND GENERATIVITY

Erikson's (1950, 1982) model of human development may be considered a mixed model. It combines elements of the individual and the contextual, the linear progressive and the cyclical. His view of development attempts to maximize the power of the human ego and stresses the concept of identity and the continuity of an individual's personality. However, unlike many other developmental theorists, Erikson does take into account the individual's context. For example, his concept of identity includes interactions with social contexts to establish a psychosocial niche in the world (McAdams, 1985). Erikson also conceives of development as a process of epigenesis, that is, a gradual, progressive unfolding with the acquisition of wisdom in old age positioned as the highest stage of ego integration. Therefore, his model is a stepped progressive model. However, unlike Piaget and Freud, who overestimated childhood and neglected developmental changes after aging, Erikson focused on adulthood and old age as well. Along with Carl Jung (1961), who valued integration in the latter half of life, Erikson was a pioneer in extending development across the entire life span. Regrettably his understanding of the ideal "successful life" was quite similar to other life-span researchers. Erikson neglected the natural loss of power or ability in old age and the appreciation of death in human life.

Erikson presents a theory in which development is more complex than the models based on a scheme of linear, quantitative functions. His model may be likened to a textile interwoven with warps and woofs. It is not a tree model in which progress, ascent, and differentiation take place linearly, but a model of a woven textile—a textured fabric made up from crossings of coetaneous lines from society to the individual and temporal lines from the past to the future. Still, his term *epigenesis* implies a linear unidirectional time perspective, reflective of a Western sensibility. Yet, from an Eastern perspective, one might ask: Does life "complete itself" within each individual, as indicated by the title of Erikson's (1982) last book, *The Life Cycle Completed*? The idea that a single human life has both an origin and an ultimate goal seems to be an expression of the West, and in particular, Judeo-Christian cosmology. The origin is the starting point where every creature is created, and the end is the completed conclusion or the terminal point of the Last Judgment. One's life is assumed to be similar to this time perspective that completely divides time between the origin and the goal. Though the term Erickson used is *life cycle*, this time perspective is used in linear models of development.

Erikson defined *generativity* as creating and producing things, people, and outcomes that are aimed at benefiting the next generation (see also McAdams & de St. Aubin, 1998). Generativity is a word coined by Erikson from the words *generation* and *generate*. This concept suggests the process of life succession from the parents' generation to that of the children in the sequence of generations: transmission of life to the next generation. Generativity involves concern in establishing and guiding the next generation and is connected with intergenerational relations beyond the ego of the individual (Kim & Harrison, 1999; Yamada, 1999, 2000). Generativity is a critical concept throughout the entire lifetime, though it is particularly meaningful in the latter half of life (McAdams & de St. Aubin, 1998). It is related to communication between generations, educational processes, genetic transmission, and even concerns with global issues. It suggests we should care for not only our own generation but also for the next and future generations. Generativity captures the process of creating a vision of our responsibilities for future generations and societies.

THE GENERATIVE LIFE CYCLE MODEL:
AN ILLUSTRATION OF AN APPLE'S LIFE

My own generative life cycle model (GLCM) integrates Erikson's concept of generativity with a Japanese folk image. To show the typical illustration of GLCM, I offer here an example from my research. I sought to understand how young people visualized the life course by having them construct drawings that depict their own life stories (e.g., Yamada, 1988). The participants were 137 Japanese university students. They were directed to draw a map of their life and to draw their images freely, without regard for drawing skill. They were encouraged to include a variety of images in their drawings. Many students conceptualized their lives using images of progress and ascent. However, there were a number whose images were classified as representing a circular model, such as the image in Figure 7.2. Figure 7.2 shows an image of the cyclical nature of the life of an apple. Although Figure 7.2 is an especially unique drawing, it is illustrative of the GLCM's concepts, especially in regard to generativity.

The six stages of a self's life are listed below and are illustrated by the example in Figure 7.2 of Japanese youths' images of their lives (Yamada, 1999).

1. (There is a tree.)
2. The tree begins to bear fruits. The first fruits are very beautiful. My fruit (myself) has not appeared yet.
3. My fruit (myself) appears at this stage.
4. My fruit is not picked and I remain on the tree.
5. I have stayed behind, but I have fallen to the earth.
6. The earth is nourished (by my fruit).

The GLCM is defined as a way of looking at human development based primarily on the following five concepts:

1. Cycle model: Time perspectives and transitions of an individual's life and generations' lives are circular, spiral, and/or recurrent.
2. Changing process: In the cycle model, the concept of changing process itself is fundamental. It is compared with the linear model wherein the beginning (the origin) and the ending (the goal or purpose) are important.
3. Generating and dying: The changing process of generating, growing, decaying, dying, and regenerating is a naturally transitional function of the vital life.
4. Contextualism: The core concept is not the individual, the self, or the entity but the contextual relationships. An individual life is fundamentally related with others' lives, such as former and latter generations and other living things in nature.

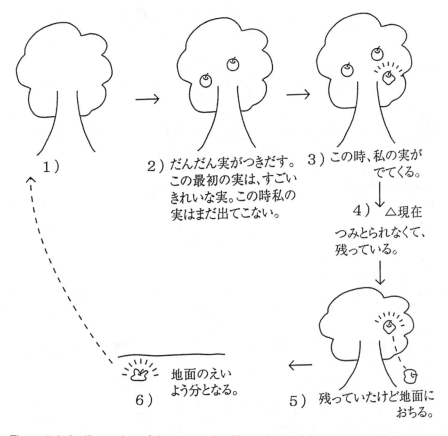

1)

2) だんだん実がつきだす。
この最初の実は、すごい
きれいな実。この時私の
実はまだ出てこない。

3) この時、私の実が
でてくる。

4) △現在
つみとられなくて、
残っている。

6) 地面のえい
よう分となる。

5) 残っていたけど地面に
おちる。

Figure 7.2. An illustration of the generative life cycle model: An apple's life cycle.

5. Meaning of life: No phase of an individual's life has a privileged status over any other phase because each phase has its
own flavor, taste, and meaning.

In Figure 7.2, time is regarded as a cycle. In this conceptualization, the
participant has chosen to represent his life by an apple. The Japanese word
mi, which stands for "fruit," has the same pronunciation and the same origin
as the Japanese word *mi*, meaning self and body. Therefore, the use of an
apple as a metaphor for the self has a deeply symbolic meaning. Furthermore,
the apple represents not only the self but also the dual meaning of the child
and the parent: a symbol of maturity, fertility, and generativity (Yamada,
1988). An apple is a "child" of an apple tree and matures into an edible fruit;
in its flesh are nested the seeds, its "children." An apple means both a child
to the tree and a parent to the next generation. In this circular depiction of
an apple's life, the fall of an apple does not represent a useless death but
shows how the dropped fruit produces new life as the next generation. We

can imagine a larger life cycle beyond a person's individual life or ego identity.

A self's life does not begin with birth. Rather, the self is part of a circle of successive generations. In Figure 7.2, "my life" does not begin with the birth of the self as an individual. A tree, representing the larger environment or the place that gives birth to apples, is drawn first, followed by the initial two fruits, which are supposed to represent the parents. Then, "myself (my fruit)" as the third motif is born. "My apple" and other apples are not distinguishable from each other. The uniqueness or identity of myself is not emphasized. A self is one member of the family of apples and one part of a connected chain of generations of apples. According to this circular generative image, the question, "Which is the origin: the parent or the child?" is meaningless. A child is born by the parents; he or she then becomes a parent, who in turn gives birth to a child. From the Japanese perspective, attention is paid not to the beginning or the end, but to the movement of transition and succession and to the process of generating and regenerating. The generative process has a spontaneous function that vitalizes and renews a life. In the GLCM, individuals coexist in a circle of a nested ecosystem. Figure 7.2 shows a contextual model in which a self lives interactively as a coexistence within its ecosystem (Yamada, 1988). A life of an apple is embedded in a larger system of life, like the tree on which it grows, and a tree is enclosed in larger life cycles such as seasonal changes. Thus, one's life is nested within a series of interconnected, concentric life cycles.

Another claim in the GLCM is that decline and descent should not be viewed negatively, as there is an emphasis on the natural cycle of transition. The model of progress or ascent assumes that time flows straight in one direction and that descent and regression have negative connotations. In the circular model, which imagines time as a cyclic, recurrent process, even descent and regression lead to comeback or rebirth, so that the meanings between the positive and the negative are relative. When the self is viewed at the individual level in the progressive model, time is irreversible and rebirth is impossible. Figure 7.2 includes descent and decline rather than ascent and progress; and the former does not have negative connotations. The apple's dropping to the ground was included as one of the life phases because it is an integral part of how the participant understands the life cycle. Contrast these images with progressive linear models (see Levinson, 1978 and Figure 7.1) in which the self must aggressively climb up against the force of gravity. The person needs to acquire the power to climb over obstacles, overcome difficulties, and successfully attain a higher position. Along the way, he or she develops a series of skills and virtues that work to assure success and well-being. Indeed, Erikson's listing of stage virtues—from hope (Stage 1: Trust vs. Mistrust) to wisdom (Stage 8: Ego Integrity vs. Despair)—suggests a progressive developmental journey. Over time the protagonist of the story gains more and more resources to meet the challenges of aging and, finally, the despair of facing death. By contrast, the images in Figure 7.2 show no motifs such as will, struggle, conquest, or success. The drawing shows a self naturally accepting a decaying self, instead of a self resisting or trying to conquer aging and death.

Figure 7.2 represents the notion that "my life" does not end with "my death." A life containing seeds does not end with death. In the last phase of the apple's life in Figure 7.2, the decayed apple is under the ground, invisible from above. The comment on the drawing is, "The apple becomes a nutrient for the earth." The dotted line in the drawing indicates that "myself in the earth" serves as nutrition for a subsequent life. The seeds of my fruit (my self) return to the earth, and the seeds will realize a succession to new lives of blossoms that will bear fruit in the future. When we think of the succession of life, it is interesting to note that the metaphor chosen is a fruit, specifically an apple. If the metaphor had been a flower, it would have emphasized the spring season of life in which the sexes have their initial encounter. By contrast, the fruit emphasizes the autumn season with a connotation of reproduction and generativity.

IMPLICATIONS AND DISCUSSIONS ABOUT GLCM

The progressive model reflects the view of Western culture from the 19th century, when modern science and industry developed. By contrast, the cyclical model reflects the naturalistic view that was the basis for premodern agricultural society. The concept of cycle is connected with the concept of ecological time that reflects seasonal changes as recurrence. At the same time, the cycle is connected with the concept of birth and rebirth as abstracted from plants that die in winter and sprout in spring. This kind of circular image of human life frequently has been seen in traditional culture. Tuboi (1984) analyzed Japanese rites of passage in the form of a circular chart showing how the human life cycle was regarded as overlapping with the cycle of the growth of rice plants. The Japanese word *toshi* (age) means both crops such as rice plants and an age including a year and a time. In this way, crops, which nurture human lives, were analogized to human beings. It was assumed that rice plants develop in the following sequence: sprouting, growing, bearing fruit, death in seed, sprouting, and so on. Modern scientific thinking has ignored organic cosmology as "unscientific," "primitive," or "premodern." Japan is no longer a society whose main economic activity is agriculture. We are in a highly sophisticated age of information technology. The GLCM does not imply a nostalgic revival of the images of a simpler agricultural society. However, the GLCM does suggest elegance and truth in the cyclical patterns of the natural order that may apply to human life as well as all other living things.

The GLCM is also based on notions drawn from Buddhist cosmology. But it is crucial to note that the meaning of the cycle in GLCM is also different from that in Buddhism. In Buddhism, *cycle* refers to transmigration of souls, or the wheel of life. Buddhism accepts the Indian presupposition that living beings are trapped in a continual cycle of birth and death, with rebirth determined by one's previous actions. The release from this cycle of rebirth and suffering is the transcendence called *Nirvana*. This is considered a fundamental precept of Buddhism, but it is not really germane to conceptualizing the vital cyclical relationship between generating and regenerating in the GLCM.

Another key concept of Buddhism that is integrated in the GLCM is the idea of transition or impermanence. The concept of transition is that everything—every function, energy, and power—appears and disappears, one after another, and that the universe is not constant but continuously moving. The *Abhidharma-kosa*, an important Buddhist text, teaches that the process of appearance and disappearance (birth and death) consists of four phases. The first phase is *jati*, generating; the second, *sthiti*, staying or being at rest; the third, *jara*, transforming, changing or declining; and the fourth, *anityata*, perishing or decaying (Saigusa, 1977). This life cosmology is in striking contrast to that of the West, as represented in the Judeo-Christian perspective. The Judeo-Christian life story is characterized by the creation of creatures by the Creator, the active selection of purpose or the right way of one's life, and attaining permanent or immortal life by going up to Heaven at the end of life.

The GLCM incorporates the continuity of life or the immortality of life that members of every culture maintain. Humans have always contemplated what happens when one's physical existence ends in death. When we confront the dying process, we cannot neglect images of the soul and the spirit. In another study, I asked 327 Japanese university students and 234 French university students to construct images of "the soul" (Yamada & Kato, 2001). The students were asked to draw an image of the relationships between the people in this world and those in the next world and of the soul's passage from this world to the next world and from the next world to this world. Among the interesting results in this study was the finding that the majority of Japanese students (63.7%) imagined the soul returning to this world after visiting the next world, whereas only 37.8% of the French students made such drawings. The majority of all students who conceived of the eventual return of the soul from the next world back to this one depicted souls being reborn into human wombs or as babies. The key concept of these images is making the connection between former generations and future generations. We should note how the Japanese students' depiction of the soul after death differs from Western traditional ideas, such as Plato's "immortality of the soul." Plato's concept of immortality dualistically contrasts the integrity of the immaterial soul with the decomposition and dissolution of the material body. Since Plato, much of Western traditional thinking has considered the soul as an eternally unchanging, ultimate entity (Vernette, 1998). Yet, the Japanese regard the soul as a changing, renewing, and recurring spirit.

In the images of circular cosmology found in our research (Yamada & Kato, 2001), Japanese depict rebirth into human beings, including dead ancestors and future newborn babies. This interaction with their ancestors allows them to feel that they occupy a certain position in a long succession of related lives. Japanese share some conceptualization of ancestors with East Asian people. This concept of the succession of generations is different from the Chinese concept of kinship, however, which is a linear model like a string or a thread of the permanent existence of the kin (Loewe, 1999). It is essential for the GCLM that people feel their lives are an animate part of a larger cycle of life from generation to generation—an ongoing project.

CONCLUSION

Recall the generative image in Figure 7.2 that interconnects death and rebirth: The seeds hidden in the earth suggest an implicit connection indicated by the dotted line. I suggest that the circular concept of one's life story that constructs a linkage from death to the following birth is a generative function. The Japanese construct generativity as one generation's caring for and linkage not only to the succeeding generation but also to preceding generations. The apple story (Figure 7.2) emphasizes that the chain of life remains constant, whereas individual life is transient. What transcends the limit of one's life is not the image of "eternal life" but the image of "a continuing cycle of life." Continuity of life is not equal to immortality; continuity of life assures that the life cycle of human beings persists. The cycle of life never ends in individual death because each individual and each generation is born anew out of the previous generation, just as the apple became a nutrient for a tree in the ecosystem and was passed on to the generation of new lives. Individual life and death are thus interwoven into the large, continuing cycle of life.

I suggest that generativity concerns not only future generations for which we cannot care directly. It seems to me that generativity should be interpreted as an intergenerational life cycle or in an even broader sense as a spiritual life cycle implying continuity of life that stretches both forward and *backward*. I do not mean that we should accept the existence of the soul, the spirit, reincarnation, or an afterlife. Rather, I think that we should acknowledge that the question of afterlife may be a universal dilemma for all of humankind. Every culture throughout time has developed images and stories related to the roles of life, death, and afterlife. A redefined generativity responds to humankind's deepest need for the succession of life by acknowledging the continuity of life through death and rebirth. Again, we should not expect a redefinition of generativity to encompass a belief in reincarnation. Yet, a redefined generativity considers, as the traditional Japanese conception does, a feeling of being closely interrelated with past generations, one's

ancestors, and nature. Also, we should note that for the Japanese, importance is placed on generations more than individual family and kinship. The
redefined generativity allows a conceptual shift away from individualism,
anthropocentrism, and egocentrism toward a way of conceptualizing the self
that is centered on one's role as a link in culture and history, as well as how
one relates to living nature or the ecosystem. Thus, a redefined generativity
places an emphasis on the generation, rather than the individual, and asserts
that both individuals and generations are embedded in their psychosocial
contexts, reaching forward into future, unborn generations and back into
past generations of ancestors. This definition of generativity is the building
block of the GLCM.

The GLCM suggests a new view of human development, particularly in
its conceptualization of time, the generative process, the shift in emphasis
from individual to generation, and the insistence that all phases of the life
cycle have appropriately important meanings. When time is construed as
cyclical, rather than unidirectional, generational care and societal concern
go both back into the past and forward into the future. The GLCM argues for
a conceptual shift from individualism and egocentrism to a way of thinking
centered on the generative life cycle that leads to respect for all generations,
past, present, and future. The GLCM also redefines old age and death. According to the GLCM's perspective on decline and death, the old are valued
as much as children and youths, especially because the elderly pass on their
gifts of memory and tradition to the following generations.

We live in a sophisticated technological society in which we are surrounded by mounting ecological and social problems. There is now, more
than ever, the critical need to develop the concept of generativity for the
survival of our future generations. A redefined generativity emphasizes the
nonlinearity of time, and the vital function of generating and regenerating.
In so doing, the generations are linked, forward and backward, in never-
ending cycles of birth and rebirth. It is hoped this emphasis on the generative process may lead to reverence for every cycle of life on earth. That is,
similar to rebirth stories that are thought to encourage people to care for
generations yet unborn and younger people to care for ancestors they have
never seen, a generativity that respects all generations would also honor all
of human history and the natural world in which history unfolds. When we
conceptualize our lives as the linkage between the past and the present, we
take on the responsibility for providing a safe and healthy world in reverence
for all past generations and in hope for all future ones.

REFERENCES

Amino, Y., Onishi, H., & Satake, A. (Eds.). (1999). *Jinsei no Kaidan* [The staircase of
   life]. Tokyo: Fukuinkan Shoten.

Ariès, P. (1960). *L'enfant et la vie familiale sous l'Ancien Régime* [Centuries of childhood: A social history of family life]. Paris: Editions du Seuil.

Baltes, P. B. (1987). Theoretical propositions of life-span developmental psychology: On the dynamics between growth and decline. *Developmental Psychology, 23,* 611–626.

Baltes, P. B., & Baltes, M. M. (1990). Psychological perspectives on successful aging: The model of selective optimization with compensation. In P. B. Baltes & M. M. Baltes (Eds.), *Successful aging: Perspectives from the behavioral sciences* (pp. 1–34). Cambridge, England: Cambridge University Press.

Bandura, A. (1977). *Social learning theory* (2nd ed.). Morristown, NJ: Prentice-Hall.

Bronfenbrenner, U. (1994). Ecological models of human development. In T. Husten & T. N. Postlewaite (Eds.), *International encyclopedia of education* (2nd ed.). New York: Elsevier.

Elder, G. H., Jr. (1995). The life course paradigm: Social change and individual development. In P. Moen, G. H. Elder, Jr., & K. Luscher (Eds.), *Examining lives in context: Perspectives on the ecology of human development* (pp. 101–139). Washington, DC: American Psychological Association.

Erikson, E. H. (1950). *Childhood and society.* New York: Norton.

Erikson, E. H. (1982). *The life cycle completed.* New York: Norton.

Gilligan, C. (1982). *In a different voice.* Cambridge, MA: Harvard University Press.

Harris, V. (Ed.). (2001). *Shinto: The sacred art of ancient Japan.* London: The British Museum Press.

Jacques, E. (1965). Death and the midlife crisis. *International Journal of Psychoanalysis, 46,* 502–514.

Jung, C. (1961). *Memories, dreams, reflections,* New York: Vintage.

Kim, T.-C., & Harrison, R. (1999). (Eds.). *Self and future generations.* Cambridge, England: White Horse Press.

Kohlberg, L. (1969). Stage and sequence: The cognitive–developmental approach to socialization. In D. A. Goslin (Ed.), *Handbook of socialization theory and research* (pp. 347–480). Skokie, IL: Rand McNally.

Levinson, D. J. (1978). *The seasons of a man's life.* New York: Knopf.

Loevinger, J. (1976). *Ego development.* San Francisco: Jossey-Bass.

Loewe, M. (1999). Cyclical and linear concepts of time in China. In K. Lippincott (Ed.), *The story of time* (pp. 76–79). London: Merrell Holberton.

McAdams, D. P. (1985). *Power, intimacy, and the life story: Personological inquiries into identity.* New York: Guilford Press.

McAdams, D. P., & de St. Aubin, E. (1998). (Eds.). *Generativity and adult development: How and why we care for the next generation.* Washington, DC: American Psychological Association.

Miller, P. (1993). *Theories of developmental psychology* (3rd ed.). San Francisco: Freeman.

Neugarten, B. (1968). (Ed.). *Middle age and aging*. Chicago: University of Chicago Press.

Oe, K. (1986). *M/T to mori no fushigi no monogatari* [A mysterious story among M/T and the forest]. Tokyo: Iwanami Syoten.

Saigusa, M. (1977). The concept of the time in Buddhism. In F. Tagima (Ed.), *Jikan kukan* [The time and the space] (pp. 225–261). Tokyo: Iwanami Shoten.

Sampson, E. E. (1989). The challenge of social change for psychology: Globalization and psychology's theory of the person. *American Psychologist, 44*, 914–921.

Tuboi, H. (1984). Murashakai to tukagirei [Mura-community and the rites of passage]. *Nihon Minzoku Bunka Taikei, 8*, 455–506.

Vernette, J. (1998). *L'au-delà* [The afterlife]. Paris: Presses Universitaires de France.

Yamada, Y. (1988). *Watashi wo tutumu hahanarumono* [Self wrapped by the mother: Japanese mentality viewed through image drawings]. Tokyo: Yuhikaku.

Yamada, Y. (1999). *The image maps of life*. Paper presented at the 10th Congress of Japanese Developmental Psychology (p. 540). Japan Society of Developmental Psychology, Tokyo. (In Japanese).

Yamada, Y. (2000). *Jinsei wo monogataru* [Telling generative life stories]. Kyoto: Mineruba Shobo.

Yamada, Y. (2002). Models of life-span developmental psychology: A construction of the generative life cycle model including the concept of "death." *Kyoto University Research Studies in Education, 48*, 39–62.

Yamada, Y., & Kato, Y. (2001). Images of the soul and the circulatory cosmology of life: Psychological models of folk representations in Japanese and French youths' drawings. *Kyoto University Research Studies in Education, 47*, 1–27.

III

GENERATIVITY AND SOCIAL INSTITUTIONS

8

ROPE OF ASHES: GLOBAL AGING, GENERATIVITY, AND EDUCATION

RONALD J. MANHEIMER

Erik Erikson posited an emergent quality or virtue in midlife that he characterized as both a biological impulse and a psychological disposition: the orientation of care, as in to care for and care about, especially the well-being of younger, and therefore future, generations. The capacity for caring is not merely a function of reaching a certain age but is the hypothetical outcome of passing through a stage-linked developmental crises. In the manner of all of Erikson's stages, care is the successful resolution of a Hegelian-like dialectical conflict occurring in this seventh of his "eight ages of man" (Erikson, 1950) between self-preoccupation or self-indulgence (*stagnation*) and the nurturing concern for those individuals, ideas, traditions, and cultural productions that will inevitably outlive oneself (*generativity*).

In Erikson's view, the resolution of conflicting orientations in one stage leads eventually to a subsequent developmental crisis in which a new set of contesting themes emerge. Hence, in the final eighth stage of the life cycle, the attribute *wisdom*, defined as "informed and detached concern with life itself in the face of death itself" (Erikson, 1986), may result from the conflict between ego integrity and despair. Erikson presented the older adult struggling with the past in light of heightened awareness of finitude. This mortality-inspired search for meaning seems to require embracing the full course of the individual's life cycle and entails wrestling with a personal history that likely includes disappointments and shortcomings.

This retrospective evaluation is actually engaged at every step as one moves up the ladder of life stages. In his philosophical treatises on the growth of human consciousness, Hegel coined the term *aufheben* to capture the process of development as a sequence of transformations in which a prior stage (of personal development or even of world history) would be overtaken by and incorporated into a subsequent stage. Likewise, Erikson understood that generativity and caring would not cease at the gateway to old age but would be revisited and reevaluated in light of the search for meaning and the quest for wisdom. He named that reincorporated process *grand-generativity* (Erikson, 1986), suggesting not only an age-linked grandparent stage of life but also an achievement of a "grander" or more encompassing point of view. Accordingly, grand-generative individuals might come to regard all children as their own grandchildren whose well-being represents concern for the future of the whole society, indeed, the continuation of life itself.

To the dialectical function within and between each life stage, Erikson added a social dimension, pointing to those institutions, customs, laws, and traditions that could foster or hinder movement between the stages. As part of this social dimension, his theory suggests a picture of interacting life stages rather than isolated ones. This relational aspect raises a critical question about generativity, care, grand-generativity, and wisdom. These processes and virtues presuppose not only a generous giver but also a willing recipient who welcomes and needs these resources for further development. Implied in this exchange is the reciprocal effect: the younger person's need for guidance and the mature person's "need to be needed." Nurturing another may heighten self-esteem, reinforce a sense of value and identity, and enhance the feeling that one is leading a meaningful life. The interrelationship of people located at different stages of development also begs the question whether a society's institutions serve to play the necessary roles in supporting and encouraging the fulfillment of the Eriksonian virtues.

What then of a society in which younger generations disdain the gifts of a generative impulse, demonstrating a reluctance or resistance weakly captured in the term *generation gap*? And what of a culture in which the accumulated knowledge and skills of an older generation are deemed obsolete, irrelevant, or even detrimental to younger persons' hopes and ambitions? Such attitudes were highly prevalent in the youthful years of the baby-boom generation that came of age in the 1960s and 1970s. Remember the phrase: "Don't trust anyone over 30"?

The huge post–World War II birth cohort of 1946–1964 is now nearly double the venerable age of 30, reaching midlife and the brink of old age, not only in the United States but throughout Europe and in other developed countries of Asia. Will graying baby-boomers who read Erik Erikson's books while in college and saw reflected their own adolescent identity crises in the upheavals of the period now trace themselves along his developmental diagonal and embrace the ideals of midlife generativity and old age wisdom? How will they be treated by their children and grandchildren's generations? As a resource, as a treasure, or as dependent elders who are largely irrelevant to a rapidly changing society?

This chapter explores the implications of Erikson's theory of generativity and grand-generativity in the context of global aging with particular emphasis on the potential reciprocal functions of giving and receiving care between the generations. Crucial to this discussion are the frameworks and institutional pathways that might enable young and old to care about and for one another. I suggest that lifelong learning and intergenerational educational opportunities are important ways to create the necessary conditions for actualizing grand-generativity and ensuring transmission of the older generation's legacy to those younger while fostering conditions for critical receptivity. Young adults cannot play a passive role in this process. Their own struggles to harmonize an inner and outer identity, achieve mutuality in love relationships, and discover their vocation (Erikson's Stage 6) must also be engaged.

To address these issues, I (a) describe the challenges that global aging presents to the individual and society, (b) discuss the emergence of new types of lifelong learning program for older adults, (c) illustrate the development of intergenerational colearning programs, and (d) discuss challenges to connecting the generations. A traditional tale that contains a contemporary message about reciprocity between the generations serves as a gateway to these explorations.

ROPE OF ASHES

The poignant 11th-century Japanese folk legend, Obasuteyama, the Mountain of Abandoned Old People, tells the story of two brothers who are obligated by tradition to take their elderly father into the mountains where they will abandon him (Dorson, 1962). While ascending the pathway, the brothers notice their father breaking off branches. Thinking the old man is marking a return route, the brothers chastise him, asking: "Why do you do such a thing?" He replies by reciting this enigmatic poem:

> To break branches in the mountain
> Is for the dear children
> For whom I am ready to sacrifice myself[1]

The brothers have no idea what he is talking about and go on with their task. They leave the old man and decide to descend the mountain on the opposite side. Becoming lost, they find their way back to their father, who guides them down the mountain using the path marked by broken branches,

---

[1]From *Folk Legends of Japan* (p. 223), by R. M. Dorson, 1962, Boston: Charles E. Tuttle. Copyright 1962 by Charles E. Tuttle. Reprinted with permission.

thus clarifying the poem's meaning. In gratitude, the brothers take their father home, look after him, but keep him hidden. Some time later, the feudal lord of the region issues a challenge: Who can bring him a rope of ashes? He has set this task to learn whether any truly wise people remain in his realm. The brothers tell their father of the lord's request and he instructs them to take straw, braid it, soak it in salt water and, when dry, set it on fire. They make the rope of ashes and take it to the lord. When he forces them to reveal the source of their wisdom, the lord rewards them and rescinds the edict.

This famous folk tale, variations of which are found in European, Jewish, and Far Eastern cultures, apparently signifies the end of a tradition once practiced by people too poor to care for their aged parents once they had ceased being productive. The legend emphasizes the virtue of filial piety, the resourcefulness of the elderly, and the exchange of knowledge that binds generations of the old who act and speak wisely and the young who have the need and capacity to listen and understand. The poem, from the viewpoint of the elderly father, also suggests an ability to intuit the future. Now, almost 10 centuries later, the legend may still speak to us.

Though progressive social policies protect them from the threat of hunger, homelessness, and ill health, older people may be abandoned in other, more subtle ways. Forced into retirement, isolated in age-segregated housing, or forgotten by their families, older people also experience abandonment when their accumulated knowledge and resourcefulness is ignored or ridiculed. These contemporary conditions make the legend of Obasuteyama relevant today. In fact, the story has served as the inspiration for modern fiction, theater, and film (such as the 1983 Japanese film *The Ballad of Narayama*). The legend takes on new meaning in light of contemporary issues concerning responsibility between the generations and the legacy of wisdom the old may have to offer. But in what way would making a rope of ashes qualify one for wisdom?

A symbol of strength and usefulness, a rope can serve for binding, pulling, lifting, or hanging. A symbol in Japanese culture of worthlessness, inadequacy, and death, ashes are traditionally used in the making of soap. Through uniting opposites, the metaphor of the rope conjoins qualities of strength and usefulness with those of worthlessness and death, the ashes. The result is a transformed meaning in which weakness and death are turned into strength and generativity. The image suggests the Taoist paradoxical notion, "the utility of what is not," and takes on special significance in this era when societies the world over must choose whether to ignore and reject their elderly or protect and learn from them.

The legend of Obasuteyama and its rope of ashes may help us to understand the current situation. The image suggests the strength and resourcefulness that many older people may possess, even those who are frail and near to death. As a parable of generativity and transcendence, the legend suggests the conditions necessary for tapping older persons' potential contribution when they are woven into the lives of other generations. It also suggests the conditions under which those younger might be more or less receptive to an older person's knowledge. The legend is relevant to societies that are becoming predominantly middle aged.

GLOBAL AGING

Demographers call those populations whose median age is above 30 "aging societies." Aging societies predominate in Europe, the United Kingdom, North America, and many Asian countries. They are characterized by an unprecedented number and percentage of people over age 65, due mainly to longevity, and a decline in birth rates and subsequent reduction of the percentage of younger people (even to the extent of causing an overall shrinking of the population). The United States with its huge middle-aged baby-boom population is a case in point. In 2001, the median age in the United States was 36 and is predicted to reach age 40 by the year 2030. Most industrial and postindustrial societies fit this description, leading to what demographers term the "squaring" of the traditional age pyramid.

Although there is a quiet demographic revolution going on, the characteristics of people in the later years have also been changing. In many modern aging societies the activities and health status of those classified as the young-old (55–65 years) are so similar to that of middle-aged adults (35–54 years) that conventional boundaries of old age have become ambiguous and irrelevant. "Old" is more often used to denote a midlife adult in poor health than someone of a given chronological age. The rate of chronic illness in old age is also declining, leading some biologists and gerontologist to predict a "compression of morbidity," a condition in which people would commonly live healthy lives until near the very end of life.

Less physically demanding work conditions, changes in attitudes about age-appropriate behavior, and legislated entitlements for social supports have turned the early and middle years of later life (55–75 years) into a boon for many individuals. But because of high costs, these entitlements are sometimes perceived as creating a burden for society. Older persons' fair share of public funds is under debate in many countries. The discussions reveal a lack of agreement as to principles for equitable distribution of resources among age groups. Moreover, as stereotypes of aging and old age are rejected—similar to the effects of the women's rights movement—little consensus has emerged about what constitutes a good old age or meaningful roles in later life.

These trends and changing conditions have made the purpose and meaning of later life a subject of widespread debate. Hundreds of books and magazine articles appear each year claiming either that growing old is something to resist at all cost or something to embrace as the greatest time of life. Similarly, economists, historians, and political theorists argue either that the growing older population constitutes a "gray peril" (Thurow 1996) or a newfound solution to national and international problems (Freedman, 1999; Roszak, 1998).

Global aging and the new longevity have changed the way one thinks about the life course. Human development theorists have added new stages at the later end of life. They speak of older persons' potential for achieving practical wisdom (Baltes, 1993), newfound freedoms (Rosenmayr, 1980), a resurgence of creativity (Cohen, 2000; Kastenbaum, 1992), and new roles such as becoming a "spiritual elder" (Schachter-Shalomi & Miller, 1995) capable of practicing wise stewardship of the earth. Besides these optimistic attributes, it is likely that a highly visible older population will increase younger persons' awareness of the aging process and of their own mortality. This awareness could help to foster greater consciousness of life as a cycle, but it could also trigger increased fear of death, denial of mortality, and dread of aging and old age. The huge market in plastic surgery and "antiaging" drugs and ointments reflects the latter trend.

Global aging presents challenges not unlike that of conservation of resources and sustainable growth. Advocates for the elderly are pursuing social policies that would ensure that our older citizens remain a vital part of society. Researchers are looking for ways to combat the diseases and illness that most commonly afflict the elderly. But if many more of us are going to live into late old age, we do not want to be stigmatized as social problems or to perceive ourselves as irrelevant except as burdens to others. What we want to understand is how the problems of aging and later life can be turned to assets and how, as we grow older, we can continue to grow intellectually and spiritually and find new ways to benefit future generations.

If, as Erikson has argued, the generative orientation is to nurturing the next generations and to cherish that which outlives oneself, then a potential resource of generativity can be found among members of the older generation. The perspective of a long life prepares and inspires some older people to become caretakers of the future. Capable of reaching back to the past through recollection and forward to the future in hope, they are well positioned to share their knowledge with those younger, who will one day follow in their footsteps. As Erikson (1986) described "vital involvement in old age," these gatekeepers demonstrate the "capacity for one generation to entrust itself to the next, by passing on a certain shared and collective identity" (p. 63).

But, as the legend of Obasuteyama suggests, older people must be equipped to formulate and communicate the knowledge they have gained through experience. And for the relationship to be reciprocal, younger people must see the value of listening and questioning. Long before Erikson, insightful observers realized the perspectives of old age and youth were not the same. In his *Ethics*, Aristotle (1954) asserted that young people dwell in hope for the future, whereas the elderly are preoccupied with the remembered past.

Elsewhere, Aristotle argued that although young adults may be capable of achieving one kind of wisdom—theoretical knowledge—about subjects such as geometry and astronomy, the achievement of moral insight—practical wisdom—requires time and experience. But Aristotle did not subscribe to the belief that age and experience were sufficient for good judgment. Practical wisdom, he argued, can only be gained through the refining powers of reason. Thoughtful reflection helps to ensure that one learns from experience rather than repeat one's mistakes. Lacking critical insight, older people may fall into habitual reminiscing and repetitive storytelling that lead to sentimentality and even narcissism.

There is a good deal of modern scientific research to suggest that Aristotle's assessment is correct. Telling stories about the good old days does not guarantee the narrator's self-knowledge or the communication of insight to those younger. If the contact between young and older generations is to be truly generative and transforming, something more is required. Supportive frameworks are needed to help mature adults mine the ore of experience to extract the precious metal of knowledge. And younger people need attractive opportunities to discover the meaning of the life course and their place within it. Lifelong learning opportunities can help to promote present engagement with life and generative exchange between generations.

LIFELONG LEARNING

Education for older adults has enjoyed remarkable success during the last 20 years, particularly in postindustrial countries whose economies and social policies have enabled average citizens to plan for what, formerly, only the wealthy could anticipate—a lengthy period of relative leisure. As British sociologist Peter Laslett (1991) has pointed out, this historically unprecedented extension of the life course, captured by the phrase "the Third Age," is both an individual experience—a new life stage with an array of options and choices, and a social phenomenon—the institution of retirement with related entitlement, government and private sector policies, and retirement-related industries.

Such Third Age frameworks are now emerging in the form of worldwide programs for lifelong learning (Manheimer, 1998, 1999b). A response to the phenomenon of global aging, these programs can help older people discover and embrace their generativity while providing avenues for bringing young and old together in cooperative learning ventures. In the United States and Canada, close to 300 Institutes for Learning in Retirement (ILR) encourage older participants to plan curricula, teach courses, and help govern these increasingly popular organizations, usually connected to colleges and universities. The ILRs represent just one recent development, with the

European and British Commonwealth countries having hundreds of University of the Third Age organizations, China with its over 2,000 Older Persons' Universities, and Japan with its University for the Aged (Foundation of Social Development for Senior Citizens) and education programs sponsored by the Federation of Senior Citizens' Club.

Distinctive among many of these programs is a revolutionary concept: Older learners are empowered to determine their own educational goals. Senior adults are invited to help lead and run the programs for themselves rather than having courses offered to them by school administrators. This approach is especially appropriate because, in North America, the United Kingdom, and Asian countries such as Japan, an unprecedented number of retirement-age people are already college graduates and in possession of decades of professional experience and their own brand of wisdom gleaned from life experience raising families, traveling, and participating in civic activities. They are used to doing for themselves and prefer an active role in determining what they want to learn, from whom they want to learn, and how.

A national study of older learner programs in the United States (Manheimer, Snodgrass, & Moskow-McKenzie, 1995), conducted by the North Carolina Center for Creative Retirement (NCCCR), found rapid expansion among programs with the following characteristics: (a) They invited participating seniors to play major roles in designing their own curricula and determining institutional policies; (b) they charged fees for courses or membership and, consequently, were less reliant on the unpredictable financial largesse of governments or foundations; (c) they encouraged participants to serve as peer teachers and facilitators for one another; and (d) they promoted community service on the part of participants.

By encouraging self-direction and cooperation among senior adults, these programs served an "emancipatory" purpose. They enabled participants to draw on a lifetime of talents and skills, turning individual self-actualization into community-building action.

Some of these new centers have instituted programs with a generative perspective. For example, they sponsor volunteer programs through which senior adults tutor and mentor school-age children or college students. Some, like the NCCCR, a well-known learning institute that is part of the state's public university system, offer leadership programs for older people to gain in-depth knowledge of their communities while they hone existing skills and reassess knowledge gained from experience so they can find the volunteer role that best suits them. Also, like the NCCCR, a few have initiated intergenerational courses in which retirees and young college students study together in special courses that benefit from having several generations exchange perspectives on ethical dilemmas, worldviews expressed in literature and philosophy, and the challenges of an ever-changing society (Manheimer, 1998).

INTERGENERATIONAL PROGRAMS

Although the ILR programs in the United States are affiliated with institutions of higher education, few are directly involved with undergraduate or graduate education on their campuses. Age-segregated learning predominates. Occasionally, older adults serve as subjects for gerontological research conducted by students and faculty. In a few instances, older adults mentor college students or function as guest lecturers for classes. Additionally, some older adults make financial contributions to scholarship funds or, in a few instances, give large gifts for buildings and programs—another form of generativity. As a matter of United States public policy, in most states, persons over age 62 or 65 (the age varies from state to state) can register tuition-free for public university courses. However, because these policies are generally not publicized, and because many older people do not want to commit themselves to lengthy terms, relatively few choose tuition-free courses.

Great potential exists to link the experience, professional expertise, and life perspective of retirees with the search for career directions and life goals among younger students. On their part, younger students can question and challenge older adults to reexamine the meaning and implications of acquired knowledge, reevaluating assumptions in the light of contemporary issues and concerns. Colearning programs in which several generations draw on diverse historical and developmental perspectives to share in the learning process offer tremendous possibilities for types of education rarely encountered on most college campuses. My own experience leading intergenerational courses may help to illuminate the possibilities.

In the spring semester of 1996, I facilitated an intergenerational course titled "1946—The Meaning of A Year." Half of the students enrolled were traditional-age undergraduates (18–21 years) and half were "seniors" (60–75 years). The course explored events and trends marking the transition from the Great Depression period through World War II and into the beginning of the postwar years. Themes included war-time changes, the new postwar lifestyle, rise of suburbia, changes in women's roles and occupations, increased mobility, racism in the military, knowledge of the holocaust, symbols of the new affluence, and new expectations of life in the United States. A year later, a second course, "The Journey of Life," explored the metaphor of life as a journey through history, psychology, poetry, the novel, and philosophy. We examined images of the life cycle from ancient to modern times, gender issues in theories of human development, the idea of a sacred journey or quest, the journey out of slavery, and a philosopher's life story of his journey. A third course, "The Meaning of Home and the Rise of Homelessness," examined home as dwelling and as metaphor for belonging and the plight of people who have no continuous shelter. Readings drew from anthropology, sociology, documentary film, and psychology.

The courses provided a framework for young and old to study together, compare generational perspectives, assess how historical events shape values and attitudes toward life, and explore similarities and differences between generations. For many younger students, the classes marked the first time they had held sustained serious conversations with an older person. The younger students were impressed with the life experiences of the seniors and with their passion for continued learning. The seniors were impressed with the intellectual abilities of the undergraduates, their energy, and their enthusiasm. Many younger students said their earlier perception of the empty meaning of old age was changed by getting to know actual older people. Some of the seniors remarked that their negative stereotypes of young people were transformed from close contact with members of the younger generation on campus.

All of the participants in these intergenerational courses were required to write research papers, complete reading assignments, and work together on group projects. It is perhaps easier to introduce these kind of innovations into the American college classroom because higher education in the United States places considerable emphasis on student development as well as on mastering intellectual content and passing tests. This model may not fit into the culture of higher education in other countries with inflexible curricula, where competition is intense and succeeding the main goal.

Another important purpose of these intergenerational courses was to link a lifelong learning program for older adults with the central mission of the university—preparing members of the younger generation for future careers and for civic participation. Today's young college students will soon find themselves members of societies in which one person of every five (in the United States) or four (e.g., in Japan, Germany, and Sweden) is over age 65. Under these circumstances, we may see age cohorts competing with one another and living in separate sociocultural enclaves, unless it is possible to forge an age-integrated society in which members of different generation experience common cause and seek the common good together. Today's younger people need to prepare for a future of global aging and view it as an opportunity for a deeper appreciation of the life cycle. Innovative lifelong learning programs help to show the way.

An assumption underlying my intergenerational classes was that knowledge acquired under different historical circumstances by members of different age groups could be successfully communicated. Are there generational gaps that must be crossed?

CONNECTING THE GENERATIONS

In the story of Obasuteyama, the offspring relationship between father and sons exemplifies family generations and a set of culturally defined obligations between parents and children. If society had remained unchanged since the 11th century, then we would only be concerned with the biological meaning of generations. But societies do change, and historical circumstances such as wars, famines, technological revolutions and political ones, and periods of economic depression and affluence deeply influence people's lives and attitudes. The shared experience of growing up under particular historical circumstances may lead to commonly held values, attitudes, and outlooks that differ among age group. Such societal groups are called *generational cohorts*.

American historians Strauss and Howe (1991) have argued that belonging to a particular societal generation or cohort may exert greater influence on people's attitudes and values than belonging to a certain familial generation. They challenged the notion that there are fixed stages of life, rather that life stage theories reflect changing cultural values, because "each generation creates its own subjective reality, its own psychology, emotions, art" (Strauss & Howe, 1991, p. 439). Growing up under common circumstances binds contemporaries through a shared mind set. That is why some sociologists and historians apply labels to American life spans such as the GI generation, the Silent generation, the baby-boomers, Generation Xers, and so on. Presumably, related generational-cohort categories are used in other societies and cultures.

According to this view, one's knowledge is deeply influenced by the formative events of one's society during a specific period. One's interpretations of the past and expectations about the future are also shaped by generational factors. Examples abound. Those who grew up during the Depression know about hard times. As midlife adults, they tend to avoid debt, disparage credit cards, and worry about having enough in reserve for a "rainy day." Their children, who know comparatively little about economic hard times, spend more freely, are likelier to run up credit card debts, and incline toward the belief the future will take care of itself. This example suggests many others.

Differences in generational values and attitudes, "generation gaps," are not accidental. They are a product of different historical conditions that today might include growing up with television, computers, cell phones, the pervasiveness of (mainly Western) popular culture, and acceptance of rapid technological change. Had such a generation gap existed in 11th-century Japan, the brothers might not have asked their father for a solution to the rope of ashes puzzle, he might not have offered the solution, and the lord might not have put the challenge in the first place because he would not have expected to find a tradition of wisdom.

Fortunately, a way across the generation gap is reflected by the story of Obasuteyama. Despite the fact that the legend originates in a time and culture remote from our own, certain elements transcend those limitations. We may grasp from this legend that there are many ways to abandon one's aged parents, recognize that parents often make sacrifices that their children do not understand until they are older and, perhaps, in similar circumstances, and realize that the wisdom of the elderly is sometimes conveyed in enigmatic ways (e.g., a poem or a recipe for making a rope of ashes) that make little sense until we discover an attitude, an outlook on life, that may unlock the mystery as we might discover the cipher that unlocks a coded message.

In other words, there are ways available to us to become contemporary with people from another time, place, culture, language and, yes, generation. Certain insights do endure the ravages of time, cultural, and generational differences. In fact, these differences may attract our attention and lead us to wonder what persists despite change. Knowledge of that which endures is often identified with wisdom. With Aristotle, once again we ask: What enables people to grow wiser as they get older, and can this wisdom be communicated across these generation gaps?

In *America the Wise*, historian Theodore Roszak (1998, p. 5) made the bold claim that "mature ethical values [are] associated with age," and that "mass longevity" will usher in a new, enlightened cohort of earth caretakers. Roszak may be practicing wishful thinking, but his notion of the wise elder deserves our attention because we are interested in a nurturing, constructive form of generativity, which would require some form of wisdom. Indeed, we will see that the ancient and debated idea that wisdom might be the reward of advancing age has taken on new significance in the context of aging societies.

The common finding among social science researchers is that wisdom in old age is a matter of balancing human abilities that, earlier in life, were in imbalance. As Labouvie-Vief (1990) put it, wisdom involves achieving "balanced dialogue" between two modes of knowledge: *mythos*, intuitive, narrative ways of knowing and experiencing, and *logos*, conceptual, rational orientations. Transcending oppositional ways of perceiving is another characteristic of wisdom, according to Tornstam (1997, p. 117), who used the term *gerotranscendence* to capture an age-triggered shift from "a materialistic and pragmatic view of the world to a more cosmic and transcendent one." Tornstam's participants experience an intermingling of the historical past with the personal present, a blurring of sharp distinctions between self and others, identity and community. But gerotranscendence is not guaranteed. Supporting Erikson's observations, Tornstam found that mental depression and other untreated psychological maladies, social isolation, and lack of cultural opportunity for nurture and personal growth can impede growth.

But how people achieve the balance of capacities such as intuition and analysis, or thinking and feeling, remains unexplained. Though Tornstam (1997) and Roszak (1998) assumed that this integration is the direct result of living a long time, their views do not account for the process of continued growth in old age. As discussed earlier, years of experience are necessary but not sufficient to develop a refined capacity for judgment and awareness of the long-term effects of personal and societal acts and decisions. Perhaps the philosophers have the answer.

Contemporary debate among philosophers reveals a sharp division between those who regard later life as a unique vantage point from which to extract the kind of knowledge that takes a lifetime to discover (Moody, 1988) and others who reject the notion that wisdom comes with aging, arguing that such assumptions simply perpetuate stereotypes (Murphy & Longino, 1997). For many postmodernists, old age is no more prescribed than gender. Still, increased awareness of one's mortality remains unavoidable. As Rentsch (1997) put it, old age "intensifies the experience of finitude," disclosing the true mirror of human existence—"our inability to repeat the past, the irreversibility of life's direction, the unavoidability of passage through stages of development, the irrevocability of the past in memories of unattained meaningfulness, and unpredictability of the future" (p. 267). The compensation accruing to the elderly, said Rentsch, is truly "becoming oneself"; the aim of human development, attaining "a calm view, without deception," of life's finality, "the singular totality of life."

Although the main motivation of earlier stages of life seems bent on success, accumulation, ambition, acceleration of activities, and future seeking, later life can bring the awareness of finality, the radical limits of temporal becoming. Echoing the sentiments of 19th-century philosopher Schopenhauer (1890) and Erikson himself, Rentsch (1997, p. 271) claimed that only in old age does the "calm look backward help us achieve an emancipated clarification of life." Only then are we free of the illusion that happiness is within our reach. Abandoning that futile quest, we may achieve humility, self-transcendence, and an intimation of timeless being.

If recognizing the rich, complex patterns of life—the truth of the whole—requires perspective that can only be gained through long experience enhanced by reflection, what social purpose might that vision serve? If Rentsch and Schopenhauer are correct, it seems impossible for someone at an earlier stage of life to learn from older people because their unique encounters with "being final" are accessible only by abandoning the quest for achievement. How could consciousness of finality and its products—humility, renunciation, assessment of the truly important—be communicated from one generation to another?

There is a way the lessons of old age might be communicated across generations, suggested philosopher Jan Baars (1997). Taking up the theme of temporality, he argued that whereas gerontology and other sciences (both behavioral and clinical) regard the process of aging as a march through chronological time segmented by biological, psychological, and social changes, subjectively aging may produce a nonlinear awareness of inner-time consciousness and a universal way in which subjective time may be communicated—through stories.

Following French philosopher Paul Ricoeur, Baars (1997) argued that personal narrative is the mode of discourse through which temporal being is brought to language. When people write or tell their life stories, they "emplot" events and feelings into a coherent, "fragile integration of a profound discordance" (Baars, 1997, p. 291). These communicated narratives bearing "meaningful configurations" of time and experience can pass from one conscious mind to another through the transformative power of stories that transcend individual concreteness, historical context, and generational barriers. Erikson and some of his followers recognize that the impulse to create such narratives plays an increasingly important role in mid- and later life.

McAdams (2001), for example, found that generative narratives help the individual craft a sense of personal coherence and a meaningful "ending" to their life story. The motive, argued McAdams, is not to fabricate a barrier of immortality against the vicissitudes of time, change, and loss but to project endurance and continuity as one's life extends into the next generation. McAdams noted that midlife narratives of generativity take two forms: private or inner narratives in which the individual defines him- or herself as a generative person who cares about and nurtures future generations through memorializing a history of contributive acts, and public narratives through which individuals seek to share the legacy of their lives with younger generations.

Kotre (1984) further enlarged on this function of narratives of generativity. His use of in-depth interviews to elicit developmental themes (*narrative psychology*) shows him multiple forms of generativity. He characterized those engaging in "cultural generativity" as passing along an "integrated set of symbols interpreting existence," of which storytelling as a form of mentoring is one such manifestation (Kotre, 1984, p. 14). Although cultural generativity may occur throughout the adult life course, Kotre found compelling examples in late midlife and old age as the individual seeks to "transcend the finiteness" of existence (Kotre, 1984, p. 268).

McAdams and Kotre focused on narrative as inner and outer speech, but it is a small step to recognizing the embodiment of generative narratives in works of the arts and literature. Reading the legend of Obasuteyama is one such example of a story that transcends time and place as it speaks to the mutuality between generations. Works of literature such as short stories, novels, poems, and plays also communicate experiences from other times, places, and times of life. Such works provide a mirror to the self and a window into others' lives. In the modern, secular world, they supplement, and sometimes replace, sacred literature and are well suited to generate and evoke intergenerational perspectives.

Storytelling matched with critical inquiry and exchange between generations holds the potential of building a stronger sense of community among the generations. Lifelong learning opportunities and intergenerational learning experiences can make a difference by providing frameworks for cultural generativity. Here are important areas for innovative program, critical assessment, and research. Much work remains to be done if the delicate rope of ashes is to be handed from one generation to another.

REFERENCES

Aristotle. (1954). *Rhetoric* (Book 2) (W. Rhys Roberts, Trans.). New York: Modern Library.

Baltes, P. B. (1993). The aging mind: Potentials and limits. *The Gerontologist, 33,* 580–594.

Baars, J. (1997). Concepts of time and narrative temporality in the study of aging. *Journal of Aging Studies, 11,* 283–295.

Cohen, G. D. (2000). *The creative age: Awakening human potential in the second half of life.* New York: Morrow/Avon.

Dorson, R. M. (1962). *Folk legends of Japan.* Rutland, VT: Charles E. Tuttle.

Erikson, E. (1950). *Childhood and society.* New York: Norton.

Erikson, E. (1986). *The life cycle completed.* New York: Norton.

Freedman, M. (1999). *The prime of life: How baby boomers will revolutionize retirement and transform America.* New York: Public Affairs.

Kastenbaum, R. (1992). The creative process: A life-span approach. In D. Van Tassel & R. Kastenbaum, (Eds.), *Handbook of the humanities and aging* (1st ed., pp. 285–306). New York: Springer.

Kotre, J. (1984). *Outliving the self: Generativity and the interpretation of lives.* Baltimore: Johns Hopkins University Press.

Labouvie-Vief, G. (1990). Adaptive dimension of adult cognition. In N. Datan & N. Lohman (Eds.), *Transitions of aging* (pp. 3–26). New York: Academic Press.

Laslett, P. (1991). *The emergence of the third age: A fresh map of life.* Cambridge, MA: Harvard.

Manheimer, R. (1998). The politics and promise of older adult education. *Research on Aging, 20,* 391–414.

Manheimer, R. (1999a). *A map to the end of time: Wayfarings with friends and philosophers.* New York: Norton.

Manheimer, R. (1999b). Aging in the mirror of philosophy. In T. Cole, D. Van Tassel, & R. Kastenbaum (Eds.), *Handbook of the humanities and aging* (2nd ed., pp. 77–90). New York: Springer.

Manheimer, R., Snodgrass, D., & Moskow-McKenzie, D. (1995). *Older adult education: A guide to research, policy, and programs.* Wesport, CT: Greenwood.

McAdams, D. P. (2001). Generativity in midlife. In M. Lachman (Ed.), *Handbook of midlife development* (pp. 395–433). New York: Wiley.

Moody, H. R. (1988). *Abundance of life, human development policies for an aging society.* New York: Columbia University Press.

Murphy, J. W., & Longino, C. F. (1997). Towards a postmodern understanding of aging and identity. *Journal of Aging and Identity, 2*, 81–91.

Rentsch, T. (1997). Aging as becoming oneself: A philosophical ethics of late life. *Journal of Aging Studies, 11*, 263–271.

Rosenmayr, L. (1980). Achievements, doubts, and prospects of the sociology of aging. *Aging and Society, 1*, 29–49.

Roszak, T. (1998). *America the wise: The longevity revolution and the true wealth of nations.* Boston: Houghton-Mifflin.

Schachter-Shalomi, Z., & Miller, R. S. (1995). *From aging to sage-ing: A proud new vision of growing older.* New York: Warner Books.

Schopenhauer, A. (1890). *The ages of life: Counsels and maxims* (T. Bailey Saunders, Trans.). London: Swan Sonnenschein.

Strauss, W., & Howe, N. (1991). *Generations: The history of America's future: 1584–2069.* New York: William Morrow.

Thurow, L. C. (1996). *The future of capitalism: How today's economic forces shape tomorrow's future.* New York: William Morrow.

Tornstam, L. (1997). Gerotranscendence: A theory about maturing into old age. *Journal of Aging and Identity, 1*, 37–50.

9

GENERATIVITY BEHIND BARS: SOME "REDEMPTIVE TRUTH" ABOUT PRISON SOCIETY

SHADD MARUNA, THOMAS P. LeBEL, AND CHARLES S. LANIER

One of the remarkable phenomena of our time is the persistence of the belief among those in power that we can coerce people into decent behavior if only we make the punishment tough enough. We keep imagining that the problem is that young people aren't frightened enough, so we keep toughening criminal sanctions. The real problem is that our young people aren't hopeful enough. They don't see that they have it within their means to transform not merely their own lives but the society. They have the power.
—*William Raspberry, journalist and Pulitzer Prize winner (1995)*

Prisons cage parents. Prisons also warehouse mentors, teachers, leaders, and potential role models for the next generation. Indeed, whether they know it or not, the 2 million men and women in prisons and jails across the country have the power to change the future. At least, this was the message Rev. Jesse Jackson gave to the residents of Cook County jail in Chicago in a Christmas day sermon (Raspberry, 1995, p. A16). Rev. Jackson urged the prisoners to redirect their anger, let go of their bitterness, and stop feeling sorry for themselves. Instead, he suggested they follow the path of Malcolm X, who, realizing that he could not change the past, decided that he would therefore have to change the future. Raspberry (1995) wrote:

> It was not, of course, what inmates are accustomed to hearing. Generally they are excoriated as social vermin, fit only for being caged or exterminated, or else pitied as victims of social forces over which they have little control. There's truth in both versions. But there is greater truth—redemptive truth—in what Jackson preached on Christmas. (p. A16)

The exploration of this "redemptive truth"—and the role it could play in reimagining the structure and purpose of corrections—is the goal of this chapter.

For at least the last 25 years, the rehabilitation of prisoners—as a professional practice and a scientific study—has been plagued with the widespread belief that "nothing works" to improve the life chances of people in prison. This pessimism has been institutionalized on almost every level of the criminal justice system. In what Simon (1993) deemed a "waste management" approach to corrections, the primary tools of the correctional enterprise have shifted from psychotherapy and job training aimed at rehabilitation to electronic monitoring, drug testing, and super-maximum security prisons aimed at surveillance and social exclusion. Essentially, because the correctional system seems unable to "correct" the individuals in its charge, from the late 1970s on it has settled on the far less ambitious goals of controlling and containing a population deemed permanently dangerous.

We feel that this institutional pessimism regarding prisoner reform is unfounded, and itself may be responsible for exacerbating the problem of recidivism by creating a self-fulfilling prophecy of doom. After all, one of the best known facts in criminology is that nearly all offenders eventually "grow out" of criminal behaviors. Although experimentation with crime and deviance may be a fairly common aspect of earlier stages of human development, a combination of internal changes and increased societal pressures make such behaviors "off-time" for mature adults. Longitudinal, self-report studies following juvenile delinquents into later adulthood, for instance, indicate that a majority of young offenders stop committing crimes after turning 23 years old (Farrington, 1997). The predictability of self-reform with increasing age has led more than a few commentators to suggest that the best strategy for corrections would be to "just leave the kids alone" and allow them to "grow out" of criminality "on their own" (or at least with the help of informal social institutions such as employment, marriage, and family ties). Others have advocated in favor of interventions that "work in partnership with self-restorative forces where these exist" (Toch, 1997, p. 97).

One such force, we argue, is the developmental challenge that Erikson (1963) refers to as *generativity*. McAdams and de St. Aubin (1998) defined *generativity* as

> The concern for and commitment to promoting the next generation, manifested through parenting, teaching, mentoring, and generating products and outcomes that aim to benefit youth and foster the development and well-being of individuals and social systems that will outlive the self. (p. xx)

According to Erikson, generativity emerges as a key developmental theme for most individuals at approximately the same time that delinquent and criminal behaviors typically dissipate, around mid-adulthood. Maruna (2001) has argued that this correlation is not coincidental. Generative commitments seem to fill a particular void in the lives of former offenders, providing a sense of purpose and meaning, allowing them to redeem themselves from their past mistakes, and legitimizing the person's claim to having changed (see Maruna, 2001, chap. 6). For the individual engaged in generative commitments and concerns, criminal behavior either seems pointless (its role in establishing one's masculinity or toughness no longer needed) or else too risky in the sense that it could jeopardize the person's generative self-identity. Similarly, Lynne Goodstein speculated that women's traditional responsibilities for caring for children, younger siblings, and community members (i.e., their involvement in generative pursuits) may be one reason that females are so dramatically underrepresented in criminal statistics (cited in Cullen, 1994).

Instead of "nothing works," therefore, we believe there is emerging evidence that *generativity works.* As such, we believe that the development, encouragement, and facilitation of generativity should be at the center of the correctional enterprise (see especially Cullen, Sundt, & Wozniak, 2001; Toch, 2000a). Generativity is a product not only of inner desire but also of cultural demands (McAdams, Hart, & Maruna, 1998); therefore, social institutions can both foster and impede its development. We argue that no institution does a better job of hindering generativity than prisons and jails and that this obstruction of normative development may be undermining the correctional system's ability to reduce crime. We contend that if the world of corrections were to become more of a *generative society*—that is, an environment in which generative commitments were modeled and nurtured, and opportunities for generative activities were promoted and rewarded—it would simply be more effective at reducing repeat offending.

This claim is built on the assumption that, on some level, generativity is an "acquired taste." In the same way that one learns to enjoy drug use and finds this a pleasurable experience through an interactive, subcultural process, one conceivably learns generativity by *doing* generative things in a setting or niche in which such behavior is defined as rewarding and good. The latter part of this equation, the "enabling niche" (Taylor, 1997), is critical because there may not be anything inherent about parenting, productivity, or mentoring the next generation that makes these behaviors appealing. Frankly, generativity can be awfully hard work. When it is modeled and appreciated by significant others, however, one learns to intrinsically enjoy and even to need or crave the feelings one gets when doing this work. We argue that when these generative motivations become internalized through such social interactions, "rehabilitation" (or more aptly, moral reintegration) is beginning to happen.

GENERATIVITY AND CRIME

Criminological research typically focuses on the processes that lead to criminal behavior. Typically, this research is divided between macrolevel studies comparing the levels of crime in various geographic areas or historic periods and microlevel research focusing on why some individuals in a given area and time period become involved in crime. Although the intersection between generativity and crime has never been directly explored in criminology (to the best of our knowledge), recent developments in both macro- and microcriminology suggest some interesting implications for the possibility of this link.

Generativity and Crime in the Macro

Because street crime is primarily committed by the young (the peak age of offending is approximately 17 years old), macrolevel research frequently focuses on the relationships between adults and children in a culture or a community. Recent theoretical work suggests that cultures and communities characterized by strong networks of social support and informal social control (the so-called "eyes on the street") are likely to have the lowest rates of crime and the least involvement with the formal criminal justice system (see especially Braithwaite, 1989; Cullen, 1994). The argument is that in areas where residents are enmeshed in a fabric of interdependencies and social solidarity, citizens are better able to promote conformity through a mixture of positive incentives (one has "something to lose" by offending) and the shaming of deviance through gossip, social censure, and interpersonal pressures. Although there are clearly reciprocal effects at work (e.g., crime problems can themselves disrupt social cohesion), considerable research suggests that communities in which residents know and trust one another (especially across generational lines) tend to be insulated from serious crime problems (Sampson, 1999).

Anderson (1990), for instance, described a mentor–protégé relationship between "old heads" (or adult members of a community) and the neighborhood youths that he said can be found in well-bonded, relatively crime-free communities. "The old heads [are] respected older women and men of the community who, as guides and role models, encourage youth to invest in conventional culture" (p. 329). These personal relationships with "natural helpers" or "community guides" are thought to act as both a bridge and a buffer between the young person and the community, connecting juveniles to conventional opportunities and institutions (Bazemore, 1999).

As these traditional community support networks erode in a community, the state—in the form of the criminal justice system—is sometimes called on to address the issue of crime and juvenile delinquency. Although at times this quick fix can temporarily ward off a serious crime problem, Clear and Karp (1999) observed that, "Once a function is being performed by one party it becomes unnecessary for another to take it on" (p. 38). So, when the criminal justice system takes over the social control functions of a neighborhood, parents and neighbors sometimes abdicate their responsibility for young people in the community. As a result, "informal control systems may atrophy like dormant muscles" (p. 38). Anderson (1990) wrote, "The result is a form of cultural disinvestment, as old heads and young boys go their separate ways, each losing the opportunity of investment from the other" (p. 329).

Generativity and Desistance From Crime

Somewhat more direct implications for a link between generativity and rates of offending might be drawn from microlevel criminology, in particular, in the relatively new area of developmental criminology (see Piquero & Mazerolle, 2001). Developmental criminology approaches the study of crime longitudinally and situates criminal activity within the human life course. Chief among the new areas of inquiry opened up by this perspective has been the renewed attention among criminologists to the process of "aging out" or desistance from criminal behavior that seems to begin in early adulthood for most former delinquents. In the best known study of desistance, for instance, Sampson and Laub (1993) empirically demonstrated the role of steady employment, marriage, and family creation in providing young people with a route out of criminal behavior. Sampson and Laub found that former offenders who assume the responsibility of providing for their spouses and children are significantly more likely to successfully desist from crime than those who make no such social commitments. Interestingly, they also found that desistance from crime is correlated with assuming social and financial responsibility for one's aging parents or one's siblings in need as well.

More recently, Uggen and Janikula (1999) investigated the question of whether involvement in volunteer work can induce a change in a person's likelihood of antisocial conduct. Focusing on young offenders (under 21 years old) involved in a variety of secular-civic volunteer activities "exemplified by persons stocking food shelves or visiting elderly persons at a hospital" (p. 350), Uggen and Janikula found a robust, negative relationship between such volunteer work and arrest (after statistically controlling for the effects of antisocial propensities, prosocial attitudes, and commitments to conventional behavior). Citing Tocqueville's (1835/1956) argument that, "By dint of working for one's fellow-citizens, the habit and the taste for serving them is at length acquired" (p. 334 [and p. 197 in Tocqueville]), Uggen and Janikula (1999) concluded that volunteerism may reduce criminality through a gradual process of prosocial socialization (see also Van Voorhis, 1985).

Finally, Maruna's (2001) research on the phenomenology of the desistance process provides additional hints at the possible relationship between generativity and desistance. In a comparison of the autobiographical narratives of successfully and unsuccessfully reformed ex-convicts, Maruna found that the self-narratives of ex-convicts who were able to "go straight" (and stay that way) were significantly more care-oriented, other-centered, and focused on promoting the next generation. In contrast with active offenders in the sample, the reformed interviewees expressed a desire for lasting ac-complishments or "something to show" for one's life. They described newfound pleasures in creative and productive pursuits, and often expressed a special attachment or duty to some particular community, group, or cause.

Frequently, the ex-convicts in the study based their self-conceptions on identities as "wounded healers" (White, 2000). That is, they have tried to find some meaning in their shame-filled life histories by turning their expe-riences into cautionary tales or hopeful stories of redemption, which they share with younger offenders in similar situations. One participant in Maruna's (2001, p. 103) research described this as a desire to *give people my life*—you know, experiences—what I been through" (male, 31 years). Another said:

> Hopefully, I'll be something to other people. To a few people down by ours, I already am. I led through example. I get a lot of people now, everyone else's ma's whose (kid is) on drugs, have got me harassed all the time, saying "Can you help our boy, Joe, or whatever?" "What if you just come round for a couple of nights and spend time?" (male, 36 years) (Maruna, 2001, p. 105)

The stories that these ex-convicts develop out of their life histories are frequently intended, in particular, to be gifts for the next generation. One interviewee stated:

> I was saying to (my brother's) kids the other day. I'd sat both of them down the other day, and I said, "Listen, me and your dad have wasted our lives. I don't want yous to do what we've done. For 15 or 16 years, me and your dad (who also served a prison sentence) wasted our lives, and now we want you to take a leaf out of our book." (male, 33 years) (Maruna, 2001, p. 104)

Ironically, even though the speaker said that his life has been wasted, by living to tell the tale, he has in fact found a social purpose or meaning for this part of his life. It has produced a "book" that he can pass on to the next generation. Indeed, the moral heroism of the wounded healer role "serves to make acceptable, explicable and even meritorious the guilt-laden, 'wasted' portions of an Actor's life" (Lofland, 1969, p. 287). As such, they can help facilitate the difficult process of identity change involved in desisting from crime, by helping ex-convicts make sense of their past lives in crime.

Although none of the research evidence reviewed above specifically tests our hypothesis that generativity is a sort of buffer against criminality, the reviewed research is largely consistent with this view. Still, the transi-tion from the self-centeredness and self-destructiveness of criminal behavior to generative role model may sound suspicious to those of us in the social sciences. A change at the margins, perhaps from egocentrism to some small degree of empathy or consideration for others, seems the more likely transi-tion. Yet, Maruna (2001) argued that the sense of higher moral purpose that accompanies generative commitments might be necessary for sustaining desistance. For all of its problems, being a criminal provides individuals with at least momentary escapes into excitement, power, and notoriety. If going straight means little more than accepting docility, self-hatred, and stigma, there is little reason to desist from such diversions. The intrinsic rewards and social respectability of generative roles provide a more appealing alternative. Finally, it may be that a degree of "hypermoralism" on the part of ex-convicts may be required for community members, who are necessarily hesitant about rewelcoming former deviants, to accept that an ex-convict has really changed his or her ways.

LOCKING UP HUMAN DEVELOPMENT

If generativity is indeed linked to reduced criminal behavior, it seems reasonable that the correctional system might seek out every opportunity, then, to support and hasten the development of these desires among its clients. To say that this is not the reigning paradigm in corrections today would be an understatement. According to Erikson (1963), the opposite of generativity is stagnation, and there could be no better word for describing life in the contemporary prison where almost everything about the process of imprisonment seems designed to cause the "arrested development" of normative maturational processes among its residents (Toch, 1975).

Although ostensibly aimed at holding prisoners accountable for their actions, imprisonment, by its nature, promotes a sort of learned dependency antithetical to success in the real world (Lanier & Fisher, 1990). According to Toch (2000b), most prisoners face a "regime of eventlessness and a life that is redundant, monotonous, and stultifying" (p. 2). Prison programs that offer substance and meaning are hard to come by, Toch wrote, yet "programs that offer an opportunity to contribute to the world are virtually non-existent" (p. 2). This absence of opportunities for growth and "career" progression is especially troubling for the growing proportion of prisoners in the United States who are serving sentences of 10 years or longer (Flanagan, 1995). For these individuals the only real world they may ever know is the prison. As such, they can find themselves confined to a permanent state of adolescence, going around in the prison's tedious circles of hypermasculine posturing, and leaving them "off time" and at odds with the "social clock" (Neugarten & Hagestad, 1976).

Although inculcating responsibility and teaching leadership skills among convicts seem like plausible goals for the correctional system, "these are often viewed as inimical to the absolute control ethic characteristic of many total institutions" (Lanier & Fisher, 1990, p. 163). Irwin (1974) wrote:

> If a program is successful or partially so in orienting a group of prisoners toward the active conception of rehabilitation, toward being self-suffi-

cient, self-actualized, socially aware, and socially involved, the clients are perceived as threats to the unstated concerns of the [prison] organization. Some of the clients . . . will try to change established routines; criticize and generate outside criticism toward the correctional organization; make claims to moral equality or superiority; and attempt to bring themselves . . . into the organization's policy and decision-making routines. (pp. 142–143)

These activities are not typically tolerated because empowering prisoners is not a popular pursuit in contemporary corrections (Sykes, 1958).

Moreover, the inherent structure of the prison environment creates disincentives and barriers to those trying to contribute to their families or achieve personal goals. Not surprisingly, convicts working for a dollar a day have little opportunity to make financial contributions to their families, and instead become a significant financial burden both to their families and society in general. Parenting from prison in general is made enormously difficult by the emotional and psychological issues involved with bringing children into a correctional facility, the outrageously high cost of making telephone calls from a prison, and the sheer distances most families have to travel to stay in physical contact. For instance, because of overcrowding, prisoners from Washington, DC, are regularly bussed to a private prison in Youngstown, Ohio, 300 miles away from their families. Eighty percent of the prisoners in Bare Hill Correctional Facility, located 15 miles from the Canadian border in Malone, New York, are residents of New York City. To visit their fathers, children of Bare Hill prisoners would need to travel 362 miles from New York City to Malone, where one third of the town's 15,000 residents reside in one of three prisons.

A recent government survey of U.S. prisoners found that 55% of state and 63% of federal prisoners had children under the age of 18; almost half of those parents reported living with their children before incarceration (United States Department of Justice, 2000). The United States Department of Justice, Bureau of Justice Statistics (2000, p. 2) estimates that 667,900 incarcerated fathers left behind approximately 1,372,700 children under age 18. The collateral consequences of incarceration on the children, families, and communities that incarcerated parents leave behind only recently has become a topic thought worthy of more thorough study (Hairston, 1989; Lanier, 1993). There is growing support that the "children of incarcerated and released parents often become confused, unhappy, and socially stigmatized" (Petersilia, 2000, p. 4; see also Hagan & Dinovitzer, 1999). Hagan and Palloni (1990) reported that "there is an intergenerational interaction effect of the labeling of parents and sons on subsequent delinquent and criminal behavior" (p. 292). In fact, children with incarcerated parents are five times more likely to be incarcerated themselves as adults as compared with children whose parents have not been incarcerated (Beck et al., 1993).

Not surprisingly, even less is known about the impact of prison confinement on a person's identity as a parent and his or her ability to maintain parental bonds. Some research does suggest, though, that incarceration—and the consequent impairment of one's ability to contribute as a parent—can result in acute feelings of guilt and shame among prisoners (Toch, 1975). Another study found that the self-concepts of some male prisoners (i.e., self-esteem and self-efficacy) were directly related to both being a father and the status of the father–child relationship (Parker & Lanier, 1997). Incarcerated parents with the poorest parent–child relationships also seem most likely to develop the constellation of negative psychological symptoms referred to as "involuntary child absence syndrome" (Jacobs, 1986; see especially Lanier, 1993, pp. 60–61).

Far from deterring crime or "scaring" offenders "straight," these well-known deprivations and impediments to growth intrinsic to the prison experience seem primarily to breed an intense apathy and a sense of social isolation. Outcast prisoners frequently develop a sense of being doomed to a life of addiction, criminality, and prison that mirrors the pessimism society seems to harbor about their potential to reform (Maruna, 2001). Rideau (1992) eloquently described this spiritual trap:

> For most, the prison experience is a one-way ride on a psychological roller coaster—downhill. And the easiest thing to do, in a world where almost everything is an assault against you, is to permit yourself to be defeated by the overwhelming indifference and sense of hopelessness that steals into your daily existence, slowly, almost unnoticeably sapping your drive, your dreams, your ambition, evoking cries from the soul to surrender, to give up the ghost, to just drift along with the tide of time and human affairs, to not care. (p. 60)

STRENGTHS-BASED CORRECTIONS

We next describe an alternative vision of "corrections" that would place the encouragement and development of generativity at the heart of the correctional enterprise. Following the lead of social work practice, in which this philosophy seems best developed and established (e.g., Saleebey, 1997), we refer to this trend as a *strengths-based* paradigm. This should be seen as an umbrella term that encompasses numerous approaches. Indeed, strengths-based themes have been a staple of progressive criminal justice reforms for much of the last century (Erickson, Crow, Zurcher, & Connet, 1973; Grant, 1968).

We choose the term *strengths-based* also because it highlights the primary difference we see between this vision of corrections and models that we label risk-based (or control) narratives and need-based (or treatment) narratives in correctional reform (see Maruna & LeBel, 2003). Arguments in favor of tighter control or additional treatment both concentrate on convicts' deficits. The strengths-based approach asks not what a person's deficits are but rather what positive contribution the person can make. How can their lives become useful and purposeful? This shift represents a move "away from the principle of entitlement to the principle of social exchange" (Levrant, Cullen, Fulton, & Wozniak, 1999, p. 22) or to what Bazemore (1999) called "earned redemption." The strengths-based paradigm calls for opportunities for convicts and ex-convicts to make amends, demonstrate their value and potential, and experience success in support and leadership roles.

At the heart of the strengths-based approach is the *helper principle* of the 1960's New Careers Movement: It is better (i.e., more reintegrative) to give help than to receive it. The central premise of the New Careers Movement was that the disadvantaged (including ex-convicts) could be trained and placed in entry-level social service jobs that would take advantage of their life experiences as well as their geographic, cultural, and functional similarities to other persons in need. The goal of strengths-based corrections, like the New Careers Movement before it, would be to "*devise ways of creating more helpers!* Or to be more exact: how to transform receivers of help (such as welfare recipients) into dispensers of help; how to structure the situation so that receivers of help will be placed in roles requiring the giving of assistance" (Pearl & Riessman, 1965, pp. 88–89).

Even though contemporary corrections lacks a coherent or systematic vision for the promotion of generative ideals and behaviors, potentially generative projects and activities can be found (with a little effort) scattered throughout the system. Below, we review three examples of practices and activities accepted and approved by various parts of the correctional system that seem to exemplify the strengths-based vision of corrections. These refreshing (but sporadic) examples might be seen as something like flowers in the concrete of the correctional system.

Giving Something Back

Virtually every jurisdiction in the United States has had some experience with community service as a sanction, and although still quite small in scale, this experiment in sanctioning has been widely viewed as a rare penal success story. Quasi-experimental evaluations of community service sanctioning for offenders consistently show that such penalties outperform standard probation or jail time in reducing recidivism (Schneider, 1986). Participants in community service work almost always rate the experience as a positive and beneficial experience (McIvor, 1992, p. 177). Moreover, there is some evidence that this sort of coerced public service often promotes and preserves things of value for future generations and can aid in moral development and personal growth (Middleton & Kelly, 1996; Van Voorhis, 1985).

Yet, despite its origins as a rehabilitative panacea, community service no longer is justified using a strengths narrative in most jurisdictions, and instead has become "almost exclusively manual, menial and arduous" (Caddick, 1994, p. 450; see also Blagg & Smith, 1989). In a strengths-based framework, community service work would be voluntarily agreed on and would involve challenging tasks that could utilize the talents of the convicted person in useful, visible roles in the service of the community. For example,

> Probation and parole projects in which offenders visibly and directly produce things the larger community wants, such as gardens, graffiti-free neighborhoods, less dangerous alleys, habitable housing for the homeless . . . have also helped build stronger communities, and have carved channels into the labor market for the offenders engaged in them. (Dickey & Smith, 1998, p. 35)

Haphazard examples of generative opportunities can even be found in state and federal prisons, which tend to be isolated from the communities in which they are based. For instance, in a partnership program with Habitat for Humanity, convicts from 75 prisons (working alongside volunteers from the community) built over 250 homes for low-income Americans in 1999 (Ta, 2000). Last year New York State prisoners were among a contingent of community volunteers that helped repair a total of 20,229 toys, with a total value of $285,724, for a Toys for Tots program (New York State Department of Correctional Services, 2001).

Among the most impressive contributions made by prisoners is the little publicized but essential work that teams of prisoners have voluntarily undertaken in fighting the forest fires ravaging America's national parks. In fact, one in six of the crewmembers (over 2,000 individuals) fighting fires by hand (to preserve our national treasures for future generations) in the year 2000 was a convict. One person in the program said, "Being in this program makes all the difference. . . . Now I can tell my 4-year old son that his dad isn't in prison, he's out fighting fires" (Jehl, 2000, p. A1). Another convict firefighter stated that, "most of my life, I took things from people, and now it's time to give something back" (p. A1).

Prisoners in many states have been involved in the crucial work of providing respite care to fellow prisoners dying of AIDS and other illnesses in the prison system. Today there are 19 states that offer hospice care for prisoners and 14 more that have programs in development. Although the genesis of these programs are practical (due partly to the boom in life sentences being served), these hospices have had some unforeseen effects, including reported decreases in prison violence and long waiting lists of prisoners seeking to volunteer to be caregivers (Stolberg, 2001). A warden at one prison with a hospice hypothesized that its nurturing climate helps first the patients, then the volunteers, and finally the whole prison. "The philosophy changes in the setting itself. The inmates change. It changes how we look at them" (Kolker, 2000, p. H2).

Convicts as Wounded Healers

Generative activities have long been at the center of mutual help societies made up of prisoners, released prisoners, and recovering addicts. For instance, the "twelve steps" of Alcoholics Anonymous (AA) and Narcotics Anonymous (NA) explicitly allow for the transformation of identity from victim to survivor to helper. The twelve steps are premised around an explicit service orientation, codified in the Twelfth Step and the Fifth Tradition, which encourages those who have found sobriety to assist others in taking this journey. According to O'Reilly (1997), "next to avoiding intoxicants," the therapeutic power of *helping* is "the major premise upon which [AA] is built" (p. 128). AA and NA members, who have been sober for many years, often remain with the organization not so much because they need to *receive* any more counseling but because the act of counseling *others* can itself be empowering and therapeutic. Members who stay connected to the program eventually take on the role of sponsors and become the mentors and teachers of the next generation of recovering addicts.

Similarly, ex-convict Bill Sands (1964) maintained that the only way that he could find "inner peace" and a "sense of accomplishment" was to abandon a successful entrepreneurial career and dedicate himself to helping other ex-convicts change their lives. Like many former convicts and recovering addicts, Sands became a "wounded healer" (White, 2000) or "professional ex-" (Brown, 1991), defined as a person who desists from a "deviant career" by "replacing it" with an occupation as a paraprofessional, lay therapist, drug counselor, or training officer (p. 219). Although it is impossible to measure the extent of the "professional ex-" phenomenon, Brown estimated that around three quarters of the counselors working in the over 10,000 substance abuse treatment centers in the United States are former substance abusers themselves (p. 219). In addition to such professional work, thousands of long sober individuals freely volunteer their time to helping others in mutual aid groups like Sands's Seventh Step organization.

The demand for this sort of role modeling seems to be as strong for convicts while in prison as it is for ex-convicts and persons recovering from addiction (see especially Erickson et al., 1973). Prisoners frequently form informal mentoring systems, whereby older (and more experienced) convicts become parent-figures to newer, younger prisoners. Moreover, more prisoners belong to self-help groups than any other form of organization or correctional program (Hamm, 1997). Again, there is a paucity of research on such groups, even though they can be found at nearly every correctional facility that allows their formation. Based on his own experience as a prisoner, Irwin (1980) emphasizes that self-help groups help convicts realize that "they have nothing to hide or live down" and "open doors . . . to a variety of conventional endeavors" and roles (p. 94). Hamm (1997) explained, "[Self-help] group members do not see themselves as deviant, sick, or inferior. Rather they try to see themselves as kind and capable individuals, who [despite their condition of imprisonment] are able to lead fulfilling lives" (p. 219).

With little doubt, the best existing model for a strengths-based, mutual aid society for ex-convicts outside prison is the Delancey Street program based in San Francisco. Founded in 1971 by Mimi Silbert and ex-convict John Maher, Delancey Street has grown from an organization consisting of 10 recovering addicts (and one criminal psychologist) living in an apartment to a thriving organization with 1,500 full-time residents in five self-run facilities, more than 20 businesses that double as training schools, and an annual operating budget of close to $24 million (Boschee & Jones, 2000; Mieszkowski, 1998). The program is self-supporting and has no professional staff. Instead, taking an "each one teach one" approach, older residents teach and train newer arrivals who then utilize these new skills to sustain the organization once the more senior residents "graduate" into private housing and independent careers. Silbert said residents "learn a fundamental lesson . . . that they have something to offer. These are people who have always been passive. . . . But strength and power come from being on the giving end" (Boschee & Jones, 2000, p. 11).

Finally, in a more recent trend being called the "New Recovery Movement" (White, 2001), wounded healers are called on "to move beyond their personal service work and become recovery activists" (White, 2001, p. 16). According to White, New Recovery Movement advocates have joined together "not in supplication but in service; not asking for something, but offering something; not advocating for themselves, but for others; not acting as individuals, but in communion; and not seeking solutions through formal institutions but through the community itself" (p. 6). Ex-convicts similarly are increasingly organizing in favor of prison reform and other changes within the criminal justice system. These and other mutual aid efforts help to transform individuals from being part of "the problem" into part of "the solution" as they give their time in the service of helping others who are less far along in the rehabilitation process (metaphorically, the "next generation").

Parenting From Prison

Research suggests that active engagement in parenting while incarcerated may provide a "stability zone" for convicts that can reduce the psychological impact of confinement (Toch, 1975). Prior research on institutional stability and parole success suggests that "men who are tethered tightly to their families, and who are aware of their special responsibilities as parents, will act in a more pro-social manner both behind prison walls and in the free world" (Lanier, 2003, p. 174). Moreover, once released, incarcerated parents must negotiate the transition from a world of dependence to a world in which they are expected to be decisive, dependable, and nurturing members of their families and communities. Importantly, such positive transitions (e.g., providing for spouses and children) do appear to be linked to desistance from crime (Sampson & Laub, 1993). This adjustment might be made easier by the maintenance of supportive interpersonal bonds or "bridging networks" (Ekland-Olson, Supancic, Campbell, & Lenihan, 1983) during incarceration (see especially Roy, 1999).

An example of this sort of network was the prisoner-initiated Eastern Fathers' Group (EFG). This parenting program was developed in the 1980s by and for incarcerated fathers in a maximum-security New York State prison. It consisted of mutual support meetings, monthly educational seminars, and a certified parenting education course, and its aim was both educational and therapeutic. Critically, the EFG model demanded "the constructive involvement of prisoners in conceptualizing, planning, and actually facilitating all three [program] components" (Lanier & Fisher, 1989, p. 169). The program served to heighten participants' sense of accomplishment and responsibility; at the same time it helped fathers work through the grief they experienced over the loss or deterioration of family bonds.

A subsequent parenting initiative proposed a more comprehensive and institutionalized program called the Prisoners Parenting Center (PPC). The PPC program model was designed to "foster socially constructive values in incarcerated fathers who then responsibly transmit prosocial attitudes to a future generation" (Lanier & Fisher, 1990, p. 164). In short, imprisoned parents could help in the moral and social development of their children—even from behind prison walls—if provided the opportunity. Capitalizing on the parental role, then, appears to exemplify the idea that prisoners acting in this way could "benefit youth and foster the development and well-being of individuals and social systems" (McAdams & de St. Aubin, 1998, p. xx). Engaging prisoners with their families also seems analogous to immersing them in "a fabric of interdependencies," which may foster, among other socially beneficial outcomes, improved control of crime (Currie, 1985).

Parenthood offers a useful and genuine way to engage prisoners on a constellation of important issues, such as substance abuse, worthwhile employment, education, and even antisocial behavior in general. By making the parental role, rather than the offender role, central to such discussions, the focus shifts from a deficit paradigm to a recognition that the individual has a crucial role to play in the lives of others (Lanier, 2003). A concerted focus on meaningful and substantive initiatives for imprisoned parents also might result in "programs that offer an opportunity to contribute to the world," as championed by Toch (2000b, p. 2). This benefaction could come in the form of guiding and nurturing biological offspring, but also helping grandchildren, stepchildren, and children born after the prisoner's release. Transcending any benefit that prisoners might receive from such programs, then, is the potential for salutary effects on others, and particularly those in subsequent generations.

CORRECTIONS IN A GENERATIVE SOCIETY

What is to be made of these examples of apparently generative activities among prisoners and ex-prisoners? There are, of course, many possible explanations, beyond suppressed generative desires, for involvement in any of the good deeds listed earlier. Prisoners may think that participating in these sorts of activities "looks good" on their record and can help them with the parole board (in states in which parole is still an option). Perhaps convicts volunteer to do charity work because the food is better when working in the community. Maybe there are long waiting lists of prisoners wanting to volunteer in hospices because this assignment allows them to work alongside female nursing staff. Simply put, the fact that someone fights fires, attends NA meetings, or takes a course on infant CPR is hardly evidence of generativity let alone rehabilitation.

Still, these strengths-based activities have the potential to serve several important functions. First, they provide persons with "something to do"—an opportunity to find meaning and purpose in the otherwise bleak circumstances of imprisonment. The long-term prisoner in particular needs to have "the opportunity to contribute positively to one's environment and to others, to make linear progress toward realistic and important goals, and to engage in activities that foster a sense of personal worth" (Flanagan, 1995, p. 237). Flanagan suggested that long-term prisoners be given the training and opportunity to fill such roles as paramedics, accountants, master plumbers, pharmacists, tutors, teacher's aides, and eventually as instructional staff within the prison environment. An argument could be made that no person, even when serving a life sentence in prison, should be denied the opportunity to be useful to others in this way.

Second, there are the not insignificant benefits enjoyed by the recipients of these services. That is, regardless of whether generativity has anything to do with the reasons that prisoners help to build homes, spend time with their children, or counsel juvenile delinquents, these activities can have positive benefits for society. For persons who have taken from others or denied others' humanity in the ways many prisoners have, "giving something back" in this way goes some way toward restoring the harm of crime (Bazemore, 1999).

Finally, there is the utilitarian rationale for these sorts of activities. Almost every person in prison will eventually be released. As the superintendent at a prison with a strengths-based agenda (among other activities, prison volunteers sew clothing for premature babies) says, "They're learning a skill, but more important, they're learning what it feels like to be of value to society, to someone in need. Hopefully, they'll carry that feeling with them when they get outside" (Warren, 1999, p. A4). This is the central premise of the strengths-based approach. Unfortunately, most of the evidence in favor of this hypothesis is anecdotal—mainly because all of the projects described earlier are small scale and temporary. In general, these sorts of opportunities, often part of a prison public relations effort, are seen as incidental to, rather than central to the mission of the correctional establishment.

What would a truly generative correctional system look like? Most fundamentally, the transformation of individuals from being part of the problem into part of a solution requires mechanisms in which their lives (both during incarceration and after release) can become useful and purposeful. Concrete steps that corrections could adopt include the following:

- promoting reciprocal processes of mutual support (self-help groups)
- setting up structured environments (niches) in which generativity can flower
- sponsoring altruistic behavior through opportunities to voluntarily engage in public service work that the larger community needs and wants (see Toch, 2000a)
- using parenting as a mechanism so that one can foster more prosocial attitudes in prisoners as well as in their children
- fostering the development of "old heads" both residing within the prison society and now living successfully out in the community and then allowing them to act as mentors and role models for the younger generation of prisoners, those prisoners who have recently returned home, and at-risk youths in the community

However, to fully assess the strengths hypothesis, not only would the correctional system need to be reorganized, but society would also need to change. After all, providing opportunities for ex-convicts to "make good" is only the first step. Generativity—like reintegration or reciprocity—is a two-way process. The ex-convict must be willing to contribute, and society (or at least generative subcultures within society) must be willing to accept and recognize those contributions and consequently reaccept the ex-convict.

Corporations discovered long ago how useful prison labor could be for advancing their bottom lines. Prisoners can be found working as telemarketers, assembly persons, and envelope-stuffers in every state. What if charities, community organizations, and social services were to similarly discover how useful prisoners could be—as coaches, organizers, mentors, and teachers? Were these helping groups to take the same interest in working with prisoners that corporations do (for very different reasons), both the convicts and the helpers could benefit. Ideally, the relationships and interests in helping behaviors developed during imprisonment could carry on after the convict's release into the community.

The most critical goal would be to make the high walls, razor wire, and bars of the prison more permeable, allowing normative social forces "in" through the high security. For instance, when groups of Quakers or other volunteers visit prisons to befriend convicts, not only are they modeling generativity in the prison society, but they also provide a rare niche where prison residents can feel safe to show a softer or more caring side of themselves. Prisoners who volunteer alongside others from both sides of the prison walls similarly get the opportunity to discuss their experiences and find meaning in them. Empowering and enabling the children and families of prisoners to take an active part in the rehabilitation of their incarcerated fathers, mothers, husbands, and wives can also tear down the walls that can obstruct normative human development.

Although it may seem naïve or Pollyannish for society to take this sort of risk on the "strengths" of a population (prisoners) that clearly has plenty of deficits (risk factors, needs, problems), the reciprocal implications of the strengths narrative—that one needs "to do something to get something" (Toch, 1994, p. 71)—make it intuitively appealing. According to a senior probation administrator at a recent focus group on the future of community corrections:

> Let me put it this way, if the public knew that when you commit some wrongdoing, you're held accountable in constructive ways and you've got to earn your way back through these kinds of good works, . . . [probation] wouldn't be in the rut we're in right now with the public. (Dickey & Smith, 1998, p. 36)

Just as importantly, the strengths perspective has, in Raspberry's (1995) words, redemptive truth. That is, it may be empirically true that prisoners pose greater risks than nonprisoners, and that prisoners have more problems and needs (social, psychological, and spiritual) than nonprisoners. Yet these well-known truths may not provide helpful information for a convict or an ex-convict who has just been released from prison. Alternatively, involving convicts in dignified and productive activities that have real benefits for others can send "a message to the community that the offender is worthy of further support and investment in their reintegration, and to the offender that s/he has something to offer that is of value to others" (Bazemore, in press).

Mimi Silbert, cofounder of Delancey Street, summarizes the redemptive truth that has been guiding her organization's success for three decades: "Nobody makes the critical point: We need these people. The country is missing something because a huge bulk of its population is not a part of it. They have talents we need" (cited in Mieszkowski, 1998).

REFERENCES

Anderson, E. (1990). *Streetwise: Race, class and change in an urban community.* Chicago: University of Chicago.

Bazemore, G. (1999). After shaming, whither reintegration: Restorative justice and relational rehabilitation. In G. Bazemore & L. Walgrave (Eds.), *Restorative juvenile justice: Repairing the harm of youth crime* (pp. 155–194). Monsey, NY: Criminal Justice Press.

Bazemore, G. (in press). Reintegration and restorative justice: Toward a theory and practice of informal social control and support. In S. Maruna & R. Immarigeon (Eds.) *After crime and punishment: Desistance from crime and ex-convict reentry.* Albany, NY: SUNY Press.

Beck, A., Gilliard, D., Greenfeld, L., Harlow, C., Hester, T., Jankowski, L., et al. (1993). *Survey of state prison inmates, 1991* (No. NCJ 136949). Washington, DC: U.S. Department of Justice, Bureau of Justice Statistics.

Blagg, H., & Smith, D. (1989). *Crime, penal policy and social work.* Harlow, England: Longman.

Boschee, J., & Jones, S. (2000). *Recycling ex-cons, addicts and prostitutes: The Mimi Silbert story.* Retrieved October 7, 2001, from http://www.socialent.org/pubs.htm

Braithwaite, J. (1989). *Crime, shame and reintegration.* Cambridge, England: Cambridge University Press.

Brown, J. D. (1991). The professional ex-: An alternative for exiting the deviant career. *The Sociological Quarterly, 32,* 219–230.

Caddick, B. (1994). The "new careers" experiment in rehabilitating offenders: Last messages from a fading star. *British Journal of Social Work, 24,* 449–460.

Clear, T., & Karp, D. (1999). *The community justice ideal.* Boulder, CO: Westview Press.

Cullen, F. T. (1994). Social support as an organizing concept in criminology: Presidential address to the Academy of Criminal Justice Sciences. *Justice Quarterly, 11,* 527–559.

Cullen, F. T., Sundt, J. L., & Wozniak, J. F. (2001). The virtuous prison: Toward a restorative rehabilitation. In H. N. Pontell & D. Shichor (Eds.), *Contemporary issues in crime and criminal justice: Essays in honor of Gilbert Geis* (pp. 265–286). Upper Saddle River, NJ: Prentice-Hall.

Currie, E. (1985). *Confronting crime: An American challenge.* New York: Pantheon.

Dickey, W. J., & Smith, M. E. (1998). *Dangerous opportunity: Five futures for community corrections: The report from the focus group.* Washington, DC: U.S. Department of Justice, Office of Justice Programs.

Ekland-Olson, S., Supancic, M., Campbell, J., & Lenihan, K. (1983). Postrelease depression and the importance of familial support. *Criminology, 21,* 253–275.

Erickson, R. J., Crow, W. J., Zurcher, L. A., & Connet, A. V. (1973). *Paroled but not free.* New York: Human Sciences Press.

Erikson, E. H. (1963). *Childhood and society* (2nd ed.). New York: Norton.

Farrington, D. P. (1997). Human development and criminal careers. In M. Maguire, R. Morgan, & R. Reiner (Eds.) *The Oxford handbook of criminology* (2nd ed., pp. 361–408). Oxford, England: Clarendon.

Flanagan, T. J. (1995). Sentence planning for long-term inmates. In T. J. Flanagan (Ed.), *Long-term imprisonment: Policy, science, and correctional practice* (pp. 234–241). Thousand Oaks, CA: Sage.

Grant, J. D. (1968). The offender as a correctional manpower resource. In F. Riessman & H. L. Popper (Eds.), *Up from poverty: New career ladders for nonprofessionals* (pp. 226–234). New York: Harper & Row.

Hagan, J., & Dinovitzer, R. (1999). Collateral consequences of imprisonment for children, communities, and prisoners. In M. Tonry & J. Petersilia (Eds.), *Prisons* (pp. 121–162). Chicago: University of Chicago Press.

Hagan, J., & Palloni, A. (1990). The social reproduction of a criminal class in working class London, circa 1950–1980. *American Journal of Sociology, 96,* 265–299.

Hairston, C. F. (1989). Men in prison: Family characteristics and parenting views. *Journal of Offender Counseling, Services and Rehabilitation, 14,* 23–30.

Hamm, M. S. (1997). The offender self-help movement as correctional treatment. In P. Van Voorhis, M. Braswell, & D. Lester (Eds.), *Correctional counseling and rehabilitation* (4th ed., pp. 211–224). Cincinnati, OH: Anderson.

Irwin, J. (1974). The trouble with rehabilitation. *Criminal Justice and Behavior, 1,* 139–149.

Irwin, J. (1980). *Prisons in turmoil.* Boston: Little, Brown.

Jacobs, J. B. (1986). Involuntary child absence syndrome: An affliction of divorcing fathers. In J. W. Jacobs (Ed.), *Divorce and fatherhood: The struggle for parental identity* (pp. 37– 51). Washington, DC: American Psychiatric Press.

Jehl, D. (2000, September 5). Inmates battling West's fires help states and themselves. *New York Times,* p. A1.

Kolker, C. (2000, February 6). Prison hospices on increase; aid dying inmates, cut violence. *Schenectady Gazette,* pp. H1–H2.

Lanier, C. S. (1993). Affective states of fathers in prison. *Justice Quarterly, 10*(1), 49–66.

Lanier, C. S. (2003). "Who's doing the time here, me or my children?": Addressing the issues implicated by mounting numbers of fathers in prison. In J. I. Ross & S. C. Richards (Eds.), *Convict criminology* (pp. 170–190). Belmont, CA: Wadsworth.

Lanier, C. S., & Fisher, G. (1989). The Eastern Fathers' Group: An educational and mutual support program for incarcerated fathers. In S. Duguid (Ed.), *Yearbook of correctional education* (pp. 155–173). British Columbia, Canada: Simon Fraser University, Institute of Humanities.

Lanier, C. S., & Fisher, G. (1990). A Prisoners' Parenting Center (PPC): A promising resource strategy for incarcerated fathers. *Journal of Correctional Education, 41,* 158–165.

Levrant, S., Cullen, F. T., Fulton, B., & Wozniak, J.F. (1999). Reconsidering restorative justice: The corruption of benevolence revisited? *Crime and Delinquency, 45,* 3–27.

Lofland, J. (1969). *Deviance and identity*. Englewood Cliffs, NJ: Prentice-Hall.

Maruna, S. (2001). *Making good: How ex-convicts reform and rebuild their lives*. Washington, DC: American Psychological Association.

Maruna, S., & LeBel, T. P. (2003). Welcome home? Examining the reentry court concept from a strengths-based perspective. *Western Criminology Review, 4(2)*, 91–107.

McAdams, D. P., & de St. Aubin, E. (1998). (Eds.). *Generativity and adult development: How and why we care for the next generation*. Washington, DC: American Psychological Association.

McAdams, D. P., Hart, H., & Maruna, S. (1998). The anatomy of generativity. In D. P. McAdams & E. de St. Aubin (Eds.), *Generativity and adult development* (pp. 7–43). Washington, DC: American Psychological Association.

McIvor, G. (1992). *Sentenced to serve: The operation and impact of community service by offenders*. Aldershot, England: Avebury.

Middleton, E. B., & Kelly, K. R. (1996). Effects of community service on adolescent personality development. *Counseling and Values, 40*, 132–142.

Mieszkowski, K. (1998). She helps them help themselves. *Fast Company, 15*, 54–56. Retrieved October 9, 2001, from http://fastcompany.com/online/15/helpthem.html

Neugarten, B. L., & Hagestad, G. O. (1976). Age and the life course. In R. H. Binstock & E. Shanas (Eds.), *Handbook of aging and the social sciences* (pp. 35–55). New York: Van Nostrand Reinhold.

New York State Department of Correctional Services. (2001, September). Facilities building on 2000 to make a difference in 2001. *DOCS Today, 10*, 9.

O'Reilly, E. B. (1997). *Sobering tales: Narratives of alcoholism and recovery*. Amherst: University of Massachusetts Press.

Parker, E. A., & Lanier, C. S. (1997). An exploration of self-concepts among incarcerated fathers. In J. W. Marquart & J. R. Sorensen (Eds.), *Correctional contexts: Classical and contemporary readings* (pp. 335–340). Los Angeles: Roxbury.

Pearl, A., & Riessman, F. (1965). *New careers for the poor: The nonprofessional in human service*. New York: Free Press.

Petersilia, J. (2000). When prisoners return to the community: Political, economic, and social consequences. In *Sentencing and corrections: Issues for the 21st century*, 9 (No. NCJ 184253). Washington, DC: U.S. Department of Justice, National Institute of Justice.

Piquero, A., & Mazerolle, P. (2001). *Life-course criminology: Contemporary and classic readings*. Belmont, CA: Wadsworth.

Raspberry, W. (1995, January 2). Prison inmates could change America. *Houston Chronicle*, p. A16.

Rideau, W. (1992). Conversations with the dead. In W. Rideau & R. Wikberg (Eds.), *Life sentences: Rage and survival behind bars* (pp. 51–72). New York: Times Books.

Roy, K. (1999). Low income single fathers in an African American community and the requirements of welfare reform. *Journal of Family Issues, 20*, 432–457.

Saleebey, D. (1997). *The strengths perspective in social work practice* (2nd ed.). New York: Longman.

Sampson, R. (1999). What "community" supplies. In W. J. Dickens (Ed.), *Urban problems and community development* (pp. 241–291). Washington, DC: Brookings Institute.

Sampson, R. J., & Laub, J. (1993). *Crime in the making: Pathways and turning points through life*. Cambridge, MA: Harvard University Press.

Sands, B. (1964). *My shadow ran fast*. Englewood Cliffs, NJ: Prentice-Hall.

Schneider, A. (1986). Restitution and recidivism rates of juvenile offenders: Results from four experimental studies. *Criminology, 24*, 533–552.

Simon, J. (1993). *Poor discipline: Parole and the social control of the underclass, 1890–1990*. Chicago: University of Chicago Press.

Stolberg, S. G. (2001, April 1). Behind bars, new efforts to care for the dying. *New York Times*, p. B1.

Sykes, G. M. (1958). *The society of captives: A study of a maximum security prison*. Princeton, NJ: Princeton University Press.

Ta, C. (2000, October). Prison partnership: It's about people. *Corrections Today, 62*(6), 114–123.

Taylor, J. B. (1997). Niches and practice: Extending the ecological perspective. In D. Saleebey (Ed.), *The strengths perspective in social work practice* (2nd ed., pp. 217–227). New York: Longman.

Toch, H. (1975). *Men in crisis: Human breakdowns in prisons*. Chicago: Aldine.

Toch, H. (1994). Democratizing prisons. *Prison Journal, 73*, 62–72.

Toch, H. (1997). *Corrections: A humanistic approach*. Guilderland, NY: Harrow & Heston.

Toch, H. (2000a). Altruistic activity as correctional treatment. *International Journal of Offender Therapy and Comparative Criminology, 44*, 270–278.

Toch, H. (2000b). Commonality in prisons. *Relational Justice Bulletin, 7*, 1–3.

Tocqueville, A. (1956). *Democracy in America*. New York: Mentor. (Original work published 1835)

Uggen, C., & Janikula, J. (1999). Volunteerism and arrest in the transition to adulthood. *Social Forces, 78*, 331–362.

U.S. Department of Justice, Bureau of Justice Statistics. (2000). *Incarcerated parents and their children* (No. NCJ 182335). Washington, DC: U.S. Government Printing Office.

Van Voorhis, P. (1985). Restitution outcome and probationers' assessments of restitution: The effects of moral development. *Criminal Justice and Behavior, 12*, 259–287.

Warren, J. (1999, August 2). Stitches in time: Sewing project helps inmates mend lives. *Schenectady Gazette*, p. A4.

White, W. L. (2000). The history of recovered people as wounded healers: II. The era of professionalization and specialization. *Alcoholism Treatment Quarterly, 18*, 1–25.

White, W. L. (2001). *The rhetoric of recovery advocacy: An essay on the power of language*. Retrieved October 7, 2001, from http://www.defeataddiction.org/grfx/LANGUAGE.pdf

10

AMERICAN RELIGION, GENERATIVITY, AND THE THERAPEUTIC CULTURE

MICHELE DILLON AND PAUL WINK

There are strong theoretical and empirical links between religion and generativity. From a Western theological perspective, the ultimate genera-tive act may be seen in Jesus Christ dying on the cross so that through his death and redemption humankind could have eternal life. Indeed, Erik Erikson's writings on generativity invoke Christian themes. He emphasized that the generative ethic of selfless care for others had a clear parallel with Christian teachings and referred, for example, to the "perfection of charity in the words of Christ" (Erikson, 1964, p. 151). Erikson cited the prayer of St. Francis as paradigmatically expressing the "active choice" involved in generativity—"Lord, make me an instrument of thy peace; where there is hatred let me bring love . . . where there is darkness, let me bring light" and the consequence that "in giving we receive" (p. 232).

The generative act, therefore, produces mutuality; it strengthens both the doer and the recipient and thus enhances individual and collective iden-tities (Erikson, 1964). The core of generativity is enshrined in the Golden Rule summarized by, as Erikson noted, the Christian injunction to "love thy neighbor." Importantly, however, the all-inclusive Golden Rule is a basic ethical principle that transcends any one religion. Erikson emphasized the universality of its "basic formula" evident in its affinity with the Hindu idea of "maintenance of the world" and the principle of Karma (p. 220), the Kantian imperative to see people as ends rather than means, and the "simple political creed" of Abraham Lincoln: "As I would not be slave, I would not be master" (p. 221).

RELIGIOUS INDIVIDUALISM IN AMERICAN SOCIETY

The historical dominance of Christianity in American society and the iconic status of Abraham Lincoln in public culture should combine to provide powerful bedrock for the flourishing of generative ethics in American society. Yet, the same Christianity that preaches the Golden Rule is also the cultural basis of the individualism that governs all aspects of American life from the economic marketplace to family relations. American religiousness itself is characterized by a strong individualistic orientation, and from colonial times to the present the autonomy of the individual has intertwined church participation and religious vitality (e.g., Finke & Stark, 1992). The plurality of diverse denominations, churches, and sects in America both reflects and has been an engine driving the cultural emphasis on individual freedom. Americans, unlike, for example, Europeans, "shop around" for a church or congregation that suits their particular interests and freely switch churches for personal (e.g., dislike of a pastor), practical (convenience), and theological reasons. Further, notwithstanding the comparatively high rates of religious belief and church attendance in America, mainstream religious behavior tends to be characterized more by individual authority than strict adherence to church doctrines and regulations (Dillon, 1999). Many people go to church but see themselves rather than church leaders as the architects of their religious identity.

Thus one of the deeply puzzling paradoxes of American society is how a culture grounded in individualism simultaneously produces high levels of religious and communal involvement. Observers from Alexis de Tocqueville (1835–1836/1969) to contemporary writers suggest that the tension between individualism and community in America is balanced by the often precarious mix of utilitarian and ethical concerns (e.g., Bellah, Madsen, Sullivan, Swidler, & Tipton, 1985). On the one hand, Americans largely define their life goals in terms of self-seeking and a self-reliant economic success (Bellah et al., 1985). On the other hand, John Winthrop's exhortation to his fellow Puritans to "choose life that you *and your descendants* [italics added] may live" has provided a powerful cultural motif encouraging Americans to think and act beyond their own immediate self-interests and hence to fuse individualistic and communal or generative interests.

Church involvement has long been seen as tempering an instrumental or utilitarian individualism. As discussed by Bellah et al. (1985), participation in a religious tradition anchors individuals within a "community of memory" whose "practices of commitment" define the patterns of loyalty and social obligation that maintain the community's vibrancy. In this process, the individual is anchored to the past and, importantly, also to the future as a "community of hope," or what we might call a generative or regenerative community. More specifically, for many generations, religious affiliation and church membership have provided both the motivating scripts and the opportunities for realizing an ethic of social responsibility. Thus the religious autonomy of the individual, as the American sociologist Talcott Parsons (1967; following Max Weber) has argued, should not be seen as absolving the individual of responsibility; rather "the element of mutuality inherent in Christian ethics" means that the individual is responsible "for results and to other persons and collectivities" (p. 419). Consequently, as Nancy Ammerman (1997) has pointed out, American religion is about "right living more than right believing." It is a "Golden Rule Christianity" that emphasizes "practices of doing good and caring for others" (Ammerman, 1997, p. 197).

Given the Golden Rule morality institutionalized in American religion, it is not surprising that there is a positive statistical association between religiousness and concern for others across many dimensions of familial, social, and communal participation (e.g., Putnam, 2000; Rossi, 2001; Verba, Scholzman, & Brady, 1995). Frequent churchgoers have larger social networks and are engaged in more socially supportive relationships than are nonattendees (Ellison & George, 1994). They are more likely than their nonreligious counterparts to have positive intergenerational family relationships (e.g., King & Elder 1999; Pearce & Axinn, 1998); to volunteer in youth, health, and other community organizations (e.g., Rossi, 2001); and to donate more time, money, and material goods to charity (Gallup & Lindsay, 1999; Putnam, 2000). Churches are major providers of social services (e.g., for homeless individuals and families) and are increasingly active in community development projects in underprivileged urban neighborhoods (e.g., Wood, 2002). In sum, churches play a substantial role in the production of a generative society. They provide scriptural narratives of exemplary generative acts that help awaken generative interests and motivations, as well as the social networks and organized opportunities that provide the means for individuals to act on their generative concerns.

THE EMERGENCE OF SPIRITUALITY
IN A THERAPEUTIC CULTURE

In recent years, however, social scientists have observed a change in American religion. The cultural and lifestyle experimentation associated with the protest movements and social upheavals of the 1960s is seen as having a transformative impact on American religion. The 1960s, according to Robert Wuthnow (1998, pp. 53–54), "reshaped Americans' understanding of freedom itself." The religious individualism so long expressed within religious institutions began to move beyond institutional walls to improvise new ways of spiritual seeking. And this quest was made easier by a greatly expanded and innovative "spiritual marketplace" that has allowed Americans to choose from and blend together an ever-increasing array of Western and non-Western religious and spiritual resources (Roof, 1999). Consequently, since the 1960s, there has been a move away from the communal, public, cosmopolitan, and intellectual emphases of religion to a focus on personal, private, local, and emotional religious experiences (Marty, 1993). The importance of tradition-centered religious beliefs and practices (such as attending church and reading the Bible) is being displaced to some extent by an emergent popular consensus that spiritual meaning can be found outside of established places of worship and by exploring Eastern (e.g., Buddhist meditation, yoga) and mythic traditions (e.g., Celtic spirituality).

Because of the established relation between traditional forms of religious involvement (e.g., church attendance) and social commitment, some scholars have responded with considerable concern to the post-1960s' emergence of a more privatized and individuated form of spirituality. They focus attention on whether a spiritual individualism that is autonomous of institutionalized religious beliefs and practices threatens to undercut Americans' sense of social obligation (e.g., Bellah et al., 1985). The long-standing cultural emphasis on responsible individualism is seen as having shifted toward a more self-centered, narcissistic individualism bolstered by the post-1960s' therapeutic culture, the triumph of "psychological man" for whom personal well-being is an end in itself rather than an outcome of socially meaningful activities (Rieff, 1966).

A self-defined spirituality that encourages mystical withdrawal from the world, either in accord with the monastic strand within Christianity or the ascetic self-disciplined practices within Eastern spirituality, is not necessarily anathema to community. But in the contemporary American context, the concern is that a self-defined spirituality is essentially a mechanism to glorify the self, a sort of "cosmic selfhood" wherein "God is simply the self magnified" (Bellah et al., 1985, p. 235). Because in American society historically people have sought to give expression to the self through communal ties and community participation, the new spiritual individualism raises concern that a personalized spirituality, if driven by the narcissistic needs of the self, will have little if any place for the "practices of commitment" and the attendant external obligations imposed by participation in a communal religious tradition (Bellah et al., 1985). The narcissistic individualism associated with spiritual seeking is seen as significantly altering the balance between individualism and community that a socially responsible religious individualism has been able to hold, but that a spiritual individualism because of its privatization and autonomy from formal communal expectations and practices may not. On this view, American spiritual individualism, a religion befitting the contemporary therapeutic culture, is perceived as causing a decline in American generativity. It is seen as directly resulting in a decline in communal participation and care for others and, indirectly, by fostering a self-centered and self-satisfied view that nothing is wrong with the world and therefore nothing needs fixing (Bellah et al., 1985; Wuthnow, 1998). Thus instead of fostering a critical reflexivity and broad social perspective, a self-seeking spirituality can instead suppress awareness of social inequalities and the motivation to try to ameliorate them.

This rather bleak assessment of the social implications of spirituality has begun to be questioned as a result of new empirical studies. Roof's (1999) research among middle-age baby-boomers challenges the purported narcissistic implications of spirituality. Roof conceded that the focus of today's religious energies has shifted from a concern with issues of social belonging to an emphasis on personal meaning. At the same time, however, he found that baby-boomers who have had spiritual experiences are far more likely to value self-giving than those who have not. Openness to self-growth, Roof argued, translates into a predisposition toward more generative personal and interpersonal social relations on the part of individuals who are spiritually engaged. On this view, spiritual individualism does not necessarily threaten communal involvement (Roof, 1999). Rather, spirituality, similar to other personalist ideologies (Lichterman, 1995), can be nurturing of communal-oriented commitments. After all, spirituality usually means that the individual has developed an awareness of a sense of connectedness between self and others and the world at large (Underwood, 1999). Consequently, spirituality should be conducive to achieving the broader societal perspective that leads to generativity, although as argued by Bellah et al. (1985), the "romantic and psychological pantheism" reflected in belief in the unity of all living things offers only the "vaguest prescriptions about how to live in an actual society" (p. 81). Nonetheless, the newly emerging attention to the positive communal implications of spirituality highlights the idea that although a spiritual quest energizes the autonomy of human agency, it may also lead to practices that encourage the communal integration of the self (Bakan, 1966; Kotre, 1996).

The expectation that spirituality should lead to an increase in generative interests fits well with diverse psychological theories that link spiritual growth to higher levels of cognitive development and self-actualization. Both Jungian (Jung, 1964) and postformal (e.g., Sinnott, 1994) theories of development see spirituality as intertwined with the maturational processes and life experiences (McFadden, 1996; Stokes, 1990) associated with the second half of adulthood. This is because the development of spirituality requires the kind of personal autonomy and awareness of contextual relativism that typically develop only around midlife, once the individual has established his or her place in society and begins to experience physical signs of aging (Jung, 1964). Adult development theories thus emphasize the relation between spirituality and a sense of human connectedness, integration of the self, and openness to new experiences (Erikson, 1963; McFadden, 1996; Sinnott, 1994). According to Tornstam (1999), gerotranscendence, the spiritual-based progression toward maturation that is characterized by a heightened awareness of the connection between the self and earlier generations, a decline in self-centeredness, and a decreased focus on this-worldly success and material assets, is a phenomenon of older adulthood. This psychological portrait of spirituality captures well the essence of classical formulations of the personal implications of humanistic religion (Fromm, 1950) and self-actualization (Maslow, 1954).

The view that both an individuated spirituality and a more communally anchored religiousness can lead to generativity fits with the idea that there is, in fact, more than one type of generative impulse or motivation. Recent theories of generativity emphasized that it fuses agential and communal interests (e.g., MacDermid, Franz, & De Reus, 1998; McAdams & de St. Aubin, 1992). As postulated by McAdams and Logan (this volume, chap. 2), generativity springs from both selfish and selfless desires, or from what we suggest might be seen as self-expanding and communal orientations. On the one hand, the more self-directed or agential generative impulse originates in a variety of sources, including the desire to outlive the self and attain immortality (Kotre, 1996), the need for power and impact on others (McAdams, 1995), and creativity (Erikson, 1963). In this sense, an important aspect of generativity entails a healthy transformation of narcissism (Kohut, 1977). On the other hand, generativity is also a manifestation of a deeply felt need for nurturance, caring, and fusion with others that is the hallmark of communion (Bakan, 1966).

Although there is a large body of empirical data supporting the links between religious involvement and generativity or caring for others, the empirical relation between spirituality and generativity has not been systematically investigated. This gap exists in part because, as indicated, spirituality is a relatively new concept in the social sciences and existing research projects have been slow to include questions on spirituality notwithstanding its popularity in public culture and its prominence in scholarly debates about individualism and community. The other, and perhaps more challenging, obstacle to research assessing the impact of spirituality on social behavior is a lack of consensus as to how spirituality should be defined. The conceptual ambiguity is due primarily to the multiple meanings of the term spirituality, which can be applied equally aptly to a pious individual who expresses devotion within the context of a traditional religious institution (Pargament, 1999), a New Age seeker (Roof, 1999), a person who has mystical experiences (Atchley, 1997), and a nonreligious individual who seeks answers to life's existential dilemmas (Stifoss-Hanssen, 1999). Clearly, because of the complexity in the relation between religiousness and spirituality, it is impossible for any one definition to capture all the nuances of both constructs (Moberg, 2002).

RELIGIOUS DWELLING AND SPIRITUAL SEEKING

In our research we have investigated religiousness and spirituality as two dimensions of individual difference using Wuthnow's (1998) distinction between dwelling and seeking. According to Wuthnow, *religious dwellers* tend to accept traditional forms of religious authority; they inhabit a space created for them by established religious institutions and relate to the sacred through prayer and public communal worship. By contrast, for *spiritual seekers*, individual autonomy takes precedence over external authority (Wuthnow, 1998) and the hold of tradition-centered religious doctrines. They are explorers who create their own space by typically borrowing elements from various religious and mythical traditions, and they frequently blend participation in institutionalized Western religious activities with Eastern religious practices. Unlike religious dwellers, spiritual seekers place a greater emphasis on self-growth, emotional self-fulfillment, and the sacredness of ordinary objects and everyday experiences. They typically construe their religious beliefs in terms of a connectedness with a sacred Other (e.g., God, Higher Power, nature, other individuals; Underwood, 1999). What differentiates dwellers and seekers is their relation to religious authority and tradition but not necessarily the seriousness of effort to intentionally incorporate the sacred in their lives. It is important to note that both dwellers and seekers, especially when they engage in intentional practices (that may be privatized or communal), can grow in their faith; they simply tend do so in different ways.

Wuthnow's (1998) model, of course, does not capture all the nuanced meanings embedded in the distinction between religiousness and spirituality, but it does offer a salient understanding of how the two constructs are used in public culture (e.g., Farina, 1989; Marty, 1993). Equally important, because it requires that an individual systematically engage in intentional religious or spiritual practices, it avoids the undisciplined, ad hoc, and idiosyncratic forms of spirituality that tend to inform much of the scholarly discussion about the narcissistic motivations and implications of spiritual seeking (Bellah et al., 1985).

In our research we have explored the relations of religiousness and spirituality to social participation and psychosocial functioning in a longitudinal sample of close to 200 older-age American men and women who were born in the 1920s. Participants in the study, which originated at the Institute of Human Development (IHD) at the University of California, Berkeley, were studied intensively in childhood and adolescence and interviewed in depth about all aspects of their lives in early, middle, late middle, and, most recently in late adulthood when two thirds of the study participants were in their late 60s and one third were in their mid-70s (see Clausen, 1993; Eichorn, Hunt, & Honzik, 1981; Wink & Dillon, 2002). Although there is a good distribution of social class, almost all of the interviewees are White, most still live in California, and the majority are members of mainline Protestant churches. The generalizability of findings from our research to the larger population is thus restricted by the absence of ethnic, religious, and regional diversity. The strength of the study, however, lies in the richness of its interview data and the fact that the same people were followed over 60 years of the life course. Further, because California was and continues to be at the vanguard of the cultural shift in American society that had its origins in the 1960s, the IHD participants offer an excellent opportunity to compare the psychological and sociological implications of adherence to institutionalized or tradition-centered religious beliefs and practices with engagement in spiritual beliefs and practices that are relatively autonomous of institutionalized traditions.

SUMMARY OF EMPIRICAL FINDINGS

In our quantitative research on the implications of religiousness and spirituality in late adulthood, we found that both constructs were associated with various indicators of positive functioning (e.g., Wink & Dillon, 2001). Of direct relevance to the themes discussed in this chapter, we found that both religiousness (dwelling) and spirituality (seeking) were positively associated with well-being in older adulthood (Wink & Dillon, in press). But as might be expected, highly religious individuals were more likely to derive well-being from mutual interpersonal and social activities, whereas highly spiritual individuals were more likely to derive their well-being from an emphasis on personal growth, a difference reminiscent of Bakan's (1966) distinction between communion and agency. Similarly, we found that both religiousness and spirituality were positively related to scores on the self-report Loyola Generativity Scale (McAdams & de St. Aubin, 1992) and the California Adult Q-Set (Block, 1978) Generative Realization scale (Peterson & Klohnen, 1995), with high scorers on both religiousness and spirituality tending to see themselves and to be described by others as generative. However, once the overlap between religiousness and spirituality was taken into consideration (i.e., statistically removed), only high scorers on religiousness tended to be described by observers as giving toward others, protective of those close to them, ethically consistent, and productive, whereas only high scorers on spirituality tended to describe themselves as being engaged in activities that have an impact on others, feeling needed and wanted by others, and involved in creative activities (Dillon, Wink, & Fay, in press). They also believed that their legacy would continue to be recognized after their death. Observers tended to describe highly spiritual individuals as being socially incisive and able to see to the heart of important problems.

On closer examination, and by way of summary, it was apparent that religiousness was significantly more likely to be associated with the communal and interpersonal caring aspects of generativity, whereas spirituality was more strongly related to the self-expansive and creative activities that enable generative individuals to "outlive the self" (Kotre, 1996). Our findings also showed that there was long-term stability in the relations between religiousness, spirituality, and generativity. In other words, we found that if an individual scored high on religiousness in early adulthood (age 30s) or high on spirituality in late middle adulthood (late 50s/early 60s), they would also score high on generativity in late adulthood (age 70s), time intervals of close to 40 and 15 years, respectively (Wink & Dillon, in press).

Further, despite the purported association between narcissism and spirituality (e.g., Bellah et al., 1985), our research findings showed no connection between spirituality and narcissism. There was a negative, but statistically nonsignificant, relation between spirituality and narcissism and a negative and statistically significant relation between religiousness and narcissism (Wink & Dillon, in press). Overall then, findings from our study indicating a positive relation between religiousness, spirituality, and generativity and a negative relation to narcissism should help dispel concerns about the excessive self-absorption of spiritual seekers (e.g., Bellah et al., 1985).

GENERATIVE LIVES IN A CHANGING CULTURE

As a way of illustrating and elaborating the statistical patterns that have emerged in our research, we now discuss three lives to show how both traditional religiousness and newer types of spiritual engagement can nurture and facilitate the realization of generative behavior.[1] We first introduce and compare two women, Laura and Jane, who have fairly similar social backgrounds and personalities. Both scored high on generativity in late adulthood, but whereas Laura was one of the most religious individuals in our study, Jane was one of the most spiritual. Then, because the empirical link between spirituality and generativity is less well established than for religiousness, we introduce Peter, one of the more spiritual men in the study and who over time became generative.

Both Laura and Jane were born in 1928 to middle-class parents, and they grew up in economically comfortable families unimpeded by the Great Depression. Religion was not emphasized in either family. Both went to col-

---

[1]Names and other personally identifying information has been changed to preserve the interviewees' anonymity.

lege where they met their respective husbands who subsequently forged successful business careers, and reflecting post–World War II American demographic trends, both had four children. Laura and Jane also had somewhat similar personalities; each from an early age was independent, strong, and resourceful, and both enjoyed athletics and outdoor activities. Both of Laura's parents were very active socially and highly involved in political and community affairs, and although Jane's father was socially reserved, her mother was very active in the community. Laura's and Jane's early life experiences sensitized them too to emotional loss. Laura's adored father died when she was in her early teens, whereas loss in Jane's life dates to her birth not long after an older sibling's death left a huge emotional gap in her mother's life that Jane assumed she had to fill. At age 8, a childhood illness meant that Jane had to spend 6 months out of school, a period she experienced as a time of emotional and social isolation.

Notwithstanding their sociobiographical similarities, Laura and Jane show quite different trajectories and patterns of generativity. Laura's generativity is tied to her religiousness, and like her religiousness, it is relatively stable, socially responsive, and action-oriented. Jane's spirituality develops in late middle adulthood and is dialectically related to the cultural changes of the 1960s and 1970s in a way that Laura's is not. Jane's generativity is grounded in a relatively privatized quest toward understanding the self and therapeutically connecting with others. It is expressed in creative activities and also, like Laura, in caring for others, but the context of care frequently intertwines Jane's inner needs.

Laura

The 1950s stand out as a high point in American religiousness (Wuthnow, 1998) and like so many young mothers of her generation, Laura was very active in the church during this decade. She was attending weekly Episcopalian services, something she had started doing while in junior high school, and, among other activities, was directing the church's youth group. Religion was her "wonderful crutch," but it also bolstered her strong sense of social responsibility and commitment to living out rather than simply professing Christian values. Illuminating American Golden Rule Christianity, Laura emphasized how much she tried to be a good "practicing" Christian by helping out in various church and community activities. She commented that she tries "to see the best in everyone . . . to look at things in a positive way and give people the benefit of the doubt" (1958, at age 30), a worldview aided by her belief that God gave each of her "children and perhaps everyone in the world something special." It was evident that Laura admired self-giving people such as her mother, whom she described as someone who "sort of dedicates her life for others." Demonstrating moreover the mutuality that is so characteristic of generativity (Erikson, 1964; McAdams, Diamond, de St.

Aubin, & Mansfield, 1997), Laura, at age 42, observed how getting a middle-ear infection and temporarily losing her hearing had been a positive experience for her because she "came out with a totally beautifully new understanding of deaf people."

The church and Laura's deep religious faith was a constant resource for her throughout her adult life, and when in her mid-40s she was confronted with her unexpected divorce, prayer and religious books helped her cope with the emotional and financial losses she incurred. In view of Erikson's use of the prayer of St. Francis as an exemplar of generativity, it is noteworthy that when asked about her usual response to trouble, Laura, at midlife, referred to that prayer as one of the "beautiful things" to which she turns for strength. Although Laura experienced chronic and debilitating health problems throughout adulthood, the focus of her generative concerns was invariably communal rather than agentic or self-oriented. Thus, for example, after a close relative was tragically killed, Laura and her husband had the bereaved children live with them for several years.

Up until midlife, Laura's social clock followed the typical "feminine" role pattern of marriage, mothering, and church involvement, and her caring for others was defined within these traditional contexts. But Laura did not need to read *The Feminine Mystique* (1963) to alert her to alternative role possibilities for women. Already in 1958, 5 years before Betty Friedan's best-selling book exploded the myth of the happily passive housewife, Laura made no bones about her independence even as she intimated her awareness that this was culturally renegade:

> Well I'm one of those awful people; I feel I'm me and no one can run my life. I tell him [husband] if I feel it's not his jurisdiction. I've maintained my own independence. . . . I'm certainly more emotionally independent than dependent. . . . I've always felt that if something should happen to [husband] I could take care of myself. That gives a clue to how independent I am.

It was not until she was in her 40s, however, that Laura expanded her social roles. Buoyed perhaps by the spirit of the Women's Movement, Laura started teaching in the late 1960s and subsequently received her diploma in special education. "Physically and mentally exhausting," Laura's occupational decision to teach "superdependent" emotionally troubled children and adolescents was clearly generative. Her subsequent work showed an even broader communal orientation when in 1980 she and her second husband, catching the rebounding wave of public concern about the environment (e.g., Putnam, 2000), started a nature store in the Southwestern United States. They saw the store not as a money-making enterprise but in terms of service to a larger good. As Laura said: "It's a thrilling store and we don't look to it as a means of making money. We feel very good about what we're doing. If it's just a message to the public and we can scrape out a living from it, that's all we want"

(1982, at age 54). Fifteen years later, Laura and her husband were still working full time in their low-profit nature store despite her continuing health problems. Weekly church attendance and daily prayer continued to be a central part of her life, but as she also pointed out, her religion was very much "the here and now and on earth." Thus, not surprising, Laura was still emphatic about her social responsibility to do good, to "contribute to society," and to make a difference in the world. She commented:

> We have made a living for ourselves but not much more than that. We're very happy with what we're doing. We believe in what we're doing. One of our major things is trying to make people aware, particularly children and the young generation, how fortunate we are to have this beautiful world and to try and take better care of it. (1997, at age 69)

Jane

The generative resources that Laura drew from established religion, Jane had to achieve through an inner journey of self-discovery and healing. If generativity, as Erikson noted, means loving thy neighbor as thyself, Jane's life can be seen as an illustration of the psychosocial insight that one has to learn to love and accept oneself before having the capacity to be self-giving toward others. When interviewed at age 30, Jane described her late-20s as the "absolute low" of her life brought on by the death of her father, her "steady rock" to whom she had been very close. His death, moreover, occurred at the same time as one of her children was diagnosed with a serious illness. To deal with her despair, Jane sought psychiatric counseling, and during the 1958 interview, was somewhat optimistic: "I feel I'm on the way to some sort of solution and understanding of [the depression]. . . . I have to accept my life as it is." At the same time, Jane was wistful that she did not share her husband's strong Catholic convictions, something she felt that anchored him in ways that she was not. Although involved in their children's religious education, Jane said she was unable to bring herself to adopt such beliefs. For Jane, God was "some nebulous force behind the universe," and as she commented, she did "not feel responsible to a God."

Jane's continuing journey toward self-insight and self-acceptance took her into psychotherapy in the late 1960s, and she also started participating in the newly expanding range of encounter groups. Illustrating how sociocultural change can impact individual change, Jane emphasized how important therapy had been in advancing her self-understanding. She commented:

> I feel that my life has just completely changed. My feelings about myself, like about what I'm doing here on earth. And I'm still growing. I don't think it will ever stop now. . . . I've never felt better about myself. I'm more confident and I feel very strongly my identity, and I feel I can do pretty much what I want to do. . . . I feel I'm worth something. (1970, at age 42)

Further reflecting the therapeutic culture of 1970s' America (Bellah et al., 1985) and her belief in inner-awareness as a pathway to personal growth, Jane, when asked about future goals for her children, said she would like to teach them "to be able to be in touch with themselves and their feelings."

Paralleling her experiences in psychotherapy and encounter groups, Jane's process of self-growth also included an expanded spiritual awareness. In the mid-1970s she became interested in Eastern meditation practices that at the time were still relatively new to American society. Pointing to the cultural intertwining of spiritual and therapeutic interests, Jane attended a lecture for mental health professionals given by an Eastern guru. As described by Jane:

> Something happened the first time I walked into that place, into the ashram. It's an indescribable something, but I felt a real internal shift inside me. Something profound was happening and I didn't understand it but I knew it felt really good. (1982, at age 54)

After a couple of return visits to the ashram, Jane subsequently started to learn meditative practices and subsequently began to experience intensive meditation. These "profound experiences in meditation" brought her, she said, "a strength and a peacefulness and a protection" that she had never before experienced, and "all of it came from within." Jane continued to do intensive meditation and 20 years later, in her 70s, meditation and other spiritual rituals continued to be a very meaningful part of her life.

The reason Jane attended that first Eastern spirituality lecture was that she herself had trained to become a family therapist in the early 1970s. For Jane, being a clinician was rewarding not just because she was helping others but because she also found it integral to her self-growth. At the time of the 1982 interview, Jane was doing group therapy with families; she was enjoying the work immensely and also found it to be "part of [her] own healing."

Like Laura, Jane responded to the increased structural and cultural opportunities for women's employment in the 1970s and expanded her social roles at midlife. Although both women entered caring professions, it is noteworthy that whereas Laura chose the more traditional domain of teaching as the initial productive outlet for her more communal interests, Jane chose the more culturally fashionable and inner-directed, therapeutic domain. Nonetheless, Jane's spiritual and therapeutic experiences helped her achieve a broader communal perspective and thus enhanced the realization of generative behavior in older age. She carved a productive career training other therapists and traveling extensively giving workshops until she retired in the early 1990s. Following her retirement Jane became more involved in her long-standing artistic pursuits, especially working in her garden where she had created some natural shrines, spaces that she regularly used for meditation. She also spent a lot of time writing poetry, painting, and sculpting, thus accumulating a creative legacy. It is important to note that Jane had also become an active volunteer. Prior to her husband's cancer and subsequent death in the mid-1990s, she had taught English to immigrants, worked with undereducated adult prisoners, and ran a caregivers' group for families of patients with Alzheimer's disease.

Like Laura, Jane too was proud of the contribution of her work to others' well-being and to a larger social good, but in Jane's case, there was additional pride in how it also reflected on her own self-growth:

> I think the [family counseling] work I did when I was working was terribly important. . . . And I feel really good about that. And the people I helped along the way. And then it's who I have become that I feel proud of too. . . . I have come to a greater depth of understanding and forgiveness. And I'm in a whole different place through it.

It is thus that Jane gives realization to Erikson's (1968) emphasis that the generative ethic "commands us always to act in such a way that the identities of both the actor and the one acted upon are enhanced" (p. 316).

Peter

Unlike Laura and Jane whose social roles maintained a good fit with American cultural expectations over successive decades, Peter, born in 1929, had a hard time carrying the role mantle of a dominant, independent, and high-achieving male. Although highly intelligent, charming, healthy, and handsome, Peter suffered chronically low self-esteem from childhood through most of his adult years. Both his parents were college graduates, and his father owned a successful business that he had taken over from his father-in-law but that became very badly hit by the Depression. Financial difficulties and insecurity, exacerbated by the spending and social habits of Peter's status-conscious mother, characterized Peter's life until junior high school when his family's economic situation improved considerably. In addition, both parents had suffered nervous breakdowns in their late adolescent years, and the legacy of this emotional instability endured into Peter's upbringing. Religion did not figure prominently in Peter's family, but his mother occasionally attended Congregational and Unitarian church services and was an active volunteer in the community (notwithstanding the family's economic straits). Peter went to a Christian Science Sunday school for a while when he was 9, and he was also a member of the Boy Scouts at the local Episcopalian church. But as a socially awkward and curious child, he was much more interested in magic and doing chemistry experiments for the transformations they caused. In adolescence he described himself as agnostic.

Peter's sole and older brother, who was boisterous and troublesome to his parents, was Peter's "friend and protector" and got him into a high school fraternity that greatly improved his social life. Nonetheless, Peter felt "socially inadequate and generally incompetent" as an adolescent. Unable to achieve the high grades his parents expected, midway through college, Peter was drafted into the army. After basic training, which to his surprise he enjoyed, he returned to Berkeley, married a woman whom he did not know so well, and after a week's honeymoon, went to Korea. He was assigned to a logistics division at headquarters and found the desk work frustrating, and getting commendations for it, hypocritical.

On returning from Korea, Peter went back to college, changed his major from physics to business administration, and got better grades. After graduating in 1955, Peter went to work with his father in his wholesale deep-freeze business. Commenting on this decision when interviewed in 1958, Peter said that if he were "more mature and self-confident" he would quit working for his father although he nonetheless felt some loyalty to him and his business. Work was not the only source of frustration for Peter; his marriage was also in trouble. His wife had a troubled personal background and was suffering from depression. Peter himself felt sexually incompetent and was further frustrated because having built his wife and young son "a new home with all mod cons," he thought this would improve their relationship, but it had not.

When interviewed in 1970, Peter's life had spiraled downward. He and his wife, although they had adopted a son and daughter, divorced in 1967; and he had been very depressed, out of work, and living in a boarding house for a few months prior to the interview. His brother, moreover, had had a nervous breakdown. Although Peter had found work managing a frozen foods wholesale branch, he was in debt as a result of his prior unemployment and experienced bouts of depression. Nonetheless, Peter was trying to take hold of his life and give it some direction. Like Jane who found new resources and opportunities for self-growth in the newly expanding therapeutic culture, Peter, and indeed most of his friends, were involved in a Transactional Analysis (TA) therapy group that met once a week. Peter felt that the TA helped him deal with his depression, and as well as looking into yoga and meditation, he was even thinking of going back to college to become a therapist. It was clear that Peter was quite taken with TA and throughout the interview he frequently drew on its therapeutic vocabulary in trying to explain his own self-perception and behavior. He explained, for example:

> One of the concepts they have is that of a good guy. . . . The good guy is somebody who's too worried about their image and functions in terms of how they think other people want them to function . . . so that rather than doing what they feel is the right thing to do, they look and say "I wonder what so-and-so would think, if I did this, would they like it?" . . . I think I have a tendency to be a good guy . . . one of my contracts [tasks] in TA is to get over being a good guy because I don't particularly like it. Over the years I have found it very destructive. (1970, at age 41)

It was through church that Peter had first found out about TA: Some friends at the Unitarian church that he had been attending on and off for several months first told him about it. What he liked about Unitarianism, he said, was that he "didn't have to have all kinds of religious beliefs to fit in."

Twelve years later, Peter's life seemed to have taken a positive turn. After selling a service station that he had owned for a few years, Peter had gone back to college and received a master's degree in ecosystem management and technology. With the new opportunities that, as we saw with Laura, had become available in the post-1970s environmental-friendly marketplace, Peter had at last found a vocational niche. He had set up a small wood stove business and was also engaged in other alternative energy projects and organic farming. Peter was also in another marriage, his third, after a second short and stormy marriage in which he had another son. His second wife had been active in the Bahai religion, and she in turn got him involved; it was through Bahai activities that he subsequently met his current wife. Both had subsequently left the Bahai religion because of what they felt was its hypocrisy, especially over women's equality. As Peter explained, in the personally authoritative and self-oriented language that Bellah et al. (1985) knew so well, "we replaced the faith with our beliefs regarding energy and self sufficiency. And how we want to handle our own lives and where we are going" (1982, at age 53). His wife, a nurse, was younger than him, but "mature and level headed"; they had a son together and seemed to have carved a happy and cohesive family life.

When interviewed in late adulthood, Peter was still happily married and had a very close relationship with his youngest son, although he was not close to any of his older children. Describing his marriage as "very good," Peter did not invoke the therapeutic language one might have anticipated based on past interviews but used a more old-fashioned vocabulary, commenting: "Finally I recognize that what it takes for a marriage to work is commitment, almost more than anything else." At this time in his life, Peter was also very committed to community participation. Although "a neo-pagan" who regularly engaged in nature spirituality practices, he also attended the Unitarian church most weeks, was on its board, and had served on its worship committee. He was also an organizer of a local farmers' market for organic foods, ran a wholesale foods buying club for 12 families, and was on the board of the community hall and of the local conservation district. Given all of these activities, it is not surprising that Peter described his values thus:

> My values tie in right with this earth's spirituality. . . . I think my values
> are very, very environmental and I'm very concerned that we as human
> beings are destroying our home, our earth. And I'm concerned that it's
> going to affect my son's life and my grandchildren's lives. Not mine nec-
> essarily. . . . So my values are very much values of attempting to live
> lightly with the earth. (1998, at age 69)

For someone who in adolescence and early adulthood had felt deeply inadequate, it is clear that from middle adulthood onward, and after many work-related troubles and personal calamities brought on by his lack of maturation, Peter carved a stable and committed life. His dabbling in various religions (Congregationalism, Unitarianism, Bahai) illustrates well the cafeteria-type religious shopper whom we might expect would end up dissatisfied with all religions and disconnected from the "practices of commitment" that link individuals to communities beyond the self. Yet, Peter managed to commit to Unitarianism and an earth-centered spirituality whose obligations in turn connected him to a whole web of personal and communal relations. By late adulthood, his generative concerns and activities encompassed his family, the local community, and the environment at large. Accordingly, self-growth for Peter achieved the Eriksonian demand that the self be a relational self, one that meaningfully incorporates and integrates others into its orbit.

We do not rule out the possibility that Peter's achievement of a generative and integrated identity may have resulted from the maturational or aging process itself. We are struck, however, that changes in the post 1960s' cultural environment provided mechanisms that enabled Peter to journey toward the creation of a purposeful and generative lifestyle. Although his parents' mental health histories may in any case have motivated Peter to seek psychotherapy at some point, the cultural accessibility of TA in the 1970s and its apparent suitability to Peter's specific needs may have enhanced his growth and maturation. Similarly, the expanded range of religious options in post-1970s America including, for example, the increased visibility of the Bahai religion and of unconventional forms of spirituality such as paganism, also played a critical role in creating new resources and social opportunities for Peter. At the same time, the culture's new environmental consciousness, and perhaps the increased societal recognition that not all men need to be "organization men," provided a legitimate outlet for his comparatively less utilitarian avocational interests.

CONCLUSION: SPIRITUALITY AND COMMUNAL COMMITMENT IN A THERAPEUTIC SOCIETY

The cultural transformation of the 1960s toward a narcissistic and therapeutic individualism and the emergent popularity of spiritual vocabularies and practices that are autonomous of tradition-centered religion raise concern that spiritual individualism may undercut Americans' social commitments. It is this broadly changed cultural context that we have used to probe the relation between religiousness, spirituality, and generativity in our research among White Christians who were born in the 1920s.

In thinking about cultural change, it is important first of all to point out that one should be cautious not to overstate the popularity of new forms of spirituality. Although there is no shortage of spiritual groups, books, and materials in the public culture, the data on the extent of the new religious–spiritual transformation are somewhat ambiguous. There has been a relatively small but statistically significant decline in religious affiliation and church attendance in America over the last several years (Hout & Fischer, 2002). At the same time, however, although the proportion of Americans who identify with non Judeo-Christian religions has increased considerably since the 1970s, the most recent reliable survey evidence suggests that less than 3% of American adults report either having a "personal religion" or follow⋯ ⋯ ⋯ (⋯ Smith, 2002) Certain skepticism there-fore, ⋯ ⋯ ation of the ⋯

tersh⋯ ⋯ indi-vidua⋯ ⋯ ⋯ e im-porta⋯ ⋯ ms of religi⋯ ⋯ links to th⋯ ⋯ that spirit⋯ ⋯ spects of ge⋯ ⋯ both, none⋯ ⋯ found no ev⋯ ⋯ s evi-dent, ⋯ ⋯ stem-atic, ⋯ ⋯ marily defin⋯ ⋯ limsy, and self-indulgent as is intimated frequently in popular ⋯

Our studies highlight the importance of recognizing that just as generativity is itself a multidimensional concept, so also there are multiple pathways toward its realization. Although involvement in a religious tradition provides individuals with more structured and socially accessible ways of engaging and realizing generative concerns, the individual journeying and self-growth associated with spirituality are also conducive to the development of the sense of connectedness and social commitment that expresses and enhances generativity. As we saw with both Peter and Jane, spirituality provided the social merger and connectedness yearned for from childhood and enabled both to become generative older adults. Their spiritual journeying was clearly self-seeking and therapeutic, but its outcome resulted in social participation rather than disengagement. In this, perhaps they illuminate the power of American culture to orient action in a pragmatic and this-worldly rather than a more mystical and inner-worldly manner. Accordingly, just as American religion has historically emphasized socially responsible action in the everyday world, so too it would seem that American therapeutic culture, if harnessed to a disciplined spirituality, can lead to a socially responsible expression of the newfound self. In this, both tradition-centered institutionalized religion and newer forms of spirituality may share more in common than is assumed by scholars who are concerned about the possible negative social consequences of spirituality (Bellah et al., 1985). If spirituality has gained in prominence among members of the baby-boom generation (Roof, 1999; Wuthnow, 1998), then our research findings augur well for the aging boomers' ability to transcend the therapeutic self and to care for others in a generative way.

It is also important to recognize that the ways in which generativity is expressed are contingent on sociocultural context. It is not coincidental that Americans' community involvement and church attendance peaked during the 1950s decade of post–World War II suburban family affluence. At the height of the Cold War, having "faith in faith" and showing one's religious (as opposed to one's atheistic or "communist") identity by going to church (Herberg, 1960) expanded the opportunities for voluntary activity both within the church (e.g., teaching Sunday school) and through church-related community service. This kind of religious involvement provided the motivation and outlet for much of Laura's generativity as a traditional mother in the 1950s. Her subsequent generative behavior, however, was in part influenced by sociocultural changes in role expectations. Both she and Jane, similar to many other American women who responded to the changes in women's status, entered the world of work in the 1970s, getting involved in caring professions. It was the loosening of gender role boundaries that also, in part, enabled Peter to settle on work commitments (alternative energy and organic farming) that might be seen as more expressive than utilitarian. The realization of these roles was in turn contingent on changing structural and cultural resources and their accessibility. Thus, whereas Jane and Peter were directly influenced by the post-1960s' therapeutic culture, and by the expanded range of spiritual resources publicly available in post-1960s' American society (e.g., Eastern meditation and Bahai rituals), Laura and Peter availed of new opportunities stemming from the post-1960s' environmental awareness movement.

In sum, our research shows that both religiousness and spirituality are associated with the development and realization of generativity. Connecting with a sacred Other, so long as it involves discipline and systematic practices, would appear to be conducive to transcending the self and caring for others, and thus to appreciating the interdependence of self, society, nature, and ultimate reality (Bellah et al., 1985). Therefore, although cultural change and associated changes in the religious and spiritual landscape necessarily alter the shared social and physical context in which people live their lives, generative behavior can endure. Its narratives and outlets may change, but such change is not necessarily the harbinger of the decline of a generative society.

REFERENCES

Ammerman, N. (1997). Golden Rule Christianity: Lived religion in the American mainstream. In D. Hall (Ed.), *Lived religion in America* (pp. 196–216). Princeton, NJ: Princeton University Press.

Atchley, R. (1997). Everyday mysticism: Spiritual development in later adulthood. *Journal of Adult Development, 4,* 123–134.

Bakan, D. (1966). *The duality of human existence.* Chicago: Rand McNally.

Bellah, R., Madsen, R., Sullivan, W., Swidler, A., & Tipton, S. (1985). *Habits of the heart: Individualism and commitment in American life.* Berkeley: University of California Press.

Block, J. (1978). *Lives through time* (2nd ed.). Berkeley, CA: Bancroft.

Clausen, J. (1993). *American lives.* Berkeley: University of California Press.

de Tocqueville, A. (1969). *Democracy in America.* New York: Doubleday. (Original work published 1835–1836)

Dillon, M. (1999). *Catholic identity: Balancing reason, faith, and power.* New York: Cambridge University Press.

Dillon, M., Wink, P., & Fay, K. (in press). Relation between religiousness, spirituality and two types of generativity. *Journal for the Scientific Study of Religion.*

Eichorn, D., Hunt, J., & Honzik, M. (1981). Experience, personality, and IQ: Adolescence to middle age. In D. Eichorn, J. Clausen, N. Haan, M. Honzik, & P. Mussen (Eds.), *Present and past in middle age* (pp. 89–116). New York: Academic Press.

Ellison, C., & George, L. (1994). Religious involvement, social ties, and social support in a Southeastern community. *Journal for the Scientific Study of Religion, 33,* 46–61.

Erikson, E. (1963). *Childhood and society* (2nd ed.). New York: Norton.

Erikson, E. (1964). *Insight and responsibility.* New York: Norton.

Erikson, E. (1968). *Identity: Youth and crisis.* London: Faber & Faber.

Farina, J. (1989, Spring). The study of spirituality: Some problems and opportunities. *U.S. Catholic Historian,* 15–31.

Finke, R., & Stark, R. (1992). *The churching of America, 1776–1990.* New Brunswick, NJ: Rutgers University Press.

Friedan, B. (1963). *The feminine mystique.* New York: Norton.

Fromm, E. (1950). *Psychoanalysis and religion.* New Haven, CT: Yale University Press.

Gallup, G., & Lindsay, M. (1999). *Surveying the religious landscape.* Harrisburg, PA: Morehouse.

Herberg, W. (1960). *Protestant, Catholic, Jew.* Garden City, NY: Anchor Books.

Hout, M., & Fischer, C. (2002). Why more Americans have no religious preference: Politics and generations. *American Sociological Review, 67,* 165–190.

Jung, C. (1964). *Memories, dreams, reflections.* New York: Vintage.

King, V., & Elder, G. (1999). Are religious grandparents more involved grandparents? *Journal of Gerontology: Social Sciences, 54*(Suppl.), 317–328.

Kohut, H. (1977). *The restoration of the self.* New York: International Universities Press.

Kotre, J. (1996). *Outliving the self* (2nd ed.). New York: Norton.

Lichterman, P. (1995). Beyond the see-saw model: Public commitment in a culture of self-fulfillment. *Sociological Theory, 13,* 275–300.

MacDermid, S., Franz, C., & De Reus, L.A. (1998). Adult character: Agency, communion, insight, and the expression of generativity in mid-life adults. In A. Colby, J. James, & D. Hart (Eds.), *Competence and character through life* (pp. 205–229). Chicago: University of Chicago Press.

Marty, M. (1993). Where the energies go. *Annals of the American Academy of Political and Social Science, 553,* 11–26.

Maslow, A. (1954). *Motivation and personality.* New York: Harper & Row.

McAdams, D. (1995). *Power, intimacy, and the life story.* New York: Guilford Press.

McAdams, D., & de St. Aubin, E. (1992). A theory of generativity and its assessment through self-report, behavioral acts, and narrative themes in autobiography. *Journal of Personality and Social Psychology, 62,* 1003–1015.

McAdams, D., Diamond, A., de St.Aubin, E., & Mansfield, E. (1997). Stories of commitment: The psychosocial construction of generative lives. *Journal of Personality and Social Psychology, 72,* 678–694.

McFadden, S. (1996). Religion, spirituality, and aging. In J. E. Birren & K. W. Schaie (Eds.), *Handbook of the psychology of aging* (4th ed., pp. 162–177). San Diego, CA: Academic Press.

Moberg, D. (2002). Assessing and measuring spirituality: Confronting dilemmas of universal and particular evaluative criteria. *Journal of Adult Development, 9,* 47–60.

Parsons, T. (1967). *Sociological theory and modern society.* New York: Free Press.

Pargament, K. (1999). The psychology of religion and spirituality? Yes and no. *International Journal for the Psychology of Religion, 9,* 3–16.

Pearce, L., & Axinn, W. (1998). Family religious life and the mother–child relationship. *American Sociological Review, 63,* 810–828.

Peterson, B., & Klohnen, E. (1995). Realization of generativity in two samples of women at midlife. *Psychology and Aging, 10,* 20–29.

Putnam, R. (2000). *Bowling alone: The collapse and revival of American community.* New York: Simon & Schuster.

Rieff, P. (1966). *The triumph of the therapeutic: Uses of faith after Freud.* New York: Harper & Row.

Roof, W. C. (1999). *Spiritual marketplace.* Princeton, NJ: Princeton University Press.

Rossi, A. (Ed.). (2001). *Caring and doing for others.* Chicago: University of Chicago Press.

Sinnott, J. (1994). Development and yearning: Cognitive aspects of spiritual development. *Journal of Adult Development, 1,* 91–99.

Smith, T. (2002). Religious diversity in America. *Journal for the Scientific Study of Religion, 41,* 577–585.

Stifoss-Hanssen, H. (1999). Religion and spirituality: What a European ear hears. *International Journal for the Psychology of Religion, 9,* 25–33.

Stokes, K. (1990). Faith development in the adult life cycle. *Journal of Religious Gerontology, 7,* 167–184.

Tornstam, L. (1999). Late-life transcendence: A new developmental perspective on aging. In L. E. Thomas & S. Eisenhandler, (Eds.), *Religion, belief, and spirituality in late life* (pp. 178–202). New York: Springer.

Underwood, L. (1999). Daily spiritual experiences. In *Multidimensional measurement of religiousness/spirituality for use in health research: A report of the Fetzer Institute/ National Institute on Aging working group* (pp. 11–17). Kalamazoo, MI: John E. Fetzer Institute.

Verba, S, Scholzman, K., & Brady, H. (1995). *Voice and equality: Civic voluntarism in American politics.* Cambridge, MA: Harvard University Press.

Wink, P., & Dillon, M. (2001). Religious involvement and health outcomes in late adulthood. In T. Plante & A. Sherman (Eds.), *Faith and health* (pp. 75–106). New York: Guilford Press.

Wink, P., & Dillon, M. (2002). Spiritual development across the life course: Findings from a longitudinal study. *Journal of Adult Development, 9,* 79–94.

Wink, P., & Dillon, M. (in press). Religiousness, spirituality, and psychosocial functioning in late adulthood: Findings from a longitudinal study. *Psychology and Aging.*

Wood, R. (2002). *Faith in action: Religion, race, and democratic organizing in America.* Chicago: University of Chicago Press.

Wuthnow, R. (1998). *After heaven: Spirituality in America since the 1950s.* Berkeley: University of California Press.

11

GENERATIVITY AND GENDER: THE POLITICS OF CARE

BONNIE J. MILLER-McLEMORE

Erik Erikson's notoriety in the 1950s and 1960s centered around his concept of identity crisis. But today it is his idea of generativity that has real potential. His own struggle to determine his place—as a Jew in a Danish household and later as an artist in scientific circles, a man with gifts for working with children, and a European in the United States—gave him particular insight into a widely shared struggle. Today, renewed interest in generativity arises partly as a result of a sweeping cultural problem that Erikson, as a man of his own times, did not directly have to confront: contemporary generativity crises.

Many factors within today's rapidly changing postmodern, postindustrial society conspire to disrupt previously unquestioned, conventional patterns of generativity in the workplace and home that reigned at the height of the modern industrial era. Dramatic changes in gender relations, including the growing vocational aspirations of women and the heightened domestic de-

Parts of this chapter are based on research done for chapter 2 of *Also a Mother: Work and Family as Theological Dilemma*, by B. J. Miller-McLemore, 1994, Nashville, TN: Abingdon Press. Copyright 1994 by Abingdon Press. Adapted with permission.

mands on men, have sparked complicated efforts to redefine family and work life and the relationship between them (see, e.g., Stewart & Ostrove's 1998 study). The push for equality between the sexes in particular has provoked unprecedented conflicts between women and men. But beneath many everyday scuffles over gender roles, child care, and equal salaries lies a deeper crisis of generativity that has not only psychological but also social, political, and religious dimensions.

In this chapter, I argue that for generativity to remain a useful psychological construct, it needs to be significantly rethought in terms of gender. More specifically, important developments in psychology, ethics, and religion reveal an often hidden and unevaluated gender "politics of generativity" that distorts caregiving. Feminist studies challenge generative-unfriendly economic and social structures and suggest new understandings of adult development that explore the complicated problems of managing a "double" generativity of relationships and occupation (Aisenberg & Harrington, 1988; Daniels, 1985; Franz & White, 1985; Gilligan, 1982; Jordan, Kaplan, Miller, Stiver, & Surrey, 1991; Mahony, 1995; Miller, 1976; Okin, 1989; Roberts & Newton, 1987; Sidel, 1990; see also Miller-McLemore, 2000). Studies in ethics and religion recognize generativity not simply as a psychological concept but also as an ethical and religious construct that has the potential to define for society the good, the right, and the just parameters of work and love (Bellah, Madsen, Sullivan, Swidler, & Tipton, 1991; Browning, 1975, 1987, 2000; Miller-McLemore, 1994; Snarey, 1993; see also Greenspan, 1983; Ricoeur, 1970; Rieff, 1966; Sturdivant, 1980). And, finally, Christian feminist studies challenge religious views of loving self-sacrifice that have exempted men from household chores and exacted the costs of domestic dedication from women and children (Anderson, 1997; Andolsen, 1981; Dunfee, 1989; Gill-Austern, 1996; Gudorf, 1985, 1996; Miller-McLemore, 1989, 1991, 1994; Ruether, 1975, 1983; Saiving, 1988).

This chapter essentially develops the thesis that this body of research calls for a more just and balanced distribution of the tasks of generativity between women and men and for the social and cultural changes necessary to make such redistribution possible. Human well-being rests on a fuller enactment of aspects of both breadwinning and childrearing by both men and women than is currently attainable under the present social structures and mores. Although generativity as a psychological goal of the seventh stage of Erikson's life cycle is an important idea, psychological understandings have ignored to their detriment wider social and cultural factors that impede or that might enable a fuller embodiment of genuine generativity by both women and men in occupational and familial spheres.

The United States and the rest of the world face immense generative challenges. Dominant social premises continue to relegate the public tasks of real "work" to men and the domestic chores of genuine "love" to women. Cultural mores, driven by the values of a market economy, prize material productivity while discounting the nonmaterial, hidden structures of domestic labor on which productivity rests. These same values make it almost impossible for the "haves" of the Northern Hemisphere even to notice the increasingly difficult generative plight of the "have-nots" of the Southern Hemisphere. Meanwhile, statistics indicate that a smaller and smaller percentage of the U.S. population bears direct responsibility for biological generativity, possibly disrupting the heretofore natural contagion between activities of parental generativity and involvement in acts of social generativity (Ahlburg & De Vita, 1997; Lesthaeghe, 1983; Smith, 2001; see also Kotre, 1984; Snarey, 1993).

In such a troubled context, the term *generativity* has immense normative and even prophetic potential, not just in the realm of adult development but also in the economic and social realms of labor. Full generativity, as Erikson defined it, involves mastery of two essential but all-too-often gender-stratified tasks: occupational or creative and relational or procreative. To attain genuine generativity in today's world will require much greater concerted efforts to establish a state of justice, shared responsibility, and mutuality between women and men in the generative tasks of family life not just on a personal level but also on a broader social and perhaps global scale.

ERIKSON ON GENERATIVITY AND WOMEN

Erikson's legacy on questions of generativity is ambiguous. He both replicated the commonly accepted stereotypes of men and women of his era and significantly challenged them. Distinct from others who disagreed with Freud's interpretation of women's desire, pointing to the social rather than instinctual pressures on women, Erikson offered one of the most compelling challenges to psychoanalytic developmental theory, connecting development to social influences while still managing to remain within the fold. Never satisfied with Freud's claim that the potential for development was set in the first few stages of life or wholly determined by internal psychic forces, Erikson spent his years attempting to elaborate and fine-tune Freud's schema. He proposed that healthy, mature adults must successfully adjudicate the tensions of two focal developmental crises: first, the clash between intimacy and isolation, and then, the clash between generativity and stagnation. In two pivotal articles, "Womanhood and the Inner Space" (Erikson, 1968) and "Once More the Inner Space" (Erikson, 1974), written later on invitation from Jean Strouse as a critical response to the first essay, he defined how these developments play out more specifically in the "inner space" of women's bodies and psyches.

True to United States society in the 1950s, the crux of female identity for Erikson involves a woman giving up attachments to her own parental family and committing herself to a man and to the care of his children. Her well-being rests on her outward appearance, the success of her "search for the man . . . by whom she wishes to be sought" (Erikson, 1968, p. 310), and finally, the particular characteristics of her children. Motherhood stands at the center of a woman's identity in a way that fatherhood does not for men. A woman's generative identity depends on the private world of intimacy, children, and home, whereas a man's generative verification comes from "labor's challenge" and a "man's *love for his works and ideas*" (Erikson, 1964, pp. 131–132). A woman gives and receives through the labors of love and a man through the love of labor. A woman has few other loves, whereas a man has multiple generative avenues. As Plato argued long before Erikson, men give birth to products, whether works of art or ideas; women give birth to children (see McAdams, 2001).

As the debate over gender roles raged even as Erikson issued his thoughts, Strouse invited Erikson to make his own contribution to a collection, *Woman and Analysis: Dialogues on Psychoanalytic Views of Femininity*. The volume pairs major articles on women by Freud, Abraham, Horney, Jung, and so forth with evaluative responses by recent theorists, such as Juliet Mitchell and Robert Coles. Uniquely, Erikson was the only person in the volume who had the opportunity to assess his own initial views. In the second essay, Erikson defended himself as a man and as a Freudian, observing that "I couldn't possibly be anywhere else and . . . considering where I came from, I was doing all right being where I was" (Erikson, 1974, pp. 321–322). As he said in *Insight and Responsibility*, he wanted to include women in his theorizing: "When I speak of man," as he put it, "I emphatically include woman" (Erikson, 1964, p. 132).

Yet, true to his words, Erikson included women in a new way. He admitted men's strong envy of women's capacity to give birth, something Freud did not confess, even if Erikson's depiction of this maternal capacity is a bit romanticized. At some point, he noted, every boy and man is disquieted by women, who "produce what in all its newborn weakness, is and remains, after all, the most miraculous human creation in the universe: and it breaths!" (Erikson, 1974, p. 332). While this marvel at a woman's pursuit of the activities "consonant with the possession of ovaries, a uterus, and a vagina" (Erikson, 1968, p. 303) seemed to blind him to other sources of female identity, it also suggested fresh appreciation for women's distinctive contributions.

Where Freud ignored the pregnant body's potency, Erikson almost got carried away with it. But in getting carried away, Erikson at least moved beyond Freud and checked the distortions of Freud's reading. Where Freud saw a lack and a defect—penis envy—and damned the potential of women to develop fully, Erikson (1968) saw a gain and a capacity—the "existence of a productive inner-bodily space safely set in the center of female form and carriage" (p. 296). Although depicting female generativity in terms of an empty cavity at her center had obvious limitations, he at least attempted to correct for the failures of psychoanalytic theory to grapple adequately with female generativity.

Women have potential for a maturity that involves more than the passive, masochistic existence and "ubiquitous compensation neurosis" (Erikson, 1968, p. 306) of Freud's women or the complete rejection of motherhood of some early feminists. Although motherhood has sometimes enslaved women, the solution, Erikson (1974) believed, is not "to claim that there is no instinctual need for parenthood and that parenthood is *nothing but* social convention and coercion" (p. 336). Instead he gave the particular generative act of parenthood a certain preeminence. As Pamela Daniels observed on a personal note, when she applied for a teaching fellow position in Erikson's undergraduate course on the life cycle, "motherhood somehow enhanced" rather than detracted from her qualifications (Daniels, 1977, p. 61).

Although a variety of generative activities contribute to society, parenthood affords for many the first and the most fundamental experience. Without this or a comparable challenge, people fall prey to the "mental deformation of self-absorption" (Erikson, 1964, p. 130). Long before the term *ecology* acquired its current popularity, Erikson made clear that procreative generativity fosters distinctive ecological attitudes. An ecology built around the "fact that the human fetus must be carried inside the womb for a given number of months, and that the infant must be suckled or, at any rate, raised" (Erikson, 1974, p. 308) challenges the modern male ecology. In Erikson's (1968) opinion, the latter is aimed at conquering the outer spaces through escalating, materialistic acquisition and has brought the Western world to the brink of disaster. Society is endangered by its fascination with self-aggrandizing technological advancement. Although he exaggerated what the "mothers of the species" can do to correct this destructive downward spiral of modern productivity, he was not wrong to hope that the experience of parental generativity might bring a new kind of vision.

On the one hand, therefore, with a only a slight change of phrase from Freud, Erikson (1968) said a woman's fulfillment rests upon filling her "inner space" with the offspring of "chosen men." Yet, on the other hand, with this inner space comes "a biological, psychological, and ethical commitment to take care of human infancy" (p. 295). This commitment to care is not a duty placed on women alone but an essential and highly prized virtue for all human beings. Learning how to care, enacting care, and fostering care are human activities that ground life. All mature adults must acquire the virtue of care, the "widening concern for what has been generated by love, necessity, or accident," and overcome the ambivalence that naturally adheres to the work one has generated. The *strength of the generations*—one of his favorite phrases—depends on it. Generativity or the "concern for establishing and guiding the next generation" defines adult maturity for women *and* men (Erikson, 1950/1963, p. 267; Erikson, 1964, p. 131). In this final respect, Erikson *was* "doing all right being where [he] was."

RECONSTRUCTING GENERATIVITY: TOWARD A JUST DISTRIBUTION OF THE LABORS OF WORK AND LOVE

Although male-dominated interpretations of women's development have received criticism (Ehrenreich & English, 1978; Gilligan, 1982; Greenspan, 1983; Sturdivant, 1980; Weisstein, 1971), and recent scholars have offered a range of new readings of generativity (see McAdams, 2001), the impact of gender, sexism, and sexual politics on the development of generativity needs further serious exploration. Although the psychological concept of generativity is compelling, there are problems. There are problems in Erikson's original conceptualization, in its later psychological interpretations and enactment in contemporary society, and in the religious values that frame that enactment.

Erikson's Original Conceptualization

When Erikson (1950/1963) first defined the "eight stages of man," men and women in modern Western societies had quite distinct roles. Simply put, women bore almost sole responsibility for affective love (caring for relationships, children, and household), whereas men turned to instrumental work (bringing home the paycheck). Ideally, together these two well-defined roles of homemaker and breadwinner complemented one another, making the home a haven from the rest of the world. This assumptive world fostered two primary oversights in Erikson's theory.

First, Erikson (1950/1963) assumed in his eight stages that the virtue of care for what one has generated does not emerge fully until one reaches the second to last stage of adulthood. Most women, however, confront generative dilemmas long before mid-to-late adulthood and long before questions of identity and intimacy are resolved. They are at least faced physiologically with early biological generative premonitions during the onset of menses in puberty, and then are regularly reminded of the potential for motherhood throughout the very earliest phases of adulthood. One recent study of college-educated women of the 1960s, in fact, discovered that by midlife (40s), generativity desires declined perhaps because women had already accomplished some of their generative hopes (Stewart & Vandewater, 1993). But more importantly, society still places primary responsibility for conception and contraception on women's shoulders. Young women, more than men, regularly ask themselves questions about the timing of motherhood and the rhythms of paid employment. They manage what Daniels (1985) described as the "logistical and chronological intricacies" of a "double generativity" (p. 435).

Second, even if it were true that authentic generativity must await late adulthood, Erikson also failed to account for just how such a capacity to produce, care, and nurture can emerge out of a series of stages that prioritize instead the values of self-assertion and independence. It is not entirely clear how generativity develops out of a childhood centered on autonomy and will, initiative and purpose, and industry and competence. In the last stage, for instance, the child, or actually the boy, focuses on individual "industry" or "work roles" in "line with the *ethos of production*" (Erikson, 1982, p. 75), learning to master the technical tools of the trade. Here and in the other childhood stages, Erikson explored the antecedents and consequences of autonomy and identity, but he neglected the genesis and import of relational intimacy and attachment. As Harvard professor Carol Gilligan (1982, p. 12) observed, if "only the initial stage of trust versus mistrust suggests the type of mutuality that Erikson means by intimacy and generativity," how can intimacy or generativity suddenly appear in adulthood? All the stages between the initial stage and the adult stages promote separateness and have individuation, not connection and relationship, as their ultimate goal (Franz & White, 1985).

The first problem has received attention in recent empirical and longitudinal studies. Researchers, such as Dan McAdams (2001), have called for greater differentiation in the types and life-cycle course of generativity (see also Stewart & Vandewater, 1993). John Kotre (1975, 1984) distinguished four types of generativity that emerge progressively during different adult phases with different emphasis: biological, parental, technical, and cultural. John Snarey (1993) modified these to the three categories of biological, parental, and societal that best capture the various ways that fathers gradually participate in generative activities. In general, then, the empirical status of generativity as a distinctive midlife stage is under review. Theorists call for more investigation into its usefulness as a developmental construct. However, here, and with the second conceptual oversight of development antecedents to generativity, insufficient research has been directed toward the gender politics that shape the actual enactment of generativity. Many psychologists, such as Daniel Stern (1985), Carol Gilligan (1982), and Jean Baker Miller (1976), have argued for the importance of more research on the developmental dynamics of attachment and affiliation. But few have extended this research to the ways in which cultural norms and biases about gender influence the actualization of generativity in the lives of women and men.

Generativity's Psychological Enactment and Interpretation

Erikson used the term generativity broadly as a metaphor for an adulthood centered on relationships and not simply as another term for career advancement. Generativity includes productivity and creativity. These popular synonyms, he insisted, cannot and should not replace it (Erikson, 1950/1963, 1964, 1964/1968). But, in fact, they often do.

Studies of the enactment of generativity in the lives of men are quite revealing. According to developmental psychologist Daniel J. Levinson and his colleagues in *Seasons of a Man's Life* (1978), the typical pattern for "normal" men involves "becoming one's own man" or climbing the ladder of success in the hierarchical public world of labor. Begun in 1967 and published 11 years later, Levinson's empirical survey of male development through interviews with 40 men ages 17 to 47 illustrates that many men display a steady drive for vocational productivity with care of relationships, children, and domicile almost an afterthought.

Levinson's (1978) study captured an essential feature of the patterns of male development during this time period: In U.S. society, as early as age 17, the products of a man's work are *the* foremost "vehicle for the fulfillment or negation of central aspects of the self" (p. 9). These adult men have few intimate relationships. When they choose to pursue them, they are often by-products of development and sometimes an instrumental means to another end but seldom the goal. They help support "the Dream" but are not essential to its fulfillment. The wife, "special (loved and loving) woman," is the "true mentor" principally because she furthers her husband's advancement:

> Her special quality lies in her connection to the young man's Dream. She helps to animate the part of the self that contains the Dream. She facilitates his entry into the adult world and his pursuit of the Dream . . . . shares it, believes in him as its hero, gives it her blessing, joins him . . . and creates a "boundary space" within which his aspirations can be imagined and his hopes nourished. (Levinson, 1978, p. 109)

That a man might learn to give comparable support for a woman's dreams is socially less acceptable. Or, at least it does not appear an essential aspect of development in the lives of the men studied. Writing about the same time as Levinson's study, psychologist Jean Baker Miller (1976) observed that women strive to foster such space and base their self-image around the question, "Am I giving enough?" Men ask instead "Am I a doer?" Giving becomes an "added luxury" after a man has paid his dues in productivity (Miller, 1976, p. 49). Generativity in its fuller sense does not truly determine action until much later in the lives Levinson studied, often after a "midlife crisis" awakens a sense of the importance of previously neglected relationships.

Other researchers, such as developmental psychologist Douglas C. Kimmel, author of the textbook *Adulthood and Aging* (1974), and George Vaillant in *Adaptation to Life* (1977), join Levinson as examples of the increasing constriction of Erikson's term as a normative ideal for care of others and community. Kimmel (1974, pp. 189–190) defined generativity as a "sense of productive accomplishment" sought in work or as a parent "so that there will be something one has done that will outlive oneself." But is a child simply "something one has done"? Odder still, Kimmel did not even mention generativity in his chapter on "Families and Singles." He actually placed rearing children and managing a home in parentheses when listing factors, such as success and satisfaction in one's job, that help resolve the crisis of generativity. Raising children, ordering the home, preserving family traditions, and securing friendships and community are parenthetically reserved for women. For Vaillant (1977), men postpone truly generative concerns until their 50s, focusing until then on the achievements and rewards of a midlife stage he called *career consolidation*. According to Vaillant, many of these men never move beyond this stage to a richer generativity.

These studies demonstrate a progressive restriction of the ideal of generativity and a related failure to attend to gender disparities. Generativity, including the generation of offspring, is increasingly focused on the generation of products while the complicated details of caring for children regularly drop out of the picture. Driven in part by the mechanisms of a market economy, male-dominated psychological and moral theory as well as male-run institutions often think about generativity largely in terms of *producing*. Adulthood means generativity, but now defined largely in a technical, product-oriented sense. Societies can rearrange gender roles all they want. But until the perception of generativity as material productivity most evident in Levinson's study but also noted in other studies (Dittes, 1985; Ehrenreich, 1983; Halper, 1989; Roberts & Newton, 1987; Vaillant, 1977) is challenged, productivity will thrive at the expense of generativity within communities, relationships, and families.

In a helpful effort to rescue from obscurity the findings of four unpublished dissertations that extend Levinson's theory to women's development, Roberts and Newton (1987) observed that men and women share similar developmental phases and transitions but noted that women have more difficulties defining and enacting vocational dreams. Unlike men, family and career goals often stood in conflict or in mutually exclusive relationship with one another for women. The complex nature of women's often more relational dreams, oriented around husbands, children, and colleagues rather than purely occupational goals, led to a greater sense of instability, tentativeness, and dissatisfaction. In fact, in contrast to Levinson's sequence of alternating periods of transition and stability, women remained highly unsettled in early adulthood (from age 22 to 28) and again in the "settling down" years (from age 33 to 40). Occupational formation extended well into middle age, giving women a "10- to 20-year disadvantage" compared with men (Roberts & Newton, 1987, p. 159). The majority of women in all four studies saw themselves as supporters of their husbands' dreams and not the other way around. Indeed, most notably, it was husbands who appeared to be the "greatest obstacle to the realization of the individualistic components of their wives' dreams" (pp. 158–159), with many husbands actively thwarting such interests.

In *Women of Academe*, Aisenberg and Harrington (1988) illustrated well the importance of recognizing generativity's gender complexity. Although their observations are based on interviews with 64 tenured and displaced academic women, their generalizations about vocational and generative turmoil extend beyond their immediate participants. The perception of sweeping changes in gender relations in the last few decades is greater than the reality. In the lives of their participants, two basic life plans persist: (a) the "marriage plot" that defines a woman's primary sphere as private and domestic; and (b) the "quest" or "adventure plot" that reserves an assertive public life for men only (Aisenberg & Harrington, 1988, p. 6).

When Levinson himself undertook a second study of women's life "seasons" in the late 1970s, published posthumously in 1996, he also divided his population into two groups: the "homemaker sample" and the "career women sample." Even though we may be, as Levinson (1996) said, in "the early stages of a vast historical transition" (p. 7), a more forceful "gender splitting" or oppositional relationship divides the generative worlds of women and men. People who deviate from these gender-differentiated plots know the stigma. Although marriage, home, and children may no longer be a viable profession for women, old social scripts of these jobs as women's work linger. Levinson's study, just like Aisenberg and Harrington's (1988), reveals the hardship, anguish, obstacles, and stressful and traumatic experiences for those who try to rewrite this script.

In Aisenberg and Harrington's (1988) findings, many women who pursued a job or higher education had a double agenda before they took their first job. They faced not one, but two significant hurdles. Adulthood involved the developmental task of determining the place of work in their life and learning the trade or acquiring the credentials, degrees, recommendations, and other proofs of accomplishment. But most women had an additional hurdle: They not only entered upon the external process of vocational change from lay to trained person but also entered upon an internal process of transformation of their core identity from private to public worker.

For some women, this entailed a "great internal drama" in which they had to reenvision themselves radically and who they have understood themselves to be (Aisenberg & Harrington, 1988, p. 26). They had to break repeatedly the restricting chains of all the old "can'ts" and "don'ts" of bygone norms. Some of the character virtues of the marriage plot—patience, receptivity, accommodation, unselfishness, modesty, passivity—had to be challenged and transformed, and previously forbidden virtues of assertiveness, initiative, competence, public visibility, and leadership had to be assumed. Women had to learn to use educational knowledge as a tool for personal advancement and power. In contrast to the more formulaic career patterns of many men, women often "veered and tacked" (p. 23) from project to project in the attempt to create new norms. They appeared indecisive and hesitant. In Daniels's (1985) research on generative development, women experience a sort of generative "drift" as they struggle to find a way to interweave family and work in their life Dream, whereas the "Dream" for men is often pursued single-mindedly and remains almost indistinguishable from occupational goals.

Even when some generative resolution was reached by women in Aisenberg and Harrington's (1988) study, events like marriage and childbirth often reignited the internal drama and resurfaced formerly resolved issues. The number of women who successfully integrated their home and work lives well was "minuscule" (p. 133). Unforeseen generative troubles such as a divorce, a sick child, a husband's move, an elderly parent, or less serious problems became major roadblocks.

Although Aisenberg and Harrington (1988) focused on only one particular "great internal drama" for particular women, the concept could be generalized. Many people now face some kind of similar double agenda that requires acquiring not only the necessary job skills but also some kind of self-transformation. Serious vocational and developmental challenges of identity, intimacy, and generativity bombard many adults as they make more mundane decisions about who will work what hours and who will watch the kids.

Ruth Sidel (1990) offered some empirical confirmation of this claim. Few issues are of graver concern, she discovered in 150 interviews with young women across the country of diverse class, race, ethnic, and educational backgrounds, than the "question of how to combine work and child rearing" (p. 193). Despite progress in role change, there is still a scarcity of models and resources for combining work and family.

In the last decade, all of these problems—the earlier onset of generative crises, the logistical nightmares of arbitrating between generative options, and the paucity of role models—are problems now shared by many men. In the United States, many people, women and men alike, struggle to attain an integrated work and home life. Many blame themselves. But the real locus of the generative crises lies in inhospitable work environments, unjust distribution of domestic labor, absence of a national family policy, and ideologies about work and love related to all three. Most important for this chapter, the energy the drama consumes is "particularly great where conservative religious values prevail" (Aisenberg & Harrington, 1988, pp. 27) because they tend to reinforce the conventional plots.

Ethical and Religious Values and Generativity

Although many 19th- and 20th-century working-class people and educated women did not comply with the breadwinner–homemaker arrangement, it still pervaded modern consciousness as a standard by which people judged themselves. Popular media depicted what happy homes looked like. Religious doctrine in Catholic, Protestant, and Jewish circles endorsed gender complementarity as both a natural fact of creation and a biblical mandate. And early developmental theory, going back to Freud, gave these premises about proper gender roles the stamp of scientific approval (Freud, 1931/

1963a, 1925/1963b; Weisstein, 1971). With such powerful cultural and religious support, these ideas held amazing sway over the hopes and dreams of daily life. In some ways, they still do.

Psychological "facts" about women's less-developed moral nature in Freud and others simply took up where classical theological and philosophical doctrines about women's inferiority had left off, but with the added claim that they represented objective, scientific truth (Ruether, 1975). They were not just ideas based on faith; they were empirical, verifiable science. More troubling, they displaced Jewish and Christian values that espoused the created worth of every human being "in God's image" regardless of differences and instead claimed a "value neutrality" that feigned avoidance of normative considerations. Psychology, however, not only described what is but also often shaped "what should be" for women and men (Ricoeur, 1970; Rieff, 1959, 1966), prescribing through both therapy and scholarship optimal adult development (Greenspan, 1983; Sturdivant, 1980).

When Erikson (1964) said that psychology often functions as a positive ethical science, however, he departed from orthodox psychoanalysis. The moral role of psychology definitely influenced his ideas about generativity. On occasion he discussed generativity using the term *mutuality* or as a modern version of the Golden Rule: "Truly worthwhile acts enhance a mutuality between the doer and the other—a mutuality which strengthens the doer even as it strengthens the other" (Erikson, 1964, pp. 231–233).

It took a scholar in religion, however, to point out the implicit moral and religious assumptions at the core of Erikson's psychology. In *Generative Man*, practical theologian Don Browning (1975) claimed that Erikson's moral and quasi-religious hopes about the care of generations shaped his psychological construction of the life cycle through and through. Generativity is not just a phase of adult growth. It is an encompassing orientation to life. When Erikson first articulated his idea of generativity and stagnation in the 1950s, he happened upon a psychological concept that has wider normative implications than he himself may have realized. Moreover, as a moral assumption, generativity and its promotion of the "culture of care" are more adequate than the normative assumptions behind some Freudian, humanistic, and behavioral approaches and their respective cultures of detachment, joy, and control (Browning, 1987). Generativity is particularly well suited to the challenges of modernity.

Browning (2000) amplified his claim in a more recent paper. Although Erikson did not attempt to establish the ethical relevance and adequacy of his concept of generativity, Browning saw within it elements of three major ethical philosophies: an ethics of principle or universalizable rules, an ethics of virtue or character formation, and a narrative ethic. Measured against these standards, generativity is an especially complex and powerful construct, even if it is thereby more susceptible to distortion and misunderstanding. Although generativity numbers among one of many instinctual needs that motivate human action, it also depends heavily on the symbolic elaboration it receives through culture and the formative processes of specific communities.

Others in psychology and theology have seen generativity's ethical potential and social importance. Snarey (1993), in fact, used it as a key unifying perspective by which to assess men's care in families. His longitudinal study of the immense benefits of generative fathering confirms the richness of Erikson's idea. Parenting is, Snarey believed, an incredibly important moral enterprise. He advocated for institutional and ideological changes that would encourage a greater paternal investment in child rearing and an increased value for doing so. Not only is good fathering satisfying and demanding, but it is also a "royal road" (p. 310) to an even more significant adulthood milestone of social generativity that affects the "future of *all* children" (p. 23). Inversely, societal generativity is more difficult without the experience of parenting. Snarey identified this as "the most important finding" of his study (p. 353). A study by McAdams and Ed de St. Aubin (1992) confirmed that "men who were not fathers . . . showed especially low scores in generativity" (p. 418).

However, just how well suited to contemporary challenges is a moral and religious ideal of generativity primarily oriented to "generative man"? Although Browning underscored generativity's ethical dimensions, he failed to consider the powerful dynamics of gender, religion, and generativity. Snarey had the benefit of more recent gender analysis but still chose to emphasize the gender-inclusive nature of generativity and quickly bypassed the problematic social and political issues that color its enactment. McAdams proposed that the most adequate expression of generativity combines relational nurture and creative self-assertion or, referring to Kotre's distinction, communal and agentic modes or styles. Less attention is paid by both Kotre and McAdams, however, to the ways in which these different styles are socially stratified along still fairly rigid gender categories. McAdams (2001) insightfully characterized an intriguing dynamic of generativity—its "curious blend of narcissism and altruism aimed toward future generations" (p. 405). But he did not address the generative problems that arise when men are conventionally encouraged toward the first and women toward the second of each paired component—power and love, agency and communion, self-expansion and self-surrender, public and private expressions. Under current social conditions, this "motivational paradox" of generativity collapses into a sometimes divisive gender dualism.

In the last four decades, other scholars in religion have addressed these issues. They have argued that cultural demands and religious belief have powerfully shaped predominant modes of generativity in destructive ways. Central to the critique of religious sexism is the refutation of religious sanction of unjust domestic relations, male headship, subordination of women in the home, and religiously justified domestic violence and abuse. This critique has important implications for reinterpreting adulthood development and generativity.

My book, *Also a Mother: Work and Family as Theological Dilemma* (Miller-McLemore, 1994), could easily have been titled "Crises of Generativity." Its exploration of contemporary conflicts of work and family actually began with a vaguely dissatisfied appreciation for Erikson's concept. Although this term is less familiar to those outside the academy, I found generativity the only term that captures in a single word the pursuit of good work and good love particular to the life-cycle stage of adulthood. Generativity is the challenge of finding meaningful avenues of productivity, creativity, and procreativity. But as a word it means more than any one of these terms alone. Like Erikson, I used the term to underscore the integral connections between love and work. Going beyond Erikson, I stressed the essential interconnection in adult work and love between families, economics, and religion—the "politics of generativity" (see Bellah et al., 1991).

My initial disenchantment with life-cycle models turned into a more personal outcry "once I found myself inhabiting a pregnant body" (Miller-McLemore, 1994, p. 21). As the mother of three young children and as a middle-class, European American, Protestant professor and theologian, I encountered firsthand the fundamental opposition in my own young adult life between the generative demands of my children and the demands of my job. The project took on a new "life of its own" motivated by anger at the silence about the daily conflicts and the amazing devaluation of children and their care. Upon considering adult development from the perspective of religious and feminist studies, I lament a society in which the value of material productivity overrides almost every other value, especially the value of care of others. And I argue for shared responsibility, mutuality, and justice between women and men in domestic work. In particular, I call Christianity to account for its uncritical endorsement of women as primarily responsible for domestic care, its lingering support of male headship, and its general inattention to current family crises. Theologians must debunk some old and powerful myths, especially the ideal of the self-sacrificial mother, and begin to offer better values and virtues for families today.

With the words, "I am a student of theology; I am also a woman," the first sentence of Valerie Saiving's pivotal 1960 article, "The Human Situation: A Feminine View," begins an important period of revision and revolution in theology. Although she wrote under the guise of the third-person singular, her own maternal experience furnished the ground for a revelatory breakthrough in Christian theological definitions of sin and love. In an interview more than two decades later she admitted, "I wrote out of my own experience—my experience at the time I wrote and before" as a divorced mother of a 3-year-old child (Saiving, 1988, p. 100).

Saiving (1960) started her exploration of the human situation with the "central fact about sexual differences": "In every society it is women—and only women—who bear children" and who remain "closest to the infant and young child" because of "the physiology of lactation" (p. 103). She used anthropology, sociology, and psychology to explore the many meanings and implications of this statement. The power of female biological creativity challenges male creativity at this most immediate, fundamental level. That is, a man's "inability to bear children" becomes "a deficiency for which he must compensate" (p. 105). Men must strive to achieve what women already have, a direct role in creation and the existential confirmation of childbearing.

Hence the modern monuments erected to celebrate male achievements and the male temptation for pride and self-promotion. It is this proclivity toward self-centeredness that male theologians have decried, holding up in its place a sacrosanct selfless love. And it is precisely this traditional Christian view of human sin as "pride" and its inverse view of love as self-sacrifice that Saiving contested.

Mothers, Saiving (1960) argued, face a different kind of temptation. They often find their relationship with a child an "irreplaceable school" (p. 108) for the illusive virtues of care and even an avenue for religious experience. However, because hearing a child demands temporarily abandoning one's point of view, mothers are more often tempted to self-loss than self-promotion. In putting aside one's own needs to care for others, women and mothers are drawn to "triviality, distractibility, and diffuseness; lack of organizing center or focus; dependence on others for one's own self-definition . . . in short, underdevelopment or negation of her self" (p. 108).

This different temptation—to lose a sense of one's desires rather than to lord one's desires over others—requires a recasting of Christian love and human development (Miller-McLemore, 1994; see also Miller-McLemore, 1989, 1991). Rather than love as complete self-giving without any thought for oneself, generativity or the care for what or whom one has produced must incorporate self-love and self-assertion. Moments of self-giving and care must be balanced, in Saiving's (1960) words, "by moments, hours, and days of withdrawal into, and enrichment of, her individual selfhood" (p. 108).

A few decades later, theological ethicist Christine Gudorf furthered the task of recasting religious ideals related to generativity. She stood alone in 1985 in attempting to understand the nature of Christian love and justice in the midst of the unfolding developments of parenting. She was among the first Christian ethicists to discuss love as mutuality from a developmental point of view. While rearing one biological child and two adopted medically handicapped children, she found common Christian views of love and childrearing inadequate. In particular, she did not buy a common perception of her mothering as a huge self-sacrifice and instead argued against self-sacrifice as the primary model of Christian agape. She suggested instead the give-and-take of mutuality as the ultimate Christian ideal. Her love for her children was never completely selfless, disinterested, and detached from self-affirmation and self-love. Her parenting efforts "rebounded to our credit";

"failure to provide for them would have discredited us." Even more power-fully, from the beginning her children "gave to us," not only of themselves but also by making the parents new and different people (Gudorf, 1985, pp. 177–178, 181).

Care, particularly the love between parent and child, involves ample self-giving certainly, but self-giving must never become the ideal. As Gudorf (1985) discovered, "all love both involves sacrifice and aims at mutuality" (p. 182). Moments of self-diminishment, even the moment of sacrifice of the crucifixion of Jesus, are "just that—moments in a process designed to end in mutual love" (p. 186). Theological ethicist Barbara Andolsen (1981, p. 80) provided helpful criteria to ascertain when sacrifice in actions of generativity is "legitimate." There are three occasions in which sacrifice has a place: when practiced by the privileged on behalf of the oppressed, when a party in greater need has a prima facie claim on others, and when occasions of sacrifice can be balanced out over the long run.

These reflections suggest that the ethical, religious, and gender dynam-ics of generativity are far more complicated than the theories of men and nonmothers have understood thus far. The social and cultural implications are wide-ranging. When generativity is used as a psychological construct to analyze individual development, religious definitions of and gender differ-ences in generativity require greater attention. If generativity is a psycho-logical construct that often functions as a moral and religious norm, then greater understanding of the cultural influence of religion and psychology is needed. If the social tasks of generativity are still divided unjustly among women and men, then greater understanding of social gender biases are needed. If social, political, and economic structures still impede a more bal-anced enactment of both occupational and relational facets of generativity for women and men, then greater social and political efforts must be made to change structures that are destructive to healthy generativity.

In thinking about the generative society, this chapter has focused pri-marily on culture—on prominent cultural ideas that influence generativity and, in the final section, on some of the religious ideas in culture that shape adult generativity most powerfully. At the most wide-reaching cultural level, religious ideas about women and men play a more crucial cultural role in shaping hopes about adult development than most social scientists have sus-pected. Although other social critics suggest a range of concrete social changes to address current generative crises, from day care to job-sharing, I contend that broad cultural changes at the level of ideology and discourse are equally important and needed.

Bringing questions of religion and gender to bear on cultural construc-tions of generativity raises critical concerns today. Erikson (1964) himself called for a "generative responsibility toward all human beings" (pp. 131–132) that guarantees to each child a chance for full development (see also Erikson, 1982, p. 68). Yet how accountable are women and men to the children they procreate together? Women still bear an inordinate degree of responsibility and cost for "maintaining and regenerating" the cycle of generations. Religious and political norms still grant men the power to produce and entitlement to products, often excluding them from giving care and relegating the demands of caring for what or whom is produced to women. U.S. social and economic structures, from factories to offices to school systems, as well as public family policy still assume that workers have stay-at-home mothers and live-in housekeepers.

In addition, the psychological use of the concept of generativity that does not consider or question the powerful quasi-religious materialistic definitions of success and the market-dominated ideologies behind them is problematic. We have to wonder about a society in which those who do make it to the "topmost ranks" have little to do with children out of the sheer necessity of their "success." Ultimately, what are the prospects for generativity when placed in a global, market economy? What happens to the capacity to care in such a context? Genuine adherence to generativity requires rectifying the huge disparities in justice, wealth, and the use of the earth's limited resources. And it will require significant attention to the radical differences in reigning cultural definitions of generativity, religion, and gender around the world.

All told, this is no small mission. Credit for setting us off on this rather massive agenda, however, belongs at least in part to Erikson himself. Although he readily perceived the heart of America's "identity crisis," and even saw the problems caused by "generative frustration," he did not anticipate the extent of our current generative crises.

REFERENCES

Ahlburg, D. A., & De Vita, C. J. (1997). New realities of the American family. In A. S. Skolnick & J. H. Skolnick (Eds.), *Family in transition* (9th ed., pp. 21–29). New York: Addison-Wesley.

Aisenberg, N., & Harrington, M. (1988). *Women of academe: Outsiders in the sacred grove*. Amherst: University of Massachusetts Press.

Anderson, H. (1997). Between rhetoric and reality: Women and men as equal partners in home, church and the marketplace. *Word and World: Theology for Christian Ministry, 17,* 376–386.

Andolsen, B. H. (1981). Agape in feminist ethics. *Journal of Religious Ethics, 9*(1), 69–83.

Bellah, R. N., Madsen, R., Sullivan, W. M., Swidler, A., & Tipton, S. M. (1991). *The good society.* New York: Vintage.

Browning, D. S. (1975). *Generative man: Psychoanalytic perspectives.* New York: Delta.

Browning, D. S. (1987). *Religious thought and the modern psychologies.* Philadelphia: Fortress.

Browning, D. S. (2000). *An ethical analysis of Erikson's concept of generativity.* Unpublished manuscript.

Daniels, P. (1977). Birth of the amateur. In S. Ruddick & P. Daniels (Eds.), *Working it out: 23 women writers, artists, scientists, and scholars talk about their lives and work.* New York: Pantheon Books.

Daniels, P. (1985). Dream vs. drift in women's careers: The question of generativity. In J. H. Williams (Ed.), *Psychology of women: Selected readings* (2nd ed., pp. 425–436). New York: Norton.

Dittes, J. E. (1985). *The male predicament: On being a man today.* San Francisco: Harper & Row.

Dunfee, S. N. (1989). *Beyond servanthood: Christianity and the liberation of women.* Lanham, MD: University Press of America.

Ehrenreich, B. (1983). *The hearts of men : American dreams and the flight from commitment.* Garden City, NY: Anchor Press/Doubleday.

Ehrenreich, B., & English, D. (1978). *For her own good: 150 years of the experts' advice to women.* New York: Doubleday.

Erikson, E. H. (1963). *Childhood and society* (35th anniversary ed.). New York: Norton. (Original work published 1950)

Erikson, E. H. (1964). *Insight and responsibility: Lectures on the ethical implications of psychoanalytic insight.* New York: Norton.

Erikson, E. H. (1968). Womanhood and the inner space. In J. Strouse (Ed.), *Woman and analysis: Dialogues on psychoanalytic views of femininity* (pp. 291–319). Boston: G. K. Hall. (Original work published 1964 as "Inner and outer space: Reflections on womanhood," *Daedalus, 93,* 582–606)

Erikson, E. H. (1974). Once more the inner space: Letter to a former student. In J. Strouse (Ed.), *Woman and analysis: Dialogues on psychoanalytic views of femininity* (pp. 320–340). Boston: G. K. Hall.

Erikson, E. H. (1982). *The life cycle completed: A review.* New York: Norton.

Franz, C. E., & White, K. (1985). Individuation and attachment in personality development: Extending Erikson's theory. In A. Stewart & B. Lykes (Eds.), *Gender and personality: Current perspectives on theory and research* (pp. 137–68). Durham, NC: Duke University Press.

Freud, S. (1963a). Female sexuality. In P. Rieff (Ed.), *Sexuality and the psychology of love* (pp. 194–211). New York: Collier Books. (Original work published 1931)

Freud, S. (1963b). Some psychological consequences of the anatomical distinction between sexes. In P. Rieff (Ed.), *Sexuality and the psychology of love* (pp. 183–193). New York: Collier Books. (Original work published 1925)

Gill-Austern, B. L. (1996). Love understood as self-sacrifice and self-denial: What does it do to women? In J. S. Moessner (Ed.), *Through the eyes of women: Insights for pastoral care* (pp. 304–321). Philadelphia: Westminster John Knox.

Gilligan, C. (1982). *In a different voice: Psychological theory and women's development* Cambridge, MA: Harvard University Press.

Greenspan, M. (1983). *A new approach to women and therapy*. New York: McGraw-Hill.

Gudorf, C. E. (1985). Parenting, mutual love and sacrifice. In B. H. Andolsen, C. E. Gudorf, & M. D. Pellauer (Eds.), *Women's consciousness, women's conscience: A reader in feminist ethics* (pp. 175–191). San Francisco: Harper & Row.

Gudorf, C. E. (1996). Sacrificial and parental spiritualities. In A. Carr & M. S. Van Leeuwen (Eds.), *Religion, feminism, and the family* (pp. 294–309). Louisville, KY: Westminster John Knox.

Halper, J. (1989). *Quiet desperation: The truth about successful men*. New York: Warner Books.

Jordan, J. V., Kaplan, A. G., Miller, J. B., Stiver, I. P., & Surrey, J. L. (1991). *Women's growth in connection: Writings from the Stone Center*. New York: Guilford.

Kimmel, D. C. (1974). *Adulthood and aging: An interdisciplinary developmental view*. New York: Wiley.

Kotre, J. (1975, December 20). Generative humanity. *America*, pp. 434–437.

Kotre, J. (1984). *Outliving the self: Generativity and the interpretation of lives*. Baltimore: Johns Hopkins University Press.

Lesthaeghe, R. (1983). A century of demographic and cultural change in western Europe: An exploration of underlying dimensions. *Population and Development Review, 9*, 411–435.

Levinson, J. D., with Darrow, C. N., Klein, E. B., Levinson, M. H., & McKee, B. (1978). *Seasons of a man's life*. New York: Ballantine.

Levinson, D. J., with Levinson, J. D. (1996). *The season's of a woman's life*. New York: Alfred A. Knopf.

Mahony, R. (1995). *Kidding ourselves: Breadwinning, babies, and bargaining power*. New York: Basic Books.

McAdams, D. P. (2001). Generativity in midlife. In M. E. Lachman (Ed.), *Handbook of midlife* (pp. 395–443). New York: Wiley.

McAdams, D. P., & de St. Aubin, E. (1992). A theory of generativity and its assessment through self-report, behavioral acts, and narrative themes in autobiography. *Journal of Personality and Social Psychology, 62*, 1003–1015.

Miller, J. B. (1976). *Toward a new psychology of women*. Boston: Beacon.

Miller-McLemore, B. J. (1989). Produce or perish: A feminist critique of generativity. *Union Seminary Quarterly Review, 43*(1–4), 201–221.

Miller-McLemore, B. J. (1991). Produce or perish: Generativity and the question of new reproductive technologies. *Journal of the American Academy of Religion, LIX*(1), 39–69.

Miller-McLemore, B. J. (1994). *Also a mother: Work and family as theological dilemma*. Nashville, TN: Abingdon.

Miller-McLemore, B. J. (2000). Research survey: Feminist studies in psychology: Implications for practical theology. *International Journal of Practical Theology, 4*, 107–131.

Okin, S. M. (1989). *Justice, gender, and the family.* New York: Basic Books.

Ricoeur, P. (1970). *Freud and philosophy: An essay on interpretation* (D. Savage, Trans.). New Haven, CT: Yale University Press.

Rieff, P. (1959). *Freud: The mind of the moralist.* New York: Viking.

Rieff, P. (1966). *The triumph of the therapeutic: Uses of faith after Freud.* New York: Harper & Row.

Roberts, P., & Newton, P. M. (1987). Levinsonian studies of women's adult development. *Psychology and Aging, 2,* 154–163.

Ruether, R. R. (1975). *New heaven, new earth: Sexist ideologies and human liberation.* New York: Seabury.

Ruether, R. R. (1983). *Sexism and God-talk: Toward a feminist theology.* Boston: Beacon.

Saiving, V. (1960). The human situation: A feminine view. *Journal of Religion, XL,* 100–112.

Saiving, V. (1988). A conversation with Valerie Saiving. *Journal of Feminist Studies, 4,* 99–115.

Sidel, R. (1990). *On her own: Growing up in the shadow of the American dream.* New York: Viking.

Smith, T. (2001). *The emerging twenty-first-century American family* (Report from the National Opinion Research Center). Retrieved from http://www.norc.uchicago.edu

Snarey, J. (1993). *How fathers care for the next generation: A four-decade study.* Cambridge, MA: Harvard University Press.

Stern, D. (1985). *The interpersonal world of the infant: A view from psychoanalysis and developmental psychology.* New York: Basic Books.

Stewart, A. J., & Ostrove, J. M. (1998). Women's personality in middle age: Gender, history, and mid-course corrections. *American Psychologist, 53,* 1185–1194.

Stewart, A. J., & Vandewater, E.A. (1993). The Radcliffe class of 1964: Career and family social clock projects in a transitional cohort. In K. D. Hulbert & D. T. Schuster (Eds.), *Women's lives through time* (pp. 235–258). San Francisco: Jossey-Bass.

Sturdivant, S. (1980). *Therapy with women: A feminist philosophy of treatment.* New York: Springer.

Vaillant, G. (1977). *Adaptation to life.* Boston: Little, Brown.

Weisstein, N. (1971). Psychology constructs the female. In V. Gornick & B. K. Moran (Eds.), *Woman in sexist society: Studies in power and powerlessness* (pp. 133–146). New York: Basic Books.

12

GUARDING THE NEXT GENERATION: THE POLITICS OF GENERATIVITY

BILL E. PETERSON

Generativity can be defined broadly as a psychological concern with making a lasting contribution to the future, especially future generations. At this point in time, the term *generativity* is rarely used outside of academic circles; however, the prosocial ideas surrounding Erik Erikson's construct have been incorporated by political leaders into their rhetoric. For example, it is not hard to find generative imagery in the inaugural addresses of the last two U.S. Presidents. President William Jefferson Clinton spoke the following words in 1993:

> Our founders saw themselves in the light of posterity. We can do no less. Anyone who has ever watched a child's eyes wander into sleep knows what posterity is. Posterity is the world to come. The world for whom we hold our ideals, from whom we have borrowed our planet and to whom we bear sacred responsibility. We must do what America does best: offer more opportunity to all and demand more responsibility from all.

The writing of this chapter was supported in part by a faculty fellowship from the Louise B. and Edmund J. Kahn Liberal Arts Institute at Smith College.

I would like to thank Lauren E. Duncan, Kathleen McCartney, Abigail J. Stewart, and Jill de Villiers for thoughtful discussions about this chapter. Thanks also to Peter B. Pufall, who organized the 1998–1999 Kahn Institute on the Ecologies of Childhood, during which some of the ideas expressed in this chapter were first discussed. As always, I bear ultimate responsibility for the content of this chapter.

In 2001, President George W. Bush said,

> We have a place, all of us, in a long story—a story we continue, but whose end we will not see. It is the story of a new world that became a friend and liberator of the old, a story of a slave-holding society that became a servant of freedom, the story of a power that went into the world to protect but not possess, to defend but not to conquer.

Both passages are filled with images of generativity, focusing as they do on generational links, ethical responsibilities, and caregiving. Although these optimistic visions are appropriate for inaugural speeches, they do not inform us about specific policy or political agendas; the words are political rhetoric not meant to invoke discussion or debate. Generative images can be used safely by politicians to express ideas that few would disagree with. However, the relationship between generativity and politics is more complicated than these quotations suggest. In this chapter I discuss this in two ways. First, I use historical examples to demonstrate the complex relations between generativity and politics. Second, I suggest that a truly generative political agenda might focus on children and their needs.

GENERATIVITY AND POLITICAL EXPRESSION

In his theoretical model of human development, Erikson (1950) argued that the counterpart to generativity was a personal feeling of stagnation. In later theorizing, Erikson (1980) added self-absorption as the "dystonic"—or negative—end of generativity. Later still, Erikson (1982) discussed how generative goals can become authoritarian in character and actions; in other words, poor expressions of generative impulses can lead to "the rejectivity of generations," which

> express[es] itself in intrafamily and communal life as a more or less well-rationalized and more or less ruthless suppression of what does not seem to fit some set goals of survival and perfection. This can mean physical or moral cruelty towards one's children, and it can turn, as moralistic prejudice, against other segments of family or community. And, of course, it can lump together as "the other side" large groups of foreign peoples. (p. 69)

As suggested by Kotre (1995), sometimes rejectivity is expressed alongside generativity: "[Erikson's] biographies of Luther and Gandhi reveal how one can turn a deaf ear to followers and offspring, be horrified by them, vilify them, disown them, abandon them" (p. 37). Furthermore, Erikson argued that rejectivity can manifest at a collective level as a war between nations. As discussed by Peterson, Smirles, and Wentworth (1997), the example of Germany during World War II can be used to illustrate Erikson's point. Hitler and the Nazi Party intended the Third Reich to last for generations of Germans; the aftermath of the war was to usher in a period of German prosperity, which is a generative goal for a leader to have for his or her people. However, German advancement was based on a nongenerative rejectivity of all non-Aryan things. The Nazi Party's policies were based on genocide and intimidation. Most people reject Hitler as a model of generativity, although not everyone. There are people alive today who continue to support Nazi (and other absolute) ideologies; at the very least we would characterize their strivings as narrowly focused on members of their in-group. We might despise the methods and goals of such specifically targeted generativity, but according to Erikson (1982), such goals are part and parcel of larger generative impulses that can also be used to unite people within and across nations for mutual benefit. This example of negative generativity suggests that individuals within a community must carefully evaluate the political rhetoric of leaders; sometimes generative images can be used to advance societal well-being, whereas at other times generative images are used in ultimately selfish and socially destructive ways. The tensions between these two forms of generativity are not always so easy to distinguish.

Even if a mandate seems generative in the positive sense, the attempts to fulfill it can lead to unexpected (and paradoxical) ends for the progenitor. Let us consider another more lengthy historical example from Japan. In 1877, the military leader, Saigo Takamori (1828–1877) of the Satsuma domain, led the last great samurai rebellion against the new conscript army of the Meiji government—a government he was instrumental in installing into power a decade earlier. Saigo's defeat on a hillside in Kagoshima symbolized the end of the feudal order, allowing the Meiji government to pursue its modernization policy without fear of domestic dissent (Reischauer & Craig, 1989). The reasons why rebellions are instigated are many, but part of Saigo the Great's rhetoric was generative in scope, focusing as it did with the preservation of Japanese culture and way of life. Interestingly, this rhetoric was used first to install the Meiji government in 1868, before it was used to try and dismantle it in 1877.

In 1867, Saigo Takamori and other leaders from the Satsuma daimyo domain signed an agreement with the Tosa daimyo domain that outlined their goals in challenging the Tokugawa Shogunate. In part, the agreement specified,

> [Our purpose] is to restore Imperial Rule and to deal with affairs, taking the situation of the world into consideration, in so reasonable a manner as to leave nothing to be desired by posterity. . . . We must, therefore, reform our political system, restore the reins of the government to the Imperial Court, hold a conference of the Daimyos, and in concert with one another work for the purpose of lifting the prestige of the nation among the Powers of the world. (as cited in Morris, 1975, p. 240)

Whereas the first part of this quotation clearly designated a generative target—posterity—the second part of the quotation goes beyond mere generative rhetoric to outline a specific plan of action. Various daimyos had already experienced the destructive power of foreign warships, which attacked to enforce unfair trade policies with Japan. In the face of this superior military technology, Saigo and the other reformers were concerned that the antiquated Shogunate government was incapable of preserving Japan's sovereignty. Thus one of their goals for establishing a new government was to pursue policy that would allow Japan to defend itself from the encroachment of Western powers. In this sense, the incipient Meiji leaders were expressing generativity in the form of preservation, manifest as a concern with the maintenance of national identity and way of life. No doubt some of the Meiji leaders were concerned with what they could gain personally by overthrowing the current leaders, but this does not seem to be the case for Saigo.

In fact, after the defeat of the Shogunate forces, Saigo returned to his native province with the intent of living out his life in bucolic comfort (Morris, 1975). However, after a few years of active persuasion by the Meiji reformers, Saigo returned to political life. During the early 1870s Saigo found himself in conflict with many of his former colleagues.

> [Saigo] was opposed to the excessively rapid changes in Japanese society and was particularly disturbed by the shabby treatment of the warrior class. Suspicious of the new bureaucratic-capitalist structure and of the values it represented, he wanted power to remain in the hands of the responsible, patriotic, benevolent warrior-administrators. (Morris, 1975, p. 248)

His clashes with colleagues led to his second resignation from government in 1873. From Saigo's perspective, the Meiji reformers went too far in imitating the political structure of the Western powers. It seems likely that Saigo's goal in overthrowing the Shogunate government was to enhance the autonomy of the larger samurai clans, allowing each to respond more quickly to the challenges of Western powers. Instead, the Meiji reformers were working toward a centralized bureaucracy.

Although retired once again from political life, Saigo became the focus for samurai discontent. After taking power, the Meiji reformers began to abolish feudal privileges, which meant the samurai became increasingly disenfranchised (Reischauer & Craig, 1989). For example, in 1876 the samurai were ordered to discard their swords—their symbolic badge of office. Realizing Saigo's popularity among the reactionary samurai, the Meiji reformers kept a close eye on him. In fact, in an attempt to prevent a samurai uprising in Satsuma, the Meiji oligarchy secretly removed arms and ammunition from Kagoshima storehouses. Some of Saigo's followers got word of this government plot, and while Saigo was away on a hunting expedition, they impetuously attacked an imperial arsenal to steal weapons. This overt act of disloyalty to the emperor instigated the Satsuma rebellion. When Saigo returned from his hunting trip, he was reluctantly forced into the position of rebel leader.

The rebellion was a disaster for Saigo. He was outnumbered, outgunned, and outmaneuvered by the government army. In September 1877, to avoid capture, Saigo committed ritual suicide. Though branded a traitor at the time, Saigo's popularity with the people of Japan resulted in his posthumous pardon and reappointment a decade later as a court noble.

As a folk hero representing Japanese traditions and values, Saigo attained symbolic immortality, which is a form of generativity (McAdams, 1988). In addition to this personal legacy, he was also parent to the Meiji Restoration, which led directly to Japan's emergence as a contemporary economic power. Saigo's efforts to establish the Meiji government, though, resulted in consequences that he did not foresee. In 1867 he was concerned with making reforms to preserve Japan for posterity; by 1877, Saigo felt that the reforms he helped put in place were destroying the fabric of Japanese culture. Saigo's story is not just another parable reminding us to always beware of what we wish for; rather, Saigo's dilemma highlights the way that generative goals develop a life and momentum of their own. Because generativity is an interpersonal concept, one does not have complete control over the outcome. This seems especially true in the domain of politics where competing sides may agree on a generative outcome (e.g., national sovereignty) but disagree on the methods. It is interesting to note that Saigo has been venerated by liberal and conservative thinkers. As noted by Morris (1975), conservatives valued his traditional samurai ethos and strong stance against foreign powers, whereas liberals valued his humanism (e.g., his genuine attempts to limit bloodshed during war) and his stand against the oppression of the Meiji oligarchy. Thus, different kinds of political thinkers used Saigo as a generative role model depending on their needs. It is clear that generative individuals as well as generative ideas can be appropriated for political purposes.

Because opposing sides in a political conflict can adopt generative rhetoric to justify their positions, it is the duty of individual citizens to determine for themselves when generative goals advanced by politicians are genuine or not. Indeed, it is not hard to imagine that generative rhetoric can be used by a clever leader in a Machiavellian way to gain support for a policy. As a consequence, as moral individuals, we must work through the generative implications of public policy before offering personal support. But can political systems or activities be made more generative? What might we offer leaders who would be interested in advancing a politics of generativity? Given that generative rhetoric can be marshaled by either side in a conflict, a truly generative leader should be able to creatively transcend conflicting arguments when designing policy. At the very least, a political leader must be willing to deal with the complexities that differing sides bring forth. As an example of how generative leaders might conceptualize issues, let us focus on the needs of children.

CHILDREN AND GENERATIVE POLITICS

Children are an underrepresented constituency in most worldwide political systems. They are denied direct representation in politics because they lack the cognitive and emotional resources necessary to lobby alongside successful constituencies such as the elderly, big business, military veterans, school teachers, and labor unions. Thus, children depend on adults to ensure that they receive advantages that can be won in the political and economic arena such as access to high-quality education, adequate food, clothing and shelter, a clean environment, and safe neighborhoods. Because generativity involves the welfare of the next generation, it makes good sense to begin a discussion of generative politics by focusing on children and the multiple ecologies that they inhabit (e.g., family, church, school, peer group, child care). There is historical precedent in the United States for a focus on children and generativity.

Moran (1998) argued that there have been "two highly creative, generative time periods in U.S. history [for children]; the era of Puritanism . . . and the period of the American Revolution" (p. 311). Both eras represent very different kinds of generativity, but the two movements converge in their attempt to provide for children.

The Puritan movement of the 17th century, mentioned in chapters 3 and 10 of this volume, derived meaning from focusing on the family's covenant with God. God would provide everlasting rewards if family members maintained a strict allegiance to biblical teachings. The very foundation of Puritanism was built on a generative model of parenting in which it was the father's responsibility to ensure the well-being of his children (including their moral education). Indeed, Puritanism strictly enforced paternal authority and assigned mothers the secondary role of "helpmeet." From most contemporary perspectives the unequal parental powers built into the Puritan movement makes it suspect; how can Puritanism be generative if women (and girls) are systematically excluded from full participation in the community? Moran argued that the generative success of the Puritan movement must be measured by its genuine "commitments to the young"; for example, the Puritan focus on transplanting families (rather than workers) protected their children from the excesses of business and trading companies that were primarily interested in profit from the New World.

Among the child-friendly advances made by the Puritans included the education of their children (so they would not be deceived by the machinations of the Devil). At first home education was stressed, but, ultimately, public schooling was established to provide supplementary knowledge. In addition, laws were written in colonial Massachusetts that protected children from "unnatural" punishment by parents, with children given "free libertie to complaine to Authorities for redresse" (Moran, 1998, p. 319). New inheritance laws were also written to do away with primogeniture; all children, male and female, were entitled to a share of the estate. Moran argued that this attention paid to children's well-being was a strong reason why the Puritan migration to the New World was so successful in its early stages. The movement was built on a patriarchal model of generativity that stressed the importance of family relationships over time.

The Revolutionary period also offered a vision of generativity that took root and flourished. According to Moran (1998), the logic of the American Revolution demanded that the citizenry of the new Republic be capable of governing themselves. This meant educational reform was necessary so that each man could play a part in local and national governance, even if it just meant filling out a voter card responsibly. The generative focus was on preparing an enlightened citizen. During the late 18th century, the nation began a dialogue over the importance of public education, which set the groundwork for the proliferation of public schooling throughout the 19th century. Moran (1998) argued that over time an educational system developed that tried to be attentive to the cognitive and emotional development of children; one goal of a U.S. education was to prepare children to take their place in American society as free-thinking adults who could participate in local- and national-level politics.

The Puritanism of New England and the educational reforms instigated by the American Revolution represent two forms of generativity expressed at a collective level, for the benefit of children. These two examples, of course, are not meant to suggest that cultural generativity of this type is an historical footnote. Indeed, one purpose of this chapter is to suggest that nations continue to face generative issues in regard to their children that could be dealt with as part of the political process. Following are three topics that present opportunities for political expressions of generativity toward children: child care, an aging population, and immigration. Issues surrounding child care will briefly set the stage for more lengthy treatments of children in an aging population and children and immigration.

Child Care

The use of child care is an important issue for any nation that relies on the work of mothers and fathers for economic growth, and embedded within the public discourse surrounding child care are conflicting images of what is generative and what is not. Because of the existence of male and female gender roles, the implications of child care may be distorted by those who oppose or favor its use. For example, those who decry the increasing use of center-based child-care facilities argue that it is unfair to children to deprive them of a mother's love and support; the use of child care is stigmatized as an example of poor parenting. Rhetorically speaking, this stance captures the generative high ground. (It harkens back to the U.S. Puritanism with its emphasis on mother as help-meet.) However, as will be quickly pointed out by proponents of group care, it is simplistic to assume that parents who use child care are unfit. Many parents do not want to place their children in group care; however, to make ends meet and provide for their children, it is becoming increasingly necessary for parents to earn dual incomes.

Furthermore, it may very well be that high-quality child care has certain advantages for children in terms of cognitive development over everyday home care (e.g., see Lamb's, 1998, review). For a recent study examining the effects of day-care quality on child outcomes, see the National Institute of Child Health and Human Development (NICHD) Early Child Care Research Network (2002). They demonstrated that structural features (e.g., low child to adult ratios) and process features of child care (e.g., subjective ratings of caregiving quality) enhanced the cognitive competence of 54-month-old children who were in child care for more than 10 hours per week. As suggested by the NICHD authors, structural aspects of child care can be regulated successfully by federal and state agencies.

Parents make individual choices about child-care options whereas communities make collective choices. If parents are going to use child care by necessity or desire, to what extent can society facilitate parental expressions of generativity by allocating resources for child-care programs, especially for the poor?

Both proponents and opponents of child care are capable of establishing generative arguments in support of their position. Given that political arguments do not necessarily serve the best interests of children, how do we go about determining what will most benefit the growth and development of boys and girls and the families to which they belong?

Grandparents and Intergenerational Harmony

Child care is not the only issue in which questions about generativity are difficult to answer. This century has witnessed a remarkable lengthening of human life expectancy in economically developed countries. For example, at the turn of the 20th century the average life expectancy in the United States was about 47 years; by contrast, in the late 1990s, the average life expectancy is just over 75 years. Comparable alterations in life expectancy exist for other industrialized nations. Projections estimate that the number of aged throughout the world will have tripled by the year 2025. These improvements in life expectancy are due to advances in medical technology, increased emphasis on sanitation, and the improved cleanliness of urban and rural environments. These statistics have at least two implications for our understanding of generativity. One, more and more generations of family members are alive at the same time, and, two, the mean age of an industrialized country's citizens is increasing. The first implication is fairly straightforward, whereas the second has hidden meaning for a politics of generativity. A modern child is in the increasingly ubiquitous position of having two or more sets of grandparents (including step-grandparents and great-grandparents). This shift in availability of grandparents to grandchildren will offer new kinds of generative challenges to the elderly. To be sure, grandparenting is not a 21st-century phenomenon, but this century and the next will see an increase in the sheer number of healthy grandparents who can provide material and psychological resources to grandchildren. (Of course the caretaking may travel the other way as well; how much will grandchildren be expected to care for grandparents who are facing physical decline?) A moral issue to consider is to what extent are grandparents expected to provide active assistance to their children and grandchildren? This question is no longer made moot by early mortality.

Furthermore, some grandparents have no choice but to step in with childcare assistance. Roe and Minkler (1998–1999) discussed how grandparent-headed households are likely to become more common, especially in countries where there is a large gap between the wealthy and poor. They examined the challenges such grandparents face when their own children need help with child care because of factors like divorce, teen pregnancy, drug abuse, and AIDS. Thus, with respect to children, generative politics will need to deal with intergenerational issues. For example, children whose parents cannot care for them are often forced into foster care programs unless other family members can step in as surrogate parents. In the United States, the number of households in which grandparents care for their grandchildren has increased dramatically in the past 20 years (Everett, 1995). Recognizing this, federal law currently states that foster care benefits cannot be denied to grandparents just because they are relatives; however, other policy issues centered around grandparent foster care remain. Roe and Minkler (1998–1999) highlighted problems that grandchildren might encounter living with grandparents. One issue revolves around access to health care; grandchildren are often not covered by the policies held by grandparents and so the former may lack adequate levels of health care. Another potential problem facing children occurs when grandparents are socially isolated from young families with children (in some cases the sense of isolation may be exacerbated when grandparents feel embarrassment at having to care for a grandchild); this has implications for grandchildren who may have fewer opportunities to interact with others their own age. It is the task of a generative politician to decide how best these kinds of issues can be addressed at the level of public policy in an attempt to alleviate some of the pressures faced by grandparents raising the next generation.

The second implication of a nation's aging populace is that generational constituencies may find themselves pitted against each other in the political arena. The needs and concerns of the elderly do not always dovetail with the needs and concerns of children. In such conflicts of interest, when resources are scarce, children, who rely on their own parents for social power, may end up losing health benefits and educational opportunities. In the popular press version of their scholarly work, Howe and Strauss (1993) commented that members of the elderly in the United States have

> organized themselves into . . . generational lobbies to promote their own age-bracket agenda. They succeeded in shifting public and private resources, and the very definition of age-based "entitlement," away from the young and toward themselves. They became the best-insured, most leisured, and (in relation to the young) most affluent generation of elders in American history. (p. 36)

As an example of their claim, Howe and Strauss discussed how children's educational opportunities can be denied by older Americans. They may be reluctant to pay taxes for school upgrades because their own children have long since graduated. Of course there is no necessary conflict between the elderly and children, so one must ask who stands to benefit by pitting these two constituencies against each other? Some segments of the media seem expert at denying any common ground shared by different groups. A public discussion of generative responsibilities across generational lines may help ameliorate intergenerational conflicts.

For example, Waddock and Freedman (1998–1999) suggested that retired older adults are an untapped resource for public school education. At this point in the United States, schools are typically closed to the general public in the late afternoon. Rather than leave the facilities and resources unused during the afternoons and evenings, Waddock and Freedman described how schools could be used for community activities to draw in adults and children. Such activity should serve as a springboard for attracting older adult volunteers to assist with the curricular and tutorial needs of children during school hours. In this way, intergenerational bonds can be formed rather than dissolved. Variations on this model have worked in other countries. For example, the success of the Reggio Emilia Approach to schooling in Italy is based in part on the active participation of parents and community in the education of children (Edwards, Gandini, & Foreman, 1993).

Immigration and Minority Status

Another changing demographic of many societies is the increasing percentage of immigrants leaving behind their country of origin, perhaps due to war and other catastrophic events. When moving to a new country, an immigrant often faces a long list of opportunities and obstacles, many of which are centered around generativity. On the one hand, it is important to assimilate into their new culture to maximize chances for economic success; on the other hand, it may be desirable to maintain unique cultural values and traditions. Children are at the crux of this age-old dilemma. Parents want their children to be successful, which often means integrating them into "mainstream" society. However, many immigrant and minority parents also want to ensure that their children do not assimilate toxic aspects of the majority culture. This tension is fundamentally a generative one for both immigrant parents and the larger culture in which they now belong. How do minority parents deal with the transmission of language, traditions, and values to their children? How will the new host country cope with the presence of different groups of immigrant children in institutions like public schools? Different kinds of solutions have already been proposed. For example, in the United States, some political constituencies argue we must mainstream immigrant minority children immediately by making English the only language spoken in a classroom. Is this stance a generative one? Can research on language acquisition help formulate a policy that is better for children, rather than one that might be expedient for politicians and school districts?

Hakuta (1986, p. 233; see also, Bialystok & Hakuta, 1994), an expert in language acquisition, argued that "answers to many of the objections about bilingual education are available, and research largely supports the contentions of the advocates of bilingual education." As one example, it has been shown that new information (e.g., a fact, a theory) learned in one language is transferred to the second language. Thus, in the United States, the argument that hours spent learning in a minority language (e.g., Spanish) means fewer hours available for learning in English is less compelling than it otherwise might be because information learned well in Spanish (e.g., about American history) will be remembered and integrated into any new languages learned (e.g., English). Scientific findings like these will rarely change the opinion of a politician who disagrees with the implications. This is not necessarily bad because there are other grounds on which to formulate policy. However, a generative politician who makes a decision with implications for children ought to be aware of whether his or her decision is based on scientific, economic, or purely political grounds.

These three examples of children and generative politics (child care, aging population, and immigration) are not meant to be an exhaustive list of children's needs; they are just a few possible areas in which a true discourse centered on children would be informative. Other obvious areas to consider include attempts to reduce teenage pregnancy, providing access to excellent teachers and schooling, and making sure children have affordable health care. It is clear that these concerns (and many others) overlap, but they are conceptually distinct and should be considered in their own right.[1]

---

[1]No matter how well generative issues of the kinds discussed in this chapter are addressed within communities and nations, I am reminded by my own family that individuals will continue to exert generative pressures alongside any political policy. In my own childhood, issues of cultural

CHARACTERISTICS OF A GENERATIVE POLITICIAN

Because nation-states face individual crises and opportunities, it is impossible to specify a universal set of generative policies. Issues such as the ones highlighted earlier should be discussed by the citizenry of each nation in such a way that the needs of children are met. Although it may not be possible to specify a generative set of politics that could be shared by all, it might be possible to describe some of the qualities that a generative politician would possess when addressing issues like the ones discussed.

First, research and theory suggest that generative people have a fundamental belief in the human species and a faith in human potential (e.g., Erikson, 1950; Van de Water & McAdams, 1989). In other words, generativity is associated with the conviction that human beings will continue to thrive in the near and far distant future. Given the assumption that humans will continue to occupy this globe, generative politicians, in addition to satisfying immediate concerns, must also develop a long-term time perspective and trace their policy decisions beyond their expected time in office. This may be difficult in democratic societies in which decision making is often based on expediency to satisfy lobbying groups before the next election cycle; thus, immediate concerns are often addressed to the detriment of long-term concerns.

Environmental issues are obviously symbolic of this kind of generative push and pull. On the one hand are environmental groups that bring to the bargaining table a clear future-time orientation; the argument is that natural resources are finite and that we must carefully preserve them so that future generations can have access to them. On the other hand are business leaders who need natural resources to maintain their productivity; the argument is that business provides jobs for workers and products for sale, thus helping to

---

generativity were important for my mother, who is of Japanese descent. My father is a White American who served 20 years in the United States Air Force. I grew up in the suburbs of northern California where my father retired from the military at his base of preference. There was no Asian population to speak of in my hometown; my close friends at school were White and (mostly) Protestant. My parents' friends, however, were all ex-servicemen with Japanese wives. My mother made contact with these other immigrant women in part through my father, who came across others at the Air Force base who also fell in love and married in Japan. My family would celebrate national holidays with these people. The summer holidays were usually held at our house because we had a large, shady backyard and a swimming pool. At these parties, the men sat in one half of the yard near the barbecue and talked about the military and the incompetence of selected officers. The women sat at the picnic tables and spoke Japanese, about what topics I don't know. But the girls my age, the daughters of these women, they knew. For they were learning bits and pieces of Japanese, sitting with their mothers and listening. We boys were in the patio talking in English. We were not expected to learn Japanese. To our mothers, I guess it was easier to pass on the language of their ancestors to their daughters.

Although my mother participated in passing on language skills along gendered lines, she made sure that I was exposed to my Japanese ancestry in other ways, through fairy tales, art, and music. She wanted me well versed in the traditions and history of her new country—the United States—but she also wanted me to know about the traditions of her past. Her example reminds me that regardless of the larger political sphere, parents continue to make decisions on their own and within the small groups to which they belong about how to transmit what they feel is of import to their children.

maintain standards of living for current generations. Concepts such as sustainable development have been offered to balance socioeconomic well-being and ecological health (Ingman, Benjamin, & Lusky, 1998–1999), but debate between business and environmental groups continues to degenerate into name-calling. When making decisions with implications for business and the natural environment, a generative politician must be able to recognize that one polemic the two groups face revolves around time perspective: short term versus long term. Given that most elected officials possess a keen sense of short-term implications, generative politicians will be distinguished by their ability to think in the long term alongside the short term.

Second, according to Erikson (1950; see also Peterson, 2002), a generative person recognizes that humans are embedded in intergenerational communities. To promote one age group through special interest lobbying at the expense of another age group is not the hallmark of a caring society. In fact, Henkin and Kingson (1998–1999) argued that contemporary societies more than ever need to promote a healthy intergenerational social compact, whereby care and resources are transferred across age groups. On an emotional level, children and youths need elderly people to serve as role models; in turn, the elderly, in order to maintain a sense of integrity, need children to affirm that years of hard work and cultural investment are valued by the next generation and will be continued by them (Erikson, 1950). If a society does not value the rhythms of the human life cycle, then special interest lobbying groups can atomize the intergenerational social compact to promote age-related competition and conflict. A generative politician would recognize this and attempt to integrate the needs of children, young adults, middle-aged adults, and the elderly.

For example, providing adequate income for the elderly (e.g., through some kind of social security program) will have an impact on younger generations. If retired persons do not have enough money to live comfortably, then the burden of caring for them may fall to their adult children, who might still be caring for their own children. The attempts by adult offspring to provide care up and down the generational line would dilute the amount of money available for all family members. Of course such a scenario simplifies a complex situation. In the United States, social security is meant as a supplement to life savings, investments, and other forms of insurance, so it is not the only form of income available to retirees. Furthermore, if we continue to think in the imagery of the extended family, the active workers who pay out social security benefits are the very same adult children who are now caring for the grandchildren of the retirees. At least this is the case in a pay-as-you-go social security system such as the one currently used by the United States. That is, contributions made by current workers are paid to current retirees. So increasing social security benefits for retirees might necessitate an increase in social security deductions from the paychecks of current workers, thus once again taking resources away from the parents of young children. It is clear that discussions of social security do not impact the elderly alone but all members of society. Henkin and Kingson (1998–1999) reminded us about the importance of the intergenerational social compact. Speaking metaphorically, different age groups exist in a web of mutual responsibilities; it is the task of a generative politician to balance age-related needs in an equitable way so that the web is not torn or too heavily weighted on one end.

THE VIRTUE OF GENERATIVITY

The virtue of working on generative policies is that they promote the long-term survival of the human species. Erikson (1950) used generativity to focus on the responsibilities of adults to children, thus forcing us to think beyond the self. In fact, it is not hard to think of the future in terms of our children and the kind of world that they will inhabit. For example, when writing wills and planning the inheritance of an estate, most people designate their children as beneficiaries; when anticipating death we maintain a concern for the well-being of our children. In so doing, the stage is set for thinking even further into the future. For our sons and daughters will be concerned with their own children. In turn, through the process of simple projection, we can conclude that our grandchildren will place value on their own children. And so the generative cycle continues and demands (if we truly value the concerns of our own children) that we consider the possible needs of unborn generations. In articulating the notion of generativity, Erikson insisted that adults and children need each other. We are locked in a mutually beneficial relationship; to ignore our interdependence invites late-life despair in the adult and the lack of an identity in the child. In other words, when adults ignore the needs of children, this sows the seeds of cultural distress for more than just one generation.

REFERENCES

Bialystok, E., & Hakuta, K. (1994). *In other words: The science and psychology of second-language acquisition.* New York: Basic Books.

Edwards, E., Gandini, L., & Foreman, G. (1993). *The hundred languages of children: The reggio emilia approach to early childhood education.* Norwood, NJ: Ablex.

Erikson, E. H. (1950). *Childhood and society.* New York: Norton.

Erikson, E. H. (1980). *Identity and the life cycle.* New York: Norton.

Erikson, E. H. (1982). *The life cycle completed.* New York: Norton.

Everett, J. (1995). Relative foster care: An emerging trend in foster care placement policy and practice. *Smith College Studies in Social Work, 65,* 239–254.

Hakuta, K. (1986). *Mirror of language: The debate on bilingualism.* New York: Basic Books.

Henkin, N., & Kingson, E. (1998–1999). Keeping the promise. *Generations: In-depth Views of Issues in Aging, 22*, 6–9.

Howe, N., & Strauss, W. (1993). *America's 13th generation*. New York: Vintage Books.

Ingman, S., Benjamin, T., & Lusky, R. (1998–1999). The environment: The quintessential intergenerational challenge. *Generations: In-depth Views of Issues in Aging, 22*, 68–71.

Kotre, J. (1995). Generative outcome. *Journal of Aging Studies, 9*, 33–41.

Lamb, M. E. (1998). Nonparental child care: Context, quality, correlates, and consequences. In W. Damon (Series Ed.) & I. E. Sigel & K. A. Renninger (Vol. Eds.), *Handbook of child psychology: Vol. 4. Child psychology in practice* (5th ed., pp. 73–133). New York: Wiley.

McAdams, D. P. (1988). *Power, intimacy and the life story: Personological inquiries into identity*. New York: Guilford Press.

Moran, G. F. (1998). Cares for the rising generation: Generativity in American history, 1607–1900. In D. P. McAdams & E. de St. Aubin's (Eds.), *Generativity and adult development: How and why we care for the next generation* (pp. 311–333). Washington, DC: American Psychological Association.

Morris, I. (1975). *The nobility of failure: Tragic heroes in the history of Japan*. New York: Noonday Press.

National Institute of Child Health and Human Development Early Child Care Research Network. (2002). Child-care structure → process → outcome: Direct and indirect effects of child-care quality on young children's development. *Psychological Science, 13*, 199–206.

Peterson, B. E. (2002). Longitudinal analysis of midlife generativity, intergenerational roles, and caregiving. *Psychology and Aging, 17*, 161–168.

Peterson, B. E., Smirles, K. A., & Wentworth, P. A. (1997). Generativity and authoritarianism: Implications for personality, political involvement, and parenting. *Journal of Personality and Social Psychology, 72*, 1202–1216.

Reischauer, E. O., & Craig, A. M. (1989). *Japan: Tradition and transformation* (Rev. ed.). Boston: Houghton Mifflin.

Roe, K. M., & Minkler, M. (1998–1999). Grandparents raising grandchildren: Challenges and responses. *Generations: In-Depth Views of Issues in Aging, 22*, 25–32.

Van De Water, D. A., & McAdams, D. P. (1989). Generativity and Erikson's "Belief in the species." *Journal of Research in Personality, 23*, 435–449.

Waddock, S. A., & Freedman, M. (1998–1999). Reducing the generation gap and strengthening schools. *Generations: In-Depth Views of Issues in Aging, 22*, 54–57.

13

GENERATIVITY AND THE POLITICS OF INTERGENERATIONAL FAIRNESS

TAKESHI SASAKI

If a society is to be generative, it must develop an approach to politics and political institutions that prioritizes future generations. In this chapter, I consider the case of contemporary Japan. Like most political systems in democratic societies, Japanese politics is mainly concerned with the needs and the contingencies of the immediate present and the short-term future. After all, it is those living adult citizens—rather than their young children and the yet-to-be-born—who vote and pay taxes and participate actively in the political process. It is in response to the well-being of those voters that politicians and political bodies are designed to act. A *responsive* democracy must address the concerns of those citizens it represents. But a *responsible* democracy must look further into the future (Dunn, 1999; Kim & Dator, 1994; Sasaki, 1994) in an effort to represent *those generations who are yet to be*. A generative society requires a political system that is both responsive and responsible—a political system that aims to achieve some measure of intergenerational fairness.

How to achieve fairness in politics is a thorny issue everywhere. It is a theme that is endlessly dogged by controversy even among our fellow human beings on the planet at the moment. How much more complicated, then, are the problems that appear when it comes to relations with people and generations who do not yet exist? In my discussion, I start by identifying the ways in which people up till now have dealt politically with problems concerning future generations as well as their theoretical position on such problems, and then turn my attention once more to the contemporary situation. Only then will it be possible to meet this issue head on.

A POLITICAL FRAMEWORK FOR THE PROBLEM OF FUTURE GENERATIONS

The social system of the family functions as the starting point for all types of social relations. In traditional societies, political activities were carried out by representatives from among the adult members of the family and directions were determined according to the wishes of those family representatives. Problems affecting future generations were taken up and dealt with by the present generation. The problems of future generations were seen as internal family matters, and there was a tacit expectation that these could be uniformly sorted out according to private motives such as parents' feelings of concern and love for their children. Fundamentally, these were "private" affairs, which were deemed unworthy of public consideration. Erikson's (1963) concept of generativity, then, finds its main expressions in traditional societies within the private realm of family. The role of politics itself was limited to a narrow range of "public" affairs.

In modern societies, however, politics probes deeply into the "private" life of the family, affecting the way people live and plan their lives. For example, pension and social security systems are designed to assure a secure family life for people after they retire. In modern democracies, people's private needs and demands have become the never-ending problem for politics, and politics has come to concern itself mainly with the establishment of mechanisms to mobilize public authority to fulfill these private needs. The borderline between public and private, therefore, has become blurred. Just as generativity has both a private and a public dimension (McAdams & Logan, this volume, chap. 2), so too do modern political systems concern themselves with issues of both private and public concern. In Japan, the focus of the government on the private needs of citizens has become an especially strong trend since the 1950s.

Now that politics has come to immerse itself so deeply in people's private lives, what meaning does this have for future generations, and to what extent is this new situation better than what has gone before? Have things truly improved in comparison to a time when the fate of future generations was something to be dealt with by individuals as a private affair? Have the prospects of a fair politics for future generations become brighter?

There is little doubt that a democratic, interest-driven political system in Japan has brought with it tremendous benefits for Japanese citizens. Even if all people living in Japan have not received equal treatment and opportunities, the reforms in social services through institutions and policies in the second half of the 20th century have still improved life immeasurably. Furthermore, the implicit assumption behind political progress has been that improving the lives of current generations will also lead to the improvements in opportunities for the lives of future generations. Thus, widening the scope of social services is assumed to confer blessings on future generations, too. As long as the intellectual and ethical sense of the present generations vis-à-vis their successors remained strong, we have assumed, democratic progress should continue to bring advantages well into the future.

Any objective observation of contemporary life in modern democracies, however, would suggest that all has not been smooth sailing. In Japan, it has been argued that social services for the family have not inevitably led to the strengthening of family ties. Instead, signs of family decline are apparent on many fronts. Many political scientists, journalists, and other cultural observers have argued that cohesion between family members in Japan has eroded considerably in recent years, and family members' sense of responsibility and duty toward each other is nowhere near as strong as it once was. The situation has precipitated what has been described as a *generativity crisis* in Japan, and perhaps in other modern societies as well (Kim, 1999). Of course, the decline of family cohesion, and other indications of generativity problems in society, are not solely due to changes in public policy. They may also be linked to a wide range of social factors that accompany the birth of an affluent society, sexual liberation, the rapid increase in divorce, and even the further strengthening of an ethos of individualism in a society that has traditionally emphasized the collective over the individual (Markus & Kitayama, 1991). Nonetheless, many observers have suggested that a number of current social problems, including those related to how older and younger generations relate to each other, could be a result of the expanding social services that were, ironically, designed to bolster families for generations to come. Expanded social systems may have had the unintended effect of hastening the decline of families. (Similar arguments have been made in the United States for many years; see, e.g., Murray, 1984.) Whether or not these arguments are valid, it is certainly true that doubt has been cast on the once-optimistic belief that progressive democratic systems will automatically function to assure the well-being of private family life, and, by extension, the welfare of future generations.

When the social framework of the family becomes unstable, it is time to argue that politics and public organs should assume a greater and more clearly defined share of the responsibility toward future generations. Is the current political system capable of replying effectively to such a demand? A skeptical response to that question stems from the observation that Japanese politicians and political institutions find it very difficult to rise above the wishes of the present moment, as represented by a myriad of interests and demands. These demands are basically those of the present adult generation. It is the members of the present generation who are in a position to bring pressure on politics by exercising their voting rights. Of course, the political influence of all voters is not equal and it is impossible to escape imbalances and some degree of discrimination. As in any current democratic society, some individuals and groups in Japan are more enfranchised than are others when it comes to the political process. But the most disenfranchised of all, one might argue, are those citizens who have not yet been born but who will be left with the world that the enfranchised will some day leave for them.

The traditional framework whereby the problems of people in the future were dealt with indirectly by solving the problems of people in the present was based on the theory that the present generation is the *virtual representative* of future generations. Although their virtual representatives were not literally chosen by future generations, it was felt that the sense of responsibility of the former meant that it would always give due consideration to the interests and rights of those who were not yet born. However, if we do indeed face today a societal crisis in generativity, then this type of intergenerational relationship cannot be counted on to assure the well-being of future generations. Future generations may be left high and dry without any representative to plead on their behalf for their rights and interests. Yet society cannot be said to be truly generative, in my view, if these rights and interests are ignored.

It is my belief that one factor that potentially undermines the responsible politics that are necessary for a generative society is the reluctance of modern people and their governments to acknowledge intractable *limitations* in many domains of life. Twentieth-century totalitarianism may be characterized as an effort to supersede human limitation through the bold exercise of autocratic power. In Stalinist Russia, for example, ruthless social engineering plowed ahead relentlessly for decades, regardless of the millions who suffered and died as a result. By contrast, democratic societies distribute power across many different venues, and typically no single, overpowering social agenda can run roughshod over the people. Still, democratic governments are especially adept at denying limitations. For example, the habit of regarding the natural environment and natural resources as inexhaustible is deeply ingrained in our civilization.

Our tenacious pursuit of creature comforts in life scarcely acknowledges any limits. Politically, it was extremely significant that the recognition of politics as a force capable of facilitating economic growth and well-being took such firm root in the latter half of the 20th century. Whether referred to as Keynesian economics or some other name, this recognition fundamentally altered the relationship between people and politics. People came to feel that they were insulated from the blind business cycle of the market economy;

government was able to influence the economy in ways that cushioned the blows of recession and worked to promote economic well-being of citizens. Although one would be wrong to cast a negative light on these important developments in modern democracies, they have come to be associated with the public expectation of greater and greater levels of material comfortableness—another way in which limits refuse to be recognized.

In Japan and a number of other societies, the desire for comfortableness in the present generation of adults has often given rise to an imbalance between tax revenues and expenditures and led to fiscal deficits that could plague future generations. In this type of fiscal-deficit-based democracy, an intergenerational zero sum game threatens to undermine moral solidarity between generations. If totalitarianism openly attempted, by the exercise of brute force, to transcend all limits, democratic systems have worked to deny limits through the eternal pursuit of comfortableness. Yet comfortableness will eventually exact its costs—and those who may have to pay up may be those who are not yet even born.

If democratic politics, then, is ruled by the wishes of one generation and if, moreover, such wish fulfillment is pursued in a way that loses sight of one limit after another, then it is likely to become especially difficult to formulate government policies based on a long-term perspective. In other words, although people's desires should have a variety of temporal and spatial dimensions, these may be often strongly shaped by concern about the "here" and the "now." For sure, citizens of contemporary democracies have good reason to be concerned about the here and now. But the question for a generative society is whether it can filter the influx of such raw concern through intellectual reflection on and a sense of responsibility for future generations. "Now-ism" belongs to an extreme type of responsive democratic politics. It promotes an attitude of irresponsibility toward not only future generations but even to considerations that may be only a few years down the road. In a generative society, responsive politics for the here and now must be tempered and combined with the responsible politics of the long term. This is a dilemma for contemporary Japanese politics. Faced with the prospect of an aging society, the Japanese government cannot draw up plans for a future social security program because it is too heavily swayed by responsive politics, which sees no further than the next election.

The relation between a fair, responsible politics for future generations and the responsive politics of modern democracies like Japan is not, at present, a harmonious one. How might greater harmony be achieved?

CONDITIONS FOR FAIR POLITICS FOR FUTURE GENERATIONS

Let us consider two approaches to the problem of the conflict between responsive and responsible politics in the light of our hopes for a generative society. The first approach is to incorporate into politics a political mechanism to prevent extreme now-ism. The second is to clarify the limits of the authority of politics and government and to regulate, from outside, the amount of resources that can be mobilized.

The simplest and most readily comprehensible, albeit somewhat radical, argument involves establishing institutions that offer political representation to future generations (e.g., Agius, 1994). We might call such a system the *People's Tribune* for future generations. If the present generation is apt to lack self-control in its exercise of power and to exhibit a strong tendency to judge matters according to its concerns for the here and now, then such a People's Tribune would serve as a countermeasure boldly set up by the present generation to limit its own power. Democratic systems already distribute power among various groupings, such as the division of legislative, administrative, and judicial government branches, or the division between central and local government. What is being proposed here is a further distribution, but this on a temporal dimension—between representation of current and future generations.

The greatest difficulty in this first approach lies in the fact that the people of the future, by definition, do not yet exist. Consequently, it is difficult to generate guidelines for supporting and representing them. For this reason, a People's Tribune might be perceived as acting in a capricious and arbitrary manner. Certainly, important limitations on the power of a People's Tribune would be necessary if such an idea were ever to be put into practice. For example, the main role of the People's Tribune might be limited to provide clear warnings to the present generation from the point of view of people in the future, to bring a critical eye to bear on opinions and policies affecting future generations. The power of a People's Tribune might derive more from moral suasion and its appeal to public moral sentiments—even shame and guilt—rather than from the conventional exercise of political influence. Although such a political entity and process may seem unrealistic to many readers, I believe that a group of discerning people empowered to think deeply and propose boldly on behalf of future generations, perhaps including experts in science and law and other disciplines, is not outside the realm of the possible, and the feasible. Such a system would encourage livelier debates on policy, and by raising the question of the effectiveness of policies from the temporal dimension, it would also help to maintain the flexibility of policy space.

Although such a People's Tribune has not been systematically established in any democratic government to date, there is a range of groups and nonprofit organizations currently working on behalf of future generations. In some democratic societies, political parties develop on the foundations of these groups, such as the Green parties in Europe. In other cases, the groups bring pressure to bear on parties to shape policy and strategy. What sort of conditions might enable the political party system to implement policies with future generations in mind? One is that a political party should have its own clearly defined organization that retains a certain amount of autonomy from the electorate. Responsible parliamentary politics in a generative society demands that once it has won an election a government should be able to carry forth with stability and strength a program that involves long-term projects and goals. Not only must the period of political office be guaranteed a fixed term in this case, but sufficient ability to plan and enforce policies must be assured. At the same time, institutional limitations must be kept in place to assure that no elected government can act in ways reminiscent of the failed totalitarian systems of the 20th century.

Every country's political system is rooted in a specific history and culture. In Japan, a tendency toward a responsive politics of the moment seems especially pronounced. One of the reasons for this is the enormous bureaucracy that exists in the first place, which in effect reduces each political party to a pressure group agitating for short-term goals. The fact that politicians themselves have seen their principal role as dealing with petitions and taking orders for local constituents testifies to this deeply rooted political legacy. Because of frequent reshufflings of ministers, including the Prime Minister, the personal foundations of responsible politics have long been in decay in Japan. Such a situation leads to the weakening of trust in the political party system and causes politicians to embrace responsive, rather than responsible, politics more eagerly than ever.

Having presented the case for internal reforms in democratic politics and the establishment of a body like a People's Tribune, I would now like to shift the focus to the question of restrictions brought to bear from the outside. One of the major problems in the 20th century lay in the blurring of the limits of political possibilities, even on occasion the adoption of the premise that politics was omnipotent. Clarification of the limits would put a brake on the exercise of power and help to curb the self-centeredness of the present generation. It might then be possible to arouse concern for the problems of future generations.

Although the 19th and 20th centuries witnessed the rise of powerful nation-states, recent years have seen the state vie with the market economy for supremacy. We are now living in an age where the limits of government have become apparent through the expansion of the international financial markets. Government fiscal and financial policies are judged by the markets. Government bonds are subject to ranking. If the process of democratic politics is the factor that sways governmental fiscal policies, this pressure comes with market-imposed limits. Squeezed by internal and external pressures, governments face a crisis in their ability to rule. As we saw in the Asian crisis of 1998, currencies plummeted as a result of turbulence in the financial markets, interest rates soared, and governments lost their ability to preserve any stability in people's lives. The economic discipline demanded by the financial markets led to the drastic reform of nations' internal economic structures and surges in unemployment, while governments were deprived of the means to satisfy the present generation. Although this failure of democratic rule under market pressures is not to be applauded, there can be no doubt that people were made bitterly aware of the limits of the power of the state and democratic rule. Democratic politics is, in a sense, more disciplined by the markets than may have been the case in the past. To achieve monetary union, the countries of the European Union subjected their state politics to severe regulations, while in other regions discipline has been imposed through the International Monetary Fund system. The significance for future generations of this regulation of democratic rule by the markets is not necessarily clear. Still, it cannot be denied that political now-ism has been dealt a serious blow.

At the same time, markets themselves operate on their own kind of now-ism. Long-term perspectives and the problems of future generations do not occur to them. While markets may, therefore, have the ability to raise problems, this does not mean that they can solve them. In many cases, it is not a question of a choice between the market and government, but a question of how to relate the two. The rules for various types of environmental regulation, for example, were devised by governments and then developed in their various forms based on market constraints and principles. A complex mechanism of reciprocal discipline between government and markets on the basis of limits to both sides has, in many cases, been set in motion. It is the judgment of civil society that influences the form this mechanism takes.

Not only, therefore, do politics and government have limits imposed on them by the markets, but they are also kept within bounds by society's intellectual and ethical resources. It is important to point out that what is being advocated here is not a reversion to a traditional framework. The argument is not that the problems of future generations may be dismissed as "private" concerns to be solved by private care and effort. Today, the conditions that made possible the traditional sharp distinction between private and public have disappeared. The collapse of traditional social structures has meant that all private problems have ended up as problems for society. Nevertheless, just because they have moved into the public arena, these problems should not necessarily be left to politics and government, or to the markets. In forums outside government and the economy, we need to develop an extended public conversation about the responsibilities of the present generation to the future. At the same time, mechanisms for social cooperation aimed at finding appropriate solutions on the basis of a clear understanding of the limits of governments and markets must be calmly investigated.

In dealing fairly with human beings of the future, we must not leave behind or create for them intolerable environmental and social conditions. In other words, a generative society should, at minimum, strive to leave the world no worse than we found it (Slaughter, 1994). Such an injunction may seem somewhat passive and overly humble. However, the example of history shows that even conditions that may appear passive at first glance are virtually impossible to put in place without disputation as well as a great deal of cooperation. The problems of future generations are no longer completely covered by the parent–child relationship. They have become a matter for society, hence for the intellectual and ethical sensibilities of society's members. Of course, I am not opposed to the idea of leaving for future generations a glorious world with greatly improved environmental and social conditions. However, a glance back at the politics of the 20th century would suggest that it is no small achievement after all to redouble our efforts on the basis of a recognition of our own limits, rather than to ignore those limits to pursue unrealistic and ultimately destructive dreams.

REFERENCES

Agius, E. (1994). What future for future generations? The "quality of life" of the future. In T. C. Kim (Ed.), *Thinking about future generations* (pp. 55–77). Kyoto, Japan: Institute for the Integrated Study of Future Generations.

Dunn, J. (1999). Politics and the well-being of future generations. In T. C. Kim & R. Harrison (Eds.), *Self and future generations* (pp. 70–81). Cambridge, England: White Horse Press.

Erikson, E. H. (1963). *Childhood and society* (2nd ed.). New York: Norton.

Kim, T.-C. (1999, November). *Generativity crisis and our responsibilities towards future generations*. Address given at the Kyoto Forum, Kyoto, Japan.

Kim, T.-C., & Dator, J. (1994). (Eds.). *Creating a new history for future generations*. Kyoto, Japan: Institute for Integrated Study of Future Generations.

Markus, H., & Kitayama, S. (1991). Culture and the self: Implications for cognition, emotion, and motivation. *Psychological Review, 98*, 224–253.

Murray, C. (1984). *Losing ground: American social policy, 1950–1980*. New York: Basic Books.

Sasaki, T. (1994). The responsibility for politics for future generations. In T. C. Kim & J. Dator (Eds.), *Creating a new history for future generations* (pp. 87–102). Kyoto, Japan: Institute for Integrated Study of Future Generations.

Slaughter, R. A. (1994). Why should we care about future generations? In T. C. Kim (Ed.), *Thinking about future generations* (pp. 247–272). Kyoto, Japan: Institute for the Integrated Study of Future Generations.

14

VOLUNTEERISM AND THE GENERATIVE SOCIETY

MARK SNYDER AND E. GIL CLARY

Every day, large numbers of individuals express concern for other people by engaging in the helping activities known as volunteerism. Volunteers offer these important services to their communities in very direct ways, as exemplified by tutoring disadvantaged students, coaching young athletes, providing religious instruction to would-be congregants, serving as companions to the elderly, assisting in the health care of the sick, providing peer counseling to the distressed, and helping in rescue and relief efforts in response to emergencies and disasters. Others serve in less direct ways, as in cases in which volunteers support organizations with educational, athletic, religious, or rescue missions by serving as office assistants, fundraisers, and board members.

Looking at this impact in terms of the sheer volume of activity, one recent survey estimated that, in 1998 alone, 109.4 million American adults engaged in some form of volunteerism, and doing so an average of 3.5 hours per week (Independent Sector, 1999). These statistics, it should be noted,

The preparation of this chapter and the conduct of the research reported in it have been supported by grants from the Non-Profit Sector Research Fund of the Aspen Institute to E. Gil Clary and Mark Snyder and the National Institute of Mental Health to Mark Snyder.

come from a national survey that adopted a definition of volunteerism that included both formal activities such as those listed above (especially those that take place in an organization) and informal ones (such as helping a friend or neighbor). When one focuses on more formal kinds of volunteerism, especially those that involved sustained efforts, an estimated 15.7 billion hours were devoted to organized volunteer efforts, and approximately 25% of the volunteers reported spending 5 or more hours each week on volunteer activities (Independent Sector, 1996). These statistics, then, tell us that millions of Americans are contributing billions of hours to making their communities, defined locally and globally, better places to live. Furthermore, this kind of activity is not simply an American phenomenon but one that occurs in many parts of the world (Curtis, Grabb, & Baer, 1992).

Along with other students of human helpfulness, we find that these kinds of activities raise a host of intriguing questions. Why do people decide, in the first place, to serve as a volunteer? Why do some of the people continue to volunteer, often times devoting years of regular work with the same organization? And why, and this may represent the so-called bottom line, are individuals willing to commit significant personal resources (time and effort, without remuneration) to others, and others who are not family, friends, or even acquaintances? Along with the personal sacrifice that is often involved in volunteering and the fact that the recipients of volunteer services are often strangers to the volunteer, the fascination with this kind of activity also stems from the fact that volunteering can hardly be characterized as normative. After all, according to the same surveys discussed above, the proportion of adults who are volunteers is accompanied by an equally large proportion of adults who are not volunteers; and, when it comes to regular and sustained volunteering, only a relatively small percentage of volunteers are doing so.

These features of volunteering, we believe, share much in common with questions about generativity. Generativity is concerned with providing some benefit, possibly at some personal cost, possibly over a period of time, to future generations. That is, just as the recipients of volunteer services are typically not previously known to volunteers (often being assigned to volunteers by referral agencies), the recipients of generative actions, being members of future generations who may be yet to be born, are also often unknown to their benefactors. Moreover, the questions that are typically posed in the context of volunteering can also be asked in the context of concerns with generativity: Why do people decide, in the first place, to act on behalf of future generations? Why do some of the people continue to serve future generations, often times devoting years of regular work to the same cause? And, why are individuals willing to commit significant personal resources to these unknown and perhaps even unborn others?

These questions point to the possibility of intriguing connections between generativity and volunteerism. In this chapter, we explore these connections between research and theorizing on volunteerism and research and theorizing on generativity, with an overall goal of examining how each research literature can inform the other. We begin by considering the defining features of generativity and of volunteering, and the activities that represent and exemplify each construct. In so doing, we focus more closely on psychological processes and dynamics that underlie each activity, with a particular emphasis on the motivations behind acts of volunteerism and of generativity. Finally, we close with an examination of generative and volunteer activities in the larger social context, and how these socially valued qualities and actions also pose significant challenges for those who participate in and promote these activities.

GENERATIVE AND VOLUNTEER ACTIONS

As readers of this volume well know, the concept of generativity was introduced by Erik Erikson in his classic life span theory of personality development and defined as "primarily the concern in establishing and guiding the next generation" (Erikson, 1963, p. 267). A polarity between generativity and stagnation is at the core of the seventh of Erikson's eight developmental stages, a stage thought to co-occur with middle adulthood. Having formed a sense of identity and developed relationships, the middle-aged adult at the generative stage is thought to be ready to become involved in the larger sphere of society, and to work to continue it and perhaps improve it for the next generation. As contemporary generativity theorists McAdams and de St. Aubin (1992) put it, "in generativity, the adult nurtures, teaches, leads, and promotes the next generation while generating life products and outcomes that benefit the social system and promote its continuity from one generation to the next" (p. 1003).

Clearly, many of the activities that are labeled as volunteer work fit these definitions of generativity. Many of the activities of volunteers cross generational lines, as when volunteers serve as companions to elderly adults and when they provide services to children. As such, the activities of volunteers may contribute to continuity and linkages across generations. In particular, when the recipient of volunteer services is a young person, the potential contribution of volunteerism to future generations is especially evident. To better reflect the diversity and frequency of volunteer activities, Table 14.1 presents the volunteer jobs performed in the previous month as reported by respondents to a national survey of volunteering conducted in each of several years (Independent Sector, 1996). As can be seen in this table, many of the volunteer activities performed by adults are clearly directed at the next generation (as represented by current youths): for example, baby-sitting, Sunday School teacher, coach, youth group leader, and Big Brother or Big Sister. Furthermore, some activities appear to be directed at future generations, in addition to current generations, as in the case of arts organiza-

TABLE 14.1

Distribution of Volunteer Jobs in the Past Month (April–May 1996 and
1994; February–March 1992, 1990, and 1988)

	% Volunteers[a]				
Job	1996	1994	1992	1990	1988
Aide/assistant to paid employees	3.1	3.3	2.5	7.6	6.2
Informal volunteering	11.0	8.9	11.1	10.6	13.6
Assisting the elderly, handicapped, social service recipients, or homeless (not as part of an organization or group)	5.6	4.8	6.0	7.3	7.7
Baby-sitting (not as part of an organization or group)	5.4	4.1	5.1	3.3	5.9
Religion related	21.5	22.3	12.4	16.5	12.7
Aide to clergy	3.2	4.1	2.1	7.1	4.0
Choir member or director	2.9	2.1	2.5	2.3	2.0
Church usher	1.6	1.9	1.1	1.5	1.5
Deacon or deaconess	0.7	0.6	0.6	0.4	1.0
Parish visitor or missionary	0.9	1.1	0.7	3.1	0.9
Sunday School or bible teacher	4.3	4.7	3.7	2.1	3.3
Office work for religious organizations	3.2	1.8	1.7	—	—
Other religious volunteer work	4.7	6.0	4.3	—	—
Driver	2.3	2.0	3.0	4.3	2.5
Fundraising for local organizations	7.3	4.8	—	—	5.3
Board member or trustee	1.6	1.3	1.7	1.6	2.3
Office work (e.g., answering telephone, clerical work, but not for religious organizations)	2.6	2.2	2.6	2.8	2.1
Organization officer (elected or appointed)	0.8	0.8	1.4	1.0	1.3
Committee member	3.2	2.7	4.9	3.6	4.9
Campaign worker or election day worker	0.5	0.8	0.4	0.5	1.6
Cleaning or janitorial work	1.6	1.0	2.5	2.2	1.3
Assistant at blood bank or blood donation station	0.3	0.4	0.3	0.4	1.2
Hospital volunteer or assistant at nursing home	1.3	1.8	0.8	0.9	2.4
Visiting nurse	—	0.1	0.1	0.1	0.4
Fire, rescue, or first aid squad volunteer	0.4	0.6	0.2	0.4	0.7
Coach, director, or recreational volunteer	4.4	2.7	3.2	2.1	3.3
Librarian or aide in library	0.8	0.6	0.5	0.4	0.6
Teacher or tutor (not as aide to paid employee)	3.7	3.4	4.6	2.6	3.5
Youth group leader or aide	3.3	3.5	4.8	3.1	3.3
Community coordinator	1.1	1.1	0.9	0.6	1.2
Counselor (Big Brother/Big Sister, substance abuse prevention)	1.2	1.3	1.0	1.1	0.9
Social service counselor	0.2	0.9	0.8	0.8	0.6

continues

TABLE 14.1 (Continued)

Job	% Volunteers[a]				
	1996	1994	1992	1990	1988
Arts volunteer (theater, arts, and music)	2.0	1.1	1.6	1.5	1.6
Usher, guide, or tour leader	0.5	0.3	0.5	0.6	0.4
Civic or social group spokesperson	0.7	0.8	1.3	1.3	1.1
Meeting or convention planner	1.2	1.8	2.2	1.1	1.7
Poll taker	—	0.1	0.0	0.2	0.4
Telephone hotline volunteer	0.7	0.7	0.6	—	—
Unpaid blood donor	0.6	1.0	0.4	—	—
Other	4.4	10.5	9.8	5.5	1.3
Don't know	11.4	17.2	19.6	26.6	32.7

Note. Dashes indicate data were not available; the category was not included in the survey for that year. From *Giving and Volunteering in the United States: Findings From a National Survey, 1996* (Table 1.7) by Independent Sector, 1996, Washington, DC: Author. Copyright 1996 by Independent Sector. Reprinted with permission.
[a]Data are from the 39% of respondents in 1988, the 43% in 1990, the 39% in 1992, the 39% in 1994, and the 40% in 1996 who volunteered in the last month.

tions that may well have extended "lives." It is clear that adult volunteers serve youths in a variety of ways and do so in significant amounts.

Not only are some of the most frequently performed volunteer jobs directed at youths, but many of the other volunteer activities reported in Table 14.1 are very likely to target all members of the community, including youths, and as investments in the larger community constitute investments in the well-being, welfare, and quality of life of subsequent generations. In particular, arts volunteers, guides or tour leaders, fire or rescue volunteers represent this category. The remaining volunteer jobs raise an interesting issue when considered from the perspective of generative activities, namely, whether the volunteer activities directed at adult (and especially elderly adult) recipients are generative in nature. Although not directly serving future generations, activities such as assisting the elderly or performing office work do benefit the social system, have an impact on the community as a whole, and affect the general quality of life in a society—all of which may redound to the benefit of generations to come.

This list of volunteer jobs, then, informs us that from an action standpoint, as behaviors, volunteer activities and generative activities have very much in common (and, perhaps, even more points of commonality than of distinction) in their contributions not only to present, but also to future, quality of life and societal functioning. Volunteer activities, in many cases, are generative activities, and generative concerns are often expressed through volunteerism. Moreover, this set of volunteer jobs, at the risk of pointing out the obvious, tells us that volunteer and generative activities are by their nature social: Individuals work with service recipients to improve recipients' lives; these relationships often occur in the context of a formal organization;

some organizations (e.g., foundations) seek to serve other organizations (e.g., public libraries); and some organizations target all of these goals (e.g., many religious institutions). Thus, through this network of social relationships in the voluntary and nonprofit sector of a society, a society becomes a generative one.

THE PSYCHOLOGY OF GENERATIVITY AND VOLUNTEERISM

As our brief tour of the activities that are perceived as generative and volunteering suggests, there may be very little difference between generativity and volunteering. There is, of course, much more to both phenomena than just the behaviors being performed. Accordingly, we now turn to the psychological underpinnings and the motivational foundations of volunteerism and generativity.

Generativity, according to McAdams (2001; McAdams & de St. Aubin, 1992), consists of seven psychosocial features, all thought to be in the service of future generations. The motivational components are (a) agentic and communal desires to act on behalf of the future and (b) cultural demands, which are age-based, to assume responsibility for the next generation, and these lead to an explicit (c) concern for future generations. Along with a (d) belief in human goodness, these motives and values result in (e) commitments to (f) act on these concerns. And, finally, these features merge into a coherent story or (g) narration of generativity, which is a part of the individual's life story. This last feature, as we will see, certainly distinguishes generativity from other similar phenomena, including volunteerism.

Investigators who have studied volunteerism, much like those who have studied generativity, have probed the psychological structures and processes underlying this kind of activity, and a good deal of this research has focused on the motivations behind participation in volunteer work. In our own work on the psychology of volunteerism, we have sought to understand why volunteers actively seek out opportunities to help others, often making a commitment to an ongoing helping relationship that may extend over a considerable period of time and that may entail considerable personal costs of time, energy, and opportunity. To do so, we have adopted a motivational perspective, specifically one that attempts to articulate and identify the personal and social *functions* being served by a person's thoughts, feelings, and actions (Snyder, 1993).

A FUNCTIONAL ACCOUNT OF VOLUNTEERISM

In psychology, the themes of functionalism are reflected in diverse perspectives that emphasize the adaptive and purposeful strivings of people toward personal and social ends and goals. A core proposition of functionalist theorizing is that people can and do perform the same actions in the service of different psychological functions. Thus, for example, in the functional accounts of attitudes and persuasion offered by M. Smith, Bruner, and White (1956) and by Katz (1960), it is proposed that the same attitudes could serve different functions for different people. More recently, however, there has been a broadening of the domain of functionalist theorizing to include diverse cognitive, affective, behavioral, and interpersonal processes (e.g., Cantor, 1994; Snyder, 1992, 1993; Snyder & Cantor, 1998).

In the tradition of such functionalist theorizing, a functional analysis may have the potential to reveal the motivational foundations of volunteer helping activity (see Clary & Snyder, 1991; Omoto & Snyder, 1995; Snyder, Clary, & Stukas, 2000). Specifically, the core propositions of a functional analysis of volunteerism are that acts of volunteerism that are similar on the surface may be supported by different underlying motivations, and that the functions served by volunteerism reveal themselves in the unfolding dynamics of the initiation and maintenance of voluntary helping behavior.

Out of our theoretical and empirical work, we have identified six psychological functions that can be served by involvement in volunteer work:

1. Volunteering may allow individuals opportunities to express *values* related to altruistic and humanitarian concern for others.
2. Volunteering may provide *understanding* about different people, places, skills, or about oneself.
3. Volunteering may serve the *social* function of providing opportunities to engage in activities valued by important others and to fit in and get along with one's reference groups.
4. Volunteering may serve the *career*-related function of allowing individuals to acquire and develop new skills, forge professional contacts, and enhance their résumés.
5. Volunteering may serve the *protective* function of reducing guilt about being more fortunate than others and may provide the opportunity to address one's own personal problems.
6. Volunteering may serve the *enhancement* function of boosting self-promoting personal growth and development, and facilitating positive strivings of the ego.

To assess these motivations for volunteering, Clary et al. (1998) developed the Volunteer Function Inventory (VFI), an inventory that reliably and validly taps a set of motivations believed to be of generic relevance to volunteerism. With the VFI, each function is assessed by a separate, five-item scale: Values (e.g., "I can do something for a cause that is important to me"), Understanding (e.g., "Volunteering lets me learn things through direct, hands-on experience"), Career (e.g., "Volunteering allows me to explore different career options"), Social (e.g., "People I'm close to want me to volunteer"), Protective (e.g., "Volunteering is a good escape from my own troubles"), and Enhancement (e.g., "Volunteering makes me feel important"). The six-factor structure of the VFI has been identified, replicated, and cross-validated on diverse samples of volunteers and nonvolunteers; in each case, the six-factor solution, measuring the Values, Understanding, Career, Social, Enhancement, and Protective functions of volunteering, has emerged as the preferred solution (for a review, see Snyder et al., 2000).

The VFI has proved its utility in a series of investigations of the hypothesized relations between the underlying functions of volunteering and the actual processes of volunteerism. When it comes to the *initiation of volunteer activity*, functionalist theorizing generates the hypothesis that individuals will initiate volunteer behavior to the extent that they believe it can fulfill their underlying motivations. In several tests of this hypothesis (e.g., Clary et al., 1998; Clary, Snyder, Ridge, Miene, & Haugen; 1994; Omoto, Snyder, & Smith, 1999; D. M. Smith, Omoto, & Snyder, 2001), participants evaluated messages as appealing and persuasive, intended to volunteer in the future, and were more likely to respond to appeals to volunteer to the extent that the messages matched motivations of great importance to them. When it comes to actually *engaging in volunteer activity*, individuals who received benefits from volunteer work that matched their initial motivations are more satisfied (e.g., Clary et al., 1998), less likely to experience stress and burnout (Crain, Omoto, & Snyder, 1998), and perform their volunteer tasks better (Ridge, 1993) than those who received mismatched benefits. And, finally, when it comes to *sustaining volunteer activity*, intentions to continue serving as volunteer helpers are also linked to the matching of helpers' experiences as volunteers with their motivations for volunteering (e.g., Clary et al., 1998), as are the actual completion of commitments to serve a tour of duty as volunteers (e.g., Clary & Miller, 1986).

Although we have emphasized the activities of individual volunteers, it is important to recognize the larger, collective contexts in which such activities occur. After all, much volunteering occurs in the context of organizations that recruit, train, and place volunteers in service opportunities, organizations that range in size and scope from the local to the national to the global. Moreover, individual volunteerism occurs against a backdrop of societal attitudes and values that support and promote such involvement in society. Accordingly, theoretical considerations of volunteerism often have used a multilevel strategy of conceptual analysis, considering individual, organizational, and societal levels of analysis and the interplay of the perspectives provided by these levels of analysis (e.g., Omoto & Snyder, 2002). Moreover, there is very often a community context to such organizations that, in the United States at least, have often emerged as a result of community grassroots organizing (with prime examples being the community-based AIDS volunteer service organizations found in every state in the United States).

The importance of this community context is underscored by the role of community concern as an important motivator of volunteer service, as well as the role of community connection in drawing people into volunteer service, in sustaining their participation, and in promoting their effectiveness (e.g., Omoto & Snyder, 2002).

Taken together, the investigations that we have reviewed provide empirical support for a functional approach that focuses on the psychological purposes served by sustained prosocial behavior. Functional motivations have been identified and investigated in terms of their roles in guiding people toward volunteer activities (as suggested by studies of the recruitment of volunteers with persuasive messages), influencing the unfolding dynamics at play during their tenure as volunteers (as indicated by studies of the determinants of the satisfaction and task performance of volunteers), and in sustaining involvement in volunteer activities (as suggested by studies of volunteers' intentions to commit themselves to further service and by longitudinal studies of volunteers).

LESSONS AND CONTRIBUTIONS

Thus far, in our considerations of generativity and volunteerism, we have seen that these two research areas overlap considerably from the standpoint of actions, but that potential differences begin to emerge in the psychological dynamics that have been proposed to be involved in each domain. This pattern of resemblances and distinctions suggests that each research area can contribute to the other and, in doing so, deepen our understanding of both. Of course, as we draw out the lessons of one research area for the other, it is quite possible that new and promising avenues of research will appear.

Lesson 1: From Volunteerism to Generativity

One possibility, which emerges as we think about generativity from the perspective of research on volunteers' motivations, is that the same principles of matching motivations to actions may apply to many forms of generativity. Just as a diversity of motivations may underlie volunteerism, so too may apparently similar acts of generativity reflect markedly different underlying motivations. And, just as the course of volunteerism may be foreshadowed by these underlying motivations, so too may agendas for generative action reflect a corresponding pattern. Individuals may embark on a course of generative action, may derive satisfaction from it, and may sustain it to the extent that it can and does fulfill their own personal motivations for generativity.

To illustrate, let us consider one psychological feature that is common to both generativity and volunteerism: the Values function. In this case, the motivation underlying generative/volunteer activity centers on a sense of responsibility for future generations and the matching principle directs us to consider whether a volunteer feels as if his or her actions are indeed enhancing the lot of those in future generations. The straightforward prediction, of course, is that the individual whose actions satisfy this concern will be likely to continue this kind of activity, whereas the individual whose actions fail to satisfy this concern will be likely to discontinue this particular form of service to future generations.

This interplay of goals desired and goals achieved applies not only to an activity at one point in time but also to activities over time. One aspect of research on volunteers' motivations has focused on volunteerism as a process that occurs over time. By its very definition as a form of helping, volunteerism is ongoing and sustained prosocial action, action that may go on for months and years. Accordingly, theoretical perspectives on volunteerism have attempted to articulate the stages of the volunteer process as it unfolds over time; thus, one account of the volunteer process (Omoto & Snyder, 1990; Snyder & Omoto, 2000) has identified antecedents, experiences, and consequences stages of the volunteer process, with events at earlier stages leading to and setting the stage for events at subsequent stages of the volunteer process. Similarly, empirical research on volunteerism has often focused on identifying predictors of longevity of service, with functional motivations for volunteering and the match between motivations for volunteering and volunteers' subsequent experiences as volunteers emerging as predictors of length of service and commitment to volunteerism (e.g., Crain et al., 1998; O'Brien, Crain, Omoto, & Snyder, 2000; Omoto & Snyder, 1995; Penner & Finkelstein, 1998). Similar theoretical and empirical perspectives may also potentially be brought to bear on generative action, which, like volunteerism, may be extended in time (indeed, the outcomes of generative actions often may not come to pass until generations to come).

Just as it is productive to examine, from conceptual and empirical perspectives, unfolding stages of the volunteer process, it may also be productive to examine successive stages of generativity. The successive stages of generativity include the antecedent processes that lead people to generativity, the experiences of those engaged in generative action, and the consequences of generative action in the short and long terms. The ways in which events at each of these stages are connected should also be examined. For example, the motivations that lead people to embark on courses of generative action guide and direct the experiences of those engaged in generative activity, and, to the extent that those motivations are fulfilled by generativity activity, they lead to ultimate satisfaction with and continued involvement in generative activity.

Consideration of goals underlying service and the satisfaction of those goals is not simply a matter of opportunities but also one of challenges. Research on efforts to promote volunteer activity, particularly in higher education programs in which students were required to perform community service, has shown that some students' motivations for volunteering has been undermined by those requirements. For example, in one investigation of the consequences of such "mandatory volunteerism" programs, Stukas, Snyder, and Clary (1999) followed students who were required to volunteer in order to graduate from college, and they found that stronger perceptions of external control eliminated an otherwise positive relation between prior volunteer experience and future intentions to volunteer. Quite possibly, a similar undermining effect may occur in the context of generativity, in that people who feel strong social or societal pressures and obligations to engage in generative action may, in the short term, respond to those pressures and obligations but, in the long term, start to "decouple" their intentions for continued generative activity from their own prior involvement, with the possible result being an undermining both of sustained generative activity and of the associated motivation to maintain lasting habits and patterns of generativity.

Lesson 2: Emergent Contributions

Our next lesson is revealed by juxtaposing volunteerism and generativity. Specifically, this lesson begins with the fact that the motivational component in generativity centers on concern for future generations. A moment's reflection reveals that this feature of generativity actually points to a pair of differences. First, generativity concerns are clearly oriented to the future, whereas the concerns in volunteerism are most often thought to be with the present. And second, the targets of generativity are others in the future, whereas in volunteerism the target may be either others or oneself, the volunteer. Combining these two distinctions result in a fourfold table, which we offer as Table 14.2, along with a sorting of the motivational components from both generativity and volunteerism. As can be seen in Table 14.2, specific functions from the psychology of volunteers' motivations can be placed in three quadrants, whereas generative concerns clearly fit within the future-other quadrant.

Among these differences, we see again some similarities and common concerns. First, although the Values motivation for involvement in volunteerism is most typically couched in terms of current needs and problems, we see no reason why a volunteer who is motivated by a recipient's current problems would necessarily reject a concern with that recipient's future. Moreover, in previous theorizing about this function (e.g., Clary & Snyder, 1991), we have argued that this motivation is the most abstract and clearly value-based of the six functions and is the function that is most closely tied to the individual's self-conception. In other words, when one sets aside the present or future orientation, there is a great deal of similarity between the Values function of volunteerism and generative concern with future gen-

TABLE 14.2
Orientations Toward and Targets of Volunteer and Generative Action

Orientation	Target of action	
	Self	Other
Present	Understanding Social Enhancement	Values
Future	Career Protective	Generativity

erations—both are values, both involve issues that are central to the individual's self, and both represent a caring for others.

A second similarity emerges as we consider differences in the target of the concern, in which the Values function and generativity line up on the concern for others side, and the other functions tend to fall within the concern for self side. In research on volunteerism and other types of helping, this distinction recapitulates the altruism–egoism debate: Is helping another person ever done out of concern for the other or is it always performed for the sake of the helper? Our research suggests a somewhat different framing of this question, one that recognizes a somewhat broader range of concerns that may motivate helping and that allows for the possibility of multiple motivations, including the possibility that a volunteer may be both serving another and receiving benefits in the process. Moreover, the most altruistic of the set of motivations identified in functional theorizing, the Values function, consists of both an other-oriented element (concern for others in need) and a self-oriented element (feeling compelled to act on one's values).

Interestingly, a related observation has emerged in work on generativity. McAdams (2001), along with others (e.g., Kotre, 1984), has observed that at the heart of generativity is communion and altruism, on the one hand, and agency and narcissism, on the other. Accordingly, along with other-oriented concerns for future generations, generativity may have as the self-oriented aim "creating something in one's own image, a powerful act of self-expansion" (McAdams, 2001, p. 405). Thus, both generativity and volunteerism may emerge from agendas that interweave other-oriented and self-oriented goals.

Lesson 3: From Generativity to Volunteerism

Our third lesson concerns the contributions of theory and research on generativity to understanding volunteerism and volunteers' motivations. We begin with the most obvious area of overlap of generativity and volunteerism research—those instances in which generative and volunteer activities are grounded in values important to the individual. As have already noted, the Values function served by volunteerism centers on concerns for others, with the implication that the other person is faced with an immediate and present need and where this need is often in the form of a problem that needs to be solved. For example, volunteering to work a weekly shift in a soup kitchen may express one's humanitarian values and provide a direct and immediate contribution to solving several individuals' problems of hunger. In generativity, however, this concern can be for a future other and the need may not, in the strictest sense, yet be a problem (i.e., rather than resolving an existing problem, one's action may attempt to prevent a future problem). For example, nutritional programs directed at pregnant mothers include among their aims the well-being of the infants and the prevention of birth defects and other health problems.

Perhaps the most important lesson here is that there are important distinctions to be made among values. That is, there may well be significant differences between the individual who is motivated primarily by concern for a person with a problem in the present and the individual who is motivated primarily by concern with preventing a problem for a person not yet born. At the very least, these two individuals would very likely gravitate toward different volunteer activities. Moreover, this leads us to expect that these two individuals differ with respect to which recipient is "saved" and which "sacrificed." In other words, given one's resources, which are likely to be limited, the nongenerative/Values function volunteer would direct those resources to a recipient faced with an immediate need, and the generative/Values function volunteer would "spend" those resources on behalf of the future. Consider, as an illustration, the individual concerned with the health of others: Should that individual direct his or her efforts toward helping elderly people with declining health, to children with an existing health problem, or to preventing problems in unborn children? All, of course, are worthy actions, but individuals with limits on time, energy, and money must make decisions about spending those finite resources.

A second contribution coming from work on generativity is the suggestion that generative concerns may be related to volunteerism generally and to people's motivations for volunteering specifically. From an empirical standpoint, this possibility can be addressed by examining the relations between generativity (as measured by the Loyola Generativity Scale, or LGS; McAdams & de St. Aubin, 1992) and volunteers' motivations (as measured by the Volunteer Functions Inventory, or VFI; Clary et al., 1998). In preparation of this chapter, a sample of 143 university undergraduates completed both measures. Not surprisingly, given the previously discussed conceptual links between generativity and values, a correlation of the LGS and Values function emerged ($r = .26$, $p = .002$). Moreover, we also found modest associations between the LGS and the Social ($r = .244$, $p = .003$), Understanding ($r = .208$, $p = .013$), Career ($r = .194$, $p = .02$), and Enhancement ($r = .164$, $p = .05$) functions identified by the VFI. The lone exception to this pattern was the lack of association between the LGS and the Protective function ($r = .04$, ns).

We find, then, that there are empirical connections between generativity and volunteerism. These connections are perhaps best viewed from the perspective of the conceptual linkages between volunteerism and generativity that we are trying to articulate. The association between generativity and values is congruent with the commonality of generative concerns and values that we have explored. In addition, the associations between generativity and several of the relatively self-oriented functions served by volunteering may underscore the possibility that, as we have suggested, generativity may, like volunteerism, stem not only from other-oriented concerns but also from self-oriented ones. Perhaps too, with additional empirical work, it will be possible to map the linkages between hypothesized features of generativity (e.g., passing on knowledge and skills, making contributions to one's community, leaving a legacy) and specific motivations for volunteerism. For example, we might expect a particularly strong association of bettering one's community and the Values function, and perhaps also a strong association of passing along skills and the Understanding function (both involve utilizing one's skills and knowledge). Moreover, concern with a legacy (especially concern with being remembered by others) may be related to the Social and Enhancement function. Finally, interests in productivity and creativity may tap concerns related to the Career function. In any event, additional investigations seem warranted, especially as we draw on the conceptual features of generativity, as identified by McAdams (2001; McAdams & de St. Aubin, 1992), and examine their possible connection with specific goals served by volunteering.

CONCLUSIONS

We have, in this chapter, explored the commonalities that exist between theoretical and empirical aspects of generativity and volunteerism. It is clear that the commonality between these two domains begins with actions: Generative concerns are often expressed in volunteer activities, and many volunteers, intentionally and unintentionally, provide services to future generations. From the perspective of activities, then, the overlap is considerable, although the two kinds of behavior are not necessarily identical. After all, some volunteers direct their efforts at current or "earlier" generations, and some generative adults may express their concerns through their paid employment.

As we move beneath the behavioral surface, a move that is essential in both research areas in the quest to understand why people volunteer and why they are generative, we begin to find important distinctions. Clearly, our work on volunteerism is directed at one important feature of the psychological processes involved in volunteer activity: the motives that bring people to volunteer and that sustain their involvement in volunteerism over time, that is, what they hope to accomplish through their participation in volunteer service. In contrast, studies of generativity are directed at a wide range of psychological components that make up and influence generative concerns. Moreover, the two domains appear to differ with respect to time orientation and target, as research on generativity tends to focus on the future needs of others and research on volunteers' motivations tends to emphasize the present and immediate needs of both helper and recipient.

And, just as we have seen the importance of moving beneath the behavioral surface to understand the psychological underpinnings of volunteerism and generativity, we think it equally important to move the conceptual perspective in another direction, namely, to understand the larger societal and culture context within which such activities occur. We have already noted that, although the United States is marked by high rates of volunteerism (as well as membership and participation in organizations and associations), such phenomena occur in many countries throughout the world as well (Curtis et al., 1992). Yet, the world is marked by considerable cultural variation in, among other things, conceptions of individuals and their relations to society; indeed, the dimension of individualism to collectivism is a key feature in psychological theorizing about culture (e.g., Triandis, 1994). Accordingly, the motivations that underlie and promote volunteerism and generativity may show meaningful culture-to-culture variation along this dimension, with perhaps motivations linked to individual values being particularly prevalent in individualistic cultures and those associated with community concern being particularly prevalent in collectivistic culture (for a more elaborated discussion of the cultural context of motivations for volunteerism and other forms of citizen participation, see Snyder & Omoto, 2001).

In this pattern of similarities and distinctions between volunteerism and generativity as forms of prosocial action, we find other linkages and connections, particularly in terms of some of the fundamental issues about human beings and human behavior that are raised. Explorations of these linkages and connections may provide the foundations for new avenues of theoretical and empirical inquiry, and these inquiries may lead to greater explication of the phenomena and processes of both volunteerism and generativity. Finally, in both activities we find human beings attempting to connect with others, both others who exist and others who will one day exist, and in doing so, contribute to their communities and to their society.

REFERENCES

Cantor, N. (1994). Life task problem solving: Situational affordances and personal needs. *Personality and Social Psychology Bulletin, 20,* 235–243.

Clary, E. G., & Miller, J. (1986). Socialization and situational influences on sustained altruism. *Child Development, 57,* 1358–1369.

Clary, E. G., & Snyder, M. (1991). A functional analysis of altruism and prosocial behavior: The case of volunteerism. In M. Clark (Ed.), *Review of personality and social psychology* (Vol. 12, pp. 119–148). Newbury Park, CA: Sage.

Clary, E. G., Snyder, M., Ridge, R. D., Copeland, J., Stukas, A. A., Haugen, J., & Miene, P. (1998). Understanding and assessing the motivations of volunteers: A functional approach. *Journal of Personality and Social Psychology, 74,* 1516–1530.

Clary, E. G., Snyder, M., Ridge, R. D., Miene, P., & Haugen, J. (1994). Matching messages to motives in persuasion: A functional approach to promoting volunteerism. *Journal of Applied Social Psychology, 24,* 1129–1149.

Crain, A. L., Omoto, A. M., & Snyder, M. (1998, April). *What if you can't always get what you want? Testing a functional approach to volunteerism.* Paper presented at the annual meeting of the Midwestern Psychological Association, Chicago.

Curtis, J. E., Grabb, E., & Baer, D. (1992). Voluntary association membership in fifteen countries: A comparative analysis. *American Sociological Review, 57,* 139–152.

Erikson, E. H. (1963). *Childhood and society* (2nd ed.). New York: Norton.

Independent Sector. (1996). *Giving and volunteering in the United States: Findings from a national survey, 1996.* Washington, DC: Author.

Independent Sector. (1999). *Giving and volunteering in the United States: Executive summary 1999.* Washington, DC: Author.

Katz, D. (1960). The functional approach to the study of attitudes. *Public Opinion Quarterly, 24,* 163–204.

Kotre, J. (1984). *Outliving the self: Generativity and the interpretation of lives.* Baltimore: Johns Hopkins University Press.

McAdams, D. P. (2001). Generativity in midlife. In M. Lachman (Ed.), *Handbook of midlife development* (pp. 395–443). New York: Wiley.

McAdams, D. P., & de St. Aubin, E. (1992). A theory of generativity and its assessment: Through self-report, behavioral acts, and narrative themes in autobiography. *Journal of Personality and Social Psychology, 62,* 1003–1015.

O'Brien, L. T., Crain, A. L., Omoto, A. M., & Snyder, M. (2000, May). *Matching motivations to outcomes: Implications for persistence in service.* Paper presented at the annual meeting of the Midwestern Psychological Association, Chicago.

Omoto, A. M., & Snyder, M. (1990). Basic research in action: Volunteerism and society's response to AIDS. *Personality and Social Psychology Bulletin, 16,* 152–165.

Omoto, A. M., & Snyder, M. (1995). Sustained helping without obligation: Motivation, longevity of service, and perceived attitude change among AIDS volunteers. *Journal of Personality and Social Psychology, 68,* 671–686.

Omoto, A. M., & Snyder, M. (2002). Considerations of community: The context and process of volunteerism. *American Behavioral Scientist, 45,* 846–867.

Omoto, A. M., Snyder, M., & Smith, D. M. (1999). [Unpublished data]. Lawrence: University of Kansas.

Penner, L. A., & Finkelstein, M. A. (1998). Dispositional and structural determinants of volunteerism. *Journal of Personality and Social Psychology, 74*, 525–537.

Ridge, R. D. (1993). *A motivation-based approach for investigating planned helping behavior.* Unpublished doctoral dissertation, University of Minnesota, Minneapolis.

Smith, D. M., Omoto, A. M., & Snyder, M. (2001, June). *Motivation matching and recruitment of volunteers: A field study.* Paper presented at the annual meeting of the American Psychological Society, Toronto, Ontario, Canada.

Smith, M., Bruner, J., & White, R. (1956). *Opinions and personality.* New York: Wiley.

Snyder, M. (1992). Motivational foundations of behavioral confirmation. In M. P. Zanna (Ed.), *Advances in experimental social psychology* (Vol. 25, pp. 67–114). San Diego, CA: Academic Press.

Snyder, M. (1993). Basic research and practical problems: The promise of a "functional" personality and social psychology. *Personality and Social Psychology Bulletin, 19*, 251–264.

Snyder, M., & Cantor, N. (1998). Understanding personality and social behavior: A functionalist strategy. In D. Gilbert, S. Fiske, & G. Lindzey (Eds.), *The handbook of social psychology* (4th ed., Vol. 1, pp. 635–679). Boston: McGraw-Hill.

Snyder, M, Clary, E., & Stukas, A. (2000). The functional approach to volunteerism. In G. Maio & J. Olson (Eds.), *Why we evaluate: Functions of attitudes* (pp. 365–393). Mahwah, NJ: Erlbaum.

Snyder, M., & Omoto, A. M. (2000). Doing good for self and society: Volunteerism and the psychology of citizen participation. In M. Van Vugt, M. Snyder, T. Tyler, & A. Biel (Eds.), *Cooperation in modern society: Promoting the welfare of communities, states, and organizations* (pp. 127–141). London: Routledge.

Snyder, M., & Omoto, A. M. (2001). Basic research and practical problems: Volunteerism and the psychology of individual and collective action. In W. Wosinska, R. Cialdini, D. Barrett, & J. Reykowski (Eds.), *The practice of social influence in multiple cultures* (pp. 287–307). Mahwah, NJ: Erlbaum.

Stukas, A., Snyder, M., & Clary, E. (1999). The effects of "mandatory volunteerism": Satisfaction, intentions, and motivations to volunteer. *Psychological Science, 10*, 59–64.

Triandis, H. C. (1994). *Culture and social behavior.* New York: McGraw-Hill.

IV

LOOKING FORWARD,
LOOKING BACKWARD

15

AN ETHICAL ANALYSIS OF ERIKSON'S CONCEPT OF GENERATIVITY

DON BROWNING

Ever since writing *Generative Man* (1973, 1975), I have believed that Erikson's concept of generativity was more than a psychological construct that defined the nature of adult maturity (Browning, 1975). I have been convinced instead that it was a mixed concept that artfully interwove psychological, ethical, and even metaphysical levels of discourse (Browning, 1987). I also have held the conviction that his idea of generativity was philosophically defensible from an ethical point of view, even though Erikson never attempted to test it from that perspective.

Even more, I have believed that the concept of generativity has special relevance for addressing the challenges of modernity and the increased speed of social change, diversity, and potential social conflict that has come in its trail. In this chapter, I take additional steps to defend these hypotheses about the moral validity of the concept of generativity and its resources for facing the possibilities and strains of modernity.

Contemporary philosophical ethics consists of three competing models of the ethical life. Each believes it can provide the most satisfactory account of the field of ethics and be the most compelling guide to the solution of contemporary moral and social challenges. These three models can be conveniently referred to as an *ethic of principle*, an *ethic of virtue*, and a *narrative ethic*. I claim that Erikson's concept of generativity contains elements of each of these three perspectives. Although Erikson never consciously identified these different viewpoints or systematically ordered them in relation to one another, I believe they fit together in his thought and do so without contradiction. Because all three models are present in his writings, his full concept of generativity is simultaneously multidimensional, powerful, and susceptible to misunderstanding. It is also quite easy to omit one or the other of these three perspectives when discussing his views on generativity. Most interpreters in fact do this. This chapter attempts to clarify these potential misunderstandings and takes steps to show the possible contributions of generativity to an ethic for the 21st century, particularly one able to address the processes of modernization.

Leading ethics of principle—the first of the three models I discuss—can be illustrated with reference to social philosophers John Rawls and Jürgen Habermas and moral psychologist Lawrence Kohlberg (Habermas, 1990). All of them agree that tradition is no longer a trustworthy source for ethics in a modern, and perhaps, postmodern world. Nor can conflicting communities and individuals agree on the definition of the nonmoral or premoral goods that should be central to our lives together. The best we can do, these scholars insist, is to agree on a procedural morality of discourse, one based on various revisions of Kant's (1959) categorical imperative and ethics of respect. The rapid dislocations wrought by modernity's increasing reliance on technical reason can only be met by the common implementation in debates of the universal principle of treating others as ends. Coping with modernity for these philosophers comes down to socializing individuals and communities to respect one another in their various conflicting deliberations.

Ethics of virtue can be found in the well-known writings of Alasdair MacIntyre (1981) and Stanley Hauerwas (1981). They insisted that simple rational principles are not enough to either resolve conflicts or guide action toward the future. The dynamics of modernity, according to them, need to be anchored, if not countered, by tested traditions of habits and virtues. Aristotle and Thomas Aquinas—classical theorists of virtue—are their heroes, and they commend this tradition to the modern world.

MacIntyre and Hauerwas also promoted the relevance of narrative for the formation of the moral self. They are advocates—along with such diverse figures as Paul Ricoeur, Amitai Etzioni, and Robert Bellah—of the importance of communities of tradition that carry commanding narratives and form virtues in their followers that exhibit these narratives. These thinkers believe that the fragmenting dynamics of modernity must be restrained by the renewal and preservation of communities of tradition and the narratives that they carry, especially those who seem most central to the various contemporary world cultures.

Erikson had the strength of implicitly bringing these three perspectives together. Furthermore, precisely because he was a psychologist who paid attention to the rhythms of biosocial development, he contributed a theory of the "good" that is absent from the other perspectives. This theory of the good, which I sometimes call "premoral" good, comes out of his view of human development and the cycle of the generations. In short, Erikson implicitly told us that, to handle the promises and dangers of modernity, we need viable communities of tradition, but ones that actualize the goods of human development as well as exhibit the principle of respect for individuals as they struggle to grow.

THE TELEOLOGICAL SUBSTRATUM OF ERIKSON'S THOUGHT

I first illustrate the implicit ethic of principle in Erikson's idea of generativity, even though this is probably the least visible of the three models in his writings. Even careful readers of Erikson overlook that he sometimes states a summary principle that has moral meaning and yet is consistent with his larger body of psychological concepts. Ethical systems that ground themselves on some general principle can be separated, according to moral philosophers, into teleological and deontological points of view (Frankena, 1973). Even with these distinctions in mind, which I will soon define, Erikson's moral thought does not in fact precisely or purely illustrate either of these alternative ethics of principle. Rather, it implicitly exemplifies features that combine elements of both models into what moral philosophers sometimes call a "mixed deontological" model of moral obligation. Here is what I mean.

Teleological views conform to the principle that ethical duty consists of actualizing or bringing into reality increased amounts of nonmoral or premoral goods. These premoral goods might consist of anything from food, water, health, shelter, or pleasure to more sophisticated goods such as the development of human capabilities and their refinement through parental care, education, culture, or even play. The birth of a child is often thought to be a great premoral good. It would be wrong, however, to say that a child as such is a moral good; that depends on the kind of will the child develops and the pattern of habits and virtues that he or she acquires. But most people would say that children are a great good in a basic premoral sense because they are beautiful, cute, endearing, continue the species, and have great potentialities for growth into moral responsibility. Teleological principles of ethics are often thought to be associated with the utilitarianism of Jeremy Bentham or John Stuart Mill, the pragmatism of William James or John Dewey, or even the older teleological models of Aristotle and Aquinas. All of these views share at least one common ethical idea or principle: that moral action should increase the goods of life. Various teleological views of ethics differ in their theory of which goods are the most important; they also vary in their view of how the goods of life (whatever their theory of these goods happens to be) should be justly distributed.

Deontological ethical systems, in contrast, claim to ground moral obligation on reasons or principles that are intrinsically moral and totally independent of consequences that increase or decrease the premoral goods of life. Kant's (1959) categorical imperative, which says, "I should never act in such a way that I could not also will that my maxim should be a universal law" (p. 18), is often presented as the arch example of deontological ethics. His second formulation of this imperative instructs us to "act so that you treat humanity, whether in your own person or in that of another, always as an end and never as a means only" (p. 47) and is a further illustration of classic deontological ethics. These principles make respecting the rationality and personhood of both self and other the key to morality, as we saw earlier with Rawls, Habermas, and Kohlberg. The promotion of other goods such as health, wealth, pleasure, potentialities, or skills cannot, according to Kantian deontology, trump or override respect for the agency, autonomy, and rationality of persons as ends. For example, a mother may sense her son's mathematical or musical skills, but if she attempts to actualize them in ways that deride his personhood and rationality, even bringing into reality these goods must be seen as proceeding in a basically immoral way. This is true because the mother's action does not conform to the principle of respect for her son as an end who should never be reduced to a means alone.

Erikson was a mixture of both of these perspectives. But this combination was not due to his confusion. He had a defensible way of relating these two styles of ethical thinking. He was not philosophically self-conscious in the way he combined them, but he did it wisely nonetheless. Erikson was a teleologist in his emphasis on the actualization of the interacting potentialities (premoral goods) that sustain and renew the cycle of the generations. He sounds like a deontologist, however, in his concern that these goods be universalized to include each present and future child. For instance, he could speak of a "universal sense of generative responsibility toward all human beings brought intentionally into this world" (Erikson, 1964, p. 131). For him, such universalization should be accomplished in ways as to communicate respect for persons. Rather than grounding respect, however, on rationality as did Kant, Erikson is more likely to speak of the phylogenetic need for "mutual recognition of and by another face" (Erikson, 1964, p. 94). An ethic of universal justice of mutual recognition pervades Erikson's ethical psychology, giving it at times a Kantian tone if not a technical Kantian substance. Furthermore, communicating respect for the personhood of the other, in the sense of recognizing her or his face and bestowing a sense of validity through this recognition, is for Erikson the great insight of both good psychotherapy and the nonviolent ethic of *Satyagraha* (Erikson, 1969).

One's natural generative interest in the welfare of one's own offspring, as important to Erikson as it was for understanding the wellspring of ethics, was never allowed by him to trump a universal obligation to the well-being of all children. In advancing this formulation, Erikson is siding with, and giving his own twist to, the kind of mixed deontological principle of obligation found today in such different moral philosophers as William Frankena (1973), Paul Ricoeur (1992), Jürgen Habermas (1990), and Alan Donegan (1977). These perspectives share a common feature of containing and guiding various teleological theories of the good life with a superordinate concern with universal justice and respect for the other as an end or, as Erikson would say it, as a person requiring and deserving recognition and mutual regard.

THE ARCHEOLOGY OF GENERATIVITY

It should be acknowledged, however, that regardless of the presence of the deontological dimension of Erikson's ethic, from another perspective the teleological aspect is the more fundamental. The test of universal respect or recognition comes for Erikson, as it does for Paul Ricoeur, as a second step, after one has advanced preliminary claims about the good. His teleology is immediately evident in his basic definition of generativity as "the concern in establishing and guiding the next generation" (Erikson, 1963, p. 267). The word *establishing* refers to the goods of procreation and the actualization of the epigenetic timetable of human potentialities. The word *guiding* refers to the goods of education and teaching as cultural acts. The teleological elements are all the more striking in one of Erikson's many definitions of *care* (the virtue associated with generativity) as "a quality essential for psychosocial evolution, for we are the teaching species" (Erikson, 1964, p. 130). He went on to say, "Animals, too, instinctively encourage in their young what is ready for release" (Erikson, 1964, p. 130). This raises the question, just what potentialities (or goods in this sense) do parents instinctively try to release or actualize in their offspring?

Teleological perspectives on ethics are also evident in Erikson's reformulation of the golden rule. But evident as well in this new interpretation are deontological elements pertaining to justice, equality, and the recognition of others as ends. Erikson's restatement of the golden rule goes like this:

> Truly worthwhile acts enhance a mutuality between doer and the other— a mutuality which strengthens the doer even as it strengthens the other. Thus the "doer" and "the other" are partners in one deed. Seen in the light of human development, this means that the doer is activated in whatever strength is appropriate to his age, stage, and condition, even as he activates in the other the strength appropriate to *his* age, stage and condition. Understood this way, the Rule would say that it is best to do to another what will strengthen you even as it will strengthen him—that is, what will develop his best potentials even as it develops your own. (Erikson, 1964, p. 233)

This is a complex passage and a challenge to interpret from the perspective of philosophical ethics. One can say with confidence, however, that this is not a reduction of the golden rule to a simple exchange theory. Erikson is not arguing that the golden rule is telling us to actualize others *if* we can predict that they will in turn actualize us. The golden rule, in Erikson's rendition, is not a conditional contract analogous to those created to regulate transactions in the fields of business and law. It is a theory of reversible mutuality built, as we will see, on far more fundamental teleological and deontological grounds. Its reversibility, that is, the fact that it must apply equally to self and other, points to its deontological characteristic. The fact that this reversibility or mutuality interweaves fundamental developmental goods points to its teleological features.

Erikson's reinterpretation of the golden rule draws on several aspects of his psychological and moral system. The instinctual grounds of generativity are important, although not exhaustive; the concepts of *cogwheeling* and the *epigenetic ground plan* are also important for Erikson's view of the real meaning of this ancient moral principle. We must remember that Erikson believes that there is, to borrow a term from the philosopher Paul Ricoeur, an "archeology" to generativity and its associated virtue of care. By archeology, Ricoeur means an archaic desire, but one that is always filtered through a linguistic or symbolically encoded cogito or ego (Ricoeur, 1970). This means that we never know our desires directly without symbolic mediation. Ricoeur would say, and Erikson would agree, that our desires are always *interpreted* desires. Our desires become attached to objects that are themselves linguistically mediated. These objects become the teleology of our desires—the direction or aim of our desires—and when we contemplate our desires, we think about them dialectically in terms of both their push and their aim—both in terms of their archeology and their teleology. This is why Erikson (1963) preferred to speak more about modes and modalities or biosocial patterns of interaction than he did about instinctual energies as such. And in the case of Erikson, this dialectic between biological tendency and culturally meaningful object also applied just as well to the desire, need, or inclination—whichever we call it—for generativity.

By using the idea of archeology, I mean to communicate Erikson's belief that generativity and care have instinctual foundations but also give rise to and interact with a variety of objects and symbolic meanings. Desire for Erikson is more than what is implied by Freud's concept of *libido*—with all the tension-reduction and pleasure-driven features Freud assigned to it, especially in the middle period of the development of his psychodynamic theory. Erikson's theory of instinct is like that of William James (1950) and the contemporary moral philosopher Mary Midgley (1978); there is for them no master instinct from which all other motivations are derived. Even the need for generativity, although casting a gentle claim on the purpose and function of the other psychobiological fragments, does not in Erikson's psychology exercise dictatorial control over other tendencies. All basic needs and tendencies find their place in Erikson's theory of the epigenetic principle that sees human development as evolving out of a preexisting set of potentialities, each of which has "its time of origin" (Erikson, 1963, p. 65).

Erikson broadens Freud's theory of libido into a more inclusive theory of psychobiological potentials that have, with the help of what Heinz Hartmann (1958) called a supporting "average expectable environment," phase-specific moments of emergence. These potentials, according to Erikson (1963), include the pleasure-oriented sucking, holding, and expelling tendencies of the oral and anal phases of development; the wider exercise of muscles and skeleton structure between age 2 and 5; the emergence of formal cognitive operations during adolescence; increased genital sexual demands during the early teens; and, finally, maturing generative needs to procreate and teach (or the use of these urges analogously for wider tasks) in young and middle adulthood. These multiple needs and tendencies constitute the foundation of Erikson's theory of cogwheeling—the idea that the needs of the young and those of adults interlock, activate one another, and propel each other through the life cycle. One should think of this less as a calculated exchange and more as an intermeshing of gears that are finely tuned to fit one another. This intermeshing set of potentialities and needs, especially between the very young and their parents, constitutes the archeology of the teleological trajectory of Erikson's ethical psychology.

These inclinations and strivings for the goods of the life cycle constitute for Erikson what humans bring to the ethical task; they make up the premoral foundations of what ethics is all about. But ethics, even the ethics of generativity, involves for Erikson more than this archeology. Disciplined ethics entails, as we have already seen, some guiding principle of justice and universalization that extends our more parochial generative preferences to include but also go beyond our own kin and those closely associated with us. And, as discussed below, such an ethic also must give consideration to the virtues and narratives that endow with wider meaning both the objects of one's generative desires and the principles designed to order them. But before turning to these additional models of the ethical life, a further word about human generative archeology is in order.

EVOLUTIONARY PSYCHOLOGY AND ETHICS

Erikson's ethics of generativity clearly has similarities to the theory of kin altruism in contemporary evolutionary psychology, sociobiology, and the philosophical efforts to conceptualize the ethical implications of these disciplines. Some ethicists informed by evolutionary psychology believe that kin altruism is the foundation of the moral capacities of humans. James Q. Wilson in his book *The Moral Sense* (1993) provides a good example of this point of view. Citing the theories of kin altruism and inclusive fitness of biologists W. D. Hamilton and Robert Trivers, Wilson (1993) believes humans have a drive (or at least their genes have a tendency) to replicate themselves. This explains, according to evolutionary psychology, why parents are willing to care for, and sometimes even sacrifice themselves for, their offspring; it is really a way of living on into the future through their children as carriers of their genes. This constitutes the grounds of parental care and the love that leads children, in turn, to identify in gratitude with their parents' wishes and values. Evolutionary psychology has its own theory of generativity, and it has analogies to what I have called the archeology of Erikson's view of generativity. It helps ground Erikson's bold but basically unsupported assertion that parents need their children as much as children need them and his belief that humans are a teaching animal.

But evolutionary psychology, especially its more sociobiological wing, presents its theory of generativity in narrowly mathematical terms. The subtleties of Erikson's view of the symbolic levels of generativity are often lost to evolutionary psychologists. For instance, the mathematics of generativity suggest that parents may sacrifice for their offspring (and brothers and sisters for each other) because they share 50% of the same genes. But this biologically determined tendency to care declines, we are told, as the ratio of shared genes diminishes, with uncles and aunts having less inclination to sacrifice for nephews and nieces because they have fewer genes in common (Singer, 1981). Kin altruism, according to this theory, soon runs out as the circle of unrelated neighbors and strangers widens. Cooperation and care between nonkin, according to evolutionary psychology, is motivated by reciprocal altruism—the conditional exchange of goods as conceptualized by forms of exchange theory that I alluded to earlier.

Erikson is more of an instinctual and motivational pluralist than many sociobiologists and evolutionary psychologists. The need to procreate and to care for what one procreates has natural foundations in Erikson's view, but it is mixed with other motivations that have some degree of autonomy from this central goal. For instance, there are for Erikson relatively autonomous needs to know one's world and one's place within it—hence, the need to have a cohesive yet flexible sense of identity or self-definition (Erikson, 1959). But this need for identity is also fueled by an archaic need, quite biological in nature, for recognition by one's primary caretakers. This is a need one never outgrows even as one's circles of social interaction expand far beyond the boundaries of basic kinship units (Erikson, 1964). Erikson's awareness of the interaction between the drive for gene reproduction and other basic needs makes it possible for him to escape from relying too heavily on kin altruism as a motivational and explanatory theory of one's generative capacities. This, however, is a mistake commonly made in sociobiology, although perhaps less so in the newer evolutionary psychology. Nonetheless, properly used and contained, the theories of kin altruism complement and enrich Erikson's view of the archeology of generativity.

ERIKSON, NEO-ARISTOTELIANISM, AND THOMISM: TELEOLOGY AND THE GENERATIVE ANALOGY

Erikson should be understood as standing in a long line of teleologically oriented philosophers extending from Plato and Aristotle to Thomas Aquinas and that includes various contemporary pragmatists as well as many current neo-Aristotelians. Most thinkers standing in this tradition give central place to finding meaning in life through either having and raising children or extending this impulse actually and symbolically to others beyond one's immediate kin. Plato (1951) did this in the *Symposium* through Diotima's speeches about gaining immortality through one's offspring, even though he in the end subordinated this impulse to the higher immortality and permanence of abstract contemplation of the good and true. Aristotle made a slightly different use of the generative analogy when he argued that parental love and preference for kin should not be suppressed in the good city, as Plato argued in *The Republic* (1968). Rather, one should build on these impulses and extend them to others beyond the circle of immediate offspring. Kin preference, Aristotle (1941b) argued in *Politics*, constitutes the inner glue of society. Thomas Aquinas picked up the same line of argument. He saw an analogical link between a parent's preferential love for his or her offspring, God's love of all humans, and the extension of kin altruism to the distant neighbor and stranger (Aquinas, 1917). Aquinas followed Aristotle in believing that humans have a natural inclination to love their children first; children, in turn, have the same inclination with regard to their parents. But, according to Aquinas, this preferential impulse for those near and dear should be analogically extended to all humans on the belief that they are children of God, made in God's image, manifestations of God's goodness, and therefore to be loved as one should love the goodness of God.

In spite of this strong place for the analogy of generativity in Aquinas's thought, and that of his neo-Thomistic followers such as Pope Leo XIII and Pius XI, Catholicism retained into the 20th century a Platonic sensibility that subordinated in value actual parenthood to the spiritual and symbolic parenthood of the celibate priest. It is important to recognize, however, the cluster of very analogous insights into generativity found in Erikson, Aristotle, Aquinas, and evolutionary psychology. Allow me to recommend the studies of Stephen Pope (1994) as a contemporary scholar actively investigating these congruences. Furthermore, it must be observed that the spiritual world of Catholicism (as well as other religions) joins with Erikson against the flat naturalism of evolutionary psychology; they both assert in different ways that for generativity to become a cultural work, in contrast to the simple act of biological procreation, it must be elaborated within a worldview that at least finds a place for religious symbolism, if not the spiritual as such.

GENERATIVITY, VIRTUE, AND NEO-ARISTOTELIANISM

Not only is Erikson similar to Aristotle and Aquinas in understanding the importance for ethics of the analogy of generativity, but he also shares their interest in virtue as an aid to the ethical life and to the realization of teleological aims. An extensive comparison between Erikson and the Aristotelian–Thomistic view of virtue is far beyond the scope of this chapter. The following points, however, should be helpful. For both perspectives, virtue builds on and helps realize natural inclinations—extending some tendencies while guiding and redirecting others. William James, the American pragmatist, in his *Talks to Teachers on Psychology* (1899/1962) and other writings on habits, says the same thing, as does the contemporary moral philosopher Owen Flanagan (1991). Erikson and the Aristotelian–Thomistic school also understood virtue as a kind of synthesis. For Aristotle, a virtue was a *mean* between two extremes (Aristotle, 1941a); for Erikson, it is a synthesis between conflicting development tendencies (Erikson, 1964). Virtue, for Erikson, is achieved by a fortunate congruence between a supporting environment and an active ego that attempts to synthesize developmental conflicts, for example, the conflict early in life between trust and mistrust synthesized by the virtue of hope.

Hence, Erikson's mixed principle of obligation that combines justice with the teleological good is made concrete in his ethic through being supplemented by a theory of virtue and personal formation. But how is one's quest for the good, one's virtues, and one's moral principles logically related? This is an issue Erikson, who was not self-consciously an ethicist, never addressed. The work of Paul Ricoeur might be of help in understanding what Erikson was really doing. Ricoeur would say that ethics is first the quest for the good, but that one first knows the goods one seeks through the way communities of tradition shape one's practices, habits, and virtues. Ethics of principle, as Ricoeur (1992) suggested, are invoked in situations of conflict when settled teleological goods, practices, and virtues are surprised, overwhelmed, and conflict with the quests for the good by other people. This is when one asserts, or should assert, one's more deontological principles of justice and fairness. People do not derive ethics from abstract principles alone; Erikson knew this. Nonetheless, people need them to order and refine conflicts in their practices and virtues. Erikson did not know why he had both an ethics of virtue and an ethics of principle, but part of our fascination with his thought, I submit, comes from the fact that he intuited the need for each of these models of the moral life. This is also why his thought is so relevant to the needs of contemporary society and the emerging challenges of modernity.

However, just as it has become popular to say that humans cannot live by principles alone, I believe that Erikson would agree that humans cannot live by either principles or virtues alone. Erikson, as we saw, had his ethical principles (for instance, his reinterpretation of the golden rule); but he also had his theory of how virtue is formed so that people can live well in average expectable circumstances and, in addition, be motivated to apply more abstract principles when more serious conflicts arise.

NARRATIVE, IDENTITY, AND ETHICS

Finally, in addition to Erikson's psychobiology and teleology of generative motivations and inclinations, his theory of virtues, his formulation of a principle that harnesses and guides one's teleological energies and mediates between one's conflicting practices, Erikson also understood the role of narrative in forming the moral life and extending the scope of generativity. In fact, narrative constituted for Erikson something of a surrounding envelope that oriented and valorized all of these other elements: generative desires, virtues, and principles.

In contemporary philosophical and theological ethics, there are, as I indicated earlier, many powerful voices claiming that narratives and stories, more than either abstract moral principles or virtues, are the true carriers and shapers of the moral life. To handle the tensions of modernity, they argue, one needs to revive one's narrative traditions and the communities that carry them. In much of narrative ethical theory, stories repeated in the rituals of vital communities are thought to have considerable power to shape virtues. The theological ethicist Stanley Hauerwas believes that narratives form character, which in turn organizes a person's virtues into a functioning whole relevant to the features of a story with beginning, middle, and end.

Erikson illustrates how the inherited religious narratives that Luther and Gandhi both received and reinterpreted also supported their personal stories of growth toward generative maturity. Religious narratives can do at least two things to consolidate and extend generativity, although it should be confessed that not all religions function in these ways. First, they can provide a person with a faith in the goodness of life—an "ontology of creation" so to speak—that conveys a basic trustworthiness to both one's own initiatives and the world's basic tendency to respond to them in supportive and actualizing ways (Schweiker, 1995). Second, some religious narratives extend a person's sense of kinship beyond blood relations to include all of humanity, indeed, in some religions to all of creation. In addition, many religions provide symbols that extend this sense of kinship with others indefinitely into the future.

An example of this first function of religious narrative can be found in the way Luther's sudden realization of the true meaning of justification by faith reconnected him with his earliest sense of initiative first awakened by his mother's affirmation and nurture (Erikson, 1962). This trust in one's basic capacities is fundamental for the successful resolution of later developmental crises, including the crisis of generativity versus stagnation. Second, both Luther and Gandhi were formed by stories that extended the scope of their generativity to include distant others. In the case of Luther, it was the narrative of how all humans are children of God, that is, all offspring of the one Father above all other fathers. And in the case of Gandhi, his generative care was extended to all of life, as demanded by the narrative implications of the philosophy of *ahimsa,* or nonviolence toward all living things (Erikson, 1969).

These reflections on the role of narrative in an ethic of generativity should leave us with the following generalizations. First, generativity builds on natural psychobiological tendencies to procreate and sustain those who, as Aquinas would say, carry "our substance." This is an important insight of Erikson's, just as it is of evolutionary psychology and the teleological tradition of Aristotle and his followers. It suggests that although generativity should never be confined to parenthood, it must never gain too much distance from it. Second, one must remember that Erikson was an instinctual pluralist. Both he, and William James before him, understood that people's multiple and conflicting natural tendencies require the guidance and stabilization of strong communities of tradition that serve as storehouses of moral principles, virtues, and narratives. There is no possibility of creating truly generative people without inducting them into a *culture* of generativity with powerful accompanying symbols. Generativity is a tendency of nature, but it needs the support and completion of communities of tradition that contain generatively inspiring narratives.

Finally, Erikson understood the importance of the Kantian-like principle of moral respect. Religious and cultural traditions may be carriers of generativity, but they may often seek to apply them only to "those like us" or our own kin and community. Traditions carrying powerful founding narratives often need critique. Sometimes these principles of critique are within them, but sometimes not, or at least not readily available. Erikson knew that the golden rule could be used to critique a narrative tradition, and he knew that it was often located within the larger narratives of the world religions. But he also saw it stemming from the primordial cry of one's phylogenetic need for recognition. Erikson could appreciate traditions, as he did in the case of Luther and Gandhi. He also had the resources to criticize them.

However, we must not make Kant's mistake when he ransacked the world's religious and cultural traditions to affirm those that conformed to his categorical imperative and reject those that did not. We must not, in analogy to Kant, use the ethic of generativity as a straitjacket that woodenly measures the worth of older traditions and contemporary ideologies only in terms of their compatibility with the ethics of generativity. We can, however, justifiably start a dialogue between the ethics of generativity and all traditions, philosophies, and ideologies that are now vying to guide the future. This dialogue would at least attempt to determine the points of analogy between an ethics of generativity and other religiocultural perspectives—be they economic, evolutionary, Christian, Buddhist, Hindu, Confucian, or Shintoist—that claim competence to lead us into the future. Discovering webs of analogy between generativity and other philosophies and religions can help provide overlapping communities of meaning and the people and institutions needed to create and maintain the future cycle of the generations. Understanding the levels of Erikson's ethic—his archeology and teleology of developmental goods, his theory of virtue, his mixed principle of obligation, and his view of the importance of encompassing narratives—should help us proceed with this emerging world conversation and the mutual criticism that it will require.

Erikson can contribute resources that broaden the three alternative ethics I mentioned at the beginning of this chapter—the ethics of principle, the ethics of virtue, and the ethics of narrative. Here the scope of this chapter allows me only to be suggestive. First, the ethics of principle—especially as practiced by neo-Kantians such as Rawls, Habermas, and Kohlberg—can be supplemented by a theory of the premoral goods of the human life cycle that every act of justice, and every act of fair communication, should seek to actualize. Erikson's moral vision helps us both to affirm the importance of Kantian justice and to overcome its formalism and potential emptiness.

Second, theories of virtue can be both affirmed and supplemented. Erikson provides fresh understandings of how virtues build on and should in fact help actualize the epigenetic timetables of the human species. His view of the premoral goods of life helps us understand the values our virtues should enhance. This view of values and virtues can give us more concrete ways of assessing the directions of modernity and determining which possibilities should be welcomed and which should be rejected, which of them support these important values and virtues and which do not.

Third, Erikson both understood the importance of traditions of narrative for the formation of generative persons and provided frameworks for critiquing the momentary or long-term distortions of such traditions. Narrative traditions that do violence to the cycle of human development or defy the universal principle of mutual recognition are deserving of criticism. Some ethicists of narrative, in their drive to balance modernity's rush into the future with the stabilizing resources of a narrative past, are both affirmed but gently criticized by Erikson's additional appreciation for the universals of human development and the universal requirement of justice.

Although Erikson was not a professional ethicist, he had within his thought an important and loosely stated synthesis of most of the elements needed for guiding our ethical trajectories amid the opportunities and threats of modernity in the 21st century.

REFERENCES

Aquinas, T. (1917). *Summa theologica: Book II*. London: Washbourne.

Aristotle. (1941a). *Nicomachean ethics: Book II. The basic writings of Aristotle*. New York: Random House.

Aristotle. (1941b). *Politics: Book I. The basic writings of Aristotle*. New York: Random House.

Browning, D. S. (1973). *Generative man: Society and the good man in Philip Rieff, Norman Brown, Erich Fromm and Erik Erikson*. Philadelphia: Westminster Press.

Browning, D. S. (1975). *Generative man: Society and the good man in Philip Rieff, Norman Brown, Erich Fromm and Erik Erikson*. New York: Dell.

Browning, D. S. (1987). *Religious thought and the modern psychologies*. Minneapolis, MN: Fortress.

Donegan, A. (1977). *The theory of morality*. Chicago: University of Chicago Press.

Erikson, E. (1959). *The problem of ego identity: Identity and the life cycle*. New York: International Universities Press.

Erikson, E. (1962). *Young man Luther*. New York: Norton.

Erikson, E. (1963). *Childhood and society*. New York: Norton.

Erikson, E.(1964). *Insight and responsibility*. New York: Norton.

Erikson, E. (1969). *Gandhi's truth*. New York: Norton.

Flanagan, O. (1991). *Varieties of moral personality*. Cambridge, MA: Harvard University Press.

Frankena, W. (1973). *Ethics*. Englewood Cliffs, NJ: Prentice Hall.

Habermas, J. (1990). *Moral consciousness and communicative action*. Cambridge, MA: MIT Press.

Hartmann, H. (1958). *Ego psychology and the problem of adaptation*. New York: International Universities Press.

Hauerwas, S. (1981). *A community of character*. Notre Dame, IN: Notre Dame University Press.

James, W. (1950). *The principles of psychology II*. New York: Dover.

James, W. (1962). *Talks to teachers on psychology*. New York: Dover. (Original work published 1899)

Kant, I. (1959). *Foundations for a metaphysics of morals*. New York: Bobbs-Merrill.

MacIntyre, A. (1981). *After virtue*. Notre Dame, IN: University of Notre Dame Press.

Midgley, M. (1978). *Beast and man*. Ithaca, NY: Cornell University Press.

Plato. (1951). *The symposium*. London: Penguin Books.

Plato. (1968). *The republic: Book V*. New York: Basic Books.

Pope, S. (1994). *The evolution of altruism and the ordering of love*. Washington, DC: Georgetown University Press.

Ricoeur, P. (1970). *Freud and philosophy*. New Haven, CT: Yale University Press.

Ricoeur, P. (1992). *Oneself as another*. Chicago: University of Chicago Press.

Schweiker, W. (1995). *Ethics of responsibility*. Cambridge, England: Cambridge University Press.

Singer, P. (1981). *The expanding circle: Ethics and sociobiology*. New York: Farrar, Straus, & Giroux.

Wilson, J. Q. (1993). *The moral sense*. New York: Free Press.

16

ERIK ERIKSON ON GENERATIVITY: A BIOGRAPHER'S PERSPECTIVE

LAWRENCE J. FRIEDMAN

From the publication of *Childhood and Society* in 1950 through the 1970s, Erik H. Erikson was acknowledged as a major influence in American intellectual life, a figure of great academic distinction whose views on human development, culture, and society commanded widespread attention. His wide-ranging and innovative approach to a variety of questions helped to make the immediate postwar decades in the United States an unusually hospitable period for interdisciplinary inquiry and served to maintain the vital, if increasingly fragile, role in the United States of the public intellectual as social critic. *Childhood and Society* laid out Erikson's conceptual itinerary for understanding the intricate dialectic between self and society. In the book's most famous chapter ("Eight Ages of Man"), Erikson divided the human life cycle into eight stages, each defined by a central psychosocial polarity. During the 1950s and early 1960s, Erikson and his readership focused their attention mainly on the fifth stage in his eight-stage scheme: the adolescent stage of *identity*. By contrast, *Childhood and Society* devoted all of two pages to the concept of *generativity*. Twenty years later, however, the emphasis had begun to shift. In 1970, Erikson won the Pulitzer Prize and the National Book Award for *Gandhi's Truth* (Erikson, 1969), a volume that looked Eastward to the nonviolent Indian leader for alternatives to America's vast nuclear arsenals and its deepening role in the Vietnam War. The key concept for his analysis of Gandhi's life and legacy was generativity.

In this brief chapter, I draw on my full-length biography of Erikson (Friedman, 1999) to consider the origins of Erikson's concept of generativity in the context of his own life and in the social history defining his most prolific years. Generativity is a concept that links the individual and society. It is indeed fitting, therefore, that a full appreciation of generativity in society brings to one's attention the life of the man who first developed the concept of generativity and the influence of the society within which he lived.

FROM IDENTITY TO GENERATIVITY

With considerable assistance from Joan, his wife, Erikson spent the years from 1944 to 1950 working on the concept of the eight-stage human life cycle. As his view of the life cycle took shape, each of life's stages stood for a crisis in the developmental process, with a new psychic strength pitted against a new vulnerability. At the same time, each stage was psychosocial, for the crisis was acted on in encounters with other humans, beginning with the infant facing the mother. This mutuality expanded as one aged to include a widening radius of social relations.

In *Childhood and Society* and at a 1950 White House conference, Erikson released the first detailed account of his developmental model:

1. Basic Trust versus Basic Mistrust (infancy)
2. Autonomy versus Shame and Doubt (early childhood)
3. Initiative versus Guilt (play age)
4. Industry versus Inferiority (school age)
5. Identity versus Role Confusion (adolescence)
6. Intimacy versus Isolation (young adulthood)
7. Generativity versus Stagnation (middle adulthood)
8. Ego Integrity versus Despair (old age)

Unlike Freud, Erikson emphasized neither infancy nor early childhood, but the fifth or adolescent identity stage. The first four stages represented efforts to establish and consolidate a personal identity, whereas the last three stages signaled efforts to retain it in the face of aging and bodily infirmity. Moreover, identity was forged and reaffirmed through mutuality—close rapport with others. It took at least two to make an identity. For the first time since G. Stanley Hall's (1904) study of adolescence, a major personality theorist was emphasizing that period in the life cycle. Erikson retained this focus in *Young Man Luther* (1958), his next book, as he explored Martin Luther's developmental crisis of adolescence and young adulthood in conjunction with his parents and others significant to his life, as Luther helped to launch the Protestant Reformation.

Erikson continued to discuss adolescent identity issues in the 1960s, especially in conjunction with student protests on American college campuses. However, his major work of that decade, *Gandhi's Truth* (1969), focused on adult life. Erikson tried to explain how the middle-aged Mahatma organized a local labor strike in 1918 that launched his nonviolent crusade against the British rule throughout India. Because the adult stages of Erikson's psychosocial life cycle were the least developed at this point, it is hardly surprising that as his interest in middle-aged Gandhi grew (and he himself aged), he made two major modifications in his eight-stage theory. These changes allowed him to gain greater insight into he psychological meaning of adulthood.

First, he included in his collection, *Insight and Responsibility* (1964), an essay titled "Human Strength and the Cycle of Generations," which soon became conceptually relevant to the Gandhi project. In this essay, he proposed a "schedule of virtues" to correspond with each of the eight stages of the life cycle: Hope, Will, Purpose, Competence, Fidelity, Love, Care, and Wisdom. These virtues were strengths in the human organism that social environments (especially the conduct of adults toward children) could thwart or enhance. They were aspects of an evolving ethical character in the individual (coming into full fruition during adulthood) that was connected explicitly to psychological development. Erikson, increasingly interested in the concerns of adult life, was linking ethical to psychosocial development.

In 1965, Erikson presented a paper ("Ontogeny of Ritualization") to the Royal Society of London that also became germane to his Gandhi project. He related a social ritual form to each of his eight psychosocial-ethical stages. At each stage, he postulated, every society oriented its members to ways of construing the world through a universal ritual element. At the first or infancy stage of Hope, for example, there was a ritualized *numinous* encounter between mother and infant, followed at each successive stage by rituals of the *judicious*, the *dramatic*, the *formal*, the *convictional*, the *affiliative*, the *generational*, and the *integral*. The eighth or integral ritual saw the old person integrating or becoming the living testimony to the wisdom of the society's entire ritual process.

By the middle of the 1960s, then, just as he was formulating the crucial strands of a biography of middle-aged Gandhi, Erikson had linked his schedule of ethical virtues and social rituals to his eight psychosocial stages. Through the completion of *Gandhi's Truth* (and for at least the next decade), he focused on the seventh or generative stage when adults were ethically obligated to create and attend to younger generations. In terms of ethical values, adults were obligated to personally care for youths. From the standpoint of social ritualization, adults became the ritualizers responsible for teaching and conducting the whole ritualization process in an authoritative and ethical, but not an authoritarian and moralistic, manner. Through their personal presences and words and deeds, they actualized and authenticated each of society's genuine, lasting social rituals and taught them to youths. Having worked out this theoretical perspective on the meaning of adult generativity, Erikson was able to articulate Gandhi's essential contribution to younger generations. This contribution was an example of militant nonviolence (*Satyagraha*). Erikson characterized Satyagraha as a way for an adult to fulfill an ethical obligation to redress social injustice and overcome ethnic, nationalistic, and often moralistic tribalism in favor of wider, more inclusive human identities that could save humankind from wars and annihilation. Erikson portrayed Satyagraha as perhaps the most important contribution a 20th-century adult could make to younger generations—to assure their survival in an increasingly precarious world.

Following Gandhi, Erikson came to see Satyagraha as the world's greatest weapon in the struggle against the kind of thinking that bred deep prejudice and even totalitarianism. In *Gandhi's Truth*, Erikson developed the concept of *pseudospeciation* (see also Kai Erikson, this volume, chap. 4), which he characterized as a deeply rooted propensity in relatively homogeneous groups to deny the humanity of people who are outside the group—in effect, to deny that all humankind is part of the same species. Pseudospeciation made for the irrational division of the world into "us" and "them," proclaimed in slavery, caste systems, religious dogmas, and rigid ideologies. Through pseudospeciation, one group could develop an identity that made it superior to all other groups, justifying all manner of cruelty and arrogance vis-à-vis all those others who were effectively deemed less than human.

Much as Erikson, the clinician, accented psychic strengths over disabilities, he heralded *universal specieshood* over pseudospeciation. Congruent with Wendell Wilkie's (1943) *One World* and Edward Steichen's *The Family of Man* photography exhibit during the mid-1950s at the Museum of Modern Art in New York, Erikson embraced a universal cosmopolitan perspective, traced to the Enlightenment, which held that particularistic loyalties were irrational and had to be countered by reformist pedagogy. Through Satyagraha or militant nonviolence, Erikson asserted, Gandhi (as an act of generativity) had succeeded during the 1918 textile strike in Ahmedabad at reconciling the mill owners and workers financially and emotionally. Gandhi's settlement of the 1918 Ahmedabad strike enhanced worker wages without jeopardizing mill owner profits and dignified all contesting parties by appealing to their common humanity. The Mahatma proceeded to build on Satyagraha to free his country by reconciling British authorities to the idea of Indian independence as beneficial for all contesting parties. In this way, Erikson insisted, Gandhi may have performed his most generative act of all, by effectively creating a ritualization through which people might face each other with mutual confidence and trust. Gandhi equated this mutuality with the Hindu concept of *dharma*, which connected self to society for the "maintenance of the world." Erikson portrayed Gandhi's method as a ritualized process by which a man actualizes within himself and others a heightened expectation of mutuality. Two antagonistic pseudospecies thereby join their identities in a creative and generative way. Erikson hoped that a world recovering from the Holocaust and immersed in the Cold War confrontations in which nuclear weapons were brandished would heed Gandhi's example of a new universal ethics, based on universal specieshood.

ERIKSON AND GANDHI

As he worked during the mid and late 1960s at characterizing how middle-aged Gandhi had launched a successful battle for Indian independence, Erikson was essentially linking his concepts of identity, generativity, and pseudospeciation. As a mature adult, Gandhi well exemplified the seventh stage of generativity. He was giving to present and future generations of youths what was the key to human survival: Satyagraha or militant nonviolence as an ethical and effective way to avert pseudospeciation and promote universal specieshood. The way to implement Satyagraha was to extend positive individual identities into a wider sense of identity that encompassed the whole human species.

From the biographer's perspective, the concepts of identity, generativity, and pseudospeciation cohered because all three, furthermore, were integral to Erikson's own life. In the middle of composing *Gandhi's Truth* during the winter and spring of 1966–1967, Erikson experienced the first writing block of his long literary career. For a man who always wrote compulsively, skillfully, fluently, and productively, this was a very disturbing occurrence. His solution was to prepare a 25-page "Personal Word"—a public letter to Gandhi, which eventually appeared as a dramatic interlude in the text of *Gandhi's Truth*. The letter made it unmistakably clear that there was a very personal biographical agenda behind his work on Gandhi—that in characterizing Gandhi, Erikson was working through some difficult issues in his own life. Addressing the Indian leader two decades after his death, Erikson (1969) criticized Gandhi for "displaced violence when nonviolence was the professed issue" (p. 231). While professing Satyagraha as a supremely generative act, Gandhi had been cruel to people close to him. He had required young girls at Tolstoy Farm (a South African communal settlement) who had admired him to cut off their hair so as to be less alluring to the boys in residence. As well, Gandhi had tried to force literacy upon his wife and required her (against her will) to discard the bodily waste of a Christian untouchable. Finally, Gandhi had repudiated his oldest son, Harilal, when the young man sought to marry, and Harilal suffered deeply. For Erikson, all of these actions were coarse and arbitrary—certainly less than generative toward the young.

They compromised Gandhi's gift of Satyagraha because they did not involve people close to him in a voluntary mutuality in their relationships with him. Rather, Gandhi's cruel acts represented blatant aggression toward others in ways that made it difficult for them to form positive identities. Nor did his aggression facilitate the connectedness with others that could promote a wider human identity.

There can be little doubt that Erikson was drawing upon aggressive aspects of his own life as he wrote about Gandhi. For one, there were the aggressions that he had personally experienced from parental figures. His father had abandoned him before birth, and his mother had not told him anything about his father's identity. Rather, she had lied to him, telling him that her second husband, Theodor Homburger, was his birth father. The lie had been transparent to the young boy, who knew that Theodor was very reticent to adopt him (delaying the process for roughly 9 years). Thus, neither mother, father, nor stepfather had been especially generative toward young Erik; none had confirmed him in a sense of viable personal identity. Is it any wonder that, years later when he became an American citizen, he changed his surname from Homburger to Erikson—son of Erik? In a sense, the fatherless son became his own father—he literally generated himself. This underscored a rather profound and unresolved identity crisis rooted in early parental aggressions against his sense of selfhood.

Linking his own life to Gandhi's, Erikson may have also identified his own aggressions with those of the Mahatma. As his father and stepfather had been cruel to him, he had been cruel to his own children. Erikson had never been particularly generative as a parent of three physically and mentally normal children, deferring to his wife Joan on almost all aspects of parenting. In a recent article in the *Atlantic Monthly*, Sue Erikson Bloland (1999) recalled many incidents from her childhood in which her father paid her little attention and seemed emotionally absent. And he may have been as aggressive and cruel as Gandhi had been toward Harilal in his own conduct toward his youngest son, Neil, who suffered from Down's syndrome. Shortly after the boy's birth in 1944, Erikson arranged unilaterally for Neil to be transferred to institutional care. He then told two of his children that Neil had died while revealing to his eldest, Kai, that Neil was still alive. As tension in Erik's relation to his children and his wife Joan mounted, he kept Neil under institutional care in northern California while he moved his family, in 1951, to western Massachusetts. Joan visited Neil once over the next 21 years; Erik, not at all. When Neil died, Erik (then in Italy) phoned his children and instructed them to make funeral arrangements. He would not return to America for the burial of his youngest son.

Gandhi described his father's death—which occurred while Gandhi was having sexual intercourse in a nearby room—as the "Curse" of his life. Erik and Joan Erikson regarded the birth of Neil and the tumult it caused within their family as a similar curse. For a time, husband and wife nearly divorced, while the eldest son had to keep the secret that Neil had survived from his siblings. Even allowing for the fact that Down's syndrome in 1944 was not a hopeful diagnosis and children with Down's syndrome tended to be institutionalized, the Erikson family was severely damaged as a social and emotional unit. The generative process had gone amuck; for a time, it would seem that parents were not rearing any of their children in a salutary way or even caring for each other as they had in the past.

In the long run, however, a generative contribution emerged from the Down's syndrome crisis, which I have detailed in chapter 5 of my biography of Erikson (Friedman, 1999). Erik and Joan Erikson viewed Neil as a kind of prototype of developmental failure in the human life cycle. Moreover, they felt he had (unwittingly) created chaos and despair within their family. In response, they set to work in 1944 on the eight-stage life cycle model. The model became a personal map for normal human development. As a map of normalcy, it reaffirmed all members of the family except Neil in their own propriety and viability, with parents in their generative seventh stage purportedly caring for three healthy children heading toward the fifth stage—the adolescent identity crisis. Contextually, Neil became a referent for negative development—for what the others supposedly were not. As the Erikson life cycle model seemed (if temporarily) to give hope for normalcy to a much battered family, it was also a supremely generative contribution to the social-scientific community and, more generally, humankind. It provided perhaps the most helpful perspective on universal human development (and perhaps the most highly regarded) in the 20th century. Grounded in the postulate that adult generativity facilitated the developing identity of youth across cultures, its universality signaled a wider human identity. As Gandhi's campaigns for Satyagraha and Indian independence compensated, in some measure, for his failures in familial generativity, Erikson's gift of the life cycle model made an important contribution to humankind by reaffirming its essential oneness. For both Gandhi and Erikson, then, their most widely recognized generative accomplishments were inextricably linked to their biggest failings in generativity.

REFERENCES

Bloland, S. E. (1999, November). Fame: The power and cost of a fantasy. *The Atlantic Monthly*, 51–62.

Erikson, E. H. (1950). *Childhood and society*. New York: Norton.

Erikson, E. H. (1958). *Young man Luther*. New York: Norton.

Erikson, E. H. (1964). *Insight and responsibility*. New York: Norton.

Erikson, E. H. (1969). *Gandhi's truth: On the origins of militant nonviolence*. New York: Norton.

Friedman, L. (1999). *Identity's architect: A biography of Erik H. Erikson*. New York: Pantheon.

Hall, G. S. (1904). *Adolescence*. New York: Appleton.

Wilkie, W. (1943). *One world*. New York: Simon & Schuster.

17

THE GENERATIVE SOCIETY: AN EPILOGUE

ED dE ST. AUBIN, DAN P. McADAMS, AND TAE-CHANG KIM

We asked the authors in this book to move generativity scholarship beyond discussions of individual adult development. Each chapter expands and clarifies the conceptual meaning of *generativity*. Many authors do so by seeking to address generative dynamics existing at collective levels such as institution, community, or society. Other authors shape the concept by examining its relation to relevant phenomena such as the parenting–career balance or by comparing it with similar terms such as *volunteerism*. Although there are original quantitative reports included in three of the chapters and many of the authors draw from a wide assortment of empirical studies, the principal contribution of this book is theoretical.

This book marks a significant development in *generativity theory*. It also speaks to the propitiousness of examining this concept at this point in history. A host of demographic and sociocultural forces have culminated at this dawn of the 21st century that suggest the *present significance of generativity*. A third theme interwoven through several of the chapters is the potential of *applied generativity* to improve the quality of human lives. Several authors contend that social policy that follows a generative path is likely to meaningfully affect individuals and to result in closer approximations toward the good society.

GENERATIVITY THEORY

Many of the forces behind the initial creation of generativity theory are discussed in the previous chapter wherein Lawrence Friedman addresses the biographical and sociohistorical impetuses that led to Erik Erikson's writings regarding generativity. For Erikson, generativity is both a psychosocial stage of individual adult development and the cultural adhesive by which valued traditions and beliefs are created, maintained, and revitalized through intergenerational transmission. Most social scientists who have tested or contributed to generativity theory have focused on the former, concentrating on generativity as an aspect of personality development. This work has yielded many important findings, all of which are summarized by Dan McAdams and Regina Logan in chapter 2 of this book. The empirical examinations that are reviewed in that chapter locate generativity either within the individual (like a personality characteristic) or in the psychosocial space between two individuals (like parent–child attachment).

But generativity does not reside solely within the individual as an attribute of personality, nor is it located exclusively in the psychosocial space between two individuals like romantic love. At its very core, generativity is the intergenerational transmission of that which is valued. When understood in this way, it becomes evident that generativity exists in many places and on many levels. One can witness it in the courtroom proceedings that determine the custody of a child. We read of it in the government's policies regarding issues affecting future generations such as pollution control, education, and health care. We hear generativity when we listen to community leaders speak of sustainability. And we find generativity in a corporation's codified procedures and actual practices regarding maternity and paternity leaves of absence.

As the authors of this book's chapters make clear, generativity exists in all of these places and in many more. This conceptual expansion in the meaning of generativity returns scholarship in this area to Erikson's initial vision. Taking a truly psychosocial perspective, we now examine the interrelatedness of cultural dynamics, social institutions, and individual lives. Such an approach leads to examinations like that of Bonnie Miller-McLemore's (chap. 11), which investigates the manner in which current social structures hinder individual generative attempts to balance work and family caregiving.

At the same time that generativity theory is expanding to include various levels and domains, we also seek to provide focus to the concept and to define its edges. Generativity entails much, but it is not everything. Generativity is related to, but distinct from, several phenomena such as altruism, sustainability, parenting, future orientation, community development, cultural evolution, and creativity. By examining the similarities and differences that exist between these concepts, we begin the ongoing process of refining the definition of generativity. Mark Snyder and Gil Clary (chap. 14) provide an example of how this might be done as they relate generativity to volunteerism.

Another way to sharpen our conceptual focus is to use generativity in our attempts to explain significant areas of human functioning. It is a testament to the power of the notion that generativity is used here in several such endeavors: as a common denominator in the three competing philosophical models of the ethical life (Don Browning, chap. 15); as the intergenerational dynamic that accounts for sociohistorical continuity and change (Takatoshi Imada, chap. 6); as the pivotal idea that will allow life span theorists to create more contextualized and temporally relevant portraits of individual development (Yoko Yamada, chap. 7); and as one important result of both institutionalized religiosity and individual spirituality (Michele Dillon & Paul Wink, chap. 10).

Generative meanings and dynamics are being brought to bear in several areas, and these efforts aid in the theory construction process. But the development of generativity theory has in no way been completed. Large gaps currently exist in at least three areas, and we would encourage scholars to take up these challenges. First, it is not precisely clear how generativity at the individual level relates to generativity at more collective levels. Is a generative society one that contains generative individuals? Is it one that encourages generative desires? One that maintains generative stories? Or one that infuses the generative spirit into social policy? The various voices in this book speak to this issue in disparate ways. A related concern is the measurement of generativity at these more collective levels. We have some confidence that our attempts to quantify individual differences in generativity are valid and reliable, but how might we measure an institution's level of generativity? How do we place a metric unit to community generativity, or to a government's generativity?

Some simply take an aggregating approach, measuring generativity at any level by summing the generativity scores of individual adults who are members of that particular system. But this is flawed in many respects. It fails to capture the potential emergent qualities that exist in these assemblages. We need more appropriate methods of quantifying generativity at the collective level, and the search for these techniques must be driven by our endeavor to specify the relation between individual generativity and collective generativity. Rather than focus on the individual, we need to start looking for generativity in locations not typically investigated by psychologists, such as written laws, the tacit social contract, rituals, cultural customs, institutional mission statements, and social policy. Societal generativity is manifested in these areas just as individual generativity might be manifested in one's parenting styles, mentoring modes, or creative projects.

A second area of needed theory construction concerns the values inherent in the content and process of the generative enterprise. In that our working definition of generativity is the intergenerational transmission of that which is valued, we must acknowledge that generativity at any level is values-laden. Theorists need to begin the process of tracing the manner in which values influence the generative process. Value priorities at any level (individual, institutional, and cultural) partially determine how generativity is enacted, and who/what enacts it as well as who/what is the target of generativity.

There are many relatively values-free ways of speaking about people ("She has a high IQ") or collectives ("That country has a near endless supply of coal"), but assertions regarding generativity necessarily evoke values. Kai Erikson (chap. 4) worked with his father on the ideology surrounding pseudospeciation, which is the tendency to divide members of the human species according to worthiness, with some groups being viewed as composed of less-than-human members and others as valued authentic human beings. The beliefs that inform a particular brand of pseudospeciation are played out in the practice of generativity. A man who views women as less worthy (a form of pseudospeciation) will engage in a separate form of generativity than one with more egalitarian values.

Further, the values that define a culture will no doubt be implicated in the generative practices in that culture. Cultural psychologists have proposed well-validated values dimensions upon which cultures vary. Most notable here is the work of Hofstede regarding cultural variation along the dimensions of power distance, uncertainty avoidance, individualism, and masculinity (gender specificity). Generativity theorists should turn to this and related research and begin to articulate the manner in which values priorities influence the content and process of generativity.

A final direction of theory construction regards the potential dark side of generativity. Theorists have not agreed as to how this might be conceptualized. Many assume that generativity is exclusively about the intergenerational transmission of life-affirming modes. But it is often the case that one's legacy is a destructive one. Further, some forms of generativity appear to benefit one group but not others—perhaps even being detrimental to some.

Here we will need to go beyond Erikson, for he also failed to clearly articulate how we might conceptualize a negative legacy or how we might understand the intended or unintended damage that generativity might inflict on certain groups. His life-cycle model maintains that adult development is characterized by the dialectic tension between generativity and stagnation. He further suggested that stagnation may be rooted in a form of narcissism wherein one's self-love overrides one's desires to care for others. These dynamics may provide insights as we begin to examine the potential dark side of generativity at collective levels. But stagnation is not the same as creating a destructive legacy. The dark side of generativity no doubt comes in various shades. We encourage theorists to address the generativity shadow.

PRESENT SIGNIFICANCE OF GENERATIVITY

A number of chapter authors note the timeliness of studying generativity at this point in history. Just as a host of social forces merged in the 1960s in the United States to propel the concept of identity into prominence, generativity appears to be a significant idea at the present historical moment. At least three sociodemographic transformations have combined to suggest the wisdom of investigating the generative society.

First, the large U.S. baby-boom cohorts are today between the ages of 39 and 57 years, precisely at that point in the life course marked by the saliency of generativity. Thus, a large portion of the citizenship is grappling in their own lives with issues of legacy-leaving and caring for members of younger generations. These population statistics are similar to those in other industrialized countries. Such countries might be thought of in terms of "a generative society" in the same way that we understand many nondeveloped cultures as "young" (high fertility rates and high mortality rates) because the bulk of its members are indeed young.

Second, the rapidity of societal changes over the past few decades has called into question the value of the skills one generation has to pass onto the next. What happens when the expertise learned by one cohort is not adaptive for younger cohorts? Few of the technical skills adolescents possess today were taught to them by members of older generations. As Kai Erikson writes in chapter 4, such abrupt social changes call for a new form of generativity: Rather than pass on *what* to think (pieces of information), it is more relevant to educate youths in *how* to think; it becomes less meaningful to indoctrinate others into a particular belief system, but more adaptive to instill in younger cohorts the importance of integrity in maintaining a system of belief.

These societal changes are quite evident at the level of institutions—a unit of analysis examined in several of this book's chapters. As the macroeconomy has shifted from production based to more service and information based, we see the institutions of capitalism convert into more relevant modes of generativity. We have also seen institutions that support faith change to accommodate the more individual and spiritual needs expressed by contemporary adults, as opposed to the more conventional and collectively based modes of faith that existed 50 years ago. It is not only U.S. institutions that are changing in ways that affect societal generativity. As Takeshi Sasaki points out (chap. 13), the political structure and process in Japan has increasingly paid insufficient attention to the needs of future generations.

The third social force propelling societal generativity onto center stage is the deepening "social recession" documented in recent books such as Robert Putnam's *Bowling Alone* (2000) and Dave Myers's *The American Paradox* (2000). Indicators of civic health such as teen suicide, violent crime, and

rates of clinical depression show that U.S. society, while enjoying unprecedented material wealth, is currently at a low point regarding social health.
Just as generative parents nurture their children and facilitate healthy development, a generative society is one that provides the necessary scaffolding
for its inhabitants to build healthy lives—and one that dedicates resources to
the health of future generations. Such criteria suggest that the United States
in some ways is not particularly generative at this point in history. Other
indicators, however, suggest that we do indeed live in a generative society.
Philanthropy and volunteerism are at an all-time high, for instance. It may
be the mark of a complex society that the appropriate response to whether or
not the United States might be considered a generative society is both no
and yes.

We would be wise to continue our investigations of generativity and of
the generative society as we move into this next millennium. Changing demographics, rapid social transformations, and the fraying of social bonds that
once supported healthy development all demand that we gain a broader understanding of generativity. As Don Browning notes in chapter 15,
"generativity has special relevance for addressing the challenges of modernity and the increased speed of social change, diversity, and potential for
social conflict that has come in its trail."

APPLIED GENERATIVITY

A final theme in this book that we would encourage others to pursue
further is the potential of applied generativity work to significantly improve
the lives of individuals and to contribute to the maintenance of a truly generative society. To date, the only discussions of generativity applications have
been relegated to suggestions that it be infused into the process of psychotherapy. This is not to say that applied generativity does not occur beyond
that in therapy, for it certainly does. The case worker who evaluates the
suitability of a home for a child's welfare is working in a generative capacity.
The neighborhood bookstore that donates a portion of its profits to purchas-
ing coats for children is operating in a generative fashion. Yet scholars have
paid insufficient attention to the impact that such generativity has on individuals or communities. And such generative modes are rarely an explicit
part of one's job description or of an organization's policies and mission statement.

Applied generativity is the intentional infusion of generative modes
into one's practices and the evaluation of such actions. Several examples of
applied generativity are provided in the previous chapters. Maruna, LeBel,
and Lanier (chap. 9) point out that the most effective programs of crime
rehabilitation and corrections are those that facilitate the growth of individual generativity. Ronald Manheimer (chap. 8) writes of specific institu-

tional pathways of generativity (e.g., intergenerational classrooms) that promote a mutual benefiting between members of two cohorts. Both Bill Peterson (chap. 12) and Takeshi Sasaki (chap. 13) speak to the potential advantages of creating explicit generative agents to take part in the political process. Noting that children and future generations are denied representation in the current political systems active in the United States and in Japan, these authors propose to rectify this nongenerative structure. Sasaki suggests that a "People's Tribune" be instilled to represent those not yet born in current political decision making.

Applied generativity, such as these examples, is a logical extension of basic research that has increased our understanding of the concept. It is important to continue our basic scientific investigations of generativity, but we must now also begin to design, implement, and evaluate programs and policies that apply generativity to improving the quality of life within a community—and for members of future communities. For help in this endeavor, we will need to turn to a host of practitioners not typically associated with generativity scholarship: community psychologists, action researchers, empirical social work scholars, political scientists, and program evaluation specialists.

CONCLUSION

Generativity is the intergenerational transmission of that which is valued. It provides meaning to the men and women who enact it and has the potential to strengthen the human bonds in communities that support it. This book does much to promote the contention that generativity has significance beyond its existence as an adult personality attribute. Generativity speaks to the strength of social institutions and to the future orientation of a government. We encourage others to continue with theory construction efforts, because nowhere is a comprehensive articulation provided that adequately addresses the complexity and full meaning of generativity. We also encourage others to begin the work of applied generativity—to infuse generative dynamics into political processes, social policy, and corporate procedures—because it is fervent work in both basic and applied arenas that will move us forward to closer approximations of a truly generative society.

REFERENCES

Myers, D. (2000). *The American paradox: Spiritual hunger in an age of plenty.* New Haven, CT: Yale University Press.

Putnam, R. (2000). *Bowling alone: The collapse and revival of American community.* New York: Simon & Schuster.

AUTHOR INDEX

Numbers in italics refer to listings in the references.

Henkin, N., 207, 208, *209*
Herberg, W., 171, *172*
Hermans, H., 36, 45, *48*
Hester, T., *148*
Himsel, A. J., 20, *28*
Hirsch, B. J., 21, *28*
Honzik, M., 160, *172*
Hostetler, A. J., 18, *27*
Hout, M., 170, *172*
Howard, G. S., 6, *12*
Howe, N., 125, *130*, 204, *209*
Hunt, J., 160, *172*

Imada, T., 43, *48*
Independent Sector, 221–223, 225, *236*
Ingman, S., 207, *209*
Irwin, J., 137, 142, *149*

Jacobs, J. B., 139, *149*
Jacques, E., 99, *111*
James, W., 26, *28*, 246, 250, *254*
Janikula, J., 135, *151*
Jankowski, L., *148*
Jehl, D., 141, *149*
Jones, C., 46, *48*
Jones, S., 143, *148*
Jordan, B. G., 74, 75, *80*
Jordan, J. V., 176, *193*
Jung, C., 103, *111*, 157, 158, *172*

Kakinuma, M. A., 69, 71, *80*
Kameguchi, K., 69, 70, *80*
Kant, I., 242, 244, *254*
Kaplan, A. G., 176, *193*
Karp, D., 134, *148*
Kastenbaum, R., 120, *129*
Kato, 108, 109, *112*
Katz, D., 227, *236*
Kazui, M., 69, 70, *80*
Kelley, M. L., 68, *81*
Kelly, K. R., 140, *150*
Kelly, W. W., 75, *80*
Kempen, H., 36, 45, *48*
Kermode, F., 25, *28*
Keyes, C. L. M., 17, 19, 24, *28*
Kim, T.-C., 45, 46, *48*, 77, *80*, 103, *111*, 211, 213, *219*
Kimmel, D. C., 182, *193*
King, V., 155, *172*
Kingson, E., 207, 208, *209*
Kitayama, S., 9, *12*, 213, *219*
Klein, E. B., 40, *48*, *193*

Klohnen, E. C., 20, 23, *30*, 160, *173*
Kobayashi-Winata, H., 68, *81*
Kohlberg, L., 98, *111*
Kohut, H., 158, *172*
Kolker, C., 142, *149*
Kotre, J., 4, 7, *12*, 15, 16, 18, 25, *28*, 39, 42–44, *48*, 66, *80*, 93, 95, 128, *129*, 157, 158, 161, *172*, 177, 181, *193*, 196, *209*, 232, *236*
Kotre, K., 44, *48*
Kuypers, J. A., 89, *94*

Labouvie-Vief, G., 126, *129*
Lachman, M., 5, *12*
Lamb, M. E., 202, *209*
Lanier, C. S., 137–139, 143, 144, *149*, *150*
Lasch, C., 7, *12*
Laslett, P., 121, *129*
Laub, J., 135, 144, *151*
Layton, L., 15, *30*
LeBel, T. P., 140, *150*
Leighton, T., 46, *48*
Lenihan, K., 144, *148*
Lesthaeghe, R., 177, *193*
LeVine, R. A., *81*
Levinson, D. J., 40, 43, *48*, 99, 106, *111*, 181, 182, 184, *193*
Levinson, M. H., 40, *48*, *193*
Levrant, S., 140, *149*
Lewis, M., 25, *29*
Lichterman, P., 157, *173*
Lindsay, M., 155, *172*
Loevinger, J., 98, *111*
Loewe, M., 102, 109, *111*
Lofland, J., 136, *150*
Logan, R. L., 17, 19, *28*, *29*
Long, C., 40, *48*
Longino, C. F., 127, *130*
Lusky, R., 207, *209*
Lyotard, J.-F., 40, *48*

Maccoby, E., 22, *29*
MacDermid, S., 158, *173*
MacDermid, S. M., 16, *29*
MacIntyre, A., 24, *29*, 242, *254*
Macy, J., 60, *61*
Madono, K. E., 75, *80*
Madsen, R., 6, 7, *11*, 27, *27*, 154, *172*, 176, *191*
Mahony, R., 176, *193*
Makino, K., 69, *82*
Manheimer, R., 121, 122, *129*

SUBJECT INDEX

Care/caregiving
    and affective love, 180
    for children, 67–73
    and crime, 133
    Erikson's view of, 115–117, 259
    and ethics, 245
    and gender, 176, 179
    and generativity, 91, 158
    by parents, 248
    in prisons, 141
    and self-love, 189, 190
Career consolidation, 183
Career-related function, 227
Caring professions, 165
Catholic Church/Catholicism, 55, 164, 249
Cautionary tales, 42, 136
Change, 84–93, 102
Charity, 155
Chicago, 36
Child, I., 66
Childbearing, 19
Child care, 201–203
Childhood, 103
Childhood and Society (Erik Erikson), 3, 257, 258
Children, 5
    autonomy granted to, 16
    care of, in Japan and U.S., 67–73
    and culture, 46
    and grandparents, 202–204
    and immigration, 204–205
    and politics of generativity, 200–205
    of prisoners, 138, 147
    survival of, 37, 51
    as teachers, 53
    welfare of one's own, 54, 244–245
China, 122
Chinese culture, 102, 109
Christianity, 153–156, 162, 176, 186, 188, 189
Christian Science Church, 166
Chung, Y.-J., 45
Churches, 22, 154, 155, 171
Clary, E. G., 227, 231
Class, 19
Clear, T., 134
Clinical ratings, 19
Clinton, William Jefferson, 195
Cognitive development, 202
Cogwheeling, 246, 247
Cole, E. R, 22
Colearning programs, 123

Coles, Robert, 178
Collectivist cultures, 56–57, 68
Communal childraising, 71
Communal mode, 76, 158
Communal orientation, 163
Communal perspective, 165
Communal religions, 157, 158
Communication with one's children, 21
Communion, 18–19, 160
Community context, 228–229
Community(-ies)
    and crime, 134
    of hope, 155
    intergenerational, 207–208
    of memory, 155
    storytelling and creation of, 128
Community participation, 168
Community service, 140–142, 146
Competency, 72
Compression of morbidity, 119
Conger eels, 63
Congregational Church, 166
Connectedness with a sacred Other, 159
Conscious adaptation, 87
Contamination sequence, 26
Content analysis procedures, 19
Contextualism, 100–102
Contextual relativism, 157–158
Continuity, 84–93, 102
Contributing cultures, 47
Coping strategies, 23
Copybook method, 74
Corrections
    in generative societies, 145–147
    strengths-based, 139–145
Creativity, 91, 120, 160, 165, 181
Crime, generativity and, 133–137
Croatia, 58
Croats, 56, 57
Cross-cultural investigation, 65–67
Cross-fertilization, 46
Cultural absolutism, 47
Cultural capital, 92
Cultural inheritance, 87
Cultural relativity, 47
Culture(s), 35–49
    as atmosphere, 35
    continuity of, 87
    contrasting, 36–39
    and gender, 176
    generativity shaped by, 19–20
    and immigration, 204–205

investigation of cross-, 65–67
Japanese, 5–6, 65–79
living forms of, 42–44
outward-looking, 44–47
religious ideas in, 190
story types in, 39–42
traditions of, 6
values defining, 268
as web of significance, 35
Customary practices, 66–67
Custom complex, 66
Custom practices, 69, 70
Cycle of generations, 91–93
Cyclical imagery (in Japanese culture), 100–
102

Daniels, Pamela, 179, 180, 184
Deductive technique, 66
Delancey Street program, 143, 147
Democratic societies, 214–218
Deontological ethical systems, 244, 250
Dependence, 68, 72, 137
Desire, 39–40, 177, 246
Desistance (from criminal behavior), 135–
137, 144
De St. Aubin, E., 66, 132, 187
Development, human, 137–139
    Erikson's view of. See under Erikson, Erik
    Japanese view of, 100–102
    Western view of, 98–100
Developmental criminology, 135
Deviant behaviors, 88–89
Dewey, John, 243
Dharma, 261
Diotima, 249
Distal eye contact, 72
Distance-promoting equipment, 69, 72
Doi, T., 68
Domestic labor, 177
Donegan, Alan, 245
Down's syndrome, 262–263

"Each one, teach one" approach, 143
Early Child Care Research Network
    (NICHD), 202
Earned redemption, 140
Eastern Fathers' Group (EFG), 144
Eastern traditions, 156, 165
Ecology, 179
Economics, 214–215, 217–218
Education, 21, 24, 38, 70, 94, 200, 204, 205
    lifelong, 121–122

moral, 58
reform of, 201
Eels, conger, 63
EFG (Eastern Fathers' Group), 144
Ego development, 90
Einstein, Albert, 43, 44
Elderly, 117–119, 207
Election cycle, 206
Elections, 207
Emperor penguins, 63
Enabling niche, 133
Encounter groups, 164–165
Enhancement function, 227
Entitlement, 119, 204
Environment, exploration of, 69, 72
Environmental issues, 206–207
Epics, 40–41
Epigenesis, 103
Epigenetic ground plan, 246
Episcopal Church, 162
Erikson, Erik
    and adolescent identity stage, 258–259
    and caring, 115–117
    and child development, 38
    and culture, 40, 45, 46, 66
    and developmental stages, 132
    and ethics, 241–253
    and Gandhi, 259–263
    and gender, 175–181, 186–188, 190,
        191
    and generative life cycle model, 104
    generativity concept of, 3–8, 16–17, 22,
        26, 52–53, 97, 257–263, 266
    Golden Rule interpreted by, 186, 245–
        246
    and identity, 24
    identity crisis of, 175, 262
    individual's context in theories of, 102–
        103
    and intergenerational issues, 212, 223
    life-cycle theory of, 90–94, 98
    and memes, 64
    and narratives, 128
    and old age, 120
    and parenting, 67
    and politics of generativity, 196, 197,
        207, 208
    on pseudospeciation, 55–56
    and religion, 153–154
    and stagnation, 137
Erikson, Joan, 258, 262, 263
Erikson, Kai, 37, 262, 263, 268

Erikson, Neil, 262–263
Erlebnisschichtung, 86, 87
Ethics, 241–255
    and archeology of generativity, 245–247
    and evolutionary psychology, 247–249
    and gender, 186–187
    and narrative, 251–253
    of principle, 242, 243, 250, 251, 253
    teleological, 243–245, 249–250
    of virtue, 242, 250–251
Ethics (Aristotle), 120
Ethnic clusters, 58
Ethos of production, 181
Etzioni, Amitai, 242
Euro Americans, 22, 23
Europe, 53–54, 216
European Union, 218
Evolutionary psychology, 247–249
Ex-convicts, 26
Exodus, 40
Experiences, stratification of, 86, 87
Exploration of environment, 69, 72
Eye contact, 72

The Family (Edward Steichen), 260
Family(-ies), 138, 187, 212, 213
Fathers/fatherhood, 22, 70, 178, 181, 187
    duties of Puritan, 37–39
    in prison, 138, 139
Federation of Senior Citizens' Club, 122
Fellow travelers, 44
The Feminine Mystique (Betty Friedan), 163
Feminist studies, 176
Fictive kin, 74
Fidelity, 90, 91
Financial markets, 217
Firefighting, 141
Flanagan, Owen, 250
Forest fires, 141
Foster care programs, 203
Francis, Saint, 153, 163
Frankena, William, 245
Freedman, M., 204
Freud, Anna, 46
Freud, Sigmund, 44, 98, 103
    early stages emphasized by, 258
    and gender, 177–179, 185–186
    libido theory of, 246, 247
Friedan, Betty, 163
Functionalism, 226–229
Funponshugi, 74
Future generations, 25, 59–61

Gandhi, Harilal, 261
Gandhi, Mahatma, 4, 22, 55, 93, 196, 251, 252, 258–263
Gandhi's Truth (Erik Erikson), 4, 22, 93, 257–261
Gardner, H., 44
GBC (Generativity Behavioral Checklist), 66
Gender, 19, 175–194
    and child care, 201–202
    and distribution of labor, 180–191
    Erikson on generativity and, 177–179
    and Japanese culture, 206n
    and productivity vs. caring, 181–185
    and religion, 185–191
Generation, 84–85
Generational cohorts, 125
Generation as actuality (*Generationszusammenhang*), 85
Generation gap, 89, 116, 125
Generation location (*Generationslagerung*), 85
Generation unit (*Generationseinheit*), 85
Generative actions, 19, 20
Generative concern, 19, 20
Generative desire, 39–40
Generative goals, 19, 20
Generative identity, 39
Generative life cycle model (GLCM), 98, 104–110
Generative Man (Don Browning), 186, 241
Generative Realization scale, 160
Generativity, 15–31, 90, 115, 257
    applied, 270–271
    archeology of, 245–247
    culture shaping, 19–20
    definition of, 4, 16, 52
    forms of, 16
    gaps in theory of, 267–268
    individual differences in, 19–23
    life stories using, 24–25
    middle adulthood challenge of, 16–18
    negative aspects of, 268
    and parenting skills, 21–22
    present significance of, 269–270
    psychological well-being promoted with, 23–24
    redemption sequences affirming, 25–26
    and social involvements, 22–23
    and society, 4–8
    stages of, 230
    as term, 103

theory of, 266–268
Generativity Behavioral Checklist (GBC),
   66
Generativity crisis, 213
"Generativity Crisis and Our Responsibili-
   ties to Future Generations" (confer-
   ence), 5, 8
Generativity versus stagnation, 91
Geography, 70–71
Germany, 196–197
Gerotranscendence, 126
Giddens, A., 84
Gift metaphor, 76
Gilligan, Carol, 181
Giving, 160, 182
Giving back, 6, 25, 145
Global aging, 119–121
Global culture, 45
"Glocalization," 45
Goals, 165, 196
God, 159, 162, 249
Golden Rule, 153–155, 162, 186, 245–246,
   252
The "good," 243–245, 250
Goodness of life, faith in, 251
The Good Society (R. Bellah et al.), 6–7
Goodstein, Lynne, 133
Grand-generativity, 116, 117
Grandparents, 202–204
"Gray peril," 120
The Greatest Generation (Tom Brokaw), 41
Great Law of Native American Iroquois, 46
Greeks, ancient, 98
Green parties, 216
Grounded theory approach, 66
Gudorf, Christine, 189–190

Habermas, Jürgen, 84, 242, 244, 245, 253
Habitat for Humanity, 141
Hagan, J., 138
Hakuta, K., 205
Hamm, M. S., 143
Happiness, 23
"Happy accidents," 74–75
Harrington, M., 183–185
Hart, H. M., 22
Hartmann, Heinz, 247
Harvard College, 38–39
Hauerwas, Stanley, 242, 251
"Haves" and "have-nots," 177
Health care, 203, 204
Hebraic culture, 102

Hegel, G. W. F., 116
Hellenic culture, 102
Helper principle, 140
Helping, 142
Henkin, N., 207, 208
Hinduism, 154
Hitler, Adolf, 196–197
Homburger, Theodor, 262
Hope, 106, 120, 155, 259
Horney, Karen, 178
Hospice care, 141
Howe, N., 125, 204
Huayan School of Buddhism, 46
Human development. See Development,
   human
Humanlike child, 72
"The Human Situation" (Valerie Saiving),
   188
Human species, belief in, 206
"Human Strength and the Cycle of Genera-
   tions" (Erik Erikson), 259

Ideal person, image of, 72
Identity, 3–4, 17, 24, 90, 262
   of adolescents, 257
   Erikson's own crisis of, 175, 262
   master identities, 57
   and primary caretakers, 248
   species-wide, 59
   of women, 177–178, 184
Identity versus role confusion, 90
Iemoto system, 73–75
IHD (Institute of Human Development), 159
Ikigai (purpose in life), 70
ILR. See Institutes for Learning in Retirement
"Imagoes," 25
Immigration, 53–54, 204–205
Immortality, symbolic, 18, 64, 89, 199
Income (for the elderly), 207–208
Indentured servants, 36–37
Independence, 69
India, 22, 93, 259, 260, 263
Individual differences, 19–23
   and parenting skills, 21–22
   and social involvements, 22–23
Individualism, 154–157
   collectivism vs., 68, 213
   and Japanese culture, 100–102
   religious, 154–155
   in Western developmental theory, 98–
   100
Individual personality, 74

Inductive process, 66
Indulgence, 68
Industry stage, 38
Information systems, 52, 53
"Initial experience," 87
Initiative stage, 38
Insight and Responsibility (Erik Erikson), 178, 259
Instinct, 246–247
Institute of Human Development (IHD), 159
Institutes for Learning in Retirement (ILR), 121, 123
Instrumental work, 180
Integral ritual, 259
Intergenerational buffers, 44
Intergenerational communities, 207–208, 223–224
Intergenerational education programs, 123–124
Intergenerational issues, 202–204, 211–219
    conditions for fairness in, 215–219
    framework for, 212–215
    religion, 155
Internalization, 74, 86, 88
International Monetary Fund, 218
Intimacy, 4, 17, 44
"Involuntary child absence syndrome," 139
Iroquois, 46, 60
Irwin, J., 137–138, 142–143
Ise, 102
Isolation, 139, 203
Italy, 204

Jackson, Jesse, 131
James, William, 243, 246, 250, 252
Janikula, J., 135
Japan, 122
    politics in, 217
    private needs of citizens in, 212–213
    social services in, 213, 215
Japanese culture, 45, 63–82, 97–98, 206n
    artistic mentoring in, 73–77
    child care in, 67–73
    contextualism/cyclical imagery in, 100–102, 104–110
    cross-cultural investigation of, 65–67
    politics of generativity in, 197–199
    rope of ashes story in, 117–119
Japanese Ministry of Health, 70
Japanese society, 5–6
Judaism, 186
Judeo-Christian worldview, 108

Jung, Carl, 103, 157, 178

Kagoshima, 197, 198
Kami, 100
Kano painting, 74
Kanshin Jukkai Mandala Temple, 100
Kant, Immanuel, 154, 242, 244, 252
Karma, 154
Karp, D., 134
Kazui, M., 69, 70
Keepers of meaning, 43
"Keepers of the meaning," 6
Keyes, C. L. M., 24
Kim, T., 77
Kimmel, Douglas C., 182
Kin altruism, 247–249
Kingson, E., 207, 208
Kinship, 109, 251
Klohnen, C. E., 23
Kohlberg, Lawrence, 242, 244, 253
Korea, 45
Kosovo, 58
Kotre, John, 16, 18, 66, 128, 181, 187, 196
Kotre, Kathy, 44
Kuypers, J. A., 89
Kyoto Conference, 5, 8
Kyoto School, 45

Labor, distribution of, 180–191
Labor laws, 36
Labouvie-Vief, G., 126
Language, 205
Lasch, Christopher, 7
Laslett, Peter, 121
Late adolescence, 24
Laub, J., 135
Leadership, 6, 197
Leo XIII, Pope, 249
Letting go, 16, 42, 91
Levinson, Daniel J., 99–101, 181–184
LGS. *See* Loyola Generativity Scale
"Liberties of Children," 37
Life cosmology, 108
The Life Cycle Completed (Erik Erikson), 103
Life cycle model, 90, 257, 258, 263
Life Dream, 184
Life endings, 25
Life expectancy, 202
Lifelong learning, 121–122
Life span, 84
Life-span developmental psychology, 99
Life stories, 24–26, 104

National Survey of Midlife Development in the United States (MIDUS), 23, 24
Native Americans, 46
Natural attitude *(naturliches Weltbild)*, 86
Nazi Party, 197
NCCCR (North Carolina Center for Creative Retirement), 122
Neo-paganism, 168
Networks of friends, 22
New Careers Movement, 140
New England, 36–39
New Recovery Movement, 143
Newton, P. M., 183
New York State, 141, 144
Next generation, caring for the, 18
NICHD (National Institute of Child Health and Human Development), 202
Ningenrashii kodomo (humanlike child), 72
Nirvana, 108
Nongenerative adults, 73
Nonself, 100
Nonviolence, 252, 259–261
North Carolina Center for Creative Retirement (NCCCR), 122
No theatre, 74
Now-ism, 215, 216, 218
Nuclear waste, disposal of, 59–60
Nuri, 45

Obasuteyama, 117–119, 124–126
Objects, 68, 72
Obligation, 156, 250
Obsessive consumption, 7
Oe, Kenzaburo, 97
Older Persons' Universities, 122
"Once More the Inner Space" (Erik Erikson), 177
One World (Wendell Wilkie), 260
"Ontogeny of Ritualization" (Erik Erikson), 259
O'Reilly, E. B., 142
Origin myths, 40–42
Ostrove, J. M., 24
Outward-looking cultures, 44–47

Paganism, 168, 169
Palloni, A., 138
Parables, 41–42
Parenthood, 179, 252
Parenting, 67, 187, 248
  in Japan, 69
  from prison, 138, 139, 143–146

skills for, 21–22
Parenting magazines, 71
Parsons, Talcott, 88, 89, 155
Paternal authority, 200
Patriarchy, 69, 70
Peaceniks, 86
Peer groups, 44
Penguins, emperor, 63
Penis envy, 178
Pensions, 212
People's Tribune, 216, 271
Personal growth, 160
Personal narrative, 128
Peterson, B. E., 23, 196
Piaget, Jean, 98, 103
Pius XI, Pope, 249
Plato, 108, 178, 249
Political interest, 23
Political involvement, 22
"Political Youths," 86
Politics (Aristotle), 249
Politics of generativity, 6, 195–209
  characteristics needed for, 206–208
  and children, 200–205
  and expression, 196–200
  and gender, 188
Politics of intergenerational fairness. *See* Intergenerational issues
Pope, Stephen, 249
Potential, faith in human, 206
Poverty, 17
Power, 44, 158
PPC (Prisoners Parenting Center), 144
Practical wisdom, 121
Practices of commitment, 155, 156
Premoral goods, 243, 253
Primogeniture, 69, 73, 201
Prisoners Parenting Center (PPC), 144
Prison society, 131–147
  corrections in generative, 145–147
  and criminal behavior, 133–137
  and human development, 137–139
  and strengths-based corrections, 139–145
Productivity, 160, 176–177, 181, 183
Protective function, 160, 227
Proximity-promoting equipment, 67
Pseudospeciation, 8, 55–56, 260
Psychological well-being, 23–24
Psychotherapy, 164–165
Public funding, 119
"Publicness," 84

Public political actions, 22
Public schooling, 38, 200, 201, 204
Public university courses, 123
Punishment, "unnatural," 201
Puritan movement, 37–40, 44, 154, 200–202
Purpose in life, 70
Putnam, Robert, 269

Q-sort ranking procedure, 19
Quakers, 147

Radcliffe College, 24
Raspberry, William, 131, 147
Rawls, John, 242, 244, 253
Real life stories, 41
Recidivism, 140
Reciprocal altruism, 248
Recovery activists, 143
Redemption sequence, 25–26
Redemptive truth, 131–132, 147
Reggio Emilia Approach, 204
Rehabilitation, 133
Reizei, Tamehito, 73, 74
Religion, 26, 153–171
    in changing culture, 161–169
    and children, 38
    and gender, 176, 185–191
    individualism in American, 154–155
    spirituality emerging in, 155–159
    and spiritual seekers vs. religious dwell-
        ers, 159–160
Religious dwellers, 159–164
Religious narratives, 251–252
Religiousness, 160, 170
Remembered past, 120
"Renovating shrine," 77
Rentsch, T., 127
Representative (of future generations), 214,
    216
The Republic (Plato), 249
Respite care, 141
Ricoeur, Paul, 242, 245, 246, 250
Right living, 155
Ritualization, 259–260
Roberts, P., 183
Role models, 136, 142, 146, 207
Roof, W. C., 157
Rope of ashes, 117–119
Roszak, Theodore, 126
Russia, 214
Ryff, C. D., 24

Sacredness of objects, 159
Sacrifice, 190
Saigo Takamori, 197–199
Saiving, Valerie, 188–189
Sampson, R. J., 135
Samurai rebellion, 197–199
Sands, Bill, 142
San Francisco, 143
Sasaki, Takeshi, 271
Satisfaction, 70
    life, 23
    with social relationships, 22
Satyagraha, 244, 260–263
"Schedule of virtues," 259
Schooling, involvement in children's, 21
Schools, 38
Seasons, 102
Seasons of a Man's Life (Daniel J. Levinson),
    182
Selecting process, 41
Self, 45–46, 105–106
Self-absorption, 179, 196
Self-affirmation, 189
Self-ascribed protagonists, 25
Self-assertion, 189
Self-esteem, 23, 116, 166
Self-fulfillment, 159
Self-giving, 162, 190
Self-growth, 159, 165–166
Self-help groups, 142–143, 146
Selfless nurturance, 18
Self-love, 189
Self-preoccupation, 7, 17
Self-sacrifice, 176
Sense of coherence, 23
September 11, 2001 terrorist attacks, 7
Serbs, 56, 57
Seventh Step, 142
Shibano, S., 88
Shweder, R. A., 66
Sidel, Ruth, 185
Silbert, Mimi, 143, 147
Skinship, 67, 69
Slavery, 38
Smirles, K. A., 196
Snarey, John, 23, 181, 187
Snyder, M., 231
Social control, 89, 93
Social function, 227
Social involvements, 22–23
Socialization theory, 87–90, 92
Social memories, 86

Social obligation, 156
Social recession, 269
Social responsibility, 84, 93–94, 155, 162, 164
Social ritual, 259
Social security, 207–208, 212
Social services, 155, 213, 215
Social stimulation, 68, 72
Social support, 22, 119
Social temporality, 85
Social time, 84, 85
Sociology of knowledge, 85–86, 89, 92
Soul, 108–109
Sparta, 64–65
Speech, 68, 72
Spiritual elders, 120
Spirituality, 155–160, 170
Spiritual marketplace, 156
Spiritual seekers, 159–160, 164–166
Stagnation, 17, 115, 137, 196
Stalinist Russia, 214
Star Wars (film), 41
Steichen, Edward, 260
Stepped progressivism, 100, 101, 103, 107
Stern, Daniel, 181
Stewart, A. J., 22, 24, 39–40
Stories of real life, 41
Stories of redemption, 136
Storytelling, 128
Story types, 39–42
Stratification of experiences (*Erlebnisschichtung*), 86, 87
Strauss, W., 125, 204
"Strength of the generations," 179
Strengths-based corrections, 139–145
Strouse, Jean, 177, 178
Structured environments, 146
Structures of memory, 86
Stukas, A., 231
Subjective time, 127–128
Substance abuse treatment, 142
"Successful aging," 99
Support groups, 44, 134, 146
"Sustainable society," 6
Symbolic immortality, 18, 64, 89, 199
Symposium (Plato), 249

TA. *See* Transactional Analysis
Talks to Teachers on Psychology (William James), 250
Tanka poetry, 73
Taoism, 118

Technical generativity, 66, 93
Technology, 42–43, 52, 53
Teleology, 243–245, 249–250
Temporality, 127–128
Therapeutic culture, 157, 164–171
Theresa, Mother, 43
Third Age, 121
Time
    concepts of, 46
    Japanese view of, 105
    social responsibility in, 84, 85
    subjective, 127–128
    Western view of, 98, 102
Time perspective, 206–207
Timing of generativity, 19
Toch, H., 137
Tocqueville, Alexis de, 154
Tokugawa Shogunate, 69, 197
Tolstoy Farm, 261
Tornstam, L., 126, 158
Tosa daimyo domain, 197
Toys for Tots, 141
Tradition, 74, 76, 155, 156, 159, 242, 243, 252
Training by doing, 74
Transactional Analysis (TA), 167, 169
Trauma, 58–59
Travelers, fellow, 44
Triandis, H. C., 68
Trust, 21, 181
Trust stage, 38
Twelve step programs, 142

Uggen, C., 135
Understanding, 227
Union of Concerned Scientists, 6
Unitarian Church, 166–169
United States
    aging baby-boomers in, 119
    child care in, 67–73
    culture in. *See* American culture
    and immigration, 205
    life expectancy in, 202
    lifelong learning in, 121, 122
    male development in, 182
    1950's society in, 177–178
    rapid change in, 53
    social security in, 207–208
    volunteerism in, 221–222
Universal specieshood, 260, 261
University for the Aged, 122
University of California, Berkeley, 159

University of Michigan, 24
University of the Third Age, 122
"Unnatural" punishment, 201
U.S. Congress, 60–61
U.S. Department of Justice, 138
"The utility of what is not," 118

Vaillant, George, 23, 182, 183
Values, 21, 227, 230–234, 253
Vandewater, E., 39–40
VFI. *See* Volunteer Function Inventory
Virginia, 36–39, 42
Virtual representative (of future generations), 214
Virtue(s), 253
    ethics of, 242, 250–251
    schedule of, 259
Vocational dreams, 183
Volunteer Function Inventory (VFI), 227–228, 233
Volunteerism, 166, 171, 221–237
    actions of, 223–226
    by churchgoers, 155
    and crime, 135
    functional account of, 226–229
    and generativity lessons, 229–234
    mandatory, 231
    number of Americans engaged in, 221–222
    in prison, 146
    psychology of, 226
    stages of, 228
Volunteer programs, senior adult, 122
Volunteers, prison visits by, 147
Voting, 22
Voting rights, 214

Waddock, S. A., 204
Washington, DC, 138
"Web of significance," 35
Well-being, 160

Well-side conferences, 71
Wentworth, P. A., 196
Western developmental theory, 98–100
Westernization, 75, 78
Whiting, J. W. M., 66
"Who Cares? Moral Commitment and Creative Lives in Contemporary America" (conference), 8
Wilkie, Wendell, 260
Wilson, James Q., 247–248
Winthrop, John, 154
Wisdom, 52, 106, 115–121, 126, 127
Wives, 182
Woman and Analysis, 178
"Womanhood and the Inner Space" (Erik Erikson), 177
Women, 19, 22, 183–185
    caregiving by, 188–189, 191
    and crime, 133
    desire of, 177
    Erikson on generativity and, 177–179
    identity of, 177–178
    in Japan, 70
Women of Academe (N. Aisenberg and M. Harrington), 183–184
Work, instrumental, 180
Work ethic, 70
World War I, 52
World War II, 196–197
"Wounded healers," 136, 142–143
Wuthnow, R., 159

Yamada, M., 70
Young adulthood, 18, 23
Young Man Luther (Erik Erikson), 258
Youngstown (Ohio), 138
Youth Romanticists, 86
Yugoslavia, 56–58

Zuroff, D., 23

ABOUT THE EDITORS

Ed de St. Aubin, PhD, is an assistant professor of psychology at Marquette University in Milwaukee, WI. His intellectual interests in life span developmental psychology concern the study of lives over time and within context. Dr. de St. Aubin's scholarship has focused on generativity, personal ideology, family dynamics, psychobiography, crime desistance, and cultural psychology. He is founder and senior consultant of WASHED (Wisconsin Association of Self Help for Enduring Desistance), a crime prevention and desistance agency that facilitates the development of generativity in ex-offenders.

Dan P. McAdams, PhD, is the Charles Deering McCormick Professor of Teaching Excellence, professor of human development and psychology, and director of the Foley Center for the Study of Lives at Northwestern University, Evanston, IL. A fellow of the American Psychological Association (APA) and recipient of the 1989 Henry A. Murray Award, Dr. McAdams has published widely on the topics of identity and the self, intimacy, generativity and adult development, and the role of narrative and life stories in personality and developmental psychology. His books include *The Stories We Live By* (1993), *The Person: An Integrated Introduction to Personality Psychology* (3rd ed., 2001), *Generativity and Adult Development: How and Why We Care for the Next Generation* (APA, 1998, edited with Ed de St. Aubin), and *Turns in The Road: Narrative Studies of Lives in Transition* (APA, 2001, edited with Ruthellen Josselson and Amia Lieblich).

Tae-Chang Kim, PhD, president of the Institute for Integrated Study of Future Generations, devoted his early academic career to the study of how his country (Republic of Korea) could be democratically modernized. After transferring to Japan, he began his current focus on how the present generation of scholars can contribute to the well-being of future generations. His research publications cover the topics of self and other, global and intergenerationally responsible public philosophy, and private and public happiness.